A NEW SOUTH REBELLION

WITHDRAWN

A NEW SOUTH

Karin A. Shapiro

The Battle
against
Convict
Labor in the
Tennessee
Coalfields,
1871–1896

REBELLION

The
University
of North
Carolina
Press

Chapel Hill
and London

The Fred W. Morrison
Series in Southern Studies

© 1998 The University of North Carolina Press

All rights reserved

This book was set

in Minion by Keystone Typesetting, Inc.

Design by April Leidig-Higgins

Manufactured in the United States of America

The paper in this book meets the guidelines for
permanence and durability of the Committee on
Production Guidelines for Book Longevity of the
Council on Library Resources.

Library of Congress Cataloging-in-Publication Data

Shapiro, Karin A.   A New South rebellion: the battle
against convict labor in the Tennessee coalfields,
1871–1896 / Karin A. Shapiro.

p.   cm.   Includes bibliographical references and index.

ISBN 0-8078-2423-2 (cloth: alk. paper).

ISBN 0-8078-4733-x (pbk.: alk. paper)

1. Labor disputes—Tennessee—History—19th century.

2. Coal miners— Tennessee—History—19th century.

3. Convict labor—Tennessee—History—19th century.

I. Title.

HD5325.M615S48   1998   97-39125

331.5′1—dc21   CIP

02 01 00 99 98   5 4 3 2 1

For Edward

CONTENTS

MAPS

ACKNOWLEDGMENTS

Growing up and receiving my initial education in South Africa, I learned early on that political economy and social experience are inextricably intertwined. This lesson was reinforced as I began graduate study—a moment when calls for the integration of social and political history were on the rise. One of the central goals of this narrative has been to heed these scholarly pleas. One simply cannot understand the persistence of convict mining in late-nineteenth-century Tennessee, or the dynamics of unionization in the state's mining regions, or the willingness of free coal miners to take up arms against the institution of convict labor, or their unwillingness to engage state troops in outright battle, without close attention to political economy and ideology. The vagaries of state and local politics mattered in the coalfields, both to mining magnates, who came to assume that the state would help them maintain a cheap and dependable supply of labor, and to free miners, who expected a Populist government to live by its promises to safeguard what they considered the God-given rights of American workers.

Over the course of writing this book, I have received crucial assistance from a number of institutions and funding agencies. Without the financial support of the Fulbright Program, Yale University, and South Africa's Human Sciences Research Council and Ernest Oppenheimer Memorial Trust, I might never have become an American historian. Their generosity enabled me to cross the Atlantic for my graduate education. Additional grants from the American Historical Association, Yale University, the University of the Witwatersrand, and the Human Sciences Research Council funded various research trips.

Most of my excursions were to libraries and archives in the American South, where several archivists and historians went out of their way to be helpful. I particularly want to thank Marilyn Hughes, Wayne Moore, Fran Schell, and Ann Alley at the Tennessee State Library and Archives in Nashville; Steve Cotham, Ted Baehr, and Sally Polhemus at Knoxville's Lawson McGhee Library; Marvin Whiting at the Birmingham Public Library; Mary Harris at the Anderson County Courthouse in Clinton; Henry Mayer in Louisville, Kentucky; and Anne Armour at the University of the South in Sewanee, Tennessee. In Tuscaloosa, Jeff Norrell greatly aided my exploration of the University of Alabama's holdings. In Knoxville, Fred Wyatt of the Coal Creek Mining & Manufacturing Company gave me access to his company's records. John Gaventa, of east Tennessee's Highlander Center, provided me with a copy of James Dombrowski's unpublished manuscript about the mining troubles in Anderson and Grundy Counties, "Fire in the Hole." Local historians Katherine Hoskins and William Ray Turner were exceedingly generous with their time, knowledge, and resources, with the latter magnanimously sharing his remarkable photographic collection. They and Darby White of the Coal Creek Mining & Manufacturing Company made sure that I saw more of Tennessee than the state's libraries and archives. During the last few months of intense work on my manuscript, Catherine Higgs chased down many obscure bibliographic references with amazing speed and cheerfulness.

The skill and talent of the people who helped me with my research was matched by those who lent a hand in the production process. Karina McDaniel and Santu Mofokeng reproduced the photographs; their mastery in this regard speaks for itself. Phillip Stickler and Wendy Job ably generated the maps, and Celeste Mann and Arlene Harris both gave freely of their considerable computer and administrative expertise. It has been a pleasure working with such professionals.

At the UNC Press, I've had the good fortune to work with Pamela Upton and Alison Tartt, who deftly shepherded the manuscript through its final stages. I am particularly grateful to Lew Bateman, the Press's executive editor, who has manifested great faith in this study from his first encounter with it.

My scholarship has been shaped in untold ways by the intellectual communities in which I have learned my trade. As an undergraduate at the University of the Witwatersrand, I was introduced to the historical craft by Bruce Murray and Charles van Onselen, who imparted a love and respect for the discipline. Though I have wandered far from their areas of expertise, they have continued to read my work and offer valuable advice.

For old friends from my years as a graduate student in New Haven, the acknowledgment of this debt has been long in coming. Thanks are especially due to Cecelia Bucki, Jackie Dirks, Dana Frank, Toni Gilpin, Stan Greenberg, Julie Greene, Leif Haase, Yvette Huginnie, Reeve Huston, Chris Lowe, John Mason, William Munro, Silvie Murray, Gloria Naylor, Ruth Oldenziel, Karen Sawislak, Brian Siritsky, and Brenda Stevenson. John Blassingame and Gerry Jaynes welcomed me into Yale's Afro-American Studies Master's Program and guided me through my first two years of graduate work. After I began my dissertation research, Bill Cronon offered invaluable advice about statistical and census matters. More recently, friends in South Africa were wonderfully warm in welcoming back a peripatetic soul and in providing both a congenial and intellectually exciting place to write—especially Russell Alley, Ann Bernstein, Phil Bonner, Belinda Bozzoli, Jim Campbell, Peter Delius, Deborah James, Paul La Hausse, Phyllis Lewsen, Isak Niehaus, Sue Parnell, Patrick Pearson, Deborah Posel, Jane Starfield, and Sue Valentine. Encouragement from my family has also been indispensable. My siblings, Colin, Mervyn, and Deena, my mother-in-law, Carolyn Balleisen, and especially my parents, Lionel and Joy Shapiro, have provided unfailing support over the years, often from thousands of miles away.

Numerous individuals have read various drafts of the book manuscript; their illuminating commentary has made this a far better book. Steve Brier, Pete Daniel, Alex Lichtenstein, Jeff Norrell, Joe Trotter, and Jon Wiener each read the manuscript closely, enriching my arguments through their extensive knowledge of late-nineteenth-century southern history. As an outside reader for UNC Press, Edward Ayers proferred expansive comments on my dissertation that in many ways constituted a blueprint for the revised manuscript. The intellectual distance that I have traveled as a southern historian over the past few years owes much to him.

David Montgomery has served as a mentor in the classic meaning of the word, teaching me much of what I know about American history. I am profoundly grateful to him for his direction of my research, for his incisive and constructive criticism of drafts of my dissertation, and for his ongoing friendship.

Throughout the life of this project, two close friends, Eric Arnesen and Dan Letwin, have helped to shape my understanding of rebellious miners, nervous mining magnates, and self-described reformist politicians. Time and again I have turned to them to read chapters and discuss the complexities and seeming paradoxes of life in the postbellum South. Our overlapping intellectual journeys have been a source of great joy.

My final acknowledgment leaves me tongue-tied. Those who know Ed Balleisen realize how lucky I am to have enjoyed the benefits of his considerable talents as a historian and writer. He has influenced this book in more ways than I could possibly recount. It is dedicated to him.

A NEW SOUTH REBELLION

CHAPTER 1

The Convict Wars and the New South

In the moonlight of July 14, 1891, several hundred east Tennesseans emerged from homes nestled in the ridges of Anderson County. The men were mostly coal miners who worked in the towns of Briceville and Coal Creek, though they also included a number of shopkeepers, professionals, and farmers. Residents of Coal Creek gathered first. Armed with rifles and shotguns, they assumed something of a military formation and began to make their way along the five-mile railway line that curved between their town and Briceville. As they proceeded, the company swelled with the bodies of men who lived in the vicinity of the neighboring village.

Sometime around midnight—later reports disagreed about whether the action took place on Bastille Day or just after its conclusion—the band of local residents arrived at the Tennessee Coal Mining Company's jerry-built stockade, just outside Briceville. This prison housed forty convicted criminals, wards of the state who had recently been leased to the company and who toiled six days a week in its mine. After reassembling outside the stockade, the group demanded that the jail's guards immediately release the convicts. Heavily outnumbered, the watchmen quickly capitulated. With minimal fuss and no bloodshed, the crowd then escorted the inmates back to Coal Creek. There the miners and their allies placed the convict laborers on a train and sent them on a thirty-two-mile ride to Knoxville.[1] So began a rebellion against the use of convict labor in coal mines that would last over a year, involve thousands of Tennesseans and Kentuckians, and engulf five mining communities in east and mid-Tennessee.

These communities did not only resort to arms in their efforts to focus public attention on the state's well-established penal policy. The miners regularly sought the assistance of sympathetic governmental officials, such as the commissioner of labor and the attorney general. In the early fall of 1891, they forced the governor to call a special session of the legislature, at which they lobbied state legislators to abolish the convict lease and reform the criminal law. Throughout the late 1880s and early 1890s, these workingmen appealed to the courts to clarify penal practices and vindicate their contractual rights. Over the same period, they negotiated vigorously with their employers and struck on numerous occasions. Finally, Tennessee's coal miners established formal political alliances with organizations that represented urban workers and small farmers. These varied strategies were interspersed with three more attacks on the state's convict stockades, including the periodic liberation of predominantly black convicts by predominantly white miners.

After July 14, 1891, the convict question remained the state's most pressing political controversy for years. But the "convict wars," as many contemporaries called them, did not immediately achieve the miners' most cherished goal—the abolition of convict labor in coal mines. During the fourth attack, in August 1892, four militiamen were killed in skirmishes. These deaths turned public opinion sharply against the miners. Facing a greatly enlarged militia contingent and confronting a public increasingly critical of their methods, the miners surrendered. As a result, convict mining continued in competition with free labor until the lease contract expired at the end of 1895.

The story of rebellion against convict labor in Tennessee provides a series of vantage points from which one can survey the terrain of aspiration and repression that constituted the postemancipation South. In the social and economic currents that brought coal mining to postbellum Tennessee, one can discern significant evidence about the terms on which upcountry southerners experienced and responded to industrialization. At the intersection of a momentary industrial labor shortage, a paternalistic and racially oppressive approach to criminal justice, and the attempt of southern industrialists to limit the power of unions, one can glimpse the role of convict labor in the New South's embrace of the industrial world. And through the narrative of the Tennessee coal miners' economic, legal, and political struggles, one can discover a new angle on the tumultuous transformations of the 1890s—including the character of Populism, the nature and limits of late-nineteenth-century labor militance, and the impact that Jim Crow had on the southern industrial workplace.

This book chronicles Tennessee's convict wars, pausing throughout to scrutinize the rich analytical vistas that they offer. It has much to say about southern industrialization, the rise of modern southern business, convict labor in the southern economy and southern society, the southern industrial working class, southern Democrats, Republicans, and Populists, and southern race relations. But this is not a comprehensive history of any of these topics. The goal throughout is to show how these processes and protagonists shaped a coal miners' revolt and what that revolt reveals about the New South.

Most of the people who came to work in Coal Creek and Briceville migrated from surrounding counties. These upcountry Tennesseans moved from farms to outposts of the industrializing world. Like so many other nineteenth-century Americans and Europeans who migrated from rural areas to towns and cities, the newcomers to the coal mines of postbellum Tennessee had to adapt to life as wage laborers in industrial communities.

For well over a decade now, historians of the late-nineteenth-century South have argued about the impulses that led tens of thousands of southerners— both white and black—to leave agricultural work and enter the industrial labor force. Some scholars maintain that the yeomanry of the upcountry South vigorously resisted the growth of a commercial society. Residents of Appalachia, they contend, were squeezed off the land by the combination of a spreading railroad network, a consolidation of land ownership, stock and fence laws that closed the southern range for livestock, and crippling debts associated with sharecropping and crop liens. Together, these developments accelerated commercialization of the southern upcountry and weakened the independence of small-scale farmers, who profoundly resented an ever-encroaching market society. According to this view, upcountry southerners reluctantly left their homesteads to seek work in the New South's textile mills, coal mines, timber operations, and iron forges. Other historians portray these same people as all too ready to leave the drudgery and isolation of farm life, especially since population pressure on the land made it increasingly difficult for every child in an upcountry family to gain access to an economically viable piece of land. After moving away from the crowded countryside, this alternative interpretation suggests, they embraced meaningful social and economic opportunities in the growing industrial towns.[2]

The experience of the Tennesseans who came to work in the coal-rich areas of Anderson and Grundy Counties, both of which became consumed by the miners' rebellion, most closely supports the second of these historiographic accounts. The majority of residents in these two counties' coal towns did not migrate because of acute economic problems in the countryside; they did not leave crushed or destitute communities. In the twenty years preceding the rebellion, the value of farms and the agricultural goods they produced moved steadily higher in upcountry Tennessee, while almost four in five farms were worked by their owners. But by 1880, the owners of farmsteads encountered increasing difficulty in providing adequate land for all of their children. The sons of many farmers and tenants could no longer find an attractive livelihood in their immediate neighborhood. Scores of these individuals sought work in the area's coal towns.

These migrants were not alienated people ripped from a previous pastoral way of life. They came to town with substantial hopes, and many sank roots, helping to build the new municipalities, buying houses, founding churches and schools, and creating a vibrant local culture.[3] Coal Creek and the other Tennessee mining settlements were not classic "company towns," where residents owned nothing and found themselves perpetually in debt to their employer through rent obligations and store accounts.

The new communities, of course, were one-industry towns, where the primary employers retained substantial authority. If a coal miner crossed "the boss" and lost his job, he usually had no choice but to seek work somewhere else. A full realization of the aspirations held by the townspeople in Tennessee's mining settlements also largely depended on strong demand for coal, which only periodically obtained in the postbellum decades. Yet one must not lose sight of the expectations that mineworkers and their families possessed about their communities. A collective sense of possibility and belonging was an indispensable catalyst to the coal mining rebellions.

The migrants to Tennessee's coal towns experienced industrialization after the core regions of the American North and northern Europe had initiated the factory age. Many of the areas on the periphery of the industrial heartlands were beset by a shortage of skilled labor, a dearth of financial capital, and high transportation costs associated with long distances from markets. Constrained by these shortcomings, the industrial economies of outlying regions were typically founded on the exploitation of natural resources, which were sent to the industrial heartland for processing and manufacture. As scholars have long noted, the relationship between peripheral regions and the most thoroughly industrialized economies were profoundly colonial in character—even when, as in the case of the postbellum South, the colonial region was part of a single national polity.

In attempting to extract raw materials inexpensively, capitalists within colonial economies like that of late-nineteenth-century Tennessee often relied on cheap labor and, not infrequently, on various forms of unfree labor. After the Civil War, every southern state placed at least a portion of its convicted criminals in the hands of private businessmen who put the prisoners to work. One must be careful, though, not to exaggerate the significance of prison labor in Tennessee's postbellum industrial economy. Throughout the late nineteenth century, coal mining never contributed more than one-tenth of the state's industrial output or employed more than one percent of its adult male population. In this period, Tennessee's industrialization rested to a large extent on small-scale manufactories and workshops and on textile, grist, and sawmills that were dependent on water power, not coal-powered steam generators. At the same time, the toil of thousands of prisoners in Tennessee's mines was by no means marginal to the state's industrial development. The labor performed by Tennessee's convicts primed the economic pump of a pivotal extractive industry—coal mining—upon which many other industries depended.

In the aftermath of the Confederacy's surrender, a number of Tennessee's leading capitalists turned their attention to the state's coal seams, hoping to develop a large-scale mining industry. When these would-be industrialists encountered difficulties in recruiting labor for their ventures, they lobbied the state government to make convicts available for use in the mines. During the 1870s—the early years of commercial coal mining in Tennessee—mine managers perceived prison laborers to be cheap and dependable. The exertions of convicts helped to propel the new ventures underground, lowered labor costs, and indirectly assisted railway development in the state, as railroads depended on coal for both fuel and cargo.

Although prison workers may have been vital in the initial period of coal mining in the Volunteer State, within a few decades convict labor no longer fulfilled its earlier function of supplying cheap and dependable labor. By the late 1880s, Tennessee's coal operators had discovered that reliance on the labor of criminals entailed a host of indirect costs. Convict lessees were responsible for paying prison guards and rewarding those who captured escaped inmates. The coal companies also suffered losses as the result of property destroyed by prisoners. In addition, management could not lay off convicts during hot summer months when demand for coal waned, nor when the market became depressed. The cost of feeding, clothing, housing, and treating ill or injured inmates remained fixed, regardless of the ebb and flow in demand for coal. Those companies that were vertically integrated and that produced for more than one market, such as coal and pig iron, were able to employ convicts most profitably. When one market weakened, larger coal corporations could simply redeploy the prisoners under their control.

Irrespective of the structure of their operations, every coal company employing state inmates found that convict labor diminished productivity at the same time that it brought fixed and often unanticipated expenses. Many customers complained that the coal excavated by prisoners was below par. Because convicts had few incentives to mine with care, their coal was frequently "shot to pieces" or filled with slate. As a result, no Tennessee company relied solely on prisoners to mine its coal. Those mining operations that did employ convicts judiciously balanced their number of free and unfree laborers.

Why then did the Volunteer State's coal operators persist in relying on the convict lease throughout the 1880s and early 1890s? The answer lies primarily with the impact of the convict lease on labor relations in the coal industry. With convicts at the coal face, corporate managers gained significant leverage over their employees. From the early 1870s until well after the first revolt of 1891, the state's free miners lived with the understanding that strikes might prompt coal companies to bring in convict laborers as replacements. Both east and mid-Tennessee mine directors were convinced that the ready availability of convict laborers dampened the labor militance of Tennessee's free miners. Convict labor, these managers found, served both to reduce the wages they paid to free miners and to curb challenges to work rules. Thus in Tennessee the convict lease structured the psychological balance between industrial capital and labor. The institution enhanced the confidence and bargaining position of mining capitalists, while always reminding mineworkers of a threat from the degraded alternative of prison labor. Eventually, however, the rebellions of 1891 and 1892 dramatically increased the costs associated with administering the convict lease, persuading Tennessee's mining magnates that convicts no longer improved their balance sheets.

As long as convict leasing remained an integral part of Tennessee's coal industry, the institution held social as well as economic significance. In tandem with the criminal justice system that generated its laborers, the lease helped to forge a new postemancipation structure of racial subordination. Thousands of state inmates—primarily young black men who were convicted of petty theft— found their lives defined by the policy of leasing prisoners to private companies. In Tennessee's bid to enshrine individual property rights, these young men learned that there were harsh penalties for individuals who took a chicken or items of clothing that did not belong to them, especially in the state's growing cities, where most postbellum inmates had been convicted of a crime. These lessons did not come cheaply. The costs entailed in the administration of criminal justice—largely the payment of fees to sheriffs, county prosecutors, and other officials—far exceeded the sums generated by the leasing out of convicts. Though the state's financial managers occasionally noted this anomaly, the legislature repeatedly refused to reform the criminal law so as to reduce its costs, such as by limiting the number of petty crimes that constituted felonies. The people's representatives believed that the money spent on law enforcement was fully justified.

The criminal justice system and the convict lease did not simply remind Tennessee's black population that transgressing the law carried stiff penalties; they also greased patronage networks and bolstered the sense among the South's white elite that it presided over a paternalistic and even benevolent social order. The numerous people who fed, clothed, and guarded the state's convicts were invariably appointed through political intervention at the state or local level. In most of these appointments, patrons dispensed sinecures to local whites in return for social and political loyalty. Tennessee's penal system also encouraged the state's elite to help secure pardons for its inmates. The governor's correspondence files from the late nineteenth century are filled with petitions for clemency by thousands of prisoners. The vast majority of the petitions—whether filed by a black or white convict—were signed and supported by jurors, justices of the peace, judges, and local notables. Without such endorsements, the chances of a pardon were slim. With them, inmates regularly obtained substantial reductions in their sentences. The culture surrounding pardon-giving in Tennessee reinforced the dependence of black and white prisoners on the patronage of their "betters," thereby assuring Tennessee's white elite that it oversaw a paternalistic and honor-bound society.[4]

The highly personalized world of pardons and petitions recalled an antebellum past in which slaves, free blacks, and many poor whites had relied heavily on the goodwill of a white patron. Similarly, the actual practice of the convict lease, which required white prison guards to coerce hard labor from groups of mostly black prisoners, was profoundly reminiscent of slavery. But while the echoes of many older social relationships continued to reverberate in the postbellum South, the region's political context changed dramatically, especially after the late 1880s. The whirlwind of populism gave tens of thousands of southern farmers reason to believe they could successfully challenge the region's prevailing structure of political power. In addition to mobilizing farmers, the Populist crusades also proved capable of galvanizing southern workers like Tennessee's miners.

The waxing of populism in the Volunteer State provided a crucial impetus to the miners' opposition to convict labor. Members of the Farmers' Alliance, which gained statewide prominence in the late 1880s and early 1890s, spoke a political language that resonated in the hills of east and mid-Tennessee. They believed that capitalists should not be accorded special privileges; they demonized "monopolists"; they denounced government intervention on behalf of the "aristocrats" of capital; and they considered Andrew Jackson—the defender of the ordinary white man—to be their hero. Alliance leaders and newspapers combined this rhetoric with promises to bring down the "penitentiary ring" by terminating the convict lease. Thus when members of the Tennessee Farmers' Alliance won the state's governorship and a plurality of seats in the state legislature in 1890, Tennessee's coal miners had every reason to believe that the newly elected government would redress their grievances. Together, the electoral successes of Tennessee's populism, the movement's political creed, and the adoption of campaign planks friendly to labor all emboldened the state's free coal miners—even those who hailed from thoroughly Republican east Tennessee.

The Farmers' Alliance, however, ultimately failed to respond to the miners' fervent demand for the abolition of convict leasing. Internal weaknesses provide one explanation for the Populists' inability to fulfill their undertaking to end the use of prison labor in the mines. The Alliance constituted a broad church, embracing political congregants from the cotton farms of west Tennessee, the wheatlands of mid-Tennessee, and upcountry east Tennessee. Broadly pitched rhetoric and carefully created campaign platforms could hold together these very different groups of farmers, who often possessed widely diverging interests. Once in power, though, Alliance leaders experienced great difficulty in adopting and implementing specific proposals. On a host of issues, such as the convict lease, the Populist leadership encountered internal factions opposed to one course of action or another. Large-scale farmers in west and mid-Tennessee came to oppose outright termination of the lease, fearing the resulting loss of revenue to state coffers and the added expense of building and operating state penitentiaries.

Had the Alliancemen possessed more experience in political affairs, they might have cobbled together compromises to move their program forward. But acquaintance with the tactics of governance was especially lacking within their legislative caucus. The combination of internal bickering and political naïveté sapped the Alliance's momentum. Consistently outmaneuvered by mainstream Democratic legislators who possessed finely honed parliamentary skills, the Alliancemen accomplished little during their stint in the Tennessee General Assembly.

Democrats did not only hamper the Alliancemen's political efforts as a result of their long practice at government; they also bequeathed a legacy of debt and retrenchment that made reform extremely difficult. The low taxes that were the hallmark of Redeemer rule dictated the range of policy options open to the Alliancemen. The newcomers to government could not reverse the state's well-entrenched penal system without creating substantial new revenues, most likely from a hike in property taxes. An unwillingness to impose such an increase vitiated the Alliance's ability to make good on its preelection promises.

The rebellion against convict labor eventually laid bare other inherited weaknesses in Tennessee's state government. The miners managed to push their agenda as far as they did partly because of the fragmentary nature of state power. Conflicts between branches of government, between political personalities, and between state and local officials crucially shaped the course of political disputes over convict labor in the Volunteer State. The executive, the legislature, the courts, and many offices of the state's administrative branches were frequently at odds with one another, enabling Tennessee mining communities to seek allies within different branches of state government. These divisions greatly complicated the development of a coherent response to the "convict troubles." State officials, moreover, could not always count on the enforcement of dictates from Nashville. Local sheriffs in mining communities, who held elective office, regularly refused to carry out gubernatorial orders. And the state militia, ostensibly the ultimate guarantor of law and order, turned out to be a largely ineffectual and sometimes incompetent organization. The government's inability either to end the convict lease or to impose convict labor on an unwilling populace largely reflected the fractured nature of state authority. In Redeemer and Populist Tennessee, representatives of the state frequently struggled to translate policy into action.

In vigorously challenging a divided state government to eliminate the social evil of unfree labor, even to the point of taking up arms against duly constituted authority, Tennessee's coal miners joined in the intense labor conflict that wracked America during the last thirty years of the nineteenth century.

Throughout these three decades, industrial production grew dramatically, periodically outstripping the nation's ability to consume ever more iron, steel, coal, and cloth. Sharp expansions led captains of industry to expand their labor force so as to exploit spurts of strong economic growth; but when the markets turned sour, as they did from 1873 to the late 1870s, in the mid-1880s, and in the mid-1890s, industrialists came under extreme pressure to cut costs. More often than not, industrial magnates targeted labor as the chief means of reducing expenses, seeking either reductions in wages, increases in productivity through the assertion of more authority over the manufacturing process, or, as in the case of the Tennessee coalfields, reliance on convict workers.[5]

When postbellum industrial barons slashed wages or tried to limit workers' control over production, their employees reacted in a variety of ways. Most commonly, workers responded to deteriorating conditions by simply moving on, hoping to find a better deal elsewhere. With increasing frequency, however, wage reductions or the imposition of new work rules prompted union drives, boycotts, and strikes. In response, many employers used brute force to eliminate independent labor organizations from their workplaces. Corporations hired Pinkerton detectives to infiltrate unions, to attack striking workers, and to protect company property and "scab" labor; they also periodically solicited the aid of state militias and the federal army.

Once hired guns, militiamen, or federal troops became involved in late-nineteenth-century industrial disputes, violence and bloodshed resulted with great regularity. This pattern repeated itself throughout the Gilded Age, giving rise to incidents of industrial conflict that collectively verged on class war. In 1877 railway workers across the nation paralyzed the transportation system in response to severe wage cuts. By the time railway cars were moving again, thousands of federal troops and militiamen had been called to duty, millions of dollars of railway property had been destroyed, and roughly 100 people had lost their lives. Less than a decade later, the movement for an eight-hour workday ended in carnage as strikers, anarchists, and police fought a pitched battle in Chicago's Haymarket Square. The bloodshed continued well into the 1890s. In 1892 workers in the steelmaking community of Homestead, Pennsylvania, battled Pinkerton guards and state militia serving at the behest of a Carnegie Corporation determined to weaken the discretion that skilled laborers exercised in the production of steel. And in 1894 a strike against the Pullman Railroad Car Company precipitated a second labor crisis along the nation's rail lines, ending in yet more death and destruction.[6] The Tennessee coal miners' rebellion constituted one of a great many similar labor battles between the Civil War and the turn of the century, battles in which working people demonstrated a willingness to fight for their vision of America's industrial future.

Nonetheless, one must emphasize that the miners' rebellion against the use of convict labor was founded on essentially conservative premises. Tennessee's coal miners rooted their militance in a defense of homeownership and community, cultivating a public image as consummate insiders to American politics and society. Throughout the revolts, local leaders portrayed themselves as descendants of the state's frontier heroes and explicitly rejected characterizations of their cause as in any way reflecting socialist impulses like those that animated the 1871 Paris Commune. The miners did excoriate coal companies that used prison labor, whom they perceived as leviathans bent on distorting the political life and economic well-being of their state. Yet they continually spoke positively about the virtues of competitive capitalism, accepting the legitimacy of an economy founded on private property, so long as no one gained unjust advantage in the marketplace.

Seeking their place within Tennessee's industrial society, the miners of Coal Creek, Briceville, and Tracy City disdained actions, whether taken by coal operators, governmental officials, or renegade miners, that would be perceived by ordinary Tennesseans as "un-American." Though the miners assembled a military force that included scores of well-disciplined Civil War veterans, they intended to use force only as a means of influencing the political agenda. They refused to engage the ill-trained and often poorly led state militia in outright battle. In essence, the rebellions served as an especially vehement form of political petition.[7] None of the miners' leaders had the slightest desire to overthrow a legally constituted government by military means.

Two other points stand out about the miners' crusade against convict labor. First, while other unions—especially those attached to the American Federation of Labor—increasingly shied away from politics, retreating into a world of business unionism, the residents of Tennessee's mining communities continued to believe in political engagement.[8] In the midst of the Gilded Age, an era stamped by laissez-faire ideology, these east and mid-Tennesseans understood that the ostensibly disparate worlds of labor negotiations and politics were intimately connected. Tennessee's coal miners realized that the ground rules for economic activity took shape in administrative offices, legislative halls, and courtrooms; and they hoped that their initiatives would remold the contours of Tennessee politics. Second, the miners of Tennessee recognized the great dangers confronting individuals who participated in militant labor actions. Almost certainly aware of the hangman's rope that greeted the leaders of Pennsylvania's "Molly Maguires" and the anarchists blamed for the Haymarket massacre, Tennessee's miners took no chances with their leadership.[9] These workingmen took great care, especially in the early attacks on the stockades, to provide community leaders with public alibis that placed them far away from the brazen maneuvers by the rank and file.

The adeptness of the miners extended to the building of bridges across the racial divide, particularly in east Tennessee. Labor struggles on the docks of New Orleans, in the mines of the Birmingham district, and in the coal towns of east Tennessee all suggest instances of far-reaching interracial cooperation during the age of Jim Crow.[10] Like Louisiana dockworkers and Alabama miners, white and black mineworkers of east Tennessee fashioned labor organizations that noticeably restrained racism among rank-and-file white workers. These noteworthy examples, however, should not lead one to romanticize race relations in the workplaces of the New South. Discrimination on the basis of race always characterized community life and the culture of work in Appalachian Tennessee, while racial tensions eventually weakened labor organizations at crucial junctures during the rebellion and its aftermath.

The existence of differing degrees of racial cooperation in the New South's industrial workplaces raises a question about the circumstances that gave rise to intraclass collaboration. The story of the Tennessee coal miners' rebellion offers intriguing evidence about the conditions that either promoted or impeded interracial working-class alliances, since the miners of east and mid-Tennessee handled racial issues differently. The east Tennessee communities of Briceville, Coal Creek, and Oliver Springs forged far more effective links between black and white miners than did mid-Tennessee's Tracy City residents. In east Tennessee, black mineworkers were well organized into separate union locals, shared a loyalty to the regional leadership of the United Mine Workers of America, and periodically demonstrated substantial solidarity in conflicts with mine managers. In Tracy City, white mineworkers consistently shunned their black fellow workers, excluding them from union meetings and preferring an all-white workforce.

The demographics and political characteristics of the two regions largely account for this divergence. Many more free black miners lived and worked in the east Tennessee towns than in Tracy City; east Tennessee black miners also formed more settled communities and blacks lived among their white neighbors. The greater permanence of black miners and their families in Coal Creek Valley encouraged white miners to view blacks as possessing a legitimate, if still subordinate position in the coalfields. Similarly, the dominance of the Republican Party in east Tennessee removed a political barrier to peaceful racial coexistence. In Coal Creek, Briceville, and Oliver Springs, blacks and whites voted the same ticket, even if they did so with varying motives. By contrast, Tracy City's free black community was small and residentially isolated, while local whites belonged overwhelmingly to a Democratic Party that was thoroughly committed to white supremacy.

The stand of Tennessee's mining communities against the degrading oppression of convict labor was very much a New South rebellion. This episode exposes both a profound sense of new possibilities in the American South and the often cruel legacies of that region's embittered past. It also demonstrates that in the postbellum South, as in so many other historical contexts, the actions of men and women could unleash a very different future from the one they expected or for which they hoped.

CHAPTER 2

Schemes and Dreams in the Coalfields

In many ways, the Tennessee mining settlements where rebellion flared during 1891 and 1892 typified the roughly 500 company towns and 100 independently incorporated municipalities that sprang up in the postbellum Appalachian coalfields.[1] Coal Creek, Briceville, and Oliver Springs in east Tennessee and Tracy City in mid-Tennessee were each emblematic of the New South. These places, like dozens of other southern coal and lumber towns, shared a history of industrial boosterism. Most of these towns grew as the result of local extractive industries whose development depended on the integration of the southern upcountry into a regional and national economy. Entrepreneurs usually founded the postbellum South's new industrial settlements, but corporate elites were by no means solely responsible for their growth. Large numbers of ordinary southerners migrated to the New South's many outposts. The migrants came in search of economic opportunities, which at least some found; they also helped to establish community institutions such as schools, churches, and fraternal lodges.

The early history of the Volunteer State's coal towns gave their inhabitants good reason to believe that local mines would provide the basis for economic prosperity and vibrant communities. Yet for all the accomplishments of investors and residents in places like Coal Creek and Tracy City, the aspirations of these southerners often collided with the constraints of a colonial economy. When business depression and the growing reliance of coal companies on convict labor threatened their dreams, coal miners, their families, and many other locals became incensed—so incensed that they fought the institution of convict leasing with remarkable conviction.

The degree of militance associated with this anger, however, was not uniform throughout Tennessee's coal lands. Coal miners in east Tennessee demonstrated a far greater willingness to challenge state authority than their counterparts in Tracy City, especially in the early stages of the rebellion. The divergent course of labor conflict in the east and mid-Tennessee coal regions reflected crucial differences in geography, economic structure, demography, and local politics. These differences profoundly shaped the manner in which simmering disputes about convict leasing turned into open revolt.

The Wedge of Industrial Capitalism

From the 1860s until the mid-1920s, coal powered America's industrial revolution. Throughout this period, the extensive anthracite and bituminous coalfields of Pennsylvania, Illinois, Ohio, and Indiana yielded most of the nation's coal. But as early as the 1870s, the growth of the national economy led some postbellum industrialists to seek additional sources of energy in the bituminous coal regions of Appalachia. The physical accessibility of southern coal attracted numerous investors. In many parts of Appalachia, coal lay in beds near or horizontal to the surface, so excavation required neither a massive outlay of capital nor costly machinery. Mining companies could begin operations simply by driving drifts or slopes into a hillside. As a result, the start-up costs of most southern mines were much lower than those of their northern counterparts, which usually required deep shafts.[2]

Tennessee's mountains beckoned along with the rest of the previously unexploited Appalachian coalfields. Within the state, the coalfield formed an irregular quadrilateral, with the northern and southern boundaries nearly parallel and running seventy-one and fifty miles respectively. The other sides ran

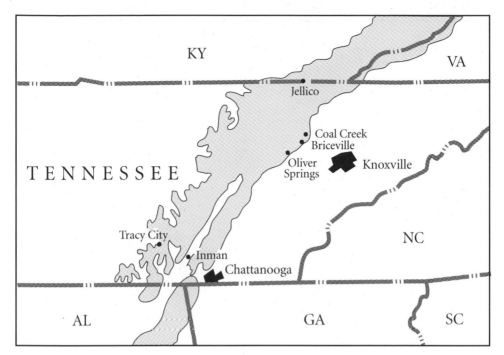

Map 2.1. The Tennessee Coalfields

diagonally through the state in a northeasterly to southwesterly direction. Coal mining was a fairly widespread activity in late-nineteenth-century Tennessee, with twenty-one counties engaged in mining. Before 1900, however, two counties—Anderson in east Tennessee and Grundy in mid-Tennessee—dominated the state's coal output. In 1890 Anderson County led the state, with Grundy County a close second. Together mines in these two counties produced almost half of Tennessee's coal.[3]

Anderson County lies partly on the Cumberland Plateau and partly in the Tennessee Valley. The rolling countryside of the valley is sharply distinguished from the deeply gashed surface of the plateau, which reaches altitudes close to 3,500 feet near Coal Creek. Parallel to the main stretch of mountains, but separated from it by a narrow vale, runs Walden's Ridge. The town of Coal Creek (now called Lake City) nestles at the eastern base of the ridge, along the floodplains of Coal Creek. The town of Briceville, five miles upstream at one of the forks of the creek, is also positioned on the valley floor, though to the west of Walden's Ridge. Grundy County, situated seventy-five miles to the southwest of Anderson, also rests partly on the Cumberland Plateau. The coal-rich mountains and sharply cut valleys of the plateau dominate the eastern part of

Map 2.2. The Coal Creek District

the county. To the west lie lowlands that form one boundary of Tennessee's central basin.[4]

The first white settlers soon learned of the coal deposits in east and mid-Tennessee. From the 1790s onward, farmers, small-time prospectors, and cartographers uncovered pockets of the southern coalfields and the iron reserves

Map 2.3. The Tracy City District (*Source:* Adapted from Wiebel, "Biography of a Business")

that lay adjacent to them. For several decades, however, these discoveries had little economic impact. Lack of transportation, limited capital, and the absence of commercial agriculture in much of the southern upcountry stymied industrial development, including mining. Though the coalfields began to draw greater attention in the 1850s, mining and iron production remained inconsequential. So long as the southern mountains remained geographically isolated, only small-scale operators made use of the region's vast mineral assets. These entrepreneurs made the best of a modest local market, supplying blacksmiths with the material from which they crafted horseshoes, hoes, plow points, and nails.[5]

Only after the great surge in railroad construction during the postbellum decades did the southern coalfields become the object of sustained interest. Indeed, the railroads and coal industry were tied together symbiotically. Southern railroads simultaneously consumed thousands of tons of coal and integrated the southern coalfields into regional and national markets, allowing southern mines to sell their coal to manufacturers in the Northeast and Midwest.

Between 1870 and 1900, four major lines penetrated the central Appalachian coalfields: the Chesapeake and Ohio into southern West Virginia, the Norfolk and Western into southwest Virginia, the Louisville & Nashville into eastern Kentucky and eastern Tennessee, and the Southern Road into North Carolina. Spur lines were just as important as the major trunk lines in opening up the South's bituminous coalfields to developers. Two lines crisscrossed the Tennessee coalfields. The East Tennessee, Virginia & Georgia connected the coal lands of Anderson County to their regional markets, while a short branch railroad linked Tracy City and other mid-Tennessee mines to the Nashville, Chattanooga & St. Louis. This road, built prior to the Civil War, ascended the Cumberland Plateau through a series of reverse curves and at a grade of 112 feet per mile.[6]

Technological advances, such as improvements in the manufacture and use of coke during the late 1860s, also boosted the coal and iron industries. Coke, the hard carbon fuel made from processed bituminous coal, was cheaper than charcoal and became an essential ingredient in the manufacture of pig iron. During the early 1870s, the Tennessee Coal and Railroad Company expanded its operation in Tracy City to include coke furnaces. Foreign entrepreneurs, especially British iron makers, also began to invest in similar operations nearby.[7]

The regional and national economies that were so important to the development of the South's bituminous coal industry subjected it to business cycles well beyond its control. Although strong national growth in the late 1860s and early 1870s underpinned investment in Tennessee mining, the panic of 1873 and the depression that followed halted industrial progress for the remainder of that decade. Iron prices improved in 1880, but plummeted again in 1882. Then from the mid-1880s, the South began to witness a boom in iron-making and the quickening of industrial development. Many southern counties and towns sought to take advantage of the prosperous economic climate, offering tax incentives to attract new industrial ventures. In 1888, for example, Anderson County exempted any company that built a factory there over the next decade from paying taxes for five years. With tax policies friendly to industry and a vibrant American economy, coal output in Tennessee multiplied fourfold between 1880 and 1890, from just under 500,000 to almost two million short tons.[8]

In spite of this striking growth, and in spite of incessant boasts by the 1880s that coal mining had become Tennessee's most important industry, the direct contribution of Tennessee's mineral products to the state's economy remained modest throughout the nineteenth century. In 1890, income from Tennessee's mining operations amounted to only $6.5 million, far below the value of the state's agricultural and manufacturing outputs, which totaled $54 million and $72 million respectively. The economic significance of mining primarily lay as a spur to railroad development and manufacturing. Mining companies provided railroads with vital freight orders, while supplying a growing number of the state's manufacturers with coal, coke, and iron. Yet for all the extra tons of coal that miners excavated from Tennessee's hillsides, and for all the machinery and bolts of cloth emerging from Tennessee's factories, the state's industrial production continued to pale in comparison to that of northern states. In 1890 Tennessee still produced less than 2 percent of the nation's coal.[9]

Tennessee's New South boosters were acutely aware of their state's low ranking in the nation's industrial sweepstakes. But this awareness only encouraged them to redouble their efforts. The examples of Britain and the industrial heartlands of the Northeast and Midwest led them to equate prosperity, progress, and civilization with coke ovens, molten metal, and flying shuttles. Coal was to be the modernizing agent. A dynamic mining industry, according to this viewpoint, would provide employment for a generation growing up after the Civil War, create a market for timber and farm products, accelerate railroad development, and stimulate growth in manufacturing. When Tennessee's New South ideologues imagined the future, they saw a landscape in which "blast furnaces" and "smokestacks" lit up "the darkness of a dead past."[10]

Tennessee's best known and most colorful New South ideologue was Arthur St. Clair Colyar. In a life that spanned most of the nineteenth century, Colyar pursued a variety of professions, engaged in numerous business enterprises, and went through several political incarnations. Born into a large east Tennessee family of limited means, he was educated by an uncle. In the decades after he became old enough to work, he at one time or another answered to all of the following descriptions: country teacher; mid-Tennessee country lawyer; slaveowner; leading Whig; staunch Unionist; member of the Confederate Congress; coal operator; convict lessee; editor of several of Tennessee's preeminent newspapers; and biographer of Andrew Jackson. These endeavors frequently led Colyar to move back and forth from the countryside to Nashville, and they brought him varying degrees of financial reward.[11]

Amid all this flux, one impulse remained constant in Colyar's life. From early adulthood, Colyar remained steadfast in his commitment to southern industrialization, even after he became a large land- and slaveowner through his wife's inheritance. When the opportunity arose in 1858, he purchased the Sewanee Mining Company, which in 1860 became the Tennessee Coal and Railroad Company. After the Civil War, he sold his plantation and put his ex-slaves to work mining Grundy County's coal. Within a short time, Colyar emerged as a leader of the Democratic faction wedded to industrialization, believing more fervently than ever that the South's future lay with the development of factories and mines.[12]

Already practiced in the use of forced labor, Colyar lobbied the state's Reconstruction government for the lease of convicts to Tennessee's emerging industrial elite. Colyar feared that if Tennessee's nascent mining industry had to rely solely on free labor, the mining regions would become little more than "outposts for Pennsylvania tramps whose principal business was to strike."[13] By 1871 his efforts paid off, and a growing number of state prisoners boarded trains bound for Tracy City's coal mines.

Whether as a coal operator employing convict laborers, a Democratic Party politician, or the editor of the *Nashville American* and *Nashville Union* during the 1880s, Colyar worked to bring industry to Tennessee. Though he never acquired the stature of the region's most famous proponents of a New South ideology, such as Henry Grady of the *Atlanta Constitution* and Henry Watterson of the *Louisville Courier Journal*, Colyar was equally adamant that the South could not continue to base its economy on agriculture in general and cotton in particular.[14]

Colyar's voice was the loudest and most persistent in promoting the growth of Tennessee's mining sector, but many others joined his chorus, including several politicians, lawyers, and bankers who invested in the state's coal mines. Though some of the emerging coal barons were born in the mining regions of the state, the majority came from outside Tennessee's mountainous areas, especially from the capital city of Nashville and the plantations of mid-Tennessee. The men at the forefront of the state's mining ventures—such as Thomas O'Connor, William Harrell Cherry, William Morrow, John Inman, Charles McClung McGhee, Nathaniel Baxter, and A. M. Shook—were all members of Tennessee's business elite. While all these New South industrialists fervently believed in the potential of Tennessee's coalfields, most did not restrict their attentions to coal mining. Instead, they diversified their holdings, investing in railroads, financial institutions, land, and cotton brokerage firms. Almost every one of these leading Tennesseans came from a family of some standing and wealth. Few were self-made men and most wielded enormous political clout, either formally or informally.[15] Contemporaries recognized the power of this small coterie of capitalists, variously referring to individuals among them as the "uncrowned ruler of the [Tennessee] legislature," a "Southern carpet bagger in Wall Street," and the "richest man in Knoxville." Such reputations resulted from careers that spanned well over two decades in coal and iron.[16]

Native Tennessee industrialists were not alone in their hopes of finding great wealth in the coal mines of Appalachia. They were joined by many northern and European financiers. Most of the outsiders stayed home, investing only money in the development of coal mining towns in east and mid-Tennessee. A few of the absentee speculators nonetheless managed to lend their names to the state's mining ventures. In mid-Tennessee, the mining towns of Tracy City and Whitwell owed their names to a New York City commission merchant, Samuel Franklin Tracy, and a renowned British metallurgist, Thomas Whitwell. In east Tennessee, the new mining hamlet of Briceville gave recognition to investor Calvin S. Brice, a U.S. senator from Ohio and a leading northern capitalist.

A handful of nonsouthern investors actually moved to Tennessee and opened mines themselves. James Bowron Jr. and E. J. Sanford were the most important of the migrant capitalists. In 1877, Bowron left a secure position as general manager of an English glass works to come to Tennessee as part of a consortium of British Quakers interested in developing the state's coal and iron lands. The consortium founded the Southern States Coal, Iron, and Land Company, concentrating its efforts in iron works at South Pittsburg and coal shafts at Whitwell. The company's directors—all based in England—ignored Bowron's constant entreaties during the early 1880s to pursue additional expansion. Instead, when the Tennessee Coal and Railroad Company sought to purchase the English-owned corporation in 1882, the directors embraced the offer. Hoping to maintain continuity in management, the board of the newly consolidated business, renamed the Tennessee Coal, Iron, and Railroad Company (TCIR), offered Bowron the position of secretary-treasurer. With few other options, Bowron readily accepted a salary less than half his previously considerable income of $7,500. So began an association with TCIR that would last more than two decades.[17]

Bowron was an astute businessman, a paternalist, and something of a political nonconformist. Meticulous in his accounting methods, he quickly mastered techniques for operating a business with limited working capital, such as

Clockwise from upper left:
A. M. Shook, James Bowron, and Nathaniel
Baxter, executives with the Tennessee Coal,
Iron, and Railroad Company (Tennessee
State Library and Archives; University of
Alabama, Special Collections)

persuading creditors to grant extensions in the payment of debts. At the same
time, he found ways to raise capital when many of his fellow southern business
leaders encountered desperate cash-flow problems for want of sufficient financial resources. In his relationship with TCIR's employees, Bowron tried to
inculcate a Christian ethic of upright conduct and self-improvement. He peri-

odically offered public lectures, seeking to instruct local workers in the virtues of piety, sobriety, and hard work. One of his primary missions was to ensure that the residents of Tracy City became small homeowners. Despite the speed with which he became a part of Tennessee's business establishment, he refused to join the state's former Whigs in swearing allegiance to the urban industrial wing of the Democratic Party. Instead, he became a staunch Republican.[18]

E. J. Sanford did not have to cross the Atlantic to reach Tennessee, but he did have to traverse a greater social distance than Bowron in order to join the ranks of the southern industrialists. A Connecticut Yankee by birth, Sanford came to Knoxville in 1853 with little but his carpenter's tools. After the Civil War, he began a meteoric rise in east Tennessee business circles. By the time of his death in 1902, he had served as director or president of several Tennessee mining, land, and railroad companies, holding most of these positions simultaneously. Sanford's background, like Bowron's, made him distrustful of the Democratic Party power structure, leading him to maintain political affiliation with the Republicans.

Sanford's pivotal role in so many industrial ventures typified the interlocking directorships that profoundly shaped the New South. He and four fellow directors of Coal Creek Mining & Manufacturing Company (CCM&MC), for example, held directorships in the East Tennessee, Virginia & Georgia Railroad—the railroad that traversed Anderson County, carrying the products of local mines to their destinations. The result was that the decisions of a relatively small number of men greatly influenced the business conditions under which coal companies and other industrial endeavors operated.[19]

These overlapping directorships also symbolized a shared belief that the New South should have a clearly defined group of men at its helm who would take the risks of industrial and finance capitalism and reap the resulting benefits. In a letter to C. M. McGhee, Sanford revealed his hope that their east Tennessee properties would yield great wealth, securing his children's future in the upper echelons of Tennessee's business world. "Coal Creek was even worth more than [TCIR]," he wrote, "and . . . it was going to be good for our children as long as any thing is good."[20] Sanford thus projected his conception of a southern elite into the future; he envisioned an unbroken connection between the power he and his fellow business leaders wielded and that which their progeny would enjoy.

Not all of Tennessee's industrialists comfortably took their place within the close-knit circles of the leading capitalists. Some of the small-scale businessmen who sought to develop patches of the Cumberland Plateau's coal lands remained outside the South's postbellum financial aristocracy. B. A. Jenkins,

B. A. Jenkins and E. J. Sanford (Tatom, "Press Clippings"; Tennessee State Library and Archives)

who hailed from Mt. Carmel, Pennsylvania, was one such entrepreneur. He never possessed the standing, influence, and connections of a James Bowron Jr. or an E. J. Sanford.

Jenkins moved south in the 1880s. With the help of relatives and business associates in Pennsylvania, he raised $50,000 in 1888 to capitalize the Tennessee Coal Mining Company (TCMC), which established a coal mine in the Anderson County town of Briceville. Jenkins and this coal mining company soon became synonymous. For a salary of $1,500 a year, he became president and general manager of the corporation, virtually running it singlehandedly. When policy decisions had to be made, Jenkins made them. When the company had a cash-flow problem—not an uncommon occurrence—Jenkins found alternative sources of credit, frequently extending personal loans to the business. Without Jenkins, the company would neither have been born nor long survived—a fact recognized by his fellow investors. Nonetheless, stockholders eventually lost confidence in their president, leading him to withdraw his financial support in late 1892. This development left the Tennessee Coal Mining Company unable to pay its debts. Jenkins, then, "fathered, conceived, organized [and] wrecked" the company, finally dragging it into court to be wound up as an insolvent corporation. Throughout Jenkins's years as a mining executive, he never acquired the faith of Tennessee's coal mining elite. These industrialists generally found him to be "obstinate, overbearing, dictatorial, and exceedingly obnoxious"—in short, a maverick who was out of step with the closely coordinated policies of the state's major industrial concerns.[21]

In several respects, the men who directed the development of Tennessee's coal industry were a diverse group. Former Whigs, urban bankers, onetime planters, politicians, and northern and international investors all stamped their mark on Tennessee's postbellum mining economy, while the political allegiances of these coal barons were split between the Democratic and Republican Parties. Yet all of these men shared a determination to wrest fortunes from the mineral deposits beneath Tennessee's mountains. Each of them combined a paternalist attitude toward the men who worked for him with a strong faith in the superiority of his class. Each fervently dreamed that Tennessee would "become the great industrial center of the South."[22] And despite the differences in background or political affiliation, most recognized the need for cooperation in the formulation of business strategies.

The Promise of the Coal Towns

Tennessee's industrialists could not have created vibrant mining communities by themselves. The dramatic growth in the state's mining operations depended on the efforts of thousands of rural Tennesseans, especially the children of small farmers. These migrants came overwhelmingly from within the state, and particularly from surrounding counties. In Grundy County, common names did not change perceptibly during the post–Civil War period, suggesting that population growth took place more by natural increase than by in-migration. Moreover, most of the men who rose through TCIR's ranks, from miner to convict guard or switchyardman, had been born and bred in Grundy County.[23] In Coal Creek, the proportion of miners born in Tennessee increased substantially between 1880 and 1900. During the early years of Tennessee's mining development, more than one-quarter of the mining workforce was foreign born or originally from the North. By 1900, almost no local miner had been born abroad or above the Mason-Dixon line and over eight in ten were native Tennesseans.[24]

Although Tennessee's postbellum miners had similar geographic origins, they were not racially homogeneous. Coal mines in the state generally provided employment for at least some blacks. Most black men who labored in Coal Creek, Briceville, and Tracy City were native Tennesseans. Migrants who came from other parts of the South followed the region's railroad routes. The Louisville & Nashville Railroad, for example, connected Alabama's black pop-

Coal Creek miners in front of a mine opening (Tennessee National Guard, *Souvenir of Company "C"*)

ulation to the coalfields of northeastern Tennessee and eastern Kentucky. African American miners may have regarded the Appalachian coalfields as a place to escape the oppression of agricultural wage labor or sharecropping.[25]

Many of the miners, both black and white, were young men who could no longer secure an agricultural livelihood in the counties of east and mid-Tennessee. These sons of tenant and small independent farmers sought work in the mines because local population growth had resulted in relative land scarcity. Local industrial ventures, and especially the new mines and iron forges, provided a means of obtaining work without requiring a move far from home.

The migrants did not head to Tennessee's coal towns because of a collapsing agricultural economy. In Anderson, Grundy, and fourteen surrounding counties, the number of farms remained essentially stable between 1880 and 1890. That decade also witnessed significant growth in the proportion of farms cultivated by their owners, from just under three out of four in 1880 to almost four out of five ten years later. Over the same decade, the value of farm implements and machinery increased 12 percent, the value of an average farm grew by almost 14 percent, and the value of farm products—primarily livestock, dairy, grain, and vegetables—rose by nearly 6 percent. Industrial development largely accounted for these measures of steady agricultural growth.

Scores of farmers embraced the opportunities created by the opening of so many coal mines to specialize in the provision of foodstuffs for the new town dwellers.[26]

Many agriculturalists, then, maintained a viable independence in and around Tennessee's coal-producing regions during the early decades of mining operations. But established farmers faced growing difficulties in providing their children with the resources to pursue the life of an independent agricultural producer. By 1880, most available land was already under cultivation; farmers who wished to give each of their children a landed birthright had either to purchase other land or divide their existing property. The first option was not so easy, as land values moved steadily upward under the pressure of population growth, even in a period when the regional and national economy experienced sustained deflation. A number of farmers evidently adopted the second strategy, as the average farm size in the counties surrounding the coal mines decreased from 150 acres in 1880 to 143 acres in 1890. Such responses, however, could not accommodate hundreds of young men and women growing up on the region's farms. These individuals had to leave the places of their youth in order to find work; as a result, counties in the coal region without working mines experienced slow rates of population growth or even small declines. By contrast, the population of mining counties boomed, growing at rates of between 35 and 63 percent during the 1880s.[27]

Although the miners of east and mid-Tennessee lost much of their access to farming as an occupation, they retained considerable autonomy over their lives outside work. Neither Coal Creek, Briceville, Oliver Springs, nor Tracy City exhibited the central traits of most postbellum company towns. In none of these settlements did a single employer possess monopolies over local housing and retail trade. The east Tennessee towns were located on land outside the vast tracts of Anderson County property that belonged to the Coal Creek Mining & Manufacturing Company, while TCIR allowed, and indeed encouraged, its employees to buy their own homes. In all four towns, independent storekeepers served the public.

The profile of homeownership in east and mid-Tennessee was not dissimilar. In the east Tennessee towns, roughly half of the adult male population owned either town lots or acres of land in the surrounding area during the late 1880s and early 1890s. The figures from mid-Tennessee were comparable. In 1892 roughly half of Tracy City's residents owned real estate. Over a third of local adult men owned a house on a small lot in town, while a further one in seven held title to nearby unimproved land.[28]

Even though none of the towns at the center of the mining rebellions were incorporated during the 1890s, extensive homeownership nonetheless placed limits on the ability of coal companies to define the contours of social interaction among their workforces. Employers could not threaten miners who held the title to their homes with eviction or increased rents. Homeownership greatly fostered the development of tightly knit communities in the Tennessee coalfields, as scores of miners came to view their residence and place of work as a permanent home.[29]

The growth of community institutions cemented a camaraderie and civic consciousness that would undergird the rebellions. During the late 1880s, newspapers in east Tennessee repeatedly commented on the explosive growth of social organizations and community networks. These associations, including churches, lodges, schools, sports leagues, literary and music societies, and unions, were usually created and nurtured by miners and their families. (Though Tracy City also boomed during the same period and its local newspaper conveyed the impression of a flourishing town with similar associations, reports there were more muted; as one of the few antebellum coal towns in Tennessee, Tracy City was well established by the late nineteenth century.)

The strongest community of mineworkers emerged in Coal Creek and Briceville, where the close proximity of the two towns led to the creation of an interlocking set of social institutions. Many local residents—Rob Roy from Briceville and N. B., Joe, Punch and Judy, E. C. P., J. Q. A. West, B. T. Sharp, and an anonymous "Miner" from Coal Creek—regularly informed local newspaper readers of town developments. These reports had a breathless quality to them: new buildings, services, and activities seemed to sprout in quick succession. Sunday services took place in Methodist, Baptist, Presbyterian, and Methodist Episcopal congregations. In addition to several schools, the towns boasted a number of fraternal and sororal organizations, including two Odd Fellows, a Knights of Pythias, a Masonic lodge, a Sons of Vulcan, and a Ladies Aid Society. Coal Creek Valley was also home to several Knights of Labor locals. These institutions sponsored brass bands, county fairs, baseball leagues, literary debates, singing competitions, and religious exercises. Many of these activities took place in the 300-seat Opera House. By the late 1880s, inhabitants along Coal Creek had developed expectations of a prosperous future. The mining town of Oliver Springs (located thirty-three miles from Knoxville in the southwestern corner of Anderson County) and Tracy City possessed similar community networks—and residents every bit as hopeful about their prospects.[30]

While much of the rich social fabric in the coal towns emerged from community institutions, work-related organizations played a central role in creating a sense of common purpose. Perhaps because of the lease system, the labor movement had a checkered history in organizing Tennessee's coal industry before 1891. In 1883 miners formed Knights of Labor locals in Coal Creek and Tracy City. Both locals consisted primarily of coal miners, although their ranks included laborers, local shopkeepers, and professionals. The emergence of Knights of Labor branches in the Tennessee coalfields occurred during the nationwide expansion of the labor federation in the mid-1880s. By affiliating with the Knights, Anderson and Grundy miners linked themselves to an organization committed to harmony among all producers as well as to the inclusion of both skilled and unskilled workers.[31]

By 1885, the Knights had footholds in several Tennessee mining towns. Two to three years later, union activity quickened, taking the form of a broader engagement with the Knights' cooperative principles, procedures, and internal politics as well as several labor actions. Throughout the latter half of the 1880s, east Tennessee locals maintained regular communication with the Knights' national officers, asking for advice about standards of behavior for leaders of a local, the obligation of unions to embark on sympathy strikes, and the fairness of taking away the membership of a union man who had accepted a job as a convict guard. In Coal Creek, unions also led unsuccessful strikes in 1887 and 1889, the first for a full accounting of the coal they mined and the second against a 10 percent wage reduction. As of 1890, all of the towns that housed branch prisons had Knights of Labor locals, and all of the east Tennessee locals were affiliated with the newly formed United Mine Workers of America.[32] The rebellion itself served as a boost to union organization; district membership of the United Mine Workers of America doubled between August 1890 and July 1892. According to William Riley, the black secretary-treasurer of the Kentucky-Tennessee area (UMWA District 19), membership had grown to 1,200 by July 1892.[33]

Workers of both races filled the membership rolls of the UMWA and Knights of Labor. Tactical considerations and an ideological commitment to interracialism led these unions to organize both black and white miners. With hundreds of black men employed by southern coal companies, unions could ill afford to ignore black miners; and the national leadership of both the Knights and the UMWA publicly proclaimed the importance of biracial unionism. Some African American leaders, in turn, responded to the promise of the UMWA and the Knights. Increasingly alienated by both the Democratic and Republican Parties, these individuals placed their hopes in these unions, offering their services as labor organizers.[34] By the early 1890s, rank-and-file miners increasingly took a similar stance. "The colored people," William Riley observed in an April 1892 letter to the *United Mine Workers Journal*, "have never had such treatment as they should have from either one of the old parties."

Largely as a result, he maintained, the majority of black miners in District 19 "are organized men, not in name only, but in principle as well."[35]

Thus the towns of Coal Creek, Briceville, Oliver Springs, and Tracy City quickly developed strong community organizations and a rich social infrastructure. Yet one should resist any temptation to portray these fast-growing settlements as bastions of secure employment and indivisible cohesion. In each of the coal towns, the dominance of a single industry constrained the independence of miners. Aside from working in a grist mill, providing board and lodging, or setting up shop in retail trade or as a professional, the townspeople had few options but to mine coal.[36] The coal companies' stranglehold over employment had significant implications for the miners' work lives and career decisions. Miners often could not choose their own checkweighman—the individual who weighed cars filled with mined coal—independent of the company's wishes. On occasion, company management attempted to coerce employees into conducting their commercial transactions in stores that the coal companies operated or in which a company superintendent had a financial interest. In addition, if a coal miner ever lost his job, he usually had little choice but to search for work elsewhere.[37]

Away from the coal shafts, the mining communities were not immune from internal conflicts. One crucial cleavage involved alcohol. Tennessee's Four Mile Law, which prohibited the sale of alcohol within a four-mile radius of any chartered school located in rural areas, applied to all four towns. This measure had warm local advocates, as a number of prominent miners were active temperance advocates. Nonetheless, lawsuits against the distributors of liquor suggest its ready availability. Bootlegging was not the only cause of tension within the mining communities. Much to the chagrin of some locals, gambling dens and bawdy houses found ready customers in towns throughout the coalfields.[38]

Colonial Realities

Postbellum Tennessee, like the rest of the postbellum South, suffered from a comparatively unskilled workforce, inadequate local consumption, relative distance to markets, technological backwardness, and reliance on a quasi-colonial structure of investment and credit. These points may seem obvious. Since the publication of C. Vann Woodward's *Origins of the New South* in 1951, historians have pored over and dissected the obstacles confronting postbellum southern businesses. But these well-explored themes bear further examination here, as they greatly influenced Tennessee's nascent mining economy. The character of rural land ownership in Tennessee posed an additional constraint on mining companies, one that would burden those enterprises either with vexing rents or the need to borrow extensively to obtain access to mineral-rich lands.

From the initial European settlement of the South through the Civil War, southern investment had concentrated overwhelmingly on the production of agricultural staples like cotton for distant markets. Because antebellum southern investors could recoup predictably good returns on land, slaves, and agriculture, they generally shied away from town-building or industrial ventures. Despite the fervent efforts of A. S. Colyar and his fellow prophets of a New South, industrial enterprises could not wish away the effects of these earlier trends. Relative to the northeastern and midwestern United States, the postbellum South continued to possess small urban populations and only scattered mills and factories. These demographic and economic realities limited the ability of Tennessee's mining companies to sell their products close to home.[39]

Nonetheless, regional buyers of Tennessee coal remained important to the state's mining companies. Mines from both east and mid-Tennessee supplied domestic consumers, southern manufacturers, southern railroads, steamboats plying southern rivers, and steamships calling at southern ports. Of these regional consumers of Tennessee's coal, households proved to be particularly erratic in their demand. As a result, larger commercial accounts made or broke these mines.[40]

Despite the many regional outlets for Tennessee coal products, the state's mine operators could not wholly surmount the limits of southern demand. As a result, those operators expended a great deal of effort to secure, maintain, and develop markets for their products. But in making these efforts, mining managers inevitably confronted another harsh economic constraint of the late-nineteenth-century South: high freight rates. As with the size of potential markets, post–Civil War southern enterprises faced regional disadvantages when shipping goods. To compete in distant markets, whether inside or outside the region, all southern producers had to price their products low enough to remain competitive after the addition of railroad charges.

Tennessee coal operators constantly badgered railroad carriers to reduce their rates. Although mineowners as a group needed to secure reasonable freight rates to compete in national markets, they pleaded individually with the railroad companies to favor the coal from their own particular mine. Railroads, for their part, drew the largest share of their profits from hauling coal and pig iron.[41] Thus railroads and mining companies were mutually dependent. Yet while their longer-term and larger interests led both kinds of enterprise to promote a southern industrial economy, in the short term they jockeyed with one another, each seeking to maximize the return to their respective industries.

In addition to bounded markets and expensive transportation, the managers of Tennessee's mining companies had to make do with scarce investment capital, at least compared with what was available to steel producers in Pittsburgh or Youngstown. Well into the twentieth century, the southern economy continued to register the disastrous impact of two and a half centuries of slavery and a cataclysmic Civil War. Comparatively scant capital reserves in the region lessened the ability of firms to weather economic downturns, pursue economic opportunities, or develop technologies that would improve productivity. These constraints bore most heavily on poorly capitalized companies, including relatively small-scale mining corporations, which were particularly likely candidates for bankruptcy.[42]

Tennessee mining enterprises faced yet other costs external to the mining process. In east Tennessee, leasing arrangements with land companies compelled coal operators to pay royalty payments on each ton of coal mined. The main coal producer in mid-Tennessee, TCIR, had to make interest payments on a massive bonded debt. These charges slashed profit margins in both regions.

By 1872, virtually all of the rich coal-bearing land of Anderson County had fallen under the control of three landholding companies that had overlapping directorships. The most important of these corporations was the Coal Creek Mining & Manufacturing Company, one of the many Tennessee enterprises for which E. J. Sanford served as a director. Owning over 60,000 acres in Anderson, Campbell, Morgan, and Roane Counties, CCM&MC dominated the region. Its name, however, did not accurately reflect its activities or interests. Early on, its directors restricted the business's activities to the leasing of coal lands. By the time the coal miners' rebellion erupted in 1891, CCM&MC had leased land to seven companies that together operated between twelve and twenty-seven mines. Three of these companies—the Knoxville Iron Company at Coal Creek, the Cumberland Coal Mining Company at Oliver Springs, and the Tennessee Coal Mining Company at Briceville—employed convict labor.[43]

CCM&MC arranged all its leases on similar terms. The contract that the corporation entered into with the Knoxville Iron Company in July 1888 was typical. The parties agreed to a thirty-year lease, during which time the lessee promised to pay CCM&MC a half cent for every eighty pounds of steam coal and one cent for every eighty pounds of domestic coal. The contract further stipulated a minimum annual payment of $4,000 in 1889 and 1890 and $8,000 thereafter, committing the mining corporation to substantial production regardless of prevailing prices.[44] Having to make such royalty payments cut into the profits of every east Tennessee mine.

In mid-Tennessee the industry's financial structure was not as complicated. There TCIR dominated both land ownership and coal production. Between 1881 and 1892, TCIR successfully expanded its operations, greatly increasing its holdings in Tennessee and extending them into Alabama. In those eleven years, the corporation bought five other mining companies. By the time TCIR had completed these acquisitions, the company owned several mines in mid-Tennessee and Alabama as well as vast tracts of undeveloped coal lands. All in all, TCIR's holdings represented more than 60 percent of coal and iron reserves in the two states.[45]

TCIR's ownership of a vast acreage of coal and iron land constituted a liability as well as an asset, absorbing much of the company's capital and creating a large debt. The company lacked the internal resources to put together its empire, necessitating the sale of company bonds to raise funds for takeover bids. These financial moves saddled the company with a heavy bonded indebtedness and fixed charges that it had to pay in good times and bad.[46]

Tennessee's location, then, placed serious pressures on the profitability of its mining enterprises. Mid- and east Tennessee coal operators faced relatively small regional markets, nettlesome and expensive transportation services, and a comparative shortage of capital. East Tennessee operators further encountered high rents for the use of their lands, while mid-Tennessee managers had to pay interest on company bonds. Thus these mining ventures confronted vexing impediments to the sale of their product and substantial fixed costs external to the mining process. The combination of these economic constraints impelled all Tennessee operators to lower production costs whenever possible.

New South Variations

Although Tracy City, Coal Creek, Briceville, and Oliver Springs were all of the New South, they were not replicas of each another. One crucial set of differences concerned the scale of mining operations in the two regions. In mid-Tennessee, TCIR, with its substantial financial resources and land holdings, dominated mining. Indeed, it was one of the South's preeminent coal and iron producers, supplying a majority of southern railroads with all or part of their energy needs, providing steam coal to seafaring ships at ports throughout the South, and shipping large quantities of pig iron to northern buyers. By 1890, the company's capitalization exceeded $16 million, a figure that would almost double in 1892 when TCIR purchased two major Alabama coal companies.[47]

East Tennessee, by contrast, was home to a substantial number of coal companies and a plethora of mines. Anderson County alone provided a base for seven mining establishments, none of which worked more than four shafts. Each of these corporations leased land from CCM&MC, and they all competed fiercely with one another to find buyers for their coal. All the Anderson County mining corporations were relatively small businesses, capitalized at between $16,000 and $300,000. The largest mining enterprise in east Tennessee, the Knoxville Iron Company, operated in unique circumstances—it mined coal primarily for use in its Knoxville rolling mill. More commonly, east Tennessee coal companies conducted business with around $100,000 in capital and restricted their efforts to mineral excavation.[48]

TCIR became so large, and the eastern mining companies stayed so small, partly because coal seams in the two regions had distinct geological qualities. East Tennessee boasted twenty-one seams, eight of which offered profitable access. The coal from these seams was very hard and easily broken into large blocks. These characteristics rendered it appropriate for use in households or for the generation of gas or steam. But for all its virtues, east Tennessee coal did not lend itself to easy conversion into coke, a profitable coal by-product essential to the manufacture of iron and steel. Anderson County miners could extract their coal only in combination with a good deal of slate. Before workers could turn this mixture into coke, they had to remove the slate through an expensive intermediary washing process. As a result, east Tennessee operators produced almost no coke, shipping essentially all of their coal.[49]

Mid-Tennessee had only one profitable vein of coal, the main Sewanee seam. But this bed of coal was substantially more valuable than its east Tennessee counterparts. In addition to being appropriate for domestic purposes and for the production of gas and steam, Sewanee coal lent itself to coke conversion. Mine managers of the Tracy City–based Tennessee Coal and Railroad Company first recognized this potential in the 1870s, when they built beehive ovens and began to turn what company officials had previously regarded as a waste product—the fine coal called slack—into coke. Thereafter the amount of the mid-Tennessee coal that workers fed to coke ovens grew rapidly. By 1894, almost one-third of the region's coal ended up as coke.[50]

The capacity to produce coke allowed the Tennessee Coal and Railroad Company to expand its field of operation and eventually laid the foundation for the vertical integration of its industrial activities. By late 1880, officials of the Tracy City company reached the conclusion that coal and coke production would not suffice if the company was to maintain its rate of growth. A year later TCR's management reincorporated the business, changing its name to the

Tennessee Coal, Iron, and Railroad Company. Shortly thereafter, TCIR acquired James Bowron's Southern States Coal, Iron, and Land Company, along with its partially developed iron ore mine at Inman, its two blast furnaces in South Pittsburg, and its coal mine and coke ovens at Whitwell. Inman, South Pittsburg, and Whitwell were all in relatively close proximity to TCIR's central Tennessee location in Tracy City. Using the coke from Tracy City and Whitwell to smelt the ore from Inman, and combining that product with limestone from a quarry near the South Pittsburg furnace, TCIR entered the pig iron business in the early 1880s. Henceforth, TCIR was able to operate in a number of different markets. In addition, TCIR now enjoyed the flexibility to increase the proportion of coal it transformed into coke whenever the market rewarded such an adjustment.[51]

The mid-Tennessee mines had topographical as well as geological advantages over their counterparts to the east. TCIR's mines were virtually all self-draining; in east Tennessee, the mines accumulated water and tended to flood when idle. If mineworkers did not expel accumulated water expeditiously, serious damage could result to entries, rooms, and mining property, potentially threatening the very existence of a given mine. To prevent such a calamity, operators had to work their mines even during periods when the market proved unfavorable.[52] With slate-filled coal seams that easily flooded, east Tennessee coal operators had far less ability to respond flexibly to changes in demand for their product.

The size of mining corporations in mid- and east Tennessee had profound implications for industrial relations and community life in the two regions. Because TCIR owned all the land and operated all the coal mines in and around Tracy City, it possessed far greater authority over its miners than did the smaller, more marginal east Tennessee companies. Like many other large American corporations in the late nineteenth century, TCIR strove to make itself the most important arbiter of community life in the towns where it operated and to win the allegiance of the company's free workers. As the major provider of economic opportunity in Grundy and several surrounding counties, TCIR wielded considerable local clout. Three-quarters of the men found worthy of inclusion in an 1898 Compendium of Biography covering the Cumberland region of Tennessee got their start in life or made their careers with TCIR. These individuals included not only executive directors and managers but also mine and convict foremen, merchants, sheriffs, blacksmiths, and switchyard engineers.[53]

In a host of ways, company managers attempted to translate TCIR's economic power into influence over the lives of Tracy City residents. One company strategy focused on housing. TCIR sought to create bonds between the company and its workforce by providing opportunities for homeownership, especially through two Tracy City building societies. The first of these mortgage lenders was founded by TCIR's secretary-treasurer, James Bowron, in 1886, and the second was incorporated in 1891 with TCIR's mine superintendent, E. O. Nathurst, as primary trustee. Bowron in particular was motivated by a combination of civic and pecuniary impulses. He wished Tracy City to develop in what he perceived as a "positive direction," to be more than another ugly mining camp. Bowron's pious upbringing and his association with the Young Men's Christian Association had much to do with his efforts to create a stable community of homeowning miners. But he also hoped that his investment in the building society would pay respectable dividends.[54]

When either of the building societies extended a mortgage or when TCIR sold houses and property outright, the company attempted to shape residential life by imposing limits on the purchaser's rights of ownership. New homeowners had to sign restrictive deeds, agreeing to neither distill nor sell liquor. In addition, buyers promised not to engage in any manufacturing process or mechanical occupation without first securing TCIR's permission. These conditions carried legal weight for ninety-nine years, irrespective of who might acquire the property.[55]

TCIR thus determined who could settle in its villages and who could operate as a business owner. "We use the power of land owners with an iron hand," Bowron noted in 1886, "to prevent the establishment . . . of any vicious or undesirable agencies." The TCIR secretary-treasurer left no doubt that "vicious and undesirable" were synonymous with labor activism and alcoholic dissipation. In his mind, mid-Tennessee's miners needed someone to provide them with guidance and look after their interests, and mine managers would serve admirably as counselors and protectors.[56]

In their efforts to distinguish between admissible and inadmissible forms of activity and to promote a settled and stable community, TCIR executives also actively fostered the development of churches and schools. For the sum of one dollar, the company sold a quarter acre of land to establish the Christian Church. Though TCIR wrote all its standard restrictions into this sale, company officials had reason to expect that the trustees would discharge their duties in line with corporate wishes. All three were reputable miners, and two of the three had bought houses from TCIR valued at $150 and $250. There were seven other houses of worship in Tracy City, all of which probably had similar links to the company.[57]

TCIR's management also took more than a passing interest in education. In

James A. Shook School, Tracy City (William Ray Turner Collection)

1889 TCIR built a large, prepossessing school under A. M. Shook's watchful eye. Shook, who had risen from store clerk to general manager and subsequently became vice president, named the institution after his father, James K. Shook, as a tribute to the years he had spent teaching in rural schools. The company put substantial resources into the project, assessing construction costs at $40,000. Elites in Tracy City and Nashville saw the school as a symbol of TCIR's benevolence.[58]

In Anderson County, coal companies had far less of a role in shaping the character of coal towns. East Tennessee miners who bought homes did so beyond the purview of their employers. Some of the companies provided houses for rent, but none set up financial mechanisms that allowed miners to purchase a permanent home; and none owned sufficient town property to take on the role of a real estate developer. In east Tennessee towns residents could buy homes without reliance on an omnipresent company.

Since coal companies did not own land in Anderson County, they also could not set the terms relating to the carrying on of local enterprises or easily prevent anyone from setting up a business. Indeed, one resident and home-owner, Eugene Merrell, established a grocery store after he had been black-listed by the company for his role in union activism. He remained in Coal Creek long after he could no longer secure a job in the mines, becoming a community leader and central figure during the Coal Creek rebellion. By the same token, mining enterprises like B. A. Jenkins's TCMC lacked the financial resources to set up religious or educational institutions. Thus east Tennessee miners and their families were not especially beholden to their employers when they bought homes, went to church, or sent their children to school. Compared with the residents of Tracy City, the citizens of Anderson County towns enjoyed a greater degree of autonomy in community life.[59]

One should not exaggerate the pervasiveness of TCIR's influence in mid-Tennessee or underestimate the authority wielded by east Tennessee mining corporations. TCIR's housing policies did make scores of its employees home-owners, and at least some Tracy City miners remained highly critical of the corporation's attempts at social engineering. One frequent letter writer to the *Weekly Toiler*, a Farmers' Alliance publication, sneered at TCIR's paternalism. "Some great monopolists," the contributor "Adolphus" intoned, "has [sic] undertaken to appease the wrath of God and gain favor in the eyes of the world by giving magnificent gifts to religions, benevolent and educational institu-tions, so the poor, they say, may have the gospel and their children may receive an education." Distinguishing between what the "monopolists" thought their employees ought to have and what working people wanted, Adolphus con-tinued: "The laboring masses are not asking for charity in money or lands, but they do ask for living wages and the right to produce."[60]

Similarly, east Tennessee mining enterprises tried to use their economic power, however limited in comparison with that of TCIR, to direct the social choices of their employees. Most important, several east Tennessee mines op-erated company stores and occasionally exerted pressure on coal miners to patronize those establishments. This pressure usually took the form of threat-ening an employee with dismissal if he or his family continued to trade with independent shopkeepers.[61]

Nonetheless, miners in Coal Creek and Oliver Springs experienced substan-tially greater independence from their employers than mineworkers in Tracy City. The symbolic meanings attached to homeownership in the various Ten-nessee towns forcefully demonstrate this difference. In Tracy City, company managers and the press, rather than local coal miners, appropriated the values associated with owning a home. In doing so, these spokesmen for capital invariably conjured up images of intelligence, sobriety, and thrift, insisting that the homeowners who demonstrated these admirable qualities owed a debt of gratitude to the company. In Anderson County mining communities, by contrast, coal miners, rather than mineowners and managers, offered the public commentary about the significance of holding the title to one's residence. East Tennessee mineworkers maintained that their own hard work had allowed so many of them to become homeowners, not the benevolence of coal operators. At the same time, these workers laid claim to the mantle of responsibility and conservatism, which they saw as intimately connected with homeownership. Explicitly linking patriotism with the stalwart defense of family, home, and property, one Coal Creek community leader insisted that "men dead to all ties of home cannot be patriotic."[62]

Just as TCIR had a greater capacity to influence the social and religious world of its employees than did the smaller companies of Anderson County, so it proved more able to mold its workforce and dictate the terms of its relationship with union representatives. The Tracy City–based company adroitly fostered divisions among its employees, especially by setting greatly varying wages for miners and mine laborers. In 1890 highly proficient miners in mid-Tennessee took home an average of $2.12 per day, while laborers netted only $1.22. This variance greatly exceeded the range of incomes in Anderson County. There miners made $1.89 per day, while laborers earned $1.65.[63] The combination of this pay discrepancy and TCIR's emphasis on homeownership allowed the company to cultivate a group of skilled miners distinct from mine laborers.

TCIR additionally encouraged division between mid-Tennessee's white and black miners. Tracy City's African Americans lived in separate residential areas and toiled in lower-paying jobs. Black residents lived in a "negro quarter" that bore the derogatory name "Happy Bottom." They were buried at "Nigger Hill" and held classes and prayer meetings in a single-room building that served as both school and church. The exact number of black miners who left this section of town in the early hours of the morning remains unclear, but they made up a tiny proportion of the mining population. Only slightly over 2 percent of Tracy City's adult male population was black, less than a third of the proportion of Grundy County's African American population and only one-tenth of the proportion of black mid-Tennesseans. Those few blacks who labored for TCIR did so as coke-drawers and furnace workers. Such opportunities resulted from the distaste the white miners generally had for working around the extremely hot coking process.[64]

The marginal status of African American miners in Tracy City was reflected in the town's high ratio of black men to black women. Over four-fifths of

Grundy County's African American residents were male, suggesting that the county's black miners were transient laborers. In this regard, the mining towns of Grundy County mirrored most postbellum southern mining communities. In places like Wise County, Virginia, McDowell County, West Virginia, and Bell County, Kentucky, single men predominated among the black population. In these settlements, as in Grundy County, few black coal miners put down significant roots.[65]

As a result of the low numbers and transience of Grundy County's black miners, their incorporation into the union local was tenuous at best. Tracy City's master workman, Tom Carrick, refused indiscriminately to accept coal miners into the Knights' locals, preferring to welcome only men of "known" character. For Carrick, who openly opposed "negro equality," one had to be white to satisfy this standard. The presence of many ex-convicts among Tracy City's black miners gave him the excuse to exclude most African American workers from the union. This stance limited the development of a biracial class-based solidarity in Grundy County.[66]

While TCIR's free workforce was beset by divisions based on skill and race, local mining unions had far more substantial links to company management than to national labor organizations. The company successfully pressured employees not to affiliate with the United Mine Workers of America after its creation in 1890, making it impossible for Tracy City locals to draw on the resources of the national union during labor disputes. At the same time, TCIR managers fostered a close relationship with the locals, based on both fraternization and thuggery. From the mid-1880s onwards, the Knights of Labor local invited company officials such as James Bowron to address its members on such topics as the "relations of labor and capital." According to one miner, H. Lee Goodman, the Knights "took anybody in. Even old Nathurst, the company superintendent, used to come over and make speeches." But the company did not solely rely on friendly relations to ensure regular cooperation. TCIR employed company toughs to spy on the union and punished individuals who advocated union militance by placing them in particularly difficult or dangerous places in the mine. This unhappy situation led Goodman to conclude that the Knights "never did anything."[67]

The configuration of Anderson County's mining workforce was far more conducive to independent labor organization. Not only was the gap in wages between miners and mine laborers relatively slight, but black men were represented in much greater numbers. Unlike the situation in Grundy County, mining in Anderson County was a particularly viable occupation for African American men. Blacks made up 16 percent of Anderson County's miners in

1891—double the proportion of African Americans in the county as a whole and 4 percent higher than the ratio of blacks in east Tennessee's population in 1890. Moreover, in contrast to several late-nineteenth-century southern coal mining towns, the mining communities of Anderson County were home to relatively settled black mineworkers. Many of the black men who migrated to Coal Creek or Oliver Springs brought wives with them; as a result, black men represented only just over half of Anderson County's adult black population.[68] The high mobility rates among southern black miners did not pertain to east Tennessee.

The African Americans living in Anderson County's mining communities were not as fully excluded from the communal, business, and union life of those towns as were their counterparts in mid-Tennessee. Black and white homes in Coal Creek stood side by side. In Oliver Springs some blacks and whites prayed and worked together. A black preacher could give "an interesting sermon at Hoskins school house" to a large audience of "both white and colored people," while a white and black pair of business partners could operate a dray-wagon firm. Anderson County's black miners were also well represented in local mining unions.[69]

The union strength of east Tennessee black miners was great enough that a handful of black men achieved positions of prominence. William Riley serves as a case in point. A black coal miner and preacher, Riley held the pivotal position of secretary-treasurer of the UMWA's southern Kentucky and east Tennessee district from the union's inception until at least the mid-1890s. He appears to have been very popular—his reelection to office in 1892 was virtually unanimous, with the single dissenting ballot coming from a black miner.[70]

Race relations in Anderson County's coalfields, however, were not wholly benign. Although men like William Riley won the support of whites in the district, white miners often refused to allow black miners to rise through the ranks to become bank-bosses or checkweighmen. Whites frequently kicked up a fuss when blacks rose above the "pick and shovel," even though they might have agreed in principle to share such positions with blacks on a proportionate basis. In addition, when the jobs of Anderson County's white miners were threatened or when they believed they had reason to distrust the commitment of black miners to union precepts, the county's white mineworkers were not beyond threatening their black counterparts with violence. Racial animosity lurked beneath the surface in Tennessee's mining communities. Given the tenor of race relations and racial politics in late-nineteenth-century Tennessee, the presence of such tensions is hardly surprising. Racially discriminatory legislation on the state level, manipulation of race by coal operators, southern custom, and a tradition of separating union locals by race all raised barriers to cooperation between white and black miners.[71] In Anderson County, then, white miners maintained shifting boundaries for the inclusion and exclusion of their black counterparts. In Grundy County the white miners more rigorously excluded their black fellow miners.

Opposing political identities further distinguished the coal-rich areas around Coal Creek from those surrounding Tracy City. The Coal Creek mines lay in a part of the state known for its pro-Union sentiment during the Civil War. One of Oliver Springs's few supporters of the Confederacy later recalled how after the Civil War he had to leave his home, since "it was not very safe for Confederate soldiers to live in Anderson Co.," a territory swarming with "Union sympathizers and bush whackers."[72] In the postbellum decades, attachment to the Union cause remained intense throughout east Tennessee and translated into fervent support for the Republican Party. The region's voters both consistently put Republicans into local offices and helped make the Grand Old Party a meaningful opposition in state politics, which was a rare occurrence in the Solid South. Grundy County, by contrast, lay in mid-Tennessee, where secession once held sway and the Democracy maintained its political supremacy.[73] James Bowron, the immigrant Quaker and Republican, was an anomaly in a section of the state that consistently elected Democratic sheriffs and judges. In state races Grundy citizens similarly voted the Democratic ticket. As in the rest of the late-nineteenth-century United States, political identifications in Tennessee were bound up with powerful emotions predicated on exclusion and opposition as much as membership. To be a Grundy County Democrat was to reject the Party of Reconstruction and "black rule"; to be an Anderson County Republican was to proclaim one's contempt for the Party of Secession.

Southern industrialization, for the most part, meant mine shafts in places like Coal Creek Valley and iron furnaces in villages like South Pittsburg. The New South was built on a foundation of rural towns. Despite the limitations of a colonial economy and the rapacity of many southern industrialists, the new communities of the New South did provide meaningful opportunities to tens of thousands of southerners, including both whites and blacks. People moved to Tracy City and Briceville and Oliver Springs because they no longer possessed a clear future on the land. But they also moved because of the promise of the new towns—the hopes of steady employment and independent homeownership; the certainties of education for children and a place to worship; and the fellowship of sports leagues, fraternal organizations, and annual dances.

The hopes, of course, did not always become realities. Steady work, reasonable wages, and company profits periodically disappeared in the face of economic slumps. Some industrial ventures never paid dividends to investors or decent wages to employees. Black residents in coal towns faced ever-present discrimination at work and in community life. But the schemes and dreams within Tennessee's coalfields did not always end in disappointment and disaster.[74]

For one group of men in the coal towns, though, the experience was less ambiguous. These individuals came to the settlements not as the result of a complicated amalgam of pushes and pulls, or with much hope of anything more than simple survival. They owed their migration to court proceedings in which a jury had found them guilty of a criminal act, and to a state government that lacked sufficient resources to house its prisoners. They were victims of the convict lease, and their presence in the coalfields eventually set off the spark of rebellion.

Coin blood into gold;
　　who cares for the cost?
There's money to make
　　though a soul may be lost.
Then cut him, and carve him;
Throw his flesh to the hog.
It is only a convict who died
　　like a dog.
—*Nashville Banner*,
　　February 7, 1885

CHAPTER 3

Measures of Southern Justice

In the four decades following the Civil War, the number of African Americans ensnared by southern justice grew tremendously. Over that same period, the majority of the southern states adopted a convict-lease system, with state governments leasing out their prisoners to private contractors for a set fee.[1] Transported to prison stockades that dotted the remote corners of the southern landscape, convicts helped the South build its railroads, mine its coal and phosphate, construct its levees, fell its lumber, and, on occasion, grow its cotton, tobacco, and corn.

The convict lease was neither a southern nor a postbellum invention; it did, however, receive its most sustained and dramatic expression in the post–Civil War South. By 1877—the year that heralded the end of Reconstruction and the entrenchment of southern home rule—Florida became the last of the southern states to begin leasing a part or all of its prison inmates. Mississippi and Georgia had led the way, leasing their convicts soon after the war ended, in 1866 and 1868 respectively. Mississippi again led the region when that state terminated its lease in 1894; Tennessee and Louisiana followed shortly thereafter. Most states ended their leases around the turn of the century and during the early years of the twentieth century. Alabama brought up the rear, not reclaiming control of its prison inmates from private entrepreneurs until 1928.[2]

The lease system emerged in an unsynchronized, makeshift fashion. Sometimes Reconstruction administrations introduced the convict lease; sometimes the institution began with the initiative of Redeemers. The shift from centralized penitentiaries to convict lessees also did not proceed along one path. Kentucky, Maryland, Missouri, Virginia, and Texas included the convict lease among other forms of penal administration; Alabama, Arkansas, Florida, Georgia, Louisiana, Mississippi, and Tennessee went further, eventually placing every state prisoner in the hands of a convict lessee.[3]

Once Tennessee officials succumbed to the convict lease as a method of penal administration, they first negotiated contracts with small operators who agreed to employ convicts in manufacturing enterprises within the main penitentiary. From 1865 to 1870, a Nashville firm employed the state's felons in the production of reapers, mowers, thrashers, plows, wagons, saddles, and cedarware. The company paid forty-three cents per day per convict; under this arrangement, the welfare of the inmates remained the responsibility of the state.[4]

In 1871 Tennessee prison officials entered into contracts with brokerage companies who paid a set fee per annum for the lease. Over the next fourteen years, these companies employed the majority of their charges beyond the walls of the Nashville pen.[5] Tennessee's white inmates, like those in other southern states, primarily stayed in the central prison and received artisanal training, while African American prisoners usually labored beyond the penitentiaries in unskilled vocations. As lessees increasingly engaged in far-flung operations, government officials gave corporate managers more and more responsibility for the detention and care of the state's inmates. Lease contracts also gradually reduced the ability of lessees to claim against the state for loss of labor caused by escapes or gubernatorial pardons.[6] Over the 1870s and early 1880s, Tennessee privatized most of the functions associated with its penal system.

With more authority over a growing number of laborers, lessees sought to maximize their investment by consolidating their wards in a small number of closely guarded prison camps and by placing convicts in employment that the lessees believed was particularly appropriate for forced labor. Once railroad development slackened in the late 1870s and Tennessee coal mining and pig iron production became more lucrative in the next decade, stripe-suited convict laborers found themselves working in and around coal mines rather than along railroad rights of way.[7]

Throughout the postbellum decades, Tennesseans of every description took the measure of the convict lease and the criminal code that filled its quota of toiling bodies. Some of these calculations involved corporate balance sheets and public deficits. Others concerned the definition of crime, the appropriate length and purpose of penal service, and the need to legitimate the state's system of criminal justice—either by tempering its harshness or by applying its provisions to the high and mighty. Still others measured the likely impact of the convict lease on the position and behavior of free workers, especially free miners. All the while, Tennessee's convicts calculated what it would take to enable them to live beyond their days as unfree laborers. Occasionally the estimations turned out to be flawed. These miscalculations put Tennessee's free miners on the path of armed revolt.

The Mining Industry and the Imperative of Cheap Labor

Convicts made their first appearance in Tennessee's mines in 1871. The Tennessee Coal and Railroad Company led the way in Grundy and Marion Counties, but over the next two decades other companies introduced state prisoners to Anderson and Morgan County mines in the eastern section of the state. The Knoxville Iron Company brought convicts to its Coal Creek Mine in 1877, leasing between 100 and 160 inmates for the next decade and a half; in 1889 the Cumberland Coal Company began using a similar contingent of prisoners at its Big Mountain Mine outside Oliver Springs.[8] The new penal system's standard-bearers, including many state officials, offered several justifications for the entry of convicts into coal shafts and coke works. They emphasized that there was a shortage of men willing to engage in mine labor during the early years of the industry's development; they trumpeted the growth of Tennessee's prosperity through the use of convict labor, since Tennessee's future lay with the coal under its ground and someone had to excavate it; and they proclaimed that Tennessee's convicts would cease to compete with urban skilled mechanics if those convicts moved to mining settlements.

The first justification received especially detailed treatment. J. T. Hill, Tennessee's representative to the 1897 meeting of the National Prison Association, recalled a dearth of free laborers who were willing to work in Tennessee's nascent mining enterprises. Hill insisted that it was "a practical impossibility

Convicts at Tracy City, 1880s (William Ray Turner Collection)

to get our native free people, either white or black, their training having been principally of an agricultural tendency, to work in the mines, rendering it necessary to send abroad for miners, and even then the demand could not be supplied." Throughout the 1870s, mine operators reported that employees were difficult to find and that those individuals who did enter the mines proved unreliable. These grievances resonated with the chief complaint of ex-slaveholders during the immediate postwar period—that an adequate supply of reliable and inexpensive labor could not be counted on.[9]

Local mining magnates further argued that the use of convict workers—whom they characterized as a cheap, dependable labor force—would stimulate growth in both mining and secondary industry. By contributing to the general development of industry in the state, the convict lease would speed up Tennessee's integration into the national economy. The result would be a greater number of coal mines, a greater number of iron furnaces, and a greater number of workshops and factories, all of which would provide employment for free Tennesseans.[10]

Finally, advocates of the convict lease's extension into mining sites sought to accommodate the interests of urban mechanics. From the 1830s onward, artisans had protested against prisoners being taught mechanical skills and called for stringent regulation of prison-made goods. Mining magnates such as A. S. Colyar continually supported the mechanics in their quest to cleanse their trades of the "polluting" and "degrading" influence of convict laborers. Like many of his contemporaries, Colyar believed that the state should show more concern about skilled workers, who attained their positions through apprenticeships, than about bituminous miners, who after a few weeks on the job were able to mine with greater or lesser skill.[11] Colyar's comments presupposed a hierarchy of labor, with the cities' white artisans deserving greater consideration than rural, upcountry whites and southern blacks.

The public rhetoric of mine managers, however, masked their most important motivation in seeking the use of convict laborers. Attracting free workers to Tennessee's mines may have been a worry in their early years of operation; but as both blacks and whites flocked to and helped build the coal towns in the 1880s and early 1890s, problems of labor supply dissipated. The desire to improve economic opportunities for Tennesseans in general and urban mechanics in particular may have been genuine, but they were secondary concerns for mine operators. These industrialists viewed the convict lease first and foremost as a means of cutting labor costs, both directly and by dampening the activity of mining unions.

Tennessee mine managers had ample reason to look for means of decreasing expenditure on labor. In addition to limited regional markets, high freight rates, restricted access to capital, and the claims of bondholders or leaseholders, coal operators confronted the turbulent, deflationary conditions of the late-nineteenth-century economy—including dramatic economic downturns after the Panic of 1873, during the mid-1880s, and even before the Panic of 1893, as well as the relentless fall in general prices. Between 1865 and 1892, coal prices dropped by one-half, and mining corporations periodically encountered serious problems in collecting from their customers or raising cash to pay their creditors. Since there was little technical innovation in postbellum mining and since labor absorbed well over half of the expenses incurred in the excavation of coal or the production of coke or iron, any significant lowering of costs had to focus on cutting the wage bill.[12]

Once Tennessee's coal companies had convicts wielding pickaxes and loading coal cars, corporate leaders gained substantial leverage over the industry's free workers. During the next two decades, from the early 1870s through to the rebellion in 1891, the state's free miners lived with the understanding that convict labor served as a club, a Sword of Damocles dangling above their heads. This role of prison labor was made patently clear by the circumstances in which coal companies introduced prisoners to mines in Coal Creek and Oliver Springs. In both instances, mining corporations turned to the convict lease as a response to strikes for higher wages by local miners.[13]

Even during the coal miners' rebellion, by which time TCIR in particular had incurred nationwide notoriety for its use of convict labor, A. S. Colyar continued to stress a theme that he had first articulated twenty years previously, when he had advocated convict leasing to prevent Tennessee from becoming an outpost for northern, strike-prone tramps. The chief reason for using convicts in TCIR's mines, in Colyar's mind, was the facility it offered for overcoming labor militance. "For some years after we began the convict labor system," Colyar maintained, "we found that we were right in calculating that the free laborers would be loath to enter upon strikes when they saw that the company was amply provided with convict labor."[14] Convict labor, operators in both mid- and east Tennessee hoped, would serve to reduce the wages they paid to free miners and curb the miners' abilities to challenge the operators' labor practices.

The introduction of convict workers was not the only strategy employed by Tennessee's mining corporations in the effort to reduce labor costs. Like industrialists throughout Gilded Age America, Tennessee mine managers regularly cut wages and periodically laid off their free workers. As a result of this latter tactic, most of the state's miners worked in conditions of chronic underemployment, especially during summer months or cyclical slowdowns. Many coal operators also manipulated the weight of coal cars, docked miners for impurities mixed in their coal, and tried to impose contracts that required employees to eschew membership in labor unions.[15]

These strategies collectively achieved significant reductions in the labor costs of Tennessee mines. The fees that convict lessees paid to the state and the expenses associated with taking care of prisoners totaled between sixty cents and one dollar per inmate per day in the twenty years after convicts first entered Tennessee's mines, far less than the daily earnings of a free miner. The earnings of mineworkers, moreover, dropped sharply over the same two decades. In some parts of the Tennessee coalfields, mine operators paid over a dollar for a ton of coal at the end of the Civil War, giving most miners the ability to earn close to four dollars for a day's work. By the early 1890s, the wage rate per ton of loaded coal had decreased by more than half, leaving the average miner with a daily pay of less than two dollars.[16]

Though Tennessee coal operators clamored for the unfree labor of prison inmates in order to achieve specific financial objectives, long-standing attitudes about race and the legitimacy of compulsory labor systems made the psychological transition to convict labor relatively easy. Some operators, like A. S. Colyar, had been slaveowners and so were experienced in coercing labor from unfree workers. Since slavery was much more than a legal institution, its legacy—the social habits acquired in the management of slaves—reinforced the attractiveness of convict miners as alternatives to free laborers.[17]

Convict Labor and Fiscal Prudence

Nascent industrialists were not alone in finding the convict lease an appealing proposition. Mine managers found common cause with state officials who wished to limit Tennessee's expenditure on penal administration and even turn the prisons into a money-making venture. The convict lease satisfied both objectives. Allowing private entrepreneurs to work prison inmates beyond the walls of the penitentiary provided the South with a far more lucrative source of revenue than the contract system employed in many northern states. In this latter system, contractors worked the prisoners within the penitentiary walls and shared disciplinary control with state officials. Northern prisons using the contract system typically earned about one-third of their total expenses, while southern states that relied on the lease generally earned well over twice the direct costs of penal administration. Of all the states leasing out convicts, Tennessee and Alabama enjoyed the most lucrative deals; by 1886, convicts brought each state over $100,000 per annum.[18] John P. Buchanan, Tennessee's governor in 1891 and a central player in the mining rebellion, modestly praised the scheme as "successful," "relieving [the state] of all business risk and expense, and paying a surplus into the treasury." Buchanan had reason to be pleased. Between 1870 and 1890, Tennessee's lessees paid over one million dollars into state coffers, four-fifths of which constituted a net surplus.[19]

Though the direct contribution that the convict lease made to state coffers should not be underestimated, its true pecuniary value lay in the savings that it represented. If the convict lease had not been in place, the state governments would have had the responsibility of transporting, housing, clothing, and feeding their prison inmates. In 1891 Buchanan estimated that transportation and maintenance alone would have required an annual expenditure of $250,000. The governor further projected that a new penitentiary would cost $300,000 and take two years to complete. Thus the actual payments associated with the convict lease represented only a part of the financial benefit that Tennessee achieved through the rental of its convicts.[20]

Such savings were greatly needed. After four years of Civil War, the Volunteer State's infrastructure lay in ruins. Returning soldiers often found their homes burned and their livestock missing. Public devastation mirrored personal loss. The state's railroads—which had, in the 1850s, symbolized progress and economic development—lay in mangled heaps of upturned iron. After the South's surrender, money was not readily available to recoup the financial losses sustained during the war. The value of agricultural products, the mainstay of the South's economy, declined drastically. In 1870 Tennessee's production of cotton and tobacco had fallen to roughly one-half of its 1860 output while the value of livestock had dropped 9 percent. In 1860 Tennessee's taxable wealth had stood at $390,000,000. By 1865 taxable property valuation had plummeted to $195,000,000; in the deflationary postwar period, it would not recover its 1860 level until 1892.[21]

The increase in Tennessee's financial obligations was as spectacular as the decline in the state's wealth. The state not only had to honor interest on loans and retire bonds secured before the war; it also contracted substantial debts in efforts to rebuild its transportation infrastructure. By 1870, Tennessee's debt stood at a staggering $40 million—the second-largest in the nation. At least half of this debt had been contracted before 1860, largely the result of assistance to railroad development. Like the antebellum debt, most postbellum financial obligations were incurred through aid issued to railroad companies. The extent of Tennessee's indebtedness in 1870 reflected the commitment of William G. Brownlow, the state's first Unionist governor, and DeWitt C. Senter, his Republican successor, to internal improvements as the basis of industrial development and economic growth.[22]

The structure of Tennessee's debt and the terms on which the state government should repay its primarily New York bondholders remained the thorniest and most contested issue in Tennessee politics until the Democratic Party eventually settled the question in 1883. Fracture lines within the Democratic and Republican Parties emerged on the basis of commitments to a "state credit" or "low tax" position. Debt and fiscal prudence—the mantra of the Redeemer governments—became the watchwords of the 1870s, overshadowing the outmoded and war-damaged penitentiary as a political issue. A similar political dynamic occurred in legislatures throughout the South.[23]

Placing prison construction toward the bottom of state agendas did not solve the problems surrounding the South's prisons. Built during the late eighteenth or early nineteenth century, these crumbling edifices of a bygone age rarely outlived the Confederacy. Some, like those in Louisiana and Virginia, were destroyed during the war; others, like Tennessee's, survived but were unequal to the task at hand. The latter state's government had erected a 200-cell penitentiary in 1829 two miles southwest of Nashville. Within a decade, prisoners teemed in overcrowded cells. Two additions to the old penitentiary proved to be temporary expedients. In 1881 the warden criticized the penitentiary as "old and dilapidated, damp and cheerless"—the result of "long use and poor ventilation."[24] By 1891, the penitentiary could hold only 400 of the state's 1,500 convicts. The convict lease, with its system of branch prisons, relieved the state governments from obligations to rebuild crumbling penitentiaries at a substantial cost to taxpayers.[25]

The unwillingness of Tennessee's voters and government to build an adequate penitentiary should not draw attention away from the state's very real financial commitment to law enforcement. Next to repayment of the public debt, which consumed between 40 and 60 percent of postbellum annual budgets, the government spent more on law enforcement and costs incurred by the judiciary than it did on social services, pensions, public administration, and a host of other governmental duties. Between 1888 and 1894, the government spent around one-fifth of taxpayers' money on the criminal justice system, including state prosecutions, the national guard, and court costs. In comparison, education, hospitals, and oversight of the state's human and physical resources together received only 14 to 21 percent of the budget.[26]

Although public officials praised the convict lease as a moneymaker, the 5 percent of state revenue that it generated covered only between a third and a fifth of costs incurred by the administration of justice, which primarily constituted the payment of fees to a host of local officials and functionaries. The greater part of the money needed to pay for maintaining law and order and other state expenditure came from property taxes, licensing fees, and corporate taxes, which provided an average of 48 percent, 20 percent, and 10 percent of the state's income, respectively.[27]

As financial discipline was a byword of Redeemer governments, the substantial shortfall between the revenue that the convict lease raised and the expenditure incurred to maintain law and order requires an explanation. One answer lies in the public's and many legislators' inability to follow the intricacies of state finance. Not surprisingly, the one group of people to draw repeated attention to the high cost of prosecutions were Tennessee's comptrollers—men with the job of balancing the state's books.[28]

Another explanation lies in the combined inertia of governmental authorities during Redemption. To lessen judicial and law enforcement costs, Tennessee's lawmakers would have had to overhaul the criminal justice system, giving substantially more responsibility to county governments. The legislature did enact some reform in 1875, when it raised the amount constituting grand larceny from ten to thirty dollars and declared petty larceny a misdemeanor. This latter shift in policy paved the way for petty criminals to serve out their sentences in county workhouses.[29] Despite these statutory changes, the distinction between a misdemeanor and grand larceny remained vague;

and while dozens of Tennessee counties built their own jails between 1877 and 1891, often at substantial cost, most county governments continued to send their misdemeanor criminals to the penitentiary in Nashville. Thus, a large majority of offenders, regardless of the nature of their crimes or the length of their sentences, found themselves enmeshed in the convict-lease system.[30]

Tennessee's Redeemers were unwilling to countenance more substantial reform because of their antipathy toward the state's African American community and their resolve to maintain white supremacy. Aside from all other considerations, the postbellum legal system played a crucial role within Tennessee's structure of racial subordination. No matter how frequently Tennessee's bureaucrats and politicians called for financial stringency from 1870 to 1890, a majority of legislators continually refused to overhaul the criminal code or penal administration.

The Making of a Prison Population

As in the rest of the South, the composition of Tennessee's convict population changed dramatically in the postbellum years. Before the Civil War, blacks seldom constituted more than one in twenty state prisoners. After emancipation, the ratio of blacks in Tennessee's prisons increased rapidly. In November 1866 blacks accounted for 52 percent of state prisoners; by 1891 the proportion of African American inmates had risen to approximately three in four. The rise in the percentage of black convicts was accompanied by an explosion in the number of persons incarcerated by the State of Tennessee. From the close of the Civil War in 1865 to 1890, the number of Tennessee's inmates grew sixfold— from 240 to 1,500; this increase dwarfed that of the state's population, which grew only by 63 percent from 1860 to 1890.[31]

State officials and other prominent whites generally agreed on an explanation for this dramatic expansion. Governor Buchanan provided a typical account, depicting the increase as an inevitable result of emancipation. In an 1891 message to the Tennessee legislature, Buchanan maintained that "when great numbers of ignorant slaves were set free from all restraints, they quickly extended our criminal list beyond the capacity of the prison to accommodate them and the ability of the State to take care of them."[32] J. T. Hill, who had "considerable experience with convict labor in the Birmingham district," similarly stressed the impact of slavery's demise. Looking back on the postemancipation period in 1897, Hill argued that with emancipation "there was suddenly precipitated upon the Southern states, a new citizen, who had theretofore been practically free from legal responsibility to the state for his moral conduct."

The burgeoning prison rolls and overflowing penitentiary were, in Hill's estimation, the inevitable result.[33]

Buchanan and Hill neglected to mention that African Americans were far more likely to find themselves subject to the supposedly salutary effects of a prison sentence than whites who committed a similar offense. Even under Reconstruction administrations, southern law enforcement was significantly biased against blacks. Throughout the postbellum South, except in areas where African Americans constituted a majority of voters and were able to elect friendly sheriffs, justices of the peace, and judges, blacks confronted a criminal justice system that was stacked against them. They encountered law officials who eagerly arrested them, county attorneys who prosecuted them with vigor, judges who afforded them little or no protection of their most basic procedural rights, and all-white juries who were rarely inclined to acquit a defendant with dark skin.[34] To many southern politicians and governmental officials, these realities mainly reflected a "more rigid enforcement" or "a more efficient administration" of the criminal law. At the same time, the desperate poverty of tens of thousands of blacks encouraged many individuals to commit petty crimes against property. Together, racial discrimination and economic deprivation ensured that prison books in many southern states bulged with the names of African Americans, especially African American men.[35]

Postbellum Tennessee's inmates tended to be young, male, uneducated, unskilled, and unmarried.[36] Throughout the post–Civil War decades, around half of the state's prisoners were convicted of petty crimes against property, which resulted in sentences of one to five years.[37] Many of the petty thefts that led to prison terms involved property with agricultural, rural overtones, such as a fence rail or a chicken. But most inmates came from counties that contained the state's urban centers—Memphis, Nashville, Chattanooga, and Knoxville. Shelby and Davidson Counties, which encompassed Memphis and Nashville, were grossly overrepresented; 45 percent of all prisoners came from these two counties at a time when well over three-quarters of Tennessee's African American population remained in the countryside.

During and after the Civil War, thousands of African Americans had fled to cities, setting up shantytowns and contraband camps. Forged during war, shantytowns such as Memphis's South Memphis and Nashville's Edgefield became permanent features on the maps of city planners. Here dreams of freedom and self-sufficiency were severely tested by overcrowding, filth, and unemployment. Comparing these shantytowns to the black hole of Calcutta, Tennessee's mainstream press frequently depicted black urban neighborhoods as overflowing with vice, slothfulness, dirt, and immorality. Although many of the people who settled on the periphery of the established cities found gainful employment and even prospered, others succumbed to conditions they could not overcome, finding crime the surest way of surviving in an uncertain world.[38]

The predominance of urban criminals in Tennessee's postbellum penal system is striking. Criminal statutes that were specifically aimed at keeping rural workers in their place rarely sent late-nineteenth-century Tennesseans to prison. Convictions of farm tenants for false pretense—the acceptance of advances in goods or cash with the intention of not fulfilling the terms of a rental or sharecropping contract—accounted for only one percent of the prison population in the twenty years after 1868. Similarly, persons convicted of stealing a horse or a mule constituted less than two percent of the state's inmates in the late 1880s.[39]

The enforcement of petty crime laws in both the cities and the countryside served to redefine property relations. In antebellum Tennessee, as in the rest of the South, slaves regularly took things that they regarded as their due, refusing in most cases to view such actions as theft. During the same period, free blacks and poor whites enjoyed access to commons for the grazing of cattle and hogs. After the Civil War, people increasingly could not simply "take" what they perceived as rightly theirs, either as payment for labor or as a result of established custom. Tennessee's postbellum system of criminal justice turned poor citizens who stole small, inexpensive items into convict laborers. With the erosion of customary rights came the criminalization of the poor and, in Tennessee especially, the urban poor.[40]

Convictions for petty thefts, of course, were not wholly responsible for Tennessee's prison population. Over one-fourth of the inmates convicted in 1888 had committed violent crimes against persons. Eleven percent had been found guilty of murder, 5 percent of rape or attempted rape, another 8 percent of attempted murder or manslaughter, and 1 percent of malicious shooting or stabbing. The remaining individuals who began prison terms in that year had been found guilty of aggravated crimes against property, such as burglary, robbery, attempted robbery, arson, or forgery, or of perjury or bigamy.[41]

Clemency and the Racial Order

Whatever their offense, thousands of inmates and their families, friends, and patrons wrote to southern governors petitioning for executive pardons. These pardons provide an unusual glimpse into the workings of southern society, suggesting public notions about extenuating circumstances in instances of crime and the political uses of power and prestige. They also reveal the con-

struction of a new racial and social hierarchy in the postemancipation South—
a hierarchy based as much on the connections between blacks or poor whites,
on the one hand, and elite whites, on the other, as on the separation of these
groups.

Prisoners, family members, public officials, and the general public petitioned for pardon on a variety of grounds. Most commonly, applicants emphasized the heavy social and economic costs associated with the incarceration
of a family member. Petitioners starkly depicted the destitution of those left
behind, stressing poverty as grounds for executive clemency. An attorney who
petitioned in 1892 for the release of Henry Martin, a white man and a young
father of four convicted of stealing two dollars worth of beef from a butcher
store, offered a typical argument. "I know of my personal knowledge," the
lawyer testified, "that the wife and four small children are in the most destitute
circumstances and one of the children in a dying condition. That the wife and
mother plys [sic] herself to washing every day for a support and spends her
nights in sleepless watch over the head of her afflicted child."[42] By granting a
pardon, the attorney suggested, the governor would enable Martin to reassert
his position at the head of his family, providing security and sustenance to his
wife and children. With a stroke of a pen, Buchanan could exercise paternalistic care for a man less fortunate than himself and restore patriarchal relationships within that man's family.

Another petitioner, a mother of eight children including eighteen-year-old
Noah Talley, who had been convicted of petty larceny and sent to the state
penitentiary for one year, explained that poverty was the cause, not just the
effect, of her family's misfortune. This woman emphasized that she and her
family "have always been poor people," without "the advantages of an education." Because of such difficult circumstances, her son "was compelled to go
out into the world to work . . . at the very commonist [sic] labor and in the
lowest walk of life." Such experience inevitably led him into "contact with
many evil influences in his tender years." Though the woman appealed to
Governor Buchanan on the basis of the family's destitution and her ill health,
she augmented her supplication with the power and prestige of the local elite.
Thirty-six people signed her petition, including the local prosecutor, the
mayor, two attorneys, two doctors, and the chairman of the local Democratic
Party Committee.[43]

The ill health of a convict also served as a solid basis on which to petition for
pardon. In some of these cases state officials and lessee representatives successfully applied for clemency. Lessees had an interest in such a prisoner's
release, since "deadheads" (the colloquial phrase for sick or injured prisoners)

could not work profitably and would inevitably become a drain on the lessee's resources. Yet some of the petitioners appear to have acted out of concern for the men themselves. In applying for the pardon for two black Tracy City prisoners sentenced for seven and five years respectively, one group of prison wardens noted that the men had "scrofula in an incurable degree and . . . [could] possibly live but a short time." They added that the inmates "are both exceptionally good prisoners and we think that Common Humanity dictates that your Excelency [sic] should grant them a pardon as we are assured that they have friends who will gladly take care of them what few remaining days they may live."[44]

In addition to pleading family hardship or ill health, some petitioners argued that the influence of alcohol exculpated a prisoner's violation of the law. A Davidson County judge wrote to Buchanan on behalf of a man his court had sentenced to a three-year term of imprisonment. One might imagine that the defendant had been a prominent citizen. But according to the judge, he was "a Rutherford county negro . . . named E. H. Liggett." Judge G. S. Ridley told Buchanan that Liggett had stolen a saddle and a few small things valued at a little over thirty dollars. The judge had sentenced Liggett to the minimum sentence he could for grand larceny. As Ridley explained, "The proof showed that Liggett was drinking at the time and was not exactly at himself." As a result, the judge promised Liggett "that if he made a good prisoner while in the Penitentiary I would ask the Governor, after a reasonable length of time to Pardon him. I enclose a letter from Mr. Bradley the Warden, and respectfully request that you now pardon Liggett." The warden at the Inman prison had certified that Liggett had indeed been an "obedient and faithful prisoner."[45] In another case, one in which the petitioner appealed solely on the basis of the inmate's inebriated state at the time of the crime, 116 people signed the petition, including the prosecutor, a witness, Tennessee's secretary of state, and its treasurer.[46]

Claims of extenuating circumstances aside from drunkenness served as the basis for still other petitions. A husband who killed a man who had raped his wife, a son who defended his mother against his father's physical abuse, and a husband who defended his wife against the attentions of a previous suitor, assaulting the man in the process, all received sympathy in their appeals for pardon.[47] In such cases, prominent men, both in and outside the legal profession, lent their weight to the petitions, which explicitly appealed to a tradition of southern honor. These applications spoke to an assumption in southern society that adult married men had both a responsibility to treat their spouses well and a proprietary claim over their women. Although many of these suppositions arose among white antebellum planters, they continued in the postbellum era and came to characterize attitudes among black as well as white men.[48]

The disposition of pardon applications makes very clear that blacks and poor whites—but especially blacks—did well to find a protector among the local elite. Young men unknown to the local community and without anyone to vouch for their integrity were most at risk in a society in which great store was placed on personal relationships. This principle applied both to the formal legal system and to the law of "Judge Lynch." Black men new to a community, without either local whites or blacks to attest for them, were most likely to be perceived as transgressing community mores; such newcomers had a much greater chance of paying for social infractions with their lives or a jail sentence.[49] Whites who were new to town did not face the same level of suspicion, but attaching themselves to local men of influence generally proved judicious.

The travails of Will White, a nineteen-year-old black man and a recent arrival to west Tennessee's largest city, demonstrates the crucial importance of having a patron. White came to Memphis to work as a railway fireman on the Louisville, New Orleans and Texas Railroad, arriving with eight dollars in his pocket. He used the money to pay his first week's board and lodging. When the railroad delayed the starting date of his work, this newcomer, in desperate straits and without a friend in Memphis, took the belongings of a fellow boarder. White pawned the items for seven dollars in order to pay his second week's board. In his court deposition, the railway fireman claimed to have had every intention of redeeming the articles and replacing them in the room from which he had taken them. The court took scant heed of White's explanation, sentencing him to four years in the state penitentiary.

White's savior, Sim L. Barinds, a reporter for the *Memphis Appeal Avalanche*, met the prisoner in the course of his work and took pity on him. In an eloquent letter to the governor, the journalist pleaded for the young man's release on the basis of his young age, honest face, and apparently respectful parents. To demonstrate his credentials, Barinds secured a number of testimonials from his superior at the *Avalanche*, a bank manager, and local lawyers, all affirming his own community standing. In this case, Barinds's plea was enough to win Will White's freedom.[50]

Usually, though, petitioners tried to secure the signatures of lawyers, justices of the peace, jurors, prosecutors, and any and all government officials. In one late-nineteenth-century short story about a young white Tennessee blacksmith's encounter with the convict lease, the protagonist's sweetheart tramps around the countryside forlorn and alone, trying to secure jurors' signatures before thrusting the petition for her lover's pardon into the governor's hand while on the hustings.[51] In Tennessee's actual criminal justice system, jurors occasionally convicted and sentenced a man with the clear understanding that once the felon demonstrated contrition and a record of honest, hard work, they would appeal for his release. In making these agreements, the jurors turned the impartiality of the law into personal relationships predicated on individual sponsorship.

Tennessee's leading citizens did not discourage such supplications. They conferred their good names to petitions for pardon in exchange for adherence to a code of social conduct that accorded with their sensibilities.[52] The patron's stature, secured largely through position and possibly wealth, could only be bolstered by assisting those less fortunate than himself. Acts of benevolence also undergirded a gentleman's sense that he presided over a paternalistic and racially segmented social order.

At the same time, the institution of gubernatorial clemency provided a means for the political establishment to demonstrate that everyone in Tennessee could receive justice. The poorest black man could receive a pardon, while a member of the white elite could have a petition denied. Although most criminals in postbellum Tennessee came from poor backgrounds, wealthier social classes occasionally found one of their number convicted of a felony. The prominence of a family, despite Tennessee's social hierarchy, did not always mean the automatic pardon of one of its members from the penitentiary.

When Henry Clay King, a lawyer and an aristocrat in Memphis society, brutally killed another respected Memphis citizen, he was convicted of murder in the first degree and sentenced to execution. The ink had barely dried on the Supreme Court's affirmation of his conviction and sentence before a petition for pardon began circulating among the city's highest social circles. While some merchants and lawyers wrote to Governor Buchanan pleading for clemency, largely out of sympathy for Mrs. King, an even larger number of Memphis's renowned citizens opposed commutation of the sentence, imploring the governor to allow the law to take its course. Many of these latter petitioners felt that a stay of execution would encourage private vendettas and "Judge Lynch." The supporters of King's execution emphasized the positive message that would be sent to ordinary working people if the state carried out the judiciary's order. "The hanging of King would have a tendency to give the poorer classes confidence in the law and our courts," wrote one upper-class protester. Another expressed similar sentiments in a slightly different way, arguing that the "infliction of such punishment will satisfy the people that all men in our State are amenable [subject] to the law without favor or distinction. The infliction of such punishment will create a healthy public sentiment of confidence in the administration of the criminal laws by the courts."[53]

For legal judgments of the courts to gain respect, ordinary Tennesseans had to believe that the legal system, if not completely impartial and wholly just, at least approximated those ideals. Full impartiality was not possible in the late-nineteenth-century South, but the culture of granting or rejecting pardons provided one means of limiting popular discontent with the established legal and social order. For many lawbreakers, clemency placed a limit on the vindictiveness and capriciousness of the law. Over the two-year period between December 1886 and December 1888, 10 percent of prison inmates received gubernatorial pardons. Relying on a governor's benevolence was not the only curb placed on the harshness of criminal sentencing. Between December 1886 and December 1888, a full 71 percent of inmates left the prison system because officials had reduced their sentences for "good behavior."[54]

These statistics suggest that judges meted out many sentences without the expectation that convicts would complete them. Once the law had been vindicated, once a prisoner had demonstrated appropriate contrition, and once the same inmate had obediently served a respectable amount of time, state officials were more than willing to return him to society. Thus the postbellum enforcement of Tennessee's criminal code by no means had the sole aim of providing cheap and reliable labor to the state's convict lessees. The criminal justice system also sought to buttress an evolving structure of racial and class subordination, strengthening the power of elites even while softening the terms of punishment.[55]

However Tennessee's convicts entered the criminal justice system and however they left it, all those men spent time as unfree laborers. For prisoners in the Volunteer State, the convict lease meant a twilight world that incorporated many elements of the old, slave South. Any understanding of postbellum Tennessee mining requires a journey to the places where these inmates toiled and bedded down for the night.

Life and Work in the Stockades

Once the Martins, Talleys, and Liggetts entered Tennessee's prison system, they boarded a train for Nashville's penitentiary. From that location most inmates found their way to branch prisons. Though the Tennessee Coal, Iron, and Railroad Company leased all the prisoners from the state by 1890, they eventually subleased almost two-thirds of them. Some 400 convicts stayed in Nashville, where local manufacturers employed them to make wagons, harnesses, and the like.[56] An additional 50 prisoners continued to work on the farm of Dr. William Morrow, a primary lessee between 1871 and 1883. TCIR employed between 400 and 500 convicts in its Grundy County mines and an additional 200 to 300 at its Inman ore mines in neighboring Marion County. East Tennessee housed the remaining felons: in 1891, Coal Creek provided work for 135 men, Oliver Springs 168, and Briceville 141.[57]

The distribution of convicts to the different stockades was not constant. Instead the lessee moved convicts from camp to camp, often in response to labor unrest. The experience of one prisoner, a black man who hailed from Dekalb County, Georgia, demonstrated the potential mobility of inmates within, and in and out of, Tennessee's prison system. Convicted of grand larceny in 1869, Bob White escaped from prison at least five times and worked in at least nine convict camps, building railroads and mining coal over the next twenty-one years.[58]

Throughout the decades after the Confederacy's surrender, Tennessee's prison administrators viewed their charges, and especially their black charges, as lacking the most basic attributes of republican citizens. Borrowing terminology and sentiments from the antebellum era, the 1868 penitentiary directors reported to the legislature that an increasing number of convicts were former slaves, without an education or trade. They were, according to the directors, "merely grown up children" "sentenced in most cases for 'taking' . . . some article of provision or clothing from their employer, who refuses to pay them." Switching from an analogy based on childhood to one emanating from the animal kingdom, the prison officials asserted that in many instances the wrongdoers had "not much more idea of criminality . . . than a dumb beast has that helps himself from his master's crib." To suggest the pettiness of their offenses—transgressions that might have been committed by a child or unthinkingly perpetrated by an animal—the directors noted that the crimes ranged from "eight cents, the value of a fence rail, to all intermediate sums not reaching $5."[59]

A quarter of a century later, many penal administrators and social commentators still thought of African Americans as "unmoral," "not vicious but undeveloped." Though writing about "the new Negro"—people born since slavery—and often comparing them unfavorably with men and women who grew to adulthood prior to emancipation, Tennessee's wardens consistently blamed petty theft on what seemed to them to be an innate characteristic of the "Negro race." Complaining that the number of prisoners had risen in the years 1893–94, one state official conceded that "the hard times" of the prevailing depression were "partially" the cause of increased crimes. Yet he insisted that dire economic conditions only brought out the natural inclinations of blacks to pilfer. The official maintained that "the poverty of the people" simply "put . . . into operation the[ir] propensity to steal and to fraudulently appropriate the property of others."[60]

J. T. Hill also expressed a view that the situation was not without its advantages, a position that acquired the status of conventional wisdom among certain sectors of southern society. The prison association delegate argued that a stint in the state's prisons would serve to inculcate Tennessee's inmates with "steady habits," "temperance," and, indeed, notions of citizenship: "To the ignorant negro, brought to manhood during the days of slavery, a term in the penitentiary was without question the best lesson he could obtain in citizenship, as it brought him to a realization of the fact that the blessings of citizenship also had its responsibilities."[61] Rather than civics lessons, however, Tennessee prisoners received a withering curriculum in backbreaking labor and survival techniques.

The convicts generally encountered horrific conditions in the mining stockades, though some gradation existed among the facilities. As a rule, stockades run by the less well capitalized east Tennessee sublessees had the most problems. Some of the sublessees, like the Knoxville Iron Company, subcontracted the care of their convicts to a third party, who generally skimped on the provision of food, clothing, and lodging whenever possible.[62] In such circumstances, the state's control over the environment in which its wards lived and worked became extremely tenuous.

Abuses of the system were commonplace. An 1893 seven-man Senate and House Joint Committee on the Penitentiary found the Coal Creek stockade consisted of "three box houses or wings." This structure, the committee reported, offered far too little space for the number of men it housed. The legislators argued that the provision would be "unsanitary in the extreme but for the somewhat open character of the construction." Though the porous nature of the building enabled those it sheltered to receive sufficient air, the only way the inmates could keep from freezing in winter was to crowd together (easily enough accomplished) and to keep a fire constantly burning. The men slept in beds "made of rough plank in a continuous row," with two men to a bed. Four feet above the beds on the floor stood a loft, consisting of a similar row of beds. Deprived of female companionship and living under such crowded conditions, prisoners, according to the prison reports, often adopted "unnatural vices."[63]

As for bedding, the legislative committee found only coverings that were "filthy to an extreme degree," smothered by "grease, grime, and coal dust." Captain John Chumbley, who was warden at Coal Creek from 1877 to 1892 and who received forty cents per prisoner per day to take care of the convicts, apparently changed the mattress and cotton blankets only every three to six months; he provided no sheets or pillows and no shirts. The men slept either naked or in their dirty work clothes. To make matters worse, prisoners had few opportunities to maintain any standards of personal hygiene. A state regulation directed the men to bathe once a week. But in Coal Creek's stockade, officials honored the regulation only in the breach; inadequate bathing facilities made any other outcome impossible.[64]

One might presume that at least the food would have been passable, since the men needed stamina to complete the work the company demanded of them. But here again the situation "was not up to the standard required by law, either in quantity or quality, variety, or method of preparation." Chumbley rarely provided any fruit, vegetables, or meat to his charges. The food available to the convicts paled in comparison with that put aside for the lessee's managers and their visitors. When William C. Tatom, the president of the Tennessee Press Association and editor of the Democratic Knoxville Tribune, visited Briceville during the rebellion, he had lunch with an agent of TCIR, the primary lessee. The pair "ate off a pine bench. Hams, beans, cabbage and coffee under such circumstances do not go bad." Tatom added that a "well behaved convict waited on us."[65]

Though Coal Creek laid claim to the worst stockade, the other sublessee-run prisons offered only variations on a theme of deplorable conditions. The stockades run by TCIR in mid-Tennessee were less inhospitable, even approaching minimal standards of decency. The substantially greater financial resources at TCIR's disposal and that company's much longer and more thorough commitment to coal mining in Tennessee probably account for the more congenial provisions for convicts in Grundy and Marion Counties.[66]

Just as living conditions varied in the different prisons, so too did the amount of work required from the convicts. Guards at the stockades also served as labor foremen, setting tasks for each inmate based on the size of the coal seam and their estimation of a prisoner's physical strength. In the coal mines, each convict who mined coal accounted for between two and one-half and four tons per day; those men who loaded coal into railroad cars were responsible for thirteen tons of ore per day; and two men working together at the coke manufactories drew coke from six ovens.[67]

When the convicts arrived at the stockades they came primarily with the skills of farms, workshops, and in some cases domestic service. They were untutored in the ways of coal mines. Free miners, though hostile to the presence of criminals in their midst, were frequently required to impart their

Convicts tending coke ovens in Grundy County, 1880s (William Ray Turner Collection)

knowledge to the convicts and work with them as "buddies." The convicts' tutelage was not a restricted one; they learned all aspects of mining, from the most elementary to the most complex. Implementing a system that echoed the use of drivers under slavery, mine managers gave some prisoners supervisory positions over their fellow inmates. These "trusties," "horns," and "police boys" worked in conjunction with white guards to ensure that ordinary convicts fulfilled their assigned tasks.[68]

At least in mid-Tennessee, the task structure of convict work provided a means for prisoners to improve their daily lot. TCIR paid the convicts an eight- to ten-cent bonus for every car they mined over and above their task.[69] Sufficient numbers of inmates received these bonuses to create a market for supplementary food, which Tracy City women met by "carry[ing] pies to the stockade and sell[ing] them to the convicts."[70]

TCIR did not rely only on the prospect of an occasional pie to induce their unfree laborers to work. In time-honored fashion the company relied heavily on the stick, or in this case the whip, when prisoners violated rules or did not meet their production quotas. "The whipping was done with a two ply strap as wide as your three fingers, tied to a staff," a prison warden recalled. "The convicts were face down with their pants off. They were whipped on the hips and legs five to twelve lashes." In both mid- and east Tennessee mines, brutal beatings of convicts occurred with great regularity.[71]

The regime of prison life in Tennessee's mines took a severe toll on inmates. Epidemics periodically visited the branch prisoners, while lice, scurvy, and tuberculosis maintained a constant presence. Convicts were also frequently hurt in the course of their daily exertions, often by explosives or rockslides. The combination of disease and work-related injuries produced appalling death rates. In the mid-1880s roughly one prisoner in ten died each year.[72]

The convicts did not remain passive in the face of harsh work demands and inhumane living conditions. Like slaves in antebellum America and serfs in pre-emancipation Russia, Tennessee's convict laborers employed a variety of strategies to limit the coercive controls over their lives. On several occasions inmates overpowered guards in the mines either as a prelude to an escape or to punish them for previous excesses in their behavior. Able to secure a variety of weapons, such as razors, sharpened pick handles, and dynamite, prisoners periodically inflicted severe damage on their overseers.[73]

The prisoners additionally demonstrated an extraordinary ability to organize large-scale attacks on the system that confined them. In the largest and most violent effort, which took place in July 1894, seventy-five Tracy City convicts lit a dynamite bomb, put it into a mining car, and shoved it down a side entry. They killed the deputy warden, wounded two guards, and refused to leave the mine until the next day. In an effort to quell the mutiny, a guard killed a convict thought to be the ringleader. Whether or not this man headed the revolt, the surviving prisoners deemed it wise to label him posthumously as their leader.[74] Revolts such as this one, though, were rare. They were also more likely to provoke a swift and intense response than resistance that was more covert and that never directly challenged power relations between convicts, state guards, and mine operators.

More commonly convicts engaged in escapes, sabotaged the mine, and shirked work. Roughly one in twelve prisoners successfully fled incarceration in one of the mining stockades. Such a high percentage reveals the generally ineffective character of stockade security. The problem became so acute that the state modified its lease contract, requiring lessees to pay a twenty-five-dollar reward for the return of any escaped convict.[75]

Sabotage took many innovative forms. Overcharging the holes with powder or engaging in "some pyrotechnic display . . . directed toward the roof" seemed to be favorite methods of damaging a mine. Inevitably officials would have to close the shaft while guards, miners, and some convicts cleared away the rubble.[76] Convicts also relied on more theatrical forms of resistance. Knowing that a mine inspector would arrive the following morning, inmates at one mine left the doors open, filling entryways with smoke. When the convicts arrived for work the next day, many of them collapsed, thereby dramatizing poor working conditions.[77] Mine inspections, though, only occasionally brought the convicts an official audience.

When visitors from state government were not on hand, inmates resorted to more subtle tactics. They "work[ed] badly" or refused to work at all. In an 1890 article entitled "Life in Southern Prisons," a *Harper's Weekly* correspondent described the convicts' attitudes to work as follows: "They naturally shirk all they can, putting in stone at the bottom and coal at the top, using coal dust in the same fashion, and in other ways overreaching their employers, for all of which a judgment waits them." An article in the mining industry's trade journal reiterated these findings. The author focused on the effect of leaving convicts to complete their tasks on their own, a system of work organization similar to that of free miners. He reported that such independence resulted in "badly laid track, badly set props . . . coal not mined at all, but simply shot to pieces, and finally, loaded up with all the slate, sulfur and other refuse at hand that would help fill up the requisite number of cars for the task."[78]

The mine operators had few options but to resort to a modified piece-rate system to eliminate forms of resistance open to workers who were required to perform so many hours of labor per day. Under the latter system, the convict could have lounged around all day; the only incentives for convicts to labor at all would have been to avoid a whipping. But where piece-rate work prevailed, resistance took the form of defective workmanship rather than slowdowns.[79]

The convict lessees, then, struggled to get inmates to work hard or with regard for quality, and yet were obligated to continue feeding and clothing them, however badly. This situation conferred certain advantages on the convicts, precisely because of their lowly status. One inmate encapsulated this irony in a work song. While the taskmasters depended on the prisoners' labor, the convicts lost little by performing poorly at the coal face:

The captain holler hurry
I'm going to take my time
Says he's making money
And trying to make time
Says he can lose his job
But I can't lose mine.[80]

Thus Tennessee prisoners were able to set certain limits on the amount of labor they were prepared to perform, how well they would do the work, and the amount of punishment they were willing to accept for violating company rules. These acts of resistance depended partially on a psychological space that

Escaped convict after capture by Tracy City guards, 1880s (William Ray Turner Collection)

the inmates created for themselves—a world in which they expressed personal preference by trading rations for goods and services and in which some black convicts challenged the southern racial order by seeing themselves as equal to their white counterparts.[81]

Though a culture of defiance probably lent many prisoners the wherewithal to survive their incarceration, one should neither romanticize their predicament nor forget the grinding realities of their daily lives. Some prisoners shied away from confrontation or disobedience, as they were fearful of hurting their chances for parole or clemency. The space that inmates created for themselves, moreover, took shape within the nooks and crannies of prison institutions, testifying as least as much to the all-encompassing and powerful nature of those structures as it did to the robust qualities of the human spirit.[82]

Economic and Social Ripples of the Convict Lease

Administration of the convict lease was far from easy. The use of prison labor also turned out to be neither as cheap nor as lucrative as coal operators had envisioned, largely as a result of the difficulties of securing quality workmanship from unfree workers. The direct cost of convict labor did stay cheaper than that of free labor. But the use of convict labor brought indirect costs of its own. Convict lessees had to pay guards, reward those who captured escaped convicts, and suffer the costs of property destroyed by convicts.

In addition, management could not lay off convicts during slack summer months or when the market became depressed, as they could free laborers. The costs entailed in the inmates' upkeep—costs that remained steady irrespective of the ebb and flow in demand for coal—gave those companies with the capacity to produce coke and pig iron greater versatility in the allocation and employment of their prison labor force. Because TCIR manufactured coke and pig iron, Grundy County miners worked more days per year than did their Anderson County counterparts and much more than the state average.[83] Access to coke and pig iron markets (opportunities shared by only one company in east Tennessee, the Knoxville Iron Company) enabled TCIR to take full advantage of convict labor. By contrast, most mining lessees in Anderson County, who could not turn to coke or pig iron production when the weather turned warm or the economy weakened, periodically found they had little work for their convicts to perform.[84] Housing, feeding, and clothing a convict, even at forty cents a day, proved expensive when the mines stood idle. In adverse economic circumstances, the east Tennessee operators adapted as best they could by cutting their work force, maintaining only a minimal number to prevent their mines from flooding. The flexibility that different companies had in deploying their prison laborers profitably would greatly influence their desire to rid themselves of the convict lease during and after the miners' rebellion.

Convict labor reduced productivity at the same time that it entailed unforeseen expenditures. By all accounts the convicts were lackluster miners. As TCIR's James Bowron observed, their performance constrained quality output at Tracy City's mine. "The convict," Bowron reflected in 1884, "or any other cheap, ignorant or degraded laborer, does not make the best or most profitable employee. The intelligent laborer cannot help but take an interest in his work; he has something at stake; he does in consequence better work. At Tracy City mines, his boxes of coal are better filled with better quality of coal." East Tennessee mine managers underscored Bowron's point, complaining that prisoners did not work efficiently or with attention to quality and noting that companies which bought convict-mined coal expressed dissatisfaction with its grade.[85] The inevitable result of coal purposefully shot to pieces and coal cars loaded with slack was damage to the profit margins of most mines that relied on prison labor.

The problems associated with convict mining eventually persuaded the major convict lessee, TCIR, to divest itself of a significant proportion of its inmates. Despite its ability to produce pig iron, TCIR's management opted by the mid-1880s to leave roughly a third of the prisoners in the main penitentiary and sublet hundreds more to competitors. Thus coal operators came to recognize the limits that a convict force placed on their bottom line.[86] No Tennessee company replaced its entire free labor force with convict miners.

The experience of Tennessee's leased convicts, though, left a historical legacy beyond the limits they imposed on the balance sheets of mining companies. The convicts' ordeal resonated with master-slave relationships of an earlier era. As journalist William Tatom's account of his meal at Coal Creek indicates, lessees could not resist the temptation to make at least some convicts the analogues of house slaves. Indeed, at times the upper echelons of company management complained that the personnel in charge of the convicts were diverting far too many inmates for such purposes. Following a visit to Tracy City's stockade, TCIR secretary-treasurer James Bowron noted in a diary entry that he had requested a reduction in the proportion of "able bodied men employed as cooks and waiters."[87]

Lessees further borrowed the techniques of slavery when trying to motivate inmates to work well. Instead of holding out the prospect of a garden plot (a strategy common to antebellum southern planters), lessees offered the possibility of wages for labor beyond the stipulated task at hand. Should such promises fail to elicit the desired response, stockade superintendents did not hesitate to wield a thick leather strap. For the convicts' part, they readily emulated the strategies of antebellum slaves, resisting both work demands, punishment, and confinement whenever possible. Finally, inmates and their families not infrequently turned to local white elites—the postbellum equivalent of the paternalist planter—for aid in petitioning the state government for pardons. Those elites often responded to such requests, interceding with the governor on behalf of the inmate and his family. Important continuities, then, connected the institutions of Tennessee's convict lease with the state's slave past.

As the convict lease created an institution evocative of slavery, it simultaneously forged a set of new economic relationships with white brokers and yeomen who benefited from the presence of convicts in their communities. Captain John Chumbley, the third party in charge of convicts' care for the Knoxville Iron Company, took advantage of his position to open a country store in Coal Creek. The company, which did not have its own store, pressured its free employees to trade at Chumbley's shop. In mid-Tennessee the impact on local producers extended beyond the enrichment of a well-placed merchant. Mrs. S. O. Saunders, a Tracy City resident, recalled that TCIR relied on the women in the local community to make convict garb. More commonly known as "Aunt Tut," Mrs. Saunders and the other young women in town made clothes for fifty cents a day. "After I was 14," she told folklorist James Dombrowski in the 1930s, "up to time I was married I made stripes. That's convict clothes. One woman had a contract and we worked for her. 50¢ a day and made from 12 to 16 shirts a day, worked from 6 to 6. The lady did the cutting and we did the sewing. Made caps, coats, shirts, pants."[88]

Local men similarly benefited from the convict lease. Guards at branch prisons frequently came from the surrounding neighborhood. Though state officials made the appointments, the lessees paid for the men's services. Both government officials and convict lessees used their authority to dispense patronage and provide employment.[89] The lease, therefore, broadened economic horizons for some residents even as it constrained the economic position of free miners. Men who worked as guards and women such as Mrs. Saunders and the "widow women" who sold pies to the convicts profited from the presence of stockades in their area.

Despite the importance of the convict lease's perpetuation of relationships reminiscent of slavery and its modification of local economies, the institution's most far-reaching consequences for mid- and east Tennessee concerned the status of free labor. The state's miners bitterly resented both the ability of coal operators to break strikes through the use of convicts and the downward pressure that prison labor placed on wages. This resentment translated into fervent opposition to the convict lease from the moment in 1871 that A. S. Colyar arranged for the first contingent of convicts to work in Tracy City. Colyar's employees immediately struck in an attempt to compel the removal of the prison laborers and even tried to dynamite the newly constructed stockade that housed them. These actions proved futile, as did the attempts of east Tennessee miners to prevent the introduction of convicts to Coal Creek and Oliver Springs. In 1877 and 1889 Anderson County miners threatened to eject convicts from Coal Creek and Oliver Springs, respectively; but they did not follow through on their threats, as Democratic governors increased the number of guards at the newly established branch prisons and made clear their intention to carry out the provisions of the lease.[90]

Throughout the 1870s and 1880s, mineworkers nonetheless sent a stream of petitions to the state legislature appealing for a halt to the use of prison labor in mining. Urban associations of mechanics, a number of middle-class prison reformers, and several newspaper editors also voiced ongoing criticism of Tennessee's penal policies, emphasizing their impact on workingmen, collusion and corruption surrounding the granting of lease contracts, and the inhumane conditions in mining camps worked by convicts. These political attacks on convict leasing were not without effect. Republican legislators from east Tennessee consistently called for the abolition of the convict lease, while Democratic leaders backed away from their initial defense of the institution as a boon to the state. As early as 1880, Democratic campaign platforms included declarations that prison labor should not compete with the state's free workers. But the shift in rhetoric did not keep Democratic legislators from extending the leasing of state inmates to mining corporations for six years in 1883, nor again for six years in 1889. On each occasion, Democratic assemblymen maintained that proposed alternatives to the convict lease—principally putting prisoners to work on county roads or building a much larger penitentiary—were too expensive. Despite widespread acceptance of the injustice and even barbarity of the lease, state prisoners remained an integral part of Tennessee's mining industry.[91]

Toward the end of 1890, east Tennessee's coal operators found themselves strapped economically. With the onset of the latest regional economic downturn, the East Tennessee, Virginia & Georgia Railroad failed to pay its creditors, including many of the local mining companies and the East Tennessee

The Briceville stockade (Tatom, "Press Clippings")

National Bank.[92] In a collective attempt to reduce costs, the small mining companies in the region banded together to eliminate checkweighmen from their district. Checkweighmen were independent weighers, chosen by local miners, whose measurements determined the wages owed to miners working for piece rates. Replacing these individuals with mine employees would greatly reduce wage payments. After a series of meetings between the operators of the region's mines, the management at Briceville's Tennessee Coal Mining Company forced a lockout over its workers' demand that they choose their own checkweighman and that the corporation pay them in legal tender.[93] Unable to secure a sufficient number of miners under financial terms he considered satisfactory, the company's president, B. A. Jenkins, eventually began to consider the importation of convict laborers.[94]

Jenkins enjoyed a unique opportunity to sublease convicts on the cheap. In October 1890 the convicts in the Nashville penitentiary set the workshops on fire, thereby destroying the workshops and many of the penitentiary buildings. The convict sublessee, Dr. William Morrow, lost substantial assets in the fire. Having bought most of his insurance policies from "wildcat" companies, Morrow proved unable to collect much on his claims. Out of business and heavily in debt, he urgently sought a sublessor for his sublease. After several months, he found an interested party in Jenkins.[95] Morrow's agent, J. E. Goodwin, promised that using prison inmates to mine 400 tons of coal per day would cost Jenkins thirty-five cents less per ton than continued reliance on free labor.[96]

The deal seemed too good for Jenkins to pass up. On July 5, 1891, Jenkins brought convict laborers into his mine. With this action, Jenkins imported the smoldering embers of the burned-out penitentiary. "All of the trouble originated," east Tennessee mining magnate E. J. Sanford later told his business partner, Colonel C. M. McGhee, "at the Jenkins mine, growing out of a fool contract which Will Morrow made with him to mine coal for almost nothing and the further foollishness [sic] of Jenkins in bragging about it all over Coal Creek. The miners thought their bread and butter was gone sure enough."[97] Once Anderson County miners became convinced that Jenkins intended to take away their livelihood, they demonstrated a steadfast resolve to protect their families from economic deprivation and to regain what they considered their most fundamental rights—as coal miners, Tennesseans, and Americans.

There is no politics in it whatever.
—Eugene Merrell,
August 1891, in Tatom,
"Press Clippings," 1:62

CHAPTER 4

Kindling Insurrection

After several days of discussions among one another and with other members of their communities, the miners of Anderson County resolved to re-move the convicts that President Jenkins had brought to Briceville as strike-breakers. Any other plan seemed insufficiently bold, given the grave threat that prison laborers posed to the interests of free mineworkers. Many residents of Coal Creek Valley also feared the consequences of delaying an eviction of the Briceville prisoners, since Jenkins was rumored to be bringing in a second con-tingent of convicts on July 15. On the night of July 14, scores of miners and several local citizens sympathetic to their cause marched on the Tennessee Coal Mining Company's newly built prison in Briceville and compelled the prison's wardens to release its forty inmates. Once the convicts were outside the confines of the mine company's stockade, the band of free miners and their local allies

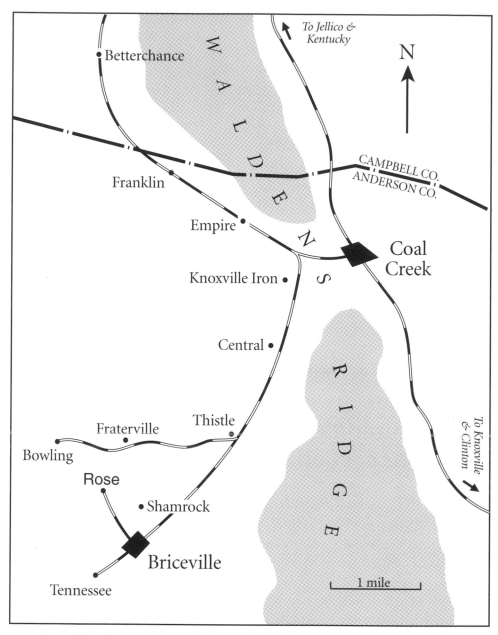

Map 4.1. The Mines in and around Coal Creek, 1890s (*Source:* Adapted from Hutson, "The Coal Miners' Insurrection, 1891–92")

hustled them to Coal Creek, placed them on a train, and ordered railway workers to transport the prisoners to Knoxville, east Tennessee's industrial center.[1]

Having dramatically excised the cancer of convict labor from Briceville, community leaders sat down to compose a telegram to Governor John Buchanan. The authors of this communication implied that the governor should fully sympathize with their militant actions. They told him that they had acted in defense of family, community, and property, fully expecting that he would find their request for intervention to be quite natural: "We the miners, farmers, merchants and property-holders of Briceville and Coal Creek and vicinity assembled to the number of five hundred, who have come together to defend our families from starvation, our property from depreciation, and our people from contamination from the hands of convict labor being introduced in our works . . . do hereby beg you, as our Chief Executive and Protector, to prevent their introduction and thus avoid bloodshed, which is sure to follow if their taking our livelihood from us is persisted in. Answer."[2]

These actions, which took place over some fourteen hours, raise three questions that go to the heart of the mining rebellions in east Tennessee. The first question stems from the cross-class alliance between the "miners, farmers, merchants and property-holders" of east Tennessee's mining towns. Both in this first act of defiance and throughout the "mining troubles," east Tennessee's free miners enjoyed steadfast support from members of the local elite. What accounts for this solidarity?

The second puzzle concerns the timing of the march on the Coal Creek stockade. Why did these citizens embark on such dramatic and determined action in 1891 and not earlier? The arrival of convict strikebreakers and the tough economic times that followed obviously sparked discontent, but they do not wholly account for the timing and nature of the action taken by the Coal Creek and Briceville communities. Convicts had replaced free miners in the past in both east and mid-Tennessee, usually during difficult economic conditions. In response, the miners had struck and lobbied the government, hoping for a change in policy. Never before, though, had they directly defied state authority.

The third quandary relates to the seemingly contradictory methods undertaken by these communities. On the one hand, armed citizens of east Tennessee marched in military formation against state prisons, securing the release of the inmates. On the other, they called on the state's governor, as their "Chief Executive and Protector," to come to their defense. How did these men justify their blatantly illegal and even insurrectionary actions? More important, how did they reconcile their march on state institutions with their supplication to the governor? The citizens of east Tennessee presumed that Buchanan would sympathize with their position, but they also gave notice that if their demands were not met, they might be forced to attack state employees and state institutions.

The first question is most easily disposed of. The community dynamics in areas of freehold title such as Coal Creek and Briceville differed markedly from those in company towns. In many postbellum southern towns, the primary employers provided the necessities of life through company-built housing and company-owned stores. As a result, there were few opportunities for people to sell clothing, food, and work equipment or for other locals to provide medical care and other services. In the east Tennessee mining towns, by contrast, companies could not dictate where and how their employees lived and shopped, nor where they prayed and spent their leisure hours. Mineworkers owned their own homes or rented from local landowners. Miners also bought a wide range of goods and services from local proprietors. Thus the populations of these towns included independent merchants, professionals, and neighboring farmers who all had a stake in the miners' steady employment. The financial well-being of these single-industry coal towns depended on the miners' having money to spend. By bringing in strikebreakers who would not earn regular wages, the company threatened the viability of the entire community—both free miners and local druggists, hoteliers, shopkeepers, liquor merchants, barbers, butchers, lawyers, doctors, and teachers. Through the introduction of convicts, B. A. Jenkins unwittingly forged a coalition of "miners, farmers, merchants, and property-holders" in Briceville and Coal Creek.

The second and third issues—those about timing and the divergent strategies embraced by the miners—present thornier questions; much of the narrative that follows is devoted to offering explanations for them. There was no single impetus behind the miners' turn to militance. The election of numerous Farmers' Alliance legislators and the organization's gubernatorial candidate in 1890 had created new expectations about the responsiveness of government to the problems of working Tennesseans, expectations that were reinforced by increasing acceptance of "labor" as an important part of Tennessee society. Growing unionization in Tennessee's mining communities simultaneously nurtured confidence in collective action. Finally, the emergence of charismatic community "elders" among the miners gave voice and leadership to their smoldering discontent. The broader political contexts, both at the level of state government and in terms of local organization, provide indispensable keys to understanding the Tennessee's coal miners' insurrection. An account of the economic conditions and specific events that set this rebellion alight only provides a starting point.

Explaining the seemingly contradictory tactics employed by the east Tennesseans requires coming to grips with them as political actors. These men possessed an ideological inheritance that both set limits on their political strategies and opened up avenues of action. This legacy shaped and justified their readiness to march in military formation as well as their willingness to embark on a series of constitutional negotiations that marked them as insiders, not outsiders. The east Tennesseans' sense of entitlement and righteousness came from an attachment to a medley of traditions, including a version of nineteenth-century civic republicanism, a defense of community most tangibly symbolized by homeownership, the legacy of the American Revolution, and a frontier heritage represented by the State of Franklin. But the political ideas these men espoused and held dear were not ideological straitjackets. The miners of Anderson County and their allies tailored their rhetoric and fitted their political strategies to circumstances, always striving to make Tennessee's political system work for them.

The First Insurrection

The miners were not alone in wiring the governor about events in Briceville. The superintendent of prisons, E. B. Wade, did not wait long before he too sought the intervention of Tennessee's chief executive officer. Wade had every reason to act in Governor Buchanan's best interests. The forty-eight-year old had secured his job as a result of his longtime political association with Buchanan. They both called Rutherford County home, had served the Democratic Party for decades, and had risen to the highest ranks of the Farmers' Alliance—the governor had captured the office of party president and Wade that of secretary.[3] The superintendent's appeal struck an ominous note. Fearing that the revolt against convict labor might spread, Wade implored Buchanan to call up one or two military companies and to send them as soon as possible.

This advice placed Buchanan in a quandary. The 1870 state constitution prohibited the governor from calling out the militia on his own initiative. Following the collapse of Reconstruction, a constitutional convention limited the power of Tennessee's chief executive officer in a direct response to what delegates perceived as the military "excesses" of the Republican governor, William G. Brownlow. Conservatives had determined that henceforth the governor could summon troops only after receiving the Tennessee General Assembly's sanction or a direct request from a county sheriff. This provision, written to curb a Reconstruction governor's reliance on the military, ironically curtailed a Democratic governor's ability to bring out the state guard in response to a revolt in Republican east Tennessee. Buchanan thus had to ask Anderson County's sheriff, Rufus Rutherford, to make a direct and urgent appeal for military intervention. Rutherford, who owned a livery stable in the county seat of Clinton, only partially complied. He declared that he was unable to enforce the law but did not explicitly request military assistance. With this careful formulation, Rutherford signaled a divided loyalty. He would be the first of a number of local officials who, because they owed their position to democratic election, would not straightforwardly serve the interests of central state authority. The governor, ignoring the cryptic nature of the message, ordered three military companies—the Lookout Rifles and Moerlein Zouaves, both from Chattanooga, and the Knoxville Rifles—to meet him at Knoxville on July 16.[4] By taking this action, Buchanan opened himself to the charge of circumventing the constitution. While his critics in the Democratic Party remained largely silent on the issue during the rebellion itself, they complained vigorously when it came time to nominate the Democratic gubernatorial candidate in 1892.[5]

After the militia companies arrived in Knoxville, Buchanan and the state guard accompanied the convicts back to Briceville. On their arrival, the governor ordered the prisoners back to the stockades and placed one of the Chattanooga companies on guard. At a public meeting in one of the mining towns, he then adopted a sympathetic but firm stand. Buchanan, or "Old Buck" as he was called, told Anderson County's citizens that his "life's service has been devoted to . . . relieve the masses of laboring men." He reminded his audience that he had appointed George Ford, a longtime labor activist and member of the Knights of Labor, as commissioner of labor. He added, however, that he remained committed to the sanctity of contracts and the maintenance of law and order. Buchanan told the miners that they should direct any grievances to the state's lawmakers and "not endeavor to take the law in their own hands." "Right or wrong," the governor continued, "the lease system was not the point at issue." Instead, the crucial political fact was that the miners "had defied the State in open insurrection, and that law and order must . . . be . . . preserved at any cost." He concluded with the suggestion that the best way for the miners to rid themselves of the convict lease was to send "good men to the Legislature."[6]

The reply fell to the chair of the meeting, Eugene Merrell, "a small man and intelligent in appearance." Though hardly a product of the Tennessee mountains, Merrell was "probably the most influential person with the miners in the valley." Born in Paris, France, as Jean Rousseau, he had come to New Orleans in 1855 with his parents at the age of six. When his father died, his mother remarried and her husband, John Merrell, adopted the young boy, giving him his family name. The family moved to Paris, Illinois, where his stepfather worked as a railway watchman and the young Merrell gained employment as a coal miner.

Merrell began his public life sometime after his marriage in 1878 at South Danville, Illinois, when the citizens there asked him to stand for city clerk. A man not given to flamboyant ways, he agreed to run but refused to campaign for the office. On election day he worked in the mine, only learning of his success at the end of the day's toil. After completing his term in office, Merrell gave up his city clerkship, preferring instead to organize miners into a Knights of Labor local. Though he achieved his objective, Merrell left South Danville for Clinton, Indiana, where he continued to organize miners. Discharged for union activity in Clinton, he lived in Kansas for a number of years before moving once again—this time to Briceville.

After working as a miner for two and a half years, Merrell was blacklisted by local coal companies for leading a protest against the use of forks in the loading of coal, a process that decreased the weight for which miners received credit. Merrell was on the verge of leaving Briceville in 1889 when a local merchant offered him a partnership in one of the town's independently owned mercantile stores. In January 1891 Merrell bought the business outright. The miner-turned-storekeeper enjoyed a steady trade, purchasing $500 worth of goods per month from Knoxville wholesalers. During the rebellion, Merrell sold his goods on credit. The tough economic times left the local inhabitants unable to make good on their debts, causing Merrell to close his store. Toward the end of the rebellion, with a $5,000 to $10,000 reward offered for his arrest, Merrell fled Tennessee. He continued his organizing efforts among the miners of Indiana and Illinois but later returned to Knoxville, where he led a successful strike at the Knoxville Woolen Mills.[7]

At the time of the first march on the Briceville stockades, Merrell acknowledged Buchanan's duty to enforce the law. He nonetheless argued that the state government had not applied the law equitably, questioning whether the governor would be so prompt to order in the militia to defend the miners' legal rights to an independent checkweighman and to payment in legal tender. The labor leader concluded his speech on an obedient but steadfast note: "The miners do not want to violate the law," he promised, "but they do want to protect themselves and their wives and children, and they intend to do so." Merrell exhibited a shrewd ability to phrase the miners' rationale for their actions in language that the governor would have difficulty countering. The

Eugene Merrell (Tatom, "Press Clippings")

"people's protector" responded virtually daily to pardon petitions from convicts who couched their appeals in similar idioms and tones. Lost for words, Buchanan could only reiterate his intention to enforce the law pertaining to the convicts. The following day the governor left Briceville while the 130-strong militia stayed behind to maintain law and order.[8]

The insurrection left matters unsettled in Anderson County. Miners in the Coal Creek Valley had accomplished nothing concrete. The convicts had returned to the stockades with three companies of the state militia standing guard over them while the Tennessee Coal Mining Company mines remained closed to free miners. Within the workingmen's ranks, calls for the renewed adoption of militant tactics grew apace.

Ignoring the governor's public appeal for order, mineworkers marched on the stockades during the morning of July 20—their second action in five days. This time a much larger contingent participated. Approximately 2,000 men from a fifty-mile radius around the Briceville and Coal Creek region descended from the hills surrounding the Tennessee Coal Mining Company's prison. Men with shotguns and rifles took their place along a line in front while those with pistols stood behind. Anyone discovered to be "under the influence of whiskey" was ejected from the party. When these men reached the stockade, an unarmed committee led by Eugene Merrell politely approached Colonel Granville Sevier, the acting adjutant general. Sevier, recognizing the futility of resistance and receiving assurance that the miners would not damage company property, agreed to relinquish the forty prisoners. Miners, guards, soldiers, and convicts then marched to Coal Creek, where the latter three groups boarded a special train to Knoxville. All of this activity was completed by 1:30 P.M. In keeping with a sense of propriety and decorum, the miners then dispersed for midday dinner.[9]

At 2:30 P.M. the crowd reassembled and approached the Knoxville Iron Company mine in Coal Creek, where they secured the release of 117 additional convicts. In a now familiar sequence of events, the miners escorted these inmates to the train station, putting them on another train bound for Knoxville. A meeting of 500 people then voted not to remove the convicts working in Oliver Springs, a small mining and resort town on the Anderson and Morgan county line, deciding to await developments at Coal Creek and Briceville.[10]

The disciplined show of force, the participation of townspeople, and the respect that the lawbreakers showed for company property were key features of both the first and second assaults on convict labor. But the raids were not identical. In the second, a large number of Kentuckians from the "tough" border town of Jellico took part. Typically described as a drinking, shooting crowd who were always ready to flout the law, their presence gave the proceedings a sharper edge.[11]

The Kentuckians' pugnacious bearing stemmed from a feeling of moral superiority, of having seen it all before. In the spring of 1886 militant opposition by Kentucky miners had successfully compelled their state government to remove convicts from two eastern Kentucky mines. Anderson County miners marched with their Kentucky compatriots in 1886, but the attack on convict labor did not spill over into the Volunteer State, where convict miners were already well entrenched in Coal Creek's Knoxville Iron Company mine. According to the rebelling miners, Tennessee had remained undisturbed largely because the initiators of the Kentucky fight—the Knights of Labor—were not well organized in Tennessee.[12] Five years later, under different circumstances and with more effective labor organizations, Anderson County miners both emulated their fellow mineworkers to the north and called on their aid.

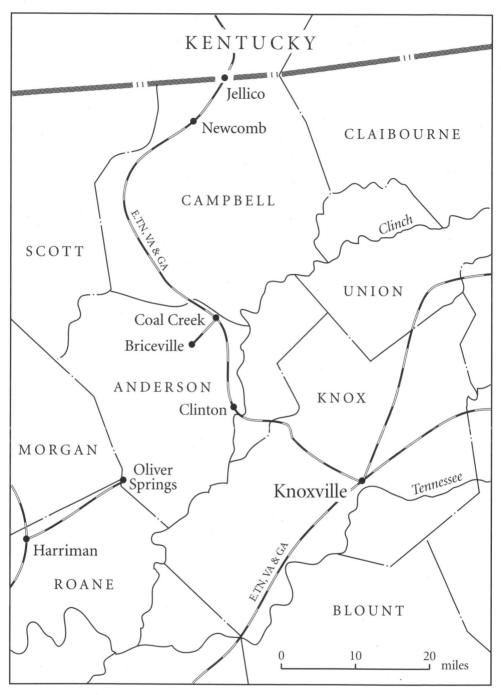

Map 4.2. Anderson County Coal Towns and Their Surroundings (*Source:* Adapted from Hutson, "The Coal Miners' Insurrection, 1891–92")

In response to the miners' second expulsion of convicts from Coal Creek Valley, Governor Buchanan mobilized another twelve companies of the state militia, comprising roughly 600 men. To minimize fraternal feelings between the local citizenry and militiamen, he judiciously called ten of these companies from Democratic mid- and west Tennessee.[13] The governor had learned a lesson from the events of the previous week. The miners had expressed minimal concern when Buchanan had first ordered the convicts back to the local prisons. "The militia are men the same as we, and they cannot help being in sympathy with us," argued one miner. "[They] did not enlist to come here among a class of hard-working men, for the purpose of shielding a gang of convicts."[14] Briceville residents had moved freely among the militia and had extended them every courtesy, whether helping the soldiers carry supplies from the train depot, guiding them over the unfamiliar and hilly terrain of east Tennessee, or entertaining them in their homes. The militiamen, mostly white workingmen from east Tennessee, explicitly declared that they would not resist the miners should the latter choose to attack the Briceville stockade for a second time.[15]

The implications of the militia's refusal to act against the miners were not lost on the editors of labor newspapers. The *United Mine Workers Journal* reprinted articles on the militia's inaction that appeared in the *Grand Rapids Workman* and the *Toronto Labor Advocate*. Both articles placed the phenomenon in historical perspective. The Michigan editor noted that "the revolution in France was not a success until the soldiers joined the revolutionists. It looks a little as if things were coming that way in this country." Toronto's commentator recalled events closer in space and time: "It will be remembered that, at the time of the Detroit street railway strike, the militia refused to act against the strikers. When capitalism can no longer depend upon its police and soldiers, its reign is drawing to a close."[16] Perhaps Governor Buchanan was well versed in recent history. Only when he had the mid- and west Tennessee troops close at hand, camped on the University of Tennessee grounds in Knoxville, did he negotiate a truce with the miners.

A People's Democrat

The committee that wired John Buchanan to request arbitration on the miners' behalf following the first attack on the Briceville stockade expected more from this governor than it would have from previous incumbents. The recently united Farmers' Alliance and Agricultural Wheel, of which Buchanan had been elected president in 1889, served as his political base. Born in 1847, the

Governor John Buchanan
(*Harper's Weekly*, August 27,
1892, Yale Collection of American
Literature, Beinecke Rare Book
and Manuscript Library, Yale
University)

young Buchanan served in the Confederate army for the last two years of the Civil War. In 1878 he moved from Williamson to Rutherford County, where he became a successful farmer and livestock breeder. By the time he rose to prominence in the Farmers' Alliance, Buchanan had amassed a tidy fortune, owning 325 acres—the fourth-largest farm in his home district. J. H. McDowell, Buchanan's election manager and editor of the Alliance's official organ, the *Weekly Toiler*, told his 10,000 subscribers that Buchanan acquired his wealth through his own hard work, common sense, and good judgment. He was, according to McDowell's inevitably supportive review, "in every sense of the word, a self-made man." When Buchanan received the Democratic Party's gubernatorial nomination, he had already gained experience in affairs of state, having served two terms as a state representative from mid-Tennessee's Rutherford County.[17]

Though Buchanan had impeccable Democratic credentials, his selection as the gubernatorial candidate came despite substantial opposition from the party's two dominant factions. Both the states' rights Democrats and the successors of the old-line Whigs reluctantly capitulated to the choice of the Jacksonian Democrats for governor. These divisions within the party had their origins in antebellum Tennessee but survived the Civil War. The miners' hopes that Buchanan would redress their grievances largely derived from his independent political base.

In the late antebellum period the states' righters, named the Harris Democrats for their Confederate governor, Isham Harris, had grown in prominence as northerners intensified their attacks on slavery. The spokesman for the great slaveholders, Harris came from cotton-growing west Tennessee. After the war, the Harris Democrats continued to distrust the federal government, generally favoring state railroad regulation and an end to tariffs. Within Tennessee, they usually opposed full payment of the state debt, insisting on low state taxes. They also had little reason to place the concerns of miners high on their agenda, caring far more about the status of crop liens and fence laws.

Though most former Tennessee Whigs joined the Democrats in secession, they commingled uneasily with their new political allies, becoming a distinct faction within the party. Following the war, little separated these men of property from moderate Republicans except the all-important race issue, as they vigorously promoted state aid to transportation projects and tax policies favorable to industrial development. By the same token, the old-line Whigs had little in common with the Jacksonian Democrats except a similar conception of how race relations should be conducted in the South. Like the Harris Democrats, former Whigs cared little for the position of mineworkers, though as the result of close links to mining corporations rather than a focus on agricultural interests.

The Jacksonian Democrats—the traditional champions of rural workingmen and small farmers against "aristocrats"—had a political philosophy far more congenial to the miners' complaint against convict labor. These Democrats had a long-standing suspicion of "monopolists" and financiers. Andrew Johnson led the Jacksonian wing of the party from the late 1860s until his death in 1875. Johnson's demise left a political void in the Jacksonian Democrats' camp. His followers, once leaderless, showed a tendency "to 'go fishing' on election days."[18]

Buchanan's independence from the two dominant factions of the Democratic Party and his 1890 affiliation with the Farmers' Alliance simultaneously rankled his powerful party colleagues and earned respect from Tennessee's miners.[19] Charles McClung McGhee, whose wide-ranging financial interests in banking, transportation, mining, and real estate made him one of Tennessee's richest men, voiced typical objections. In McGhee's view, Buchanan was "a representative of the agrarian element and his election I fear would retard future developments."[20] Buchanan's presidency of the Farmers' Alliance particularly troubled the states' righters and the old-line Whigs. Both factions strongly opposed the Alliance's subtreasury scheme—the innovative proposal to use nonperishable agricultural produce as collateral for loans to farmers, thereby alleviating the necessity to sell in glutted markets and making the money supply more flexible. Harris Democrats and the industrial wing of the party further worried about the possibility that the Alliance might serve as a platform for a third-party movement.[21]

Should the Democratic Party split, the possibility that the Republican Party would regain control of the machinery of state remained ever present. In Tennessee, unlike the rest of the South, the Republican Party survived as a substantial minority party after Redemption. Though its strength lay chiefly in east Tennessee, several pro-union counties along the Tennessee River voted Republican and three west Tennessee counties—Shelby, Fayette, and Hayward—had large black populations, which gave the GOP a foothold in that region of the state.[22] The ability of the Republicans to woo undecided white voters in any given contest rendered it a genuine threat to Democratic supremacy.

Before his nomination, Buchanan refused to be pinned down on the subtreasury plan and ducked the issue of a third-party movement. His silence on these issues did not stop the Democratic press from initially treating Buchanan's candidacy with mirth and giving him only lukewarm support. Once he became the Democratic Party's standard-bearer, several newspapers lampooned the convention that nominated the Alliance president as unsophisticated and full of political novices. One typical account characterized the assembly as "one of the wildest and wooliest . . . ever held in Nashville." According to the same reporter, "The air about the capitol that was not full of spit balls and hats was redolent with Lincoln fragrance and bucolic oratory."[23]

Having the support of journalists was all important in an age where the press served as the dominant form of mass political communication. The vast majority of Tennessee's broadsheets were politically aligned, and the editors saw themselves as important opinion makers. Editorial control of the big party newspapers—for the Democratic Party, Memphis's *Appeal Avalanche* and *Commercial*, Nashville's *Banner* and *American*, Knoxville's *Tribune* and *Sentinel*, and the *Chattanooga Times*—was seen as so important that political factions waged internecine struggles to wrest management away from one another. During the 1880s, for example, A. S. Colyar and his fellow industrialists engaged in a bitter struggle for control of the preeminent *Nashville American* with a group of states' righters—a struggle that witnessed four shifts in editorial direction in six years. The battle over the *American* was not unique. East Tennessee Republicans also immersed themselves in "paper wars," especially over those based in Knoxville, the largest city in Republican east Tennessee.[24]

The newspaper world and its political influence was not just a big-city affair. Small county broadsheets proliferated in the late nineteenth century. In 1891 Tennessee boasted 271 newspapers—including 21 dailies, 4 semiweeklies, 205 weeklies, and 31 semimonthlies, monthlies, or quarterlies. Like their city counterparts, the small country papers exhibited their particular brand of politics on their editorial pages. The growth of papers can be traced to the growing number of towns and villages as well as the emergence of syndicated news agencies. With a Chicago or New York agency providing material for a couple of pages at low cost, a local editor had only to find copy for two more sheets before he was in business. The number of subscribers ranged widely—from hundreds for village weeklies to the tens of thousands for big-city dailies.[25]

The disquiet that Buchanan induced among Democratic Party editors, like his attraction to small farmers, rural laborers, and wage workers, lay as much in what he personified, in his populist flair, as in substantial deviation from standard Democratic Party policies. In his stump speeches Buchanan proposed fiscal retrenchment, taxes on railroads, and homestead development while offering constant criticism of the high McKinley tariff and the excessive political influence of monopoly finance and capital. He further denounced Henry Cabot Lodge's Federal Election Bill, which authorized national intervention in local elections, arguing that its passage would result in "negro supremacy." This proposed piece of legislation had sparked one of the fiercest congressional debates since the end of Reconstruction, pitting northern and southern states against one another. Buchanan knew that the image of "colored heels upon white necks" would be a sure winner among his white audiences.[26]

By emulating Democratic race-baiting, Buchanan reached out to the mainstream of his party. In courting the votes of laborers and farmers, Buchanan also veered away from positions that the business elite might find abhorrent. To this end, he emphatically denied supporting "class legislation." Nonetheless, by referring to "the *legitimate* growth of mercantile, manufacturing, and railroad interests," by raising the old axiom "the greatest good to the greatest number," and by invoking the mantle of Johnson, Polk, and Jackson, Buchanan attracted sufficient electoral support to gain a comfortable victory in November 1890.[27]

On the issue closest to the hearts of east Tennessee's miners—the convict lease—Buchanan could boast only an equivocal record. As a representative to the legislature, he had voted in favor of the lease. In his 1890 campaign platform, though, Buchanan advocated the modification of the penal system "so that convict labor may not come in conflict with or antagonize the honest labor of the country." Thus, in July 1891, east Tennessee miners settled down to negotiate with a person who combined a populist style with an ambivalent attitude toward the policy of convict leasing.[28]

Negotiations with the People's Governor

For four days following the east Tennesseans' second incursion against prison labor in Anderson County, a group of miners met with a five-man committee of supportive leading Knoxvillians, as well as with the governor, his attorney general, and the commissioner of labor. Beginning on July 21, these meetings eventually thrashed out an agreement that accommodated the expectations of the rank-and-file miners and the commitments of Tennessee's leaders to the sanctity of the law.

The miners initially demanded that Governor Buchanan withdraw the convict strikebreakers from Briceville immediately and call an extra session of the legislature at which the people's representatives would repeal the convict-lease system. Following the sitting of the general assembly, the miners further expected the government to remove the remaining convicts from the east Tennessee towns of Coal Creek and Oliver Springs.[29] In responding to these demands, Buchanan had to contend with fiscal realities—especially the costs that abrogating the lease would entail—and with the vested interests that had sustained the convict lease over the preceding two decades.

During a series of meetings, both the governor and the miners' delegation adopted a number of strategies that would become typical of their tactics to secure an amicable resolution to the crisis. Buchanan attempted to reach a compromise through the office of an appointed, rather than elected, government official. Immediately after hearing of the second march on the stockades, the governor dispatched Attorney General Pickle to urge the Tennessee Coal Mining Company's president, B. A. Jenkins, and the TCIR convict broker, William Morrow, to terminate the use of convict strikebreakers in their Briceville mine. Though this maneuver proved unsuccessful, the attorney general and the commissioner of labor would both again attempt to craft solutions to the standoff between the miners and their employers.[30]

The miners also employed stratagems that they would later repeat, persuading civic leaders of both parties to form a committee supporting their cause. The leading Republicans who agreed to serve on the committee included Henry R. Gibson, an east Tennessee representative of the general assembly and chancellor of east Tennessee's Court of Chancery Appeals, William Rule, a U.S. pension agent and general manager of the *Knoxville Journal*, and Dennis Leahy, an officer in east Tennessee's Central Labor Union. Among the Democrats who joined were J. C. J. Williams, a leading Democratic attorney who would steadfastly assist the miners in various legal cases free of charge, and Major D. A. Carpenter, an ex-U.S. pension officer and local capitalist.[31] By incorporating Republicans and Democrats in its support committee, the mining community purposefully steered away from aligning themselves wholly with either major party.

Despite their careful caucusing, the miners failed to achieve their immediate objectives. On July 24 they accepted the return of convicts and the militia to the east Tennessee mining towns, in exchange for a promise that the governor would call a special session of the general assembly to address their concerns about the convict lease. The miners' committee, acting on behalf of both miners and "their friends of Briceville and Coal Creek," resolved not to "molest" the guards and convicts on their return to the mines. In a carefully worded agreement, they boosted the stature of the governor while asserting his accountability, declared their faith in the legislature to "give us the necessary relief from the oppression that now hangs over us," and promised to conduct themselves as law-abiding citizens. Lest politicians or the press cast them as malcontents, the miners reminded the governor that they had the "confidence and sympathy of the public."[32]

The compromise fell short of the miners' aspirations. Marcena Ingraham, a leader in the march on the convict stockades and a signatory to the agreement, stressed the tactical limits of the situation in explaining the miners' acceptance of the deal. Readily admitting that the short-term rapprochement was "not satisfactory to any of us," Ingraham told the press that it was "under the circumstances the best thing we could do." In his next breath he cautioned that if the legislature failed to repeal the lease, "you may expect to hear from us again."[33]

In the midst of the negotiations, the miners' representatives enlisted the assistance of their more prominent allies to build support within east Tennessee's angry mining communities for a compromise. On July 23 union leaders asked J. C. J. Williams to address a public meeting of approximately 1,000 people. Confronted by calls to "fight it out" as he rose to speak, Williams managed to allay the miners' discontent with biblical metaphors that emphasized

William Webb (Henry C. Mayer
Collection)

the dignity of laboring people, a stress on the necessity of maintaining public
support, and a report that the governor would call an extra session of the
legislature at which he would recommend the repeal of the convict lease.
William Webb, president of UMWA's District 19, repeated the plea for patience at the same gathering, maintaining that "only proper reform is obtained
through your Legislature, and when you do this you will have served yourself
proudly."[34]

Choosing Webb—known to his friends and comrades as "Billy"—for this
important task proved a stroke of genius, for the locals knew that he had led
the Kentucky miners in their successful fight against convict labor in the
mid-1880s. A native Tennessean who had adopted Kentucky as his home, Webb
began organizing coal miners for the Knights of Labor in the mid-1870s and
became the first president of the Kentucky/Tennessee district—District 19—of
the United Mine Workers of America. His strong endorsement of a peaceful
course of action solidified the willingness of rank-and-file miners to entrust
their grievances to the legislature. For the moment, the miners agreed to direct
their energies to constitutional redress.[35]

The settlement generally pleased the business community. While business leaders reserved their special scorn for those among them who had sided with the miners, such as the Republican chancellor Henry Gibson and the Democratic lawyer J. C. J. Williams, they nonetheless expressed their newfound satisfaction with Buchanan's fortitude. Colonel C. M. McGhee, who had despaired at the Allianceman's nomination, now "admire[d] very much the courage and firmness as shown by Governor Buchanan."[36] Other businessmen, concerned that the rebellion would hinder financial investment in Tennessee, paid more effusive tribute. One attorney from Memphis congratulated Buchanan for his "courageous" and "patriotic" actions, predicting that he would receive "the commendation of all good citizens."[37] To the state's businessmen and legal fraternity, Buchanan's "law and order" stance was cause for public approbation.

The miners' willingness to commit themselves to "lawful and regular methods" in the July 24 agreement reflected their hopes that the reform government, headed by a Farmers' Alliance governor, would prove to be responsive to complaints about the convict lease. Even with the election of a new government, however, the miners' acceptance of the compromise also depended on the maturation of the labor unions in the coalfields, the emergence of charismatic community leaders, and shifts in political discourse—specifically the recognition and honor accorded working people by the establishment of a state labor department and by the creation of a Labor Day as a public holiday.

The miners' leaders were able to gain unanimous endorsement for the agreement from a more militant and impatient rank and file because of the democracy within the miners' organizations, the moderating influence of the Knights of Labor, and the prestige of specific leaders. Throughout negotiations, Merrell and company regularly reported back to the rank and file, consistently refusing to make decisions without the backing of the Briceville and Coal Creek communities. The accountability of the leadership and the loyalty of ordinary miners led newspapers to predict that the workingmen would abide by the terms of the negotiations. The *New York Times* offered a typical analysis, observing that "the men are so thoroughly disciplined and so thoroughly controlled by the miners' union that it is universally conceded that the end of the trouble has come."[38] In an early August speech, Eugene Merrell also acknowledged the miners' discipline, attributing it largely to the many lessons they had learned from the Knights. Careful to distance the official organization of the Knights from illegal activities, he explained that "none of our war was carried on under the name of that order, yet most of those connected with it had been schooled in the Knights of Labor meetings."[39]

As important as experience with the Knights of Labor may have been to the

A public meeting of miners and residents of Coal Creek Valley (*Harper's Weekly*, August 27, 1892, Yale Collection of American Literature, Beinecke Rare Book and Manuscript Library, Yale University)

miners' struggle, one would be hard pressed to exaggerate the crucial roles played by such leaders as Eugene Merrell, George Irish, and Marcena Ingraham. Their stature, along with careful organization and clear enunciation of Knights of Labor principles, gave coherence and political force to the grievances of the east Tennessee miners. In much the same way that Emile Zola's Etienne gave focus and impetus to the discontent of fictional French miners in Monsou, so these men, though not native to Anderson County, and in two cases not native to Tennessee, held the respect of the rank and file and gave effective voice to their concerns.[40]

Merrell's prominence derived from a sharp mind, his previous experience in union activity, which had honed skills in public speaking, and a pivotal community role as a Briceville storekeeper. Country stores in the late-nineteenth-century South served as crucial meeting places, on the porch during the summer months or next to the stove during the winter. Locals gathered in such stores throughout the South to dream about their futures, discuss local and national politics, and whittle away their time. From the store fronts, which often served as community bulletin boards, a newcomer to town could often tell who had married in the past year, who had died, what ballgames had taken place, and what issues had brought the community together or sparked heated division. Storekeepers additionally served as an important link to the outside world. With the growth of wholesale houses located in the city centers such as Knoxville, Nashville, Chattanooga, and Memphis, southern country stores provided an effective means of distributing merchandise. Through the store-keeper, a local might order cotton for a dress, a bottle of quinine, material for a shroud, equipment for work, or slate and chalk for a child's schooling. The store supplied everything "needed in both life and death." As a proprietor, Merrell had his finger on the pulse of the community, with intimate knowledge of its stresses and strains.[41]

George Irish also owned a store in Briceville in 1891. The *Chattanooga Republican* described him as an "intelligent, good-looking man, aged thirty-five." The son of a well-to-do Knox County farmer, Irish moved to Briceville around 1880. Sometime thereafter he married, purchased a house in the town, and, along with his brother, invested in local real estate. Irish served on many of the miners' committees and developed a reputation for his particularly "conservative" disposition. Like Merrell, he proudly wore a Knights of Labor insignia on his vest lapel.[42]

Marcena Ingraham led the miners in their first march on the stockades and later lobbied for the miners' cause in the state legislature. A native New Yorker and father of six children, the forty-seven-year-old moved to Tennessee in 1884. A "small, wiry, keen-eyed man," he soon became a coal miner. Ingraham was a "faithful Knight" and proud veteran of the Grand Army of the Republic, prominently displaying a G.A.R. label on his lapel. During an impromptu 1891 gathering of lobbyists and politicians at a Nashville inn, a Farmers' Alliance-man from Grundy County chided him about the G.A.R. label, remarking that when "you doubtless thought we Southerners were in defiance of the con-stituted authorities you very promptly came down here and taught us a lesson on that subject. You ought not to compel us to teach you the same lesson thirty years after." Ingraham saw no paradox in his fighting to uphold the duly constituted authority of the United States and his willingness to lead the miners against Tennessee's government. According to the newspaper that re-ported the exchange, he was "not disconcerted . . . by such an interruption, and continued to set forth the miners' side of the question in a very effective manner."[43]

These men, together with other union and community leaders, secured

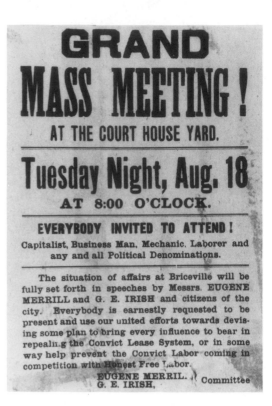

GRAND
MASS MEETING!
AT THE COURT HOUSE YARD.

Tuesday Night, Aug. 18
AT 8:00 O'CLOCK.

EVERYBODY INVITED TO ATTEND!
Capitalist, Business Man, Mechanic, Laborer and
any and all Political Denominations.

The situation of affairs at Briceville will be
fully set forth in speeches by Messrs. EUGENE
MERRILL and G. E. IRISH and citizens of the
city. Everybody is earnestly requested to be
present and use our united efforts towards devis-
ing some plan to bring every influence to bear in
repealing the Convict Lease System, or in some
way help prevent the Convict Labor coming in
competition with Honest Free Labor.
EUGENE MERRIL. } Committee
G. E. IRISH,

Poster advertising a grand mass
meeting (Tatom, "Press
Clippings")

their authority in the mining communities through a diverse set of tactics.
They arranged meetings and picnics, organized military companies, and ad-
vertised their demands on posters pasted on storefronts, always cultivating a
sense of mutual resolve and purpose.[44] Efforts to foster communal identity
could also take on a sober hue, as conveyed in the miners' secret oath of loyalty.
"You do each of you solemnly swear," the oath prescribed, "to obey all orders
committed to you, and to keep profoundly secret all our objectives and aims,
not even giving the name of any member of this company to any individual or
any inquisitorial power whatever."[45] Such oaths were far from rare in the
nineteenth century. They served at once to foster collaboration and set limits
on militant behavior. Although mining leaders periodically sought to stir
people up, they also tried to prevent individual or group action that might
endanger the interests of their organization. To this end, the east Tennessee
miners established committees to protect company property, ensure good
behavior, and urge their more militant friends from Kentucky to act in a
restrained fashion.[46] These efforts to instill an identity among working people

distinct from that of their employers was part and parcel of a broader project, or a "movement culture." Purposeful and ongoing strategies to nourish common identities and collective action were central to working-class and agrarian movements of the late nineteenth century. Economic grievances alone did not magically create unified stances at the workplace or ballot box.[47]

Newspapers across the political spectrum noted the cool-headedness and effectiveness of union and civic leaders in Coal Creek and Briceville. According to the *Nashville Herald*, had it "not been for Merrell and Irish and a few others there would have been a little hell in these valleys." The leaders themselves acknowledged their influence. Merrell remarked in 1892 that a "few of us are recognized by the miners as conservative men. They have confidence in us and we have influence to a certain extent over them."[48] By funneling the miners' more militant impulses into a negotiated settlement with the governor, the local leadership won the same accolade of being "conservative" in newspapers across the state. This image of moderation enhanced the miners' reputation as responsible workers with legitimate complaints.

The aura of respectability did not derive solely from perceptions of a prudent, sensible leadership. Changes in the structure of the state government and in political discourse strengthened the miners' claim to be honorable workingmen with reasonable concerns. Following a national trend, Governor Buchanan had created a Bureau of Labor and Mining Statistics early in March 1891. Prior to the 1890s, the miners had been without a special voice in government. Throughout the 1870s and 1880s, their criticisms about the convict-lease system had engendered little action, and their legal rights to independent checkweighmen and payment in legal tender had been honored more in the breach than in the observance. Now the miners could appeal to a friendly government office—the Bureau of Labor and Inspector of Mines. Workers in the mining industry did not serve as the sole beneficiary of Buchanan's policy; labor interests in general received attention during the governor's tenure in office. Through the legislative work of Charles Alleman, a Knoxville iron molder and the Knox County representative in the general assembly, the first Monday in September became Labor Day in Tennessee.[49] This celebration inscribed the importance of labor on the local political calendar. At the first Nashville Labor Day parade in 1891, over 15,000 people watched Anderson County miners head the procession.[50] The creation of a Bureau of Labor and the legislative and public acknowledgment of labor's honorable place in society amplified the miners' public standing while encouraging them to expect that the political system would deliver reform.

Republican Rhetoric:
The Art of Lobbying

Having called attention to their plight in the most dramatic fashion possible and having forced a reopening of the legislature, east Tennessee's mining communities did not sit back and simply let events unfold. Union leaders recognized that they now had to justify their past behavior and sell their objectives to constituencies beyond their own. Only a massive outpouring of support for the miners' cause was likely to dislodge the long-settled policy of convict leasing. East Tennessee's community leaders portrayed themselves as exemplary citizens and honest, moderate workingmen in a coordinated campaign to cultivate public opinion. Spokesmen for the miners went on speaking tours, raised money, kept an eye on press reports, and lobbied legislators and national labor organizations.

The miners sent their most polished emissaries—Eugene Merrell and George Irish—to travel around the state arguing their case and drumming up public sympathy. The two men held meetings in all the large cities—Knoxville, Nashville, Chattanooga, and Memphis—and in coal mining towns such as Tracy City, Jellico, Soddy, and Rockwood. The purpose was both to broadcast the miners' point of view—that Jenkins had initiated the conflict, that the mineworkers had no choice but to attack the convict lease forcibly, and that they had maintained remarkable discipline during the marches on the stockades—and to solicit financial assistance. In addition to collecting money in the course of their public appearances, community leaders set up an independent committee specifically to raise funds and to place advertisements requesting contributions.[51] They also tried to keep the convict-lease issue in the public mind by raising the point in letters to newspapers and in interviews with a range of journalists. Ever mindful of the kind of publicity they received, community leaders occasionally objected to reports that they considered too sensational or requested that miners' representatives be properly quoted.[52]

Community leaders knew that a sympathetic public image was particularly important during the three-week period that the legislature met in September 1891. Accordingly, they established a special committee to represent their interests in Nashville. Familiar figures such as Merrell, Ingraham, and Irish were accompanied by a newcomer to the leadership ranks, John Hatmaker, a "diminutive miner" with "brilliant" eyes. In an effort to present a united front, the Briceville and Coal Creek men were joined by labor representatives from the coal towns of Tracy City, Whitwell, Jellico, Newcomb, and Oliver Springs as well as from the capital, Nashville. During the legislative extra session, the miners closely monitored debates and public presentations of the situation in Briceville and Coal Creek. Thus when the TCMC president, B. A. Jenkins, corresponded with Senator T. J. Alexander, a lawyer from mid-Tennessee's Franklin County, suggesting that the miners were rowdy and belligerent, "Briceville Men" were quick to refute such charges.[53]

When Merrell and Irish faced an audience, they sought initially to portray themselves as innocent victims, blaming the coal operators for the current crisis and complaining about their inability to secure their legal rights in a court of law. They then tried to convince their listeners that events in east Tennessee were of central concern to all citizens of the state—and so all Tennesseans should petition the legislature and write to local newspapers urging the people's representatives to adopt a new penal policy. To achieve the desired response, Merrell and Irish couched their past actions and current desires in a vocabulary with which their audiences could identify.

The language that the miners' ambassadors used represented a concatenation of ideas and key phrases rather than a coherent ideology. Such rhetorical techniques should not come as a surprise. Merrell and Irish spoke to diverse groups of people—to urban industrial workers, property owners, and professionals as well as to their own rank and file. Merrell and Irish hoped that each of these groups would identify with the miners' grievances, noting the connections to their own disparate experiences. The work of historian Daniel Rodgers offers a useful means of contextualizing the strategies of persuasion employed by the miners' leaders as they sought to coax favorable responses from their audiences, to secure political alliances, and to create the impression that the abrogation of the convict lease would benefit all Tennesseans. Rodgers reminds historians that "political talk" is more than just linguistic window dressing; politicians use language in the hopes of moving people to action.[54] Just as the miners had used military tactics to focus attention on the convict-lease system, so their leaders now used their verbal skills in efforts to achieve more durable political objectives.

The two men frequently began their lectures with a standard rhetorical device, disclaiming any partisan motivations and assuring their listeners that they only hoped to further the common good of Tennesseans. "The question is not as to who is responsible for this iniquitous law, but who will do away with it," Merrell told an August meeting organized by the Chattanooga Federation of Trades. "There is no politics in it whatever, and the man who introduces politics into it is our enemy and the worst one we have."[55] Even though the east Tennesseans knew that the convict-lease system was steeped in politics, they nonetheless tried to sidestep party-political divisions within the state. To be aligned with the Republican Party—the party that dominated their region but constituted a minority within the state—would have doomed their attempts to have the convict lease repealed by the legislature.

The miners not only cast the abolition of the convict lease as above party politics; they also projected it as a concern for the mining industry as a whole and for the overall Tennessee economy. In an August 1891 interview, Merrell made the case that the lease issue affected a much wider geographic area: "We are not struggling to save Briceville and Coal Creek from ruin, but the coal industry of the state."[56] Because new investors could not compete with the coal companies already employing prisoners, the miners' leaders reasoned, the convict lease retarded the development of Tennessee coal lands.

Moreover, the miners argued, convict labor had an adverse impact beyond the coalfields. Foregone wages to free labor additionally damaged secondary and service industries. One frequent writer of letters to Tennessee newspapers from Tracy City discussed the implications of convict labor for industries seemingly far removed from coal mining. "XX"—the pen name of the Tracy City correspondent—argued that "the convict don't have as many clothes to wear out and his food is of the cheapest and coarsest." As a result, "he is of no benefit to anybody save his master the lessee, and what he earns his master pockets it." The free miner's earnings, by contrast, went "into circulation for food, clothes, etc. as soon as he gets it." "XX" calculated that the employment of 1,500 convicts withdrew "not less than forty-five thousand dollars monthly [from] the circulation of the country, or a loss of five hundred and forty thousand yearly." "No wonder," he concluded, "all classes cry 'hard times'; when the wage earners are deprived of this magnificent sum."[57] The miners further maintained that they were fighting for more than their prerogatives. They fought as well for the claims belonging to "legitimate capital"—coal operators who refrained from using convict labor, who did not seek to monopolize the industry, and who honored the miners' legal rights—as well as those of other industrialists and merchants whose businesses were hurt by the secondary effects of the convict-lease system.[58]

If Briceville and Coal Creek's community leaders projected their concerns as those of the coal industry as a whole, and indeed of competitive capital, they also sought to persuade small property owners that they too had a stake in the outcome of the east Tennesseans' struggle. The theme of property ownership and the community standing that it conveyed dominated the August 1891 speeches that Merrell and Irish made in Tennessee's major cities. Like the 1892 steel strikers in Homestead, Pennsylvania, who "spoke passionately" about themselves as "home-owner citizens defending their dwelling place," and with whom the east Tennesseans later identified, the citizens of Anderson County insisted that continued availability of work profoundly affected their rights to their property. The two men repeatedly stressed that many miners owned homes, proclaiming to their audiences that Anderson County miners had acquired houses through great sacrifice and "unremitted toil."[59] Eugene Merrell spoke especially eloquently of the rights of Anderson County citizens to their property: "If the convicts are not taken away from the mines where free labor has been employed every house and hamlet and all that value will be deserted. It will amount to exile for us and confiscation of the property we have labored for years to accumulate. We are fighting as much for our homes and property as for our labor."[60] For Merrell, disrespect for the miners' stake in their property carried serious consequences. At the same time, he insisted that the need to protect the rights of homeownership compelled the miners to act as they had—any other response would have marked these workingmen as "not fit for citizenship in a civilized country."[61]

Rhetorically, the theme of property ownership served the east Tennesseans well. The motifs of communal integrity, independence, and the sanctity of homeownership formed the basis of most petitions to the legislature supporting the east Tennesseans' cause. These motifs went to the heart of one message from 600 "miners, merchants and citizens of all classes" who petitioned the special session from the Rhea County mining town of Dayton. Boasting of their flourishing town with its population of 6,000, these petitioners stressed that "1,000 miners have provided for themselves little houses and have paid for them by honest toil." The signatories warned that "dark and dire disaster" would follow the introduction of convict labor and urged the legislature to change the law if it wished to "prevent a re-occurrence of trouble witnessed at our sister town of Briceville."[62]

The success of such themes in mobilizing interclass alliances was not unique to the South. During the 1880s and 1890s, railway men in Creston, Iowa, and silk workers in Paterson, New Jersey, also drew on a defense of traditional community values to build locally based cross-class alliances against the machinations of industrialists.[63] Similarly aware of tactical opportunities, the miners expressed strong respect for property belonging to the coal companies. Soon after the miners had marched on the stockades for the second time, they passed a public resolution condemning anyone who advocated the burning down or destruction of company property, pledging to guard such property against any harm.[64]

Just as appeals to property ownership could strike chords with people who had no background in mining, so it could join the diverse experiences and backgrounds of the Tennessee miners and their more widely traveled leaders, some of whom had no experience in mining. The emphasis on community and property hearkened back to the upcountry culture that most miners carried with them as they traveled from their parents' farms to the newly established coal towns of east Tennessee. This rhetoric also dovetailed with the original impulses of the Republican Party, which continued to appeal to many small businessmen and professionals. Early Republicans stressed the great worth of free labor and the centrality of economic opportunity. They argued that hard work deserved its reward in eventual ownership of one's firm, business, or home.[65] These ideas found an easy reception in Republican east Tennessee.

In addition to currying favor outside the coalfields, east Tennessee labor leaders also had to mobilize and sustain support among the rank and file. When the audience shifted from the broad public of Knoxville, Memphis, or Nashville to the workingmen of Briceville and Coal Creek, so too did the tone and emphasis of mine leaders. In reaching out to their own constituents, union spokesmen talked less of property rights and more of the just deserts earned by productive toil. A rhetorical stress on the most basic rights of workers to the full value of their labor had long served as a rallying cry for east Tennessee miners. Before the revolts of 1891, the most vexing threats to those rights had been the attempts of mineowners to appoint checkweighmen and to pay their employees in company scrip rather than legal tender.

With a checkweighman dependent on mine management, miners had good reason to fear that they would not receive full remuneration for the coal they mined. With payment in company scrip, mineworkers had their options as consumers severely curtailed. On several occasions in the late 1880s and the early 1890s, Tennessee miners demonstrated a willingness to go on strike or endure a lockout in order to keep the checkweighman independent or their pay in greenbacks. Throughout those disputes, labor leaders had asserted the claim of mine employees to a "full and just share of the wealth" that they brought out of the Appalachian hillsides.[66]

During the conflicts of 1891, and for several years thereafter, community leaders in the coal towns continued to remind their neighbors that the miners possessed rights as free workers. Dr. J. R. Adkins, a druggist in Coal Creek and editor of a local newspaper, offered typical commentary, noting a few months after the second attack on the convict stockades that "our wealth consists in the product of our labor." "When convict labor is substituted for free labor," Adkins concluded, "we"—meaning the free coal miners and the townspeople who depended on their custom—"have nothing left."[67]

As union officials and community supporters articulated their commitments to the rights of property owners and productive workers, they frequently appropriated the mantle of "manly behavior." The celebration of manliness— with its connotations of defiant egalitarianism, respectability, and dignity— enjoyed great popularity in the nineteenth century. Like workingmen through-out the country, east Tennessee's miners lambasted any "perversions" that might undermine the "rights of manhood"—whether the source of that corruption came from unjust laws or from developments in "industrial and economic affairs."[68]

While taking pains to assert their manhood, the miners also fervently proclaimed their determination to avoid its opposite—enslavement.[69] Individual workers and the miners' committee repeatedly referred to the condition of slavery in order to dramatize the social consequences of the convict lease. Alternately portraying it as "convict slavery," "negro slavery," and "judicial slavery," the residents of east Tennessee depicted the lease as undermining the economic and political viability of mining communities. Henry Gibson, the leading Republican who served on the citizens' committee supporting the miners, encapsulated this vision of looming enslavement during a July 23, 1891, meeting in Knoxville. Gibson observed that the coal operators "say they want their property protected. Very well, but the largest property of a citizen . . . is the right to be a free man. . . . We have not all one thousand acres of land or even a coal mine but we all have arms and muscles and the right to use them to support our families. The miners have a right to compete with free, not slave labor."[70] In these comments, Gibson skillfully drew together the notion of labor as property and the right that had become associated with that form of property: the right to self-government. By holding up the specter of slavery, Gibson made two distinctions: first, between those who held property in the form of land and mines and those who only owned their own labor; and, second, between those for whom property in labor ensured a capacity for independence and self-government and those who, like slaves, occupied a dependent position.[71] The miners asserted their ownership of property in the form of both homes and labor. Both attributes differentiated them sharply from unfree laborers.

In reporting on Gibson's speech, the *Coal Creek Press* praised the chancellor for honoring the worker, calling his characterization an "apotheosis to labor." Alluding to the antebellum notion that hard, menial labor was demeaning, a notion formed during the days of slavery, the reporter added a particularly southern twist to his story: "Before the war labor was regarded as degrading to the South. Now it is noble to engage in any honorable labor anywhere in the United States."[72]

The miners coupled their embrace of manliness and critique of convict slavery with an attack on the state's leading industrialists, whom they saw as "degrading" work and free society. Harking back to epithets that American patriots had hurled at English monarchy and that good Jacksonians had directed toward banks and "the money power," the miners labeled "the monopolists" (in this instance the convict lessees and the dominant coal company in the state, TCIR) as "tyrannical," "arrogant," and the greedy beneficiaries of "a shameful prosperity."[73] These workingmen were profoundly disturbed by the corrosive impact that concentrations of wealth inevitably had on the democratic process. Indeed, in an era personified by the consolidation of capital, they wondered whether the state could continue to respond to the demands of ordinary voters—whether their sacred rights as citizens might become mere sham. Miners across Tennessee's coalfields evinced pessimism, fearing that the public corruption wrought by financial monopoly precluded adequate protection of workingmen. Chancellor Gibson gave poignant voice to this pessimism in his Knoxville address of July 1891, observing that Tennessee's miners had approached a succession of governors about the insidious consequences of the convict lease. Each governor "had heard [the miners] not, for he had corporation cotton in his ears."[74]

By connecting the convict lease with assaults on small property owners and the rights of labor—with attempts to transform manly coal miners into rootless slaves—and with the corruption of state government by greedy monopolists, community leaders in the coal towns skillfully played on a range of well-worn themes in nineteenth-century American political culture. These themes both convinced the miners that their cause was just and earned that cause a hearing throughout the state of Tennessee. At the same time, the east Tennesseans' acceptance of wage labor and legitimate returns to capital reflected the realities of the lives they led in the South's rural industrial towns. The industrializing world of the late nineteenth century meant chronic unemployment for most working people. Although work retained its honorable qualities—and indeed for southern whites had newfound value, as suggested by the editorial comments in the *Coal Creek Press*—the miners' public emphasis on home-ownership suggests a shift in the measure of self-worth. Their value as working people and political actors was sustained less by independent work, as symbolized by the yeoman's cultivation or the artisan's craftsmanship of the early nineteenth century, and more by a long-term commitment to a community, with homeownership the most tangible embodiment of that commitment. Defense of that community compelled the miners to protect their rights in the marketplace. To paraphrase community leader Eugene Merrell, if the miners lost their jobs they could seek work elsewhere, but they could not take their homes with them.

The east Tennessee miners' beliefs about the rights of property owners, and to a lesser extent, those of productive workers, provided them and their local allies with the means to make sense of their world and evaluate it. These beliefs further offered guides to action, generally calling for appeal to and participation in government in order to redress wrongs. The east Tennesseans embraced such tactics. But in order to enhance their leverage in the corridors of power, the miners and their supporters peppered their public speeches and written commentary with references to the dire consequences that would follow if the government did not answer the call of justice. These warnings were not just meant for the people's representatives; they also buttressed morale in Tennessee's coal towns. The tough negotiations between the miners' committee and the governor and commentary by mine leader Marcena Ingraham indicating that the miners were not satisfied with the outcome of those discussions made clear that more militant oratory also had its place. Other cultural sources—emanating from the legacy of the American Revolution and Tennessee's frontier heritage—more directly addressed those needs.

Labor journals and their correspondents generally justified the miners' turn to militance through reference to the revolutionary ideals of the struggle for independence from Great Britain. In a defense of the miners' illegal actions, the *United Mine Workers Journal* appealed to the rights derived from the Revolution. "There is a limit to endurance," the journal intoned, "and that limit would seem to have been reached in the uprising of these American freemen to assert their God-given rights, purchased by the lives, blood and suffering of the patriots and heroes of 1776." Individual correspondents gladly took on the mantle of rebel or mob, maintaining that if contemporary law did not sanction the miners' insurrection, historical precedent did. The UMWA official S. P. Herron responded to one newspaper's characterization of the miners as "anarchist" by recalling the acts of American colonists. "What," Herron asked, "was [sic] our forefathers who rebelled against a bad system of taxation called? Was it not the modest name of rebels, traitors and the like?" One local resident more simply quipped, "It was just such a mob as founded this nation, such a mob as threw the tea into Boston harbor."[75]

Tennessee's frontier tradition also legitimated the miners' militance, at least in their own eyes and in the eyes of their supporters. The miners' committee literally swore an affidavit attesting to their local birth, demonstrating their genealogical connection to popular frontier heroes such as John Sevier, Evan Shelby, and Davy Crockett. Those men, one reporter noted, had "defended the honor of their country and their liberties, home and just laws; and their teaching is exemplified in their descendants of today."[76] To the miners, both Sevier and Shelby became mythologized in the Jacobin tradition attributed to the short-lived postrevolutionary rump state of Franklin. In a lengthy 1892 article about the events in Anderson County, the *National Labor Tribune* combined a tribute to Sevier, the onetime governor of Franklin and six-time governor of Tennessee, with both the democratic character of Franklin's original constitution and a rejection of "mountain backwardness." The article had the headline "The Mountaineer Convict Haters Come of Famous Fighting Blood" and proclaimed that in east Tennessee "every man is reared a freeman and the peer of his fellows."[77] In addition to praise for the leadership of Franklin officials, and particularly Sevier, sympathetic newspaper accounts teemed with representations of hardy, fiercely independent mountaineers who possessed a keen sense of justice. Tennessee reporters referred to Anderson County as "one of the wildest [counties] in Tennessee," its people as "no means peaceably inclined when they consider that their rights have been infringed."[78]

These values gave rise to a rough-hewn sense of justice and fierce political independence. "They are mountaineers of the liberty loving order and are traditional enemies of all government except their own," noted one C. L. Dego in an oblique reference to the State of Franklin.[79] As the *National Labor Tribune* pointed out, this independence went hand in hand with a belief "in the argument of the shotgun." Careful to tie this tradition to the miners' identity as Americans, the editor insisted that local workers were "patriots [and] lovers of freedom, who were opposed to slavery during the great war for the union."[80] The willingness of the miners to flaunt such revolutionary language, however, carried its own dangers. If they took such language too far, and especially if they opted for truly revolutionary behavior, they ran the risk of alienating the broad public opinion that was indispensable if they were to win reform through the democratic process.

When B. A. Jenkins brought in convict strikebreakers, he gravely threatened the security of Briceville's mining community. For men who had long suffered the indignities of a company that rode roughshod over their legal rights to an independent checkweighman and payment in legal tender, the new convict stockade constituted an insufferable symbol of oppression. But the introduction of prison labor to Briceville was not sufficient by itself to ignite the east Tennesseans' rebellion. The miners, and particularly their community leaders, were political actors—people who measured opportunities and risks. Just as they surveyed the political landscape when calculating their options, so must we.

The election of a Farmers' Alliance governor offered the Anderson County miners new hope, as Buchanan had few connections to the "penitentiary ring" and spoke a language with which the east Tennesseans could identify. The new governor's attacks against monopolies and class legislation and his defense of "legitimate capital" were all phrased in the same idiom as that used by the miners in their critique of the lease system. The possibilities suggested by Buchanan's election, moreover, were not limited to rhetoric. During the regular session of the legislature in early 1891, the governor signed two laws that signaled labor's legitimate place in state affairs; the first provided for a commissioner of labor, and the second declared that September 1 would be celebrated as Labor Day. These gentle quivers on the state's political seismograph, together with the presence of a Populist in the governor's mansion, rendered 1891 an opportune moment for action. In one sense, at least, Merrell and company read Buchanan correctly. In reporting to the extra session of the legislature, he acknowledged that he had no awareness of the miners' grievances before their dramatic marches on the stockades.[81]

In taking their case to the governor and the people of Tennessee, community leaders in the east Tennessee coal towns skillfully appealed to notions of loyalty, patriotism, and community. They were, as the miners' committee was once moved to declare, "neither of the school of the commune nor nihilist"; rather, they were quintessentially Tennesseans and Americans. Theirs was "not a rebellion against the stars and stripes," according to H. H. Schwartz of the Chattanooga Typographical Union, "but against those who have camped outside the constitution and polluted the flag."[82] Drawing inspiration from the values of property ownership and productive work, the example of the victors in the War of Independence, and their own narrower (and perhaps mythic) frontier tradition of justice, they sought to rid themselves, the coal industry, and the state of their nemeses—convict labor and industrial monopolists, the dependent, servile slaves and their arrogant, conspiratorial masters.

While the symbolic representations of dependent convict labor and corrupting, power-hungry monopolists had deep roots in republican ideology, they received a distinct meaning in the coal towns of late-nineteenth-century Tennessee. Unlike most southern coal towns, these communities were not owned by the coal companies. The relative freedom and independent communal life fostered by freehold title and encouraged by worker organizations enhanced the miners' and their neighbors' sense of belonging. The linkage of citizenship and commitment to community and property rights had a special resonance for the inheritors of the State of Franklin. The Franklinites had, in popular recollection, asserted the rights of small western homesteaders against an aristocratic east. But the miners of east Tennessee would soon distinguish themselves from their forebears who founded Franklin. The Franklinites, according to their proponents and detractors alike, believed only in the "law of the shotgun." The late-nineteenth-century inhabitants of east Tennessee, by contrast, would also press their claims in politically sophisticated ways to the various branches of state government.

The law of the land was a
"mighty tetchy contrivance."
—Mary Noailles Murfree,
"Drifting Down Lost Creek," 53

CHAPTER 5

An Uneasy Armistice

By the end of July 1891, the miners had forced Governor Buchanan to call a special session of the legislature and had begun adroit cultivation of public sympathy. But favorable public opinion did not ensure the reform of Tennessee's penal system or the enforcement of the miners' legal rights. Any substantial change in the convict lease, and any strengthening of laws pertaining to independent checkweighmen or payment in legal tender, required decisive action by the state government in Nashville. Ironically, the miners generally found their most steadfast allies among those public servants least dependent on public approbation. Most of the men who owed their positions to popular election either managed to avert outright attacks on the lease or to reaffirm it as necessary policy and settled law.

Friends of Labor

After the governor's initial negotiations with the miners' committee, the first governmental offices to tackle the conflict in east Tennessee were those of the commissioner of labor and the inspector of mines. Both positions were held by the indefatigable George W. Ford. Ford was born either in Massachusetts or New York, probably in 1855, and worked in the boot and shoe trade. Why he came to Tennessee in the late 1880s remains a matter of dispute. One version of his biography maintains that an employer sent him South to set up a manufacturing concern—the implication being that his commitment to the interests of labor crystallized after his arrival in the Volunteer State. Another account insists Ford's deep-seated commitment to working people in the Northeast led national labor leaders to encourage him to travel south in the hope that he would help organize Tennessee's nascent unions.[1]

Whatever the character of George Ford's early years, his life during and following his stint as commissioner of labor was committed to the rights of workers. Ford was a founder of two key labor establishments in east Tennessee—the Knoxville Central Labor Union (1889) and the *Knoxville Independent* (1894), a labor weekly and court reporter. He continued to edit the paper until his death over fifty years later.

Ford's efforts on behalf of working people won him the enduring respect of east Tennessee's miners. Several years after the miners' rebellion, Merrell still applauded Ford's steadfast dedication to wage laborers and his adherence to the "profession of unionism." Indeed, Ford's devotion to Tennessee miners and to labor in general remained a constant throughout his life. When the folklorist James Dombrowski interviewed him in the late 1930s, pictures of Samuel Gompers, William Green, and John L. Lewis graced the walls of his office. Even as he identified with later union leaders, he maintained his connection with the early history of American unionism. Sixty years after he joined the Knights of Labor, he continued to wear its badge on his jacket lapel.[2]

Ford soon encountered an opportunity to champion the miners' cause. Less than a week after the governor had negotiated the settlement with the miners, the company whose policies had sparked conflict reopened its Briceville mine using convict laborers. Still facing a shortage of working capital, the Tennessee Coal Mining Company remained in a precarious financial position and had essentially no alternative but to send the convicts back into its mine.[3] Although TCMC's action fell within the ambit of the July 24 compromise, the Briceville community viewed it as unseemly at best and provocative at worst. A number of concerned local citizens immediately contacted Ford, urging him to inspect

Commissioner of Labor George
Ford (Tennessee Commissioner
of Labor, *Annual Report*, 1892)

the mine. The coal shaft had lain idle for the previous three and a half months,
and the locals feared that the inevitable accumulation of water had rendered
the mine unfit for operation.[4] Ford obliged, conducting an inspection of the
mine with the assistance of three men on August 4 and 5.

The selection of two of his companions came as a matter of course—T. J.
Davis, the superintendent of the mine, and Charles Alleman, the assistant
commissioner of labor. Alleman probably came by this position as one of the
two mechanics in the House of Assembly and the only one from the Democratic Party. Though a Democrat, he called the east Tennessee city of Knoxville
home. Ford's third escort, William Camack, was a more surprising choice. A
miner for sixteen years, Camack was a black man, master workman of his local
in Newcomb, Tennessee, and almost certainly the union representative on the
inspection. This reliance on the technical skill of a black man suggests that
white miners at least occasionally entrusted a black miner with matters of
grave importance and that UMWA officials felt they had to sustain a carefully
negotiated alliance between black and white union members.[5]

Camack's service on the inspection committee also reflected broader political realities. During the 1880s, African American political influence waxed in Tennessee, largely because of an evenly balanced white electorate. Black politicians were able at times either to play the two major parties against each other or to play one faction within a party against other factions. In east Tennessee, Congressman Leonidas Houk and his son, Congressman John Houk, both owed some of their political success to African American constituents. Leonidas Houk in particular had successfully employed black support to counter challenges from fellow Republicans. In deference to their black constituents, then, east Tennessee politicians may have felt encouraged to include a black man in the TCMC committee, especially since convict labor was an issue of concern to this group of voters.[6]

After two long days of crawling through the tight spaces of the Briceville coal shaft, Ford roundly condemned conditions in the mine. Disdain permeated his report, as he deplored the "sickening stench" and "suffocating" character of a workplace filled with "mud, slush, and stagnant water." Ford also provided a careful assessment of mining law violations, cataloguing the company's disregard for mining standards per se, its infringements of the rights of free miners, and its indifference toward the health and safety of the prisoners under its care.

The commissioner of labor chastised the company for ignoring a host of regulations about mine operations. Its managers did not furnish a map of the mine, nor did they examine the mine before sending miners to work. The mine had only one egress, rather than the legally mandated two, and had grossly inadequate ventilation, drainage, and roof supports. Equally disconcerting, TCMC did not notify the mine inspector when accidents occurred, did not allow the miners an independent checkweighman, and did not pay its employees in legal tender. Ford ended this litany of violations with the lamentation that circumstances often forced late-nineteenth-century Americans to labor under such abominable conditions, either through fear of their employers' "rules and regulations" or the need to make a living. Reflecting on the overall conditions in the mine, Ford found it "shameful to think that any class of men, whether free or convicts, are compelled or allowed to work therein."[7]

Though Ford's official brief did not extend to the inspection of the stockades, he nonetheless made special mention of the convicts' awful living conditions. After a grueling day's labor, Ford observed, "tired, wet, and dirty" convicts had "to sleep on the floor without any change of clothing." Ford also noted that "convicts and free men are allowed to mingle indiscriminately, and work together within the mine"—yet another violation of state law and a cause of great consternation among prison authorities and reformers, who wished to maintain a racial divide within the mines.[8]

Lacking the authority to protect the convicts' or the free miners' legal rights, Ford ensured that their plight received widespread publicity. His report exposed the miserable circumstances of the prisoners' daily lives to newspaper readers throughout the state while legitimizing the complaints of mining unions. As a first step to safeguarding the liberties and interests of mineworkers, both unfree and free, the commissioner of labor recommended that the state government remove the convicts from the Briceville mine to a place of safety; he also declared that he would seek an injunction to prevent the mine's operation.[9] Ford hoped that by being a stickler about mining regulations, he would keep the pressure on east Tennessee's mine operators and convict sublessees.

Ford's exposé prompted the Board of Prison Inspectors to follow his visit a week later with a one-day inquiry of its own. Seeking to test Ford's allegations about conditions in the stockades, the board's members interviewed a variety of participants in the unfolding drama. The convicts they spoke to bore names that reflected their heritage as slaves, including Wood Diggs, Babe Hurt, Obie Lewis, and Henry Cotton. These men told of the degrading and dangerous conditions in which they lived and worked—of having to walk three-quarters of a mile through water to get to the coal face; of stultifying air, aching chests, headaches, and cramps. After a miserable day of work in the mine, the return to the stockade provided no relief—only hard beds and nothing "fit to eat." Intent on keeping the inspectors' attention on the convict lease itself, as well as on horrific living conditions, the convicts continually stressed the brutality that inevitably accompanied forced labor. Diggs, for example, remarked that he was a novice miner but that his status did not shield him from receiving a whipping at the hands of state-appointed, company-paid guards when he did not complete his daily task.[10]

Even before the prison inspectors verified Ford's findings, they sought legal counsel from Attorney General George W. Pickle about the extent of their jurisdiction over mines that used convict labor. The board members wanted to know what powers they possessed to remedy a convict lessee's violation of Tennessee's mining code and what latitude they had in protecting the lives of inmates working in such a lessee's mines. In asking for such an opinion, these appointed officers sought a remedy for the impasse in east Tennessee that circumvented the state's elected representatives—who mostly served constituents from mid- and west Tennessee.

The attorney general responded almost immediately with a written opinion that the board possessed far-reaching legal powers over the use of state prisoners in mining. This opinion argued that state officials (including the Board of Prison Inspectors) could not legally surrender responsibility for state prisoners. Pickle maintained that the inspectors had the authority to take three kinds of action if a convict lessee was found to be operating a mine illegally: to order the lessee to "remedy the existing evils"; to prohibit it from working the convicts in the illegally operated mines; or to threaten forfeiture of the contract.[11] Pickle's ruling thus furnished the state's labor commissioner and prison inspectors with substantial authority to regulate competition between free and unfree labor—an authority that was not specifically designated in the government lease contract.

Pickle's east Tennessee roots suggest the motivations behind his opinion. Pickle hailed from the mountain town of Dandridge and so almost certainly shared the region's many resentments against the politically powerful western and middle sections of the state. (Dandridge lay in Jefferson County, two counties to the east of Anderson.) More important, the office of the attorney general was traditionally held by someone from east Tennessee. This allocation resulted from the peculiar composition of the state's judicial system. The Supreme Court had five justices, one from each district and two elected from the state at large. In practice, east Tennessee elected only one Supreme Court justice, as the two at-large positions generally went to mid- or west Tennesseans. The distribution of judges reflected the institutionalized character of Tennessee's divided political geography. To compensate for the unbalanced representation in the state's highest court, the justices—under whose authority the appointment of the attorney general rested—typically selected an east Tennessean as the state's chief law enforcement officer. This position, which was not subject to popular ratification, had an eight-year term. In line with custom and legal precept, George W. Pickle became attorney general on September 17, 1886, with a term that would expire on September 16, 1894.[12] As a man with east Tennessee origins, Pickle likely sympathized with the position of Anderson County's miners; and as an official not subject to popular recall, he had an insulated position from which to act in accordance with any such sympathies.

Fortified by the counsel of the state's legal adviser, the prison inspectors ordered on August 13 that the convicts stop work immediately and that the lessees remove them from the Briceville mine and stockade to a place "where they can be properly worked and humanely treated, and securely and comfortably confined." The board further resolved that henceforth the lessees would

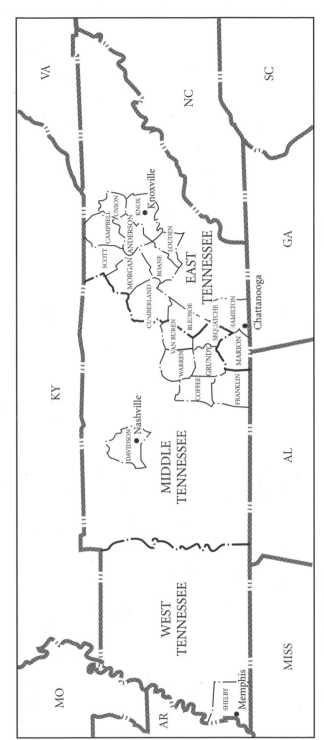

Map 5.1. Tennessee's Political Divisions

have permission to place convicts only in already established branch prisons. Should they choose to locate their wards elsewhere, the lessees and their agents would need to secure the board's sanction.[13] This ruling had far-reaching implications. The board's assertion of control over the location of new stockades promised both to reduce competition between free and unfree miners and to weaken the ability of coal operators to raise the threat of substituting convict labor for free.

The tenor of the board's decisions was not lost on the coal operators and convict lessees. All were quick to point to what they perceived as questionable motives on the part of the labor commissioner and prison inspectors. TCIR's secretary-treasurer, James Bowron, strongly opposed these rulings, remarking that the state had opted for "the easiest way of relieving it from it's [sic] duty of maintaining order and peace and guaranteeing us the use of the labor for which we were paying." B. A. Jenkins, TCMC's president, attributed a more narrowly political rationale to the Prison Board's determinations. Noting both the Democratic affiliation of the board's individual members and the political divisions within the state (west and mid-Tennessee were Democratic Party strongholds and east Tennessee a Republican citadel), Jenkins saw the prison inspectors' adjudication as a subterfuge, a transparent ploy to win Democratic Party support in east Tennessee.[14]

While some representatives of the coal producers raised suspicions about the actions of the attorney general, labor commissioner, and Prison Board, others—especially J. E. Goodwin, the agent for the convict sublessees—began a legal campaign to challenge the basis of Pickle's ruling. On August 15, 1891, Goodwin filed suit against Ford, arguing that he held his position as inspector of mines illegally and that he was incapable of acting in a neutral fashion. In this suit, Goodwin noted that the law creating the position of inspector of mines required that the incumbent have five years of practical training as a miner and that Ford had been a shoemaker by trade.[15] This first legal action failed, but it resulted in favorable press coverage for the coal companies, which linked Ford and the Knights of Labor in a conspiracy against TCMC. Several Tennessee newspapers approvingly quoted one TCMC official, who maintained that "Mr. Ford is a Knight of Labor man and belongs to the secret labor societies, and he pays special attention to our mine since the trouble."[16] This accusation was not without foundation. Most east Tennessee mines suffered from at least one of the numerous shortcomings that Ford revealed in his report on TCMC. As the reports of mine inspections throughout the 1890s make clear, few mines did not exhibit an excessive accumulation of water, stagnant air, inadequate reporting, inattention to safety laws, and insufficient and inferior timbering.

Once Goodwin proved unable to unseat Ford as inspector of mines, he aimed his next salvo at the prison inspectors. He requested that they rescind the order requiring the lessees to remove the convicts from Briceville and modify the order prohibiting the convicts from working in the mine. Goodwin based his appeal on the pecuniary losses the lessees would suffer were board members not to revoke this directive and promised to rectify conditions in the mine within the next fifteen to twenty days. Again he misfired. The members of the Prison Board refused to budge, reasoning that their decisions should be based on current conditions, not on promises of future conduct.[17]

Unable to persuade the prison inspectors to reconsider their rulings, Goodwin sued for a Chancery Court injunction against them in mid-August. In his brief—a grab bag of assertions characteristic of legal argument—Goodwin raised four issues: who could legally determine the place and character of the convicts' work; whether the veracity of Ford's report could be trusted; whether the state government was trying to avoid the expense of maintaining the law; and the high costs involved in changing settled policy. The latter three arguments simply repeated allegations previously made by Goodwin. The first, however, raised the key issue of who had jurisdiction over the state's convict laborers. Implicitly taking the attorney general to task, Goodwin argued that the lessees had legal control over the place and character of the convicts' work and that only new kinds of work, not new workplaces, required approval. Even in such situations, he asserted, only the legislature had the authority to deny permission. No matter which way Goodwin looked at the board's pair of rulings, they were, in his words, "reckless, cruel, and made without authority of law."[18]

The attorney representing the Board of Prison Inspectors responded by reasserting his client's legal authority over the branch prisons. He based his argument on the legislature's allocation of funds for the board to inspect the branch prisons and on Attorney General Pickle's opinion. The law, according to the board, gave it the responsibility of overseeing the convict lease, and its members were not about to forsake their duty.[19]

In considering the case, the Davidson County Chancery Court judge faced conflicting pressures. He had to take into account the convicts' health and safety and respect for the determination of a duly constituted government office, while recognizing the severe political and financial ramifications that would follow the removal of the convicts from Briceville. If the judge allowed Pickle's ruling to stand, there would be nothing to stop the free miners in

Oliver Springs and Coal Creek from insisting, for one reason or another, that the Board of Prison Inspectors remove the convicts from their midst. If such a situation came to pass, both the state government and the lessees would be under great pressure to accommodate the convicts at the central penitentiary or at TCIR's mines in Grundy County. Since neither prison could absorb many more prisoners, the removal would have placed the convict-lease system under great strain. In addition to weighing the implications for the current system of penal administration, the chancery judge also had to rule on which branch of state government had the final say over the convict lease. Pickle's ruling had shifted the locus of authority from the legislature to the Board of Prison Inspectors—from an elected to an appointed body. Goodwin's motion forced the chancery court to clarify which branch of government had authority to determine where and under what conditions the state's forced laborers could live and labor.

Faced with competing interests, the judge struck a compromise in his August 26 ruling. He enjoined the State Board of Prison Inspectors from removing inmates from the branch prison in Briceville but did not interfere with the order prohibiting the convicts from working in the mines.[20] This ban proved to be short-lived. Over the next week and a half, the sublessees and Commissioner Ford tussled over state standards for mining conditions. Once the lessees satisfied state requirements, the labor commissioner had no option but to permit them to reopen the mine with convict labor.[21]

The conflicts over TCMC's mine suggest both the scope of the powers enjoyed by appointed officials in Tennessee's government and the limits on those powers. The officeholders who sympathized with the miners tried to attack the convict lease through imaginative interpretations and hard-nosed enforcement of state law. The coal companies, though, could always appeal both interpretation and enforcement in the state courts. Only if state judges sustained the actions of Tennessee's public servants would their rulings have force. Administrative officials, moreover, only had the job of executing the law in Tennessee's statute books, which still included the convict lease. For Tennessee's miners to rid themselves of the lease, they would have to persuade the legislature to change the law.

September's Extra Session

After the Chancery Court ruling in Nashville, public attention shifted to the opening of the legislature's extra session on August 31, 1891. Responding to the miners' demands, Governor Buchanan called the special session primarily to discuss the crisis in east Tennessee and the overall convict-lease system.[22] The miners' expectations were high. They had dramatically focused attention on the inequities of convict labor and had mobilized widespread support for the adjustment, if not abrogation of the convict-lease contract. Throughout the latter half of July and August, Tennessee newspapers, labor unions, community leaders, and groups of citizens from every section of the state voiced sympathy for the miners' cause, if not their insurrectionary methods.[23] In addition, the discord in Tennessee politics and the apparent complexion of the legislature indicated the possibility of favorable political action.

Tennessee politics seemed even more fractured than usual in the late summer of 1891. Inter- and intraparty conflicts were rife. The Volunteer State possessed the most competitive political system in the South during the 1880s. Drawing support from blacks in agricultural (and secessionist) mid- and west Tennessee and poor whites in industrial (and Unionist) east Tennessee, the Republican Party was a strong minority party throughout the 1880s. State elections routinely brought out high voter turnouts—ranging from 63 to 78 percent—and Republicans consistently won more than 40 percent of the ballots in gubernatorial elections. In congressional elections, the Democratic Party rarely received more than 54 percent of the vote.[24]

Disunity within the Democratic Party enhanced the viability of interparty competition. The "white man's party" splintered into three distinct groups in the aftermath of Redemption: the old-line Whigs, the state's righters, and the Jacksonian Democrats. Within this fractured and volatile political context, a political organization emerged toward the end of the 1880s that enjoyed a power base independent of the Democratic Party—the Farmers' Alliance. Though a recently united movement, the Alliance was seemingly able to wrest control of the Democratic Party in the 1890 election. Campaigning on a platform of aid to the tillers of the soil, it succeeded in naming the governor and electing fifty-four state legislators—fourteen of thirty-three senators and forty of eighty-nine House members belonged to the new organization.[25]

Though the Farmers' Alliance did not enjoy legislative majorities, its members had the ability to dominate legislative decisions on specific issues, so long as they cultivated the votes of the twenty-seven Republican representatives. Between them, the Alliance and the Republicans had sufficient votes to modify the convict lease substantially or to repeal the institution.[26] Both the Farmers' Alliance and the Republican Party were on record opposing the lease in principle, and Republican legislators voted consistently against the convict lease during the extra session. Indeed, the only bill to abrogate the lease immediately came from a Republican House member representing Memphis.[27]

The Alliance's stance proved to be more complicated. Just a few weeks before the legislature met, the organization officially denounced the lease for encouraging competition between free and unfree labor, thereby oppressing "a large element of producers of wealth." This August 1891 policy statement proposed that petty criminals should stay in the counties where they were convicted, working on roads, bridges, and other public works—a position that was to gain wide support in other southern states after the turn of the century. The Alliance further suggested that more serious criminals go to state prison, with the inmates manufacturing goods that the state needed.[28]

The farmers' movement offered only an ambiguous clause on the convict lease's abolition, declaring that it "should be abolished at the earliest practicable time." If this phrasing suggests a hesitancy to terminate the lease contract immediately, the organization's resolution on the crisis in east Tennessee mines was unequivocal. The Alliance favored "the restriction of the convicts to the mines where they were worked before the late trouble until the Legislature can take action and arrangements be perfected to remove them from the mines."[29]

Articles published by the Alliance's official organ, the *Weekly Toiler*, conveyed the movement's dislike for the lease—again in principle. In one strongly worded article, the *Toiler* denounced the institution for creating "cheap competition with honest labor," corrupting government, and promoting crime: "As long as [the lease system] lasts it will be a menace to upright Government in Tennessee. As long as it lasts it will thrust itself into legislation and morality, bending the one to its base uses and diverting the other from the path of reform . . . our whole prison system is woefully benighted and at fault. Instead of being a hindrance to crime, and an extinguisher of the criminal classes, it is the prolific parent of both." "Private capital" alone, in the *Toiler*'s estimation, benefited from the lease system.[30] This editorial position was matched by several letters to the *Toiler*, which suggested adjustments to the lease system and called for its eventual repeal, and by resolutions of support from Alliance chapters that bordered mining areas.[31]

Yet for all the official and unofficial messages of sympathy, solidarity, and goodwill, there were good reasons for labor leaders to question the likelihood of the Alliance uniting around its stated opposition to the lease. Among west Tennessee's substantial farmers, many of whom were active in the Alliance, support for repeal of convict leasing was weak. In the months prior to the extra session, for example, the Bourbon-leaning *Memphis Scimitar* told its 7,500 subscribers that the Gibson County Alliance was demanding the lease law's retention. By favoring the continuation of the convict lease, large landowners in the western part of the state articulated a desire to maintain low property taxes, an unwillingness to support convicts in a state of idleness, and a belief that convict miners competed with the smallest possible number of "honest laborers."[32] In mid-Tennessee a number of substantial farmers had expressed concern for years that the withdrawal of convicts from the mines would open them to free laborers, thereby decreasing the supply and increasing the cost of agricultural labor.[33] Finally, by September 1891 the organization of Alliance chapters most hostile to convict leasing—small farmers in east Tennessee—was unraveling. On the very day on which the extra session opened, one newspaper reported on the dire condition of east Tennessee's Alliance, predicting that it would "soon be a thing of the past." The journalist believed that the farmers' movement would have probably had even "less vitality if the *Nashville American* and the bourbon press [had] stop[ped] kicking the sick body of the Alliance."[34]

Despite the stated opposition of many mid- and west Tennessee Alliancemen to the reform of the convict lease and the disorganization of Alliancemen in the eastern part of the state, the miners awaited legislative action on the convict-lease issue with substantial optimism. Governor Buchanan's opening message to the extra session further buoyed the miners' hopes. The events of July and August prompted a shift in Buchanan's political thinking. During the March regular session, the governor had urged the removal of the state penitentiary from Nashville. He argued, along with Nashville's business elite, that the current prison was wholly inadequate, while its "present site" was a "barrier" to the capital's "progress and a menace to its safety." But in early 1891 Buchanan's desire for penal reform had not included the convict labor system. Although the governor had acknowledged that an alternative prison system would diminish competition with "honest labor," he still viewed the convict lease as the best way for the state "to extricate herself from her financial embarrassments."[35] As far as Buchanan was then concerned, the state's primary consideration had to be the financial benefits of the lease system. Any effect on free labor or the convicts themselves was of secondary importance.

When Buchanan addressed the legislature's extra session in early September, however, he indicated a readiness to consider alternatives to the leasing of convicts. The governor put forth long- and short-term strategies for responding to the mining crisis. His long-term approach proposed a radical change in the criminal justice system. Maintaining that the penal statutes in force were obsolete, having been "enacted before the present conditions of society existed—when masters controlled their plantations and inflicted corporal punishment for petty offenses," Buchanan suggested that the state should draw a greater distinction between minor infractions and more serious crimes. He noted that of the current 1,500 convicts, 1,008 were black, the vast majority of whom were serving time for misdemeanors. Raising the Alliance's earlier policy suggestion, the governor then advised that these petty criminals be confined in county workhouses and that each county defray the costs of its own prisoners. In this way the "supply of criminals to the penitentiary would be cut by fifty per cent, and the prison problem rendered much easier of solution." Individuals who committed more serious crimes would be confined to a prison farm, where they would be under the control of government officials. Profits from the sale of goods produced on the farm, beyond those consumed by the prisoners, would accrue directly to the state rather than to a private company.[36]

If the legislature chose not to alter the criminal code, the governor recommended that the state buy iron and coal lands and put convicts to work there. Buchanan believed that even this secondary strategy would reduce competition between free and unfree labor, since prisoners would only labor in state mines and the coal produced would never see the open market. (Public institutions would serve as its sole consumers.) The proposal also had the virtue of guaranteeing that the 1,500 convicts would work for their keep.[37]

As a short-term solution, Buchanan advised that the legislature appoint a committee to confer with the lessees about ways to modify the current contract.[38] Governmental officials would request that the lessees restrict convicts to one or two mines—preferably worked exclusively by convicts and in areas not yet worked by free miners. Such an adjustment would alleviate the most grievous aspects of the lease system: the ability of the coal companies to rely on the threat of convict labor in contract negotiations. "It seems plain to me," the governor intoned, "that the feature of the lease system which has affected free labor most injuriously is the privilege of the lessee . . . to employ convict labor in all mines without restriction. The miners themselves say that this is their chief objection to the lease system." Finally, in an effort to grant control over the lease to a nonlegislative body, Buchanan urged that the power of the prison inspectors receive clearer statutory definition and, "if necessary, [be] increased, in order to give them the authority to say where and how the convicts should be worked."[39]

A little more than a week into the extra session, Attorney General Pickle again rendered an opinion that placed the legality of the current system in doubt. At the legislature's request, he examined the lease contract to ascertain whether subleasing was legal. Pickle maintained that as the contract did not explicitly mention the lessee's authority to sublease, the legislature did not intend to confer such power.[40] Both gubernatorial proposals and the opinion of the state's counsel pointed toward a modification of the current lease contract.

The legislature soon appointed a committee to negotiate with TCIR, hoping to confine the convicts to a few mines. Nathaniel Baxter, TCIR's vice president, responded that the company would not modify the lease, adding that such a step would require the replacement of free miners who worked in its Tracy City mines. Baxter indicated, however, that his company would be happy to lease convicts to the state to build a new penitentiary; alternatively, TCIR was willing to surrender the lease.[41] This latter proposal was nothing more than an empty gesture; Baxter knew full well that the government could not contemplate taking control of all the prisoners.

Once it became evident that these negotiations were going nowhere, legislative initiative dissipated. Legislators put forward many proposals, virtually none of which found their way into the statute books. Suggestions from Democratic and Alliance sponsors included setting up a whipping post for petty criminals; sending petty criminals to county jails to work on public highways, as the Alliance and Buchanan had proposed; improving prison conditions for young criminals; prohibiting the whipping of convicts; amending criminal law in accordance with the governor's recommendations; ensuring that larger counties pay for the cost of prosecutions within their jurisdiction; and, in accordance with the attorney general's ruling, ordering the prison inspectors to ensure the transfer of convicts from the subleased branch prisons to those belonging to TCIR.[42] To supplement these narrow, piecemeal proposals, Alliance and Democratic legislators spent substantial time trying to draft a comprehensive penitentiary bill. Again following Buchanan's counsel, legislators called for a joint committee to inquire into the purchase of coal lands and the establishment of a penitentiary thereon. This approach also failed to become law, foiled largely as a result of bickering between the legislature's two chambers.[43]

Though the coalition between Alliancemen and mainstream Democrats disappointed the miners on the issue of their deepest concern, it did offer them token relief. The general assembly reaffirmed the miners' legal right to a checkweighman and stipulated that payment be in legal tender; it also adopted a resolution expressing "the wish of the General Assembly that the state never again lease its convicts at the expiration of the present lease contract." But these actions had little impact. Without vigorous enforcement in the courts, the rights to an independent checkweighman and to payment in legal tender would not mean much; and Tennessee's Supreme Court exhibited little inclination to show increased concern for the rights of miners. Furthermore, the resolution calling for eventual abandonment of the lease was purely hortatory, and even this "toothless" declaration received only lukewarm support from Alliance members, gaining only twenty of thirty-seven votes by Alliancemen in the House.[44]

The legislature was less indecisive when it considered issues of law enforcement that the miners' actions had raised. The two chambers passed a bill making interference with state convicts a felony. Conviction would carry a sentence of one to five years. Further legislation gave the governor discretion to call out the militia "to suppress all insurrections and other like unlawful assemblages, whether existing or imminent." Alliance and Democratic support for the bill in the House was overwhelming—only one Allianceman and two other Democrats opposed the legislation. Predictably, Republicans opposed the proposal unanimously. This provision also empowered the governor to bypass the legislature in mobilizing the militia. Knowing that such a grant of power made the bill constitutionally suspect, legislators designed it specifically to suppress an anticipated uprising by the miners, having the law expire at the convocation of the next general assembly. Finally, the assembly passed a bill appropriating $25,000 for the state militia.[45]

The role that the coal operators and their lobbyists played in securing such a favorable outcome is difficult to document. There is little doubt, however, that they were involved in some legislators' attempts to discredit the miners' leaders. B. A. Jenkins wrote to one Jesse Wilson in Coal Creek, urging him to "get an affidavit to break down G. E. Irish and Eugene Merrell's character." Jenkins also allegedly gave Senator T. J. Alexander of Franklin County a $500 bribe.[46] Whether or not such a payoff took place, Alexander did propose a resolution in the Senate directing the governor to offer a reward for the "apprehension and conviction" of Merrell, Irish, Marcena Ingraham, John Hatmaker, and others "known to have actively by speeches or otherwise, aided, abetted or excited the miners to aforesaid acts of lawlessness and rebellion."[47] In one of his frequent letters to the *United Mine Workers Journal*, Billy Webb, president of District 19, portrayed Alexander as a "champion of Jenkins's cause."[48]

The coal barons were also probably behind a campaign to disparage the credentials of Commissioner of Labor Ford and his assistant, Knox County representative Charles Alleman. E. J. Sanford, president of the landholding Coal Creek Mining & Manufacturing Company, referred to Ford and Alleman as "head devils," men "untrue to the state's interests and working for the miners."[49] Legislators took such charges seriously: on the third day of the session, House members appointed a committee to investigate the two men. Legislative reports accused them of contributing to the "Briceville trouble" by encouraging and "abetting" the miners. These efforts to discredit the miners' leaders and intimidate sympathetic state officials, though, received no explicit legislative sanction.[50]

Newspapers across the political spectrum decried and mocked the legislature's incompetence. Some journalists upbraided the legislators for a series of delays—such as taking a day off from an already limited session to attend a reunion of Confederate veterans. One editor attributed legislative inaction to lawmakers being "dazed by the immensity of the task"; another contended that representatives had been dazzled by their hobnobbing experiences with the "holders of the lease and other monopolists, plutocrats and gentlemen of leisure." All commentators, though, seemed mercifully relieved when the legislators left the capital.[51] The verbal attacks extended to the mainstream Democratic press, even though the editors of papers like the *Nashville American* and the *Memphis Appeal Avalanche* viewed the legislature's inaction as a victory. Former Whigs and the states' righters had never come to terms with the success of the Alliance during the last election, and certainly did not want it to take credit for settling such a contentious issue. The widespread derision of the legislators' intelligence, including accusations that the session represented a "menagerie" and its occupants a "bunch of nincompoops," served the usually dominant factions of the Tennessee Democratic Party well.[52] Highlighting the legislature's incompetence while advocating reform of the lease was in their long-term interests.

The Alliance's legislative performance, then, diverged substantially from its presession proclamations. Unable to adopt their organization's short-term compromise position of restricting the convicts to mines where they worked prior to the rebellion, Alliance legislators achieved little more than strengthening the governor's hand against any future unrest. One explanation for the Alliance's failure to do more for the miners lies in the movement's organizational limitations. Alliance assemblymen did not caucus within the legislature. Susceptible to rhetoric that promoted Democratic Party loyalty and under attack for Buchanan's appointment of Alliancemen to valuable patronage positions, Alliance lawmakers did not unite to secure key committee positions for themselves. Partly through a lack of experience and partly because Alliancemen possessed a political style that emphasized personal relationships, Populist legislators failed to grasp the importance of cultivating party discipline.[53]

The historian Bruce Palmer invokes the homily of an Alliance contemporary, George Washington Plunkitt of New York City's Tammany Hall, to explain why Populist election victories in 1890 did not give them control of the Democratic Party or the legislature in the states where they won majorities or pluralities. As Plunkitt observed, the "fact is that a reformer can't last in politics. He can make a show for a while, but he always comes down like a rocket. Politics is as much a regular business as the grocery or the dry-goods or the drug business. You've got to be trained up to it or you're sure to fail."[54] In Tennessee, the Bourbon and Whig Democratic machines retained a firm grip on political business.

Another barrier to Alliance action against the lease system had to do with the dangers of cooperating with Republicans. The splits within the Democratic Party and the strength of the Republican Party rendered Alliance members vulnerable to accusations of not being true Democrats, or even true southern white men. Siding with the Republican proposal to end the lease would place Alliancemen in the company of "Negro-lovers," potentially jeopardizing their long-term prospects in Tennessee politics.

Yet there were also deeper reasons for the tepid response of Alliance legislators to the grievances of Tennessee's miners. Alliance leaders were strongly committed to industrial development in Tennessee, even if rank-and-file members greatly feared the power of railroads and trusts. Despite the organization's outspoken antimonopoly stance, the 1891 legislature passed no laws aimed at checking industrial enterprise, whether in transportation or manufacturing. In response to popular suspicions of big business, the general assembly did enact two moderate bills that imposed new regulations on corporations. The first required out-of-state and foreign companies doing business in Tennessee to file their charters with the secretary of state, thereby subjecting them more effectively to state jurisdiction. The second declared unlawful all trusts acting to restrain trade, production, or sale and stipulated punishment for its violation.[55] But such limited measures against large corporations and cartels did not undercut the Alliance's overall enthusiasm for the development of mining and manufacturing.

Consideration of proposals to regulate railroads was typical of the movement's legislative inclinations. One Democratic editor who favored railroad regulation recalled in 1896 that Tennessee's "Farmers Alliance Legislature" had been putty in the hands of railroad lobbyists. The editor remembered their record with indignation: "It was loudly heralded by the Legislature that every trust and corporation in the State would be torn up, root and branch. . . . Members piled in bill after bill about regulating the railroads and curbing the power of corporations. There were forty-two bills against railroads alone, and only one of them passed. That one was to provide Jim Crow cars for negroes."[56] The analogous failure of newly elected Alliancemen to take punitive measures against the coal industry was in keeping with an earlier *Weekly Toiler* editorial. "The development of the resources of our great state and the prosperity of every legitimate industry," the *Toiler* argued, "should be made a common cause in which every class is equally interested. We need more railroads, more factories and more capital to develop the hidden resources of mother earth."[57] This pre-election assertion proved to be a durable policy. An unwillingness to curb industrial growth reinforced the Alliance's ambivalence toward convict mining.

Finally, the leadership of Tennessee's Alliance possessed an ingrained reluctance to tap the pocketbooks of property-owning citizens. Buchanan, among others, cut his political teeth as a low-taxer in the early 1880s. These principles stayed with the governor and his allies and were undoubtedly reinforced by a constituency that opposed an expensive new penal system. This opposition reflected both a recognition that postbellum Tennessee's major source of revenue was property taxation and a commitment to Jeffersonian ideals of minimal, nonintrusive government. Most of the state's Alliancemen were farmers who came from mid- and west Tennessee. In addition to tenants, the organization counted thousands of wealthy, middling, and struggling landowners in its ranks. Irrespective of differences in economic position, almost all farm-owning Alliancemen in Tennessee opposed high taxes.[58]

Tennessee's version of Populism revealed itself to be much more conservative than the Alliances of the western states. Buchanan's platform had resembled national Alliance demands in only two ways—in its call for the unlimited coinage of silver and in its opposition to land grants for railroads. Unlike western Populist organizations, Tennessee's Alliance did not call for government ownership of transportation and communication. Indeed, so long as he remained as governor, Buchanan did not declare himself in favor of the subtreasury scheme. Instead, Tennessee's Alliance saw its own specific nemesis in trusts—seemingly a dangerous economic breed nurtured by protective tariffs.[59]

While the representatives of Tennessee's agricultural movement embraced minimal government and the interests of industrialists who stayed clear of cartels, they also acquiesced in measures designed to restrict the political influence of men at the bottom of the state's social structure. In the late 1880s Tennessee began a half-decade-long process of restricting voter registration. The laws that accomplished this end had their most dire effects on the black electorate, but they additionally diminished the pool of poor, illiterate white voters. As the diversity among southern voters shrank, elected officials could more easily disregard the interests and objectives of their less-advantaged constituents.

Tennessee was the first southern state to enact legislation that restricted voter registration. Its 1890 legislature passed four such election laws. The first two had virtually unanimous Democratic support, including that of Alliance legislators. They mandated that voters in districts or towns where 500 or more votes were cast in 1888 register at least twenty days before every election and that polling places provide separate ballot boxes for state and federal elections. The lawmakers' objective with the second law was to circumvent federal supervision of state elections if the U.S. Congress should pass the Lodge Bill. The third strategy, known as the Dortch Law after its sponsor, required a secret ballot and essentially authorized a literacy test. The final piece of legislation called for a poll tax.[60]

The partisan intent and racial slant of these measures were hardly disguised. Ostensibly neutral and color-blind, they served to diminish Republican and black political clout.[61] The wording of the acts themselves lacked overt reference to race, but not so the public debate surrounding their passage. The Democratic *Memphis Avalanche* applauded the Dortch Law as a solution to the "Negro Question": "The first thing to be done is to cut off the great mass of innate ignorance from its baleful influence in our elections. . . . It is certain that many years will elapse before the bulk of the Negroes will reawaken to an interest in elections, if relegated to their proper sphere, the corn and cotton fields."[62] These bills gained passage on the basis of such arguments, as well as through back-room caucusing and minor concessions to senators who feared disfranchisement of their white electorate.[63]

In 1891 and 1892 a legislature with Alliancemen as the largest faction reconfirmed the new election laws. Indeed, Buchanan had called the extra session not only to respond to the mining crisis but also to correct a mistake made by the previous legislature in amending the registration law, making it apply to counties with a "voting" population of 50,000. Since no county had voting populations of this size, the typographical error had nullified the registration and secret ballot laws.[64]

The new measures proved highly effective. In 1888, prior to the passage of the voter registration, secret ballot, and poll tax laws, 78 percent of adult men went to the polls. In 1890 this figure had dropped dramatically to 50 percent and would drop further later in the decade. Though primarily undercutting the black urban electorate, these acts reduced voter participation throughout the state.[65]

With hindsight, some Alliancemen assigned great importance to the disfranchisement laws, lamenting their passage and suggesting that these laws stood between them and long-term political success. Governor Buchanan, a man who built his support through rhetoric that appealed to small white farmers, urged in his final 1893 gubernatorial address that the legislature remove educational qualifications and rigid restrictions on the technical marking of ballots. After two years as governor, Buchanan had changed his views on these measures, coming to believe that they unfairly disfranchised uneducated Tennesseans.[66]

Throughout the late-nineteenth-century South, restrictive voting laws added to the failure of southern Populists to achieve and maintain political power.[67] Yet in Tennessee, Alliancemen helped to bring about disenfranchisement. With a weakened and narrowed electoral base, many Alliance legislators primarily looked to safeguard the class interests of larger mid- and west Tennessee farmers.[68] Fervent belief in low taxation, support for nonmonopolistic industrialization, a fear of losing farm labor to convict-free mines (particularly in mid-Tennessee), and a desire not to appear to capitulate to the miners all influenced the voting patterns of Alliance legislators.[69]

The election of 1890 had once seemed like a watershed for Tennessee politics. New faces and reform agendas made their entrance into Nashville. With them came hope for the miners. But the faces turned out to be not so fresh, the commitment to reform not so steadfast, and the legislative battle plan not so well thought out. The miners' lobbyists walked away from the session with essentially no concessions to their position. As C. Vann Woodward noted when considering an optimistic Tennessee Allianceman who suggested that the organization had captured the Democratic Party, few contemporaries recognized that just the opposite actually transpired: the Democratic Party captured the Alliance.[70]

The Miners' Fate in the Courts

In August the attempt by Ford and the Board of Prison Inspectors to remove the convicts from Briceville ran aground in one of Tennessee's courtrooms, while Attorney General Pickle's opinion that subleasing was illegal had not resulted in any substantive change in penal administration. In September the general assembly failed to provide east Tennessee's miners with any kind of meaningful relief. After wrangling with the state over convict labor for more than two months, the miners became frustrated and despondent. One Welsh miner conveyed this somber mood in a letter home, remarking that "when the deputation returned from Nashville it was obvious that loyalty to the government had declined rapidly." As the Welshman also reported, these workingmen had one final constitutional means of seeking redress open to them—to take their case into the courts and seek a ruling on the legality of subleasing.[71]

To bring the subleasing arrangement before the courts, the miners solicited the support of a state official friendly to their cause. Five days after the legislature adjourned, the miners smuggled a justice of the peace into the Briceville mines to get William Warren's signature on a writ of habeas corpus. The miners selected Warren, a white man serving a two-year sentence for manslaughter, because he happened to work in a shop guarded by a sympathetic warden, Captain Samuel W. Jack. Although Jack technically stood as the respondent in this case, he was, according to the coal company, "too friendly with the miners and citizens." Indeed, a day after the court case ended, Jack lost his job.[72]

Under the steady watch of the miners' committee, TCIR's Arthur Colyar opened the case before circuit court judge Sneed on the first day of October. Ostensibly defending Samuel Jack's authority to hold William Warren a prisoner at Briceville, Colyar's objective was to ensure that the subleasing arrangement continued unchanged. Nonetheless, Colyar chose not to base his case primarily on the terms of the lease contract. Instead, he contended that the controversy should not have come before the courts at all, as Warren lacked standing to come before the court as a party. His strategy was twofold. First, he argued that a prisoner, especially one who acknowledged the legitimacy of his conviction and imprisonment, could not file a writ of habeas corpus. Second, he challenged the courts' jurisdiction to hear the case, maintaining that "the governor and state officers had certain powers conferred upon them and as long as they conformed to these laws the courts must keep hands off." Only if they overreached their powers could the courts interfere.[73]

General J. C. J. Williams, the prominent lawyer and member of the Knoxville citizen's committee supporting the miners, volunteered to take on Warren's case for free. This offer won him the miners' gratitude, though it caused consternation in Republican Party circles. Williams, a Democrat, had previously challenged Republican stalwart John Houk for his seat in east Tennessee's second congressional district. With Williams's congressional ambitions still strong, the Republican *Knoxville Journal* suggested that his decision reflected vote-mongering more than genuine sympathy for the miners' interests.[74]

With his sights possibly set beyond the courtroom, Williams presented a series of arguments in defense of Warren's writ of habeas corpus. The general based his case primarily on the ruling that Attorney General Pickle had rendered during the special session, reiterating that the contract did not explicitly empower the lessees to sublease a portion of the convicts. He supplemented this position with a reductio ad absurdum argument. If the contract allowed such an arrangement, the general maintained, then the lessee "might sub-let the 1,500 convicts in squads of fifty or twenty five and place them in every community of the state and use them for any purpose." He further insisted that

the lease contract required state inmates to be in the hands of carefully selected, "responsible" lessees. Subleasing precluded governmental control over
the character of those individuals who would guard and care for the convicts.
Williams, in a final reference to Pickle's opinion, observed that the Board of
Prison Inspectors had never recognized the subleasing of convicts.[75]

Justice Sneed, who had won his place on the circuit court bench the previous February as a result of a recommendation from Charles Alleman, the
assistant commissioner of labor and friend of the miners, dismissed Colyar's
assertions on the day after the presentation of oral argument. The Knoxville
judge ruled that the language and spirit of the act sanctioning convict leasing
implied only one lessee. Echoing Williams's claim that subleasing resulted in
attenuated authority, Sneed held that the state could not ensure humane treatment of convicts under subleasing arrangements. His opinion further maintained that subleasing represented Tennessee's surrender of the convicts to
private individuals; "such a system," he concluded, "resembles slavery too
much to be tolerated in a free state." The judge ordered the sheriff to return
Warren to the Nashville prison or to the lessees.[76]

The decision greatly improved the spirits of miners. If this ruling stood, all
inmates working for sublessees in Coal Creek, Briceville, and Oliver Springs
could enter habeas corpus appeals. Such legal maneuvers would restrict the
convicts to the main penitentiary and to TCIR's mines in Grundy and Marion
Counties. Reaction on the part of the mineowners was of a completely different order. TCIR's secretary-treasurer, James Bowron, noted the defeat in his
diary with the simple entry, "Chancellor Sneed at Knoxville declares sub-lease
of convicts illegal."[77]

Not one to give up easily, Colyar immediately appealed the decision. By
special consent, court officials advanced the case through a crowded docket to
appear before Supreme Court chief justice Peter Turney. A mid-Tennessean
from Franklin County, an ardent secessionist before the Civil War, and a
stalwart of the mainstream Democratic Party, Turney was not well disposed
toward the miners.

In an earlier case prompted by the 1890 dispute that set off the crisis in the
east Tennessee coalfields, Turney signaled that his jurisprudential views favored the interests of industrial capital over those of labor. The mining crisis
had begun when B. A. Jenkins threatened to close his mine if the miners did
not fire their checkweighman. Jenkins claimed that the checkweighman, Hendricks Bradley, was an "obstructionist" and "agitator." The miners believed
that the threat violated an 1887 statute giving them the legal right to an independent checkweighman, and they subsequently convinced the state to sue

their employer over this issue. When the case reached the Supreme Court in early October 1891, Turney overturned a favorable lower court ruling. Since the mine belonged to Jenkins, Chief Justice Turney argued, he had the right to dispose of his property as he saw fit: "It is apparent the language of the statute does not make it obligatory on the miners to employ a checkweighman, nor upon the owners of mines to operate them if a checkweighman is employed. Each party has its election. If a checkweighman is selected as allowed by law, the mineowner is guilty of no violation of the statute in refusing to continue to work the mines. To say to the miners 'that if *they* did not discharge Hendricks Bradley he (B. A. Jenkins) would shut down and close the mines,' was but a declaration of what, under the law, he had the right to do." This decision gutted the substance of the miners' statutory right. Supreme Court justice Lea shared this assessment in his dissenting opinion, remarking that Jenkins's "object and purpose" was to discharge the checkweighman and thus "render . . . nugatory the statute."[78]

Despite the acuity of Lea's criticism, Turney's decision in the checkweighman case did not reflect a departure from the jurisprudence of late-nineteenth-century America. Rather, that ruling was part and parcel of a growing legal tradition that sought to justify employers' absolute right to discipline their employees. The "employment at will doctrine" held that both employer and employee could terminate employment at any time without reason or explanation. An 1884 Tennessee Supreme Court decision on labor contracts laid out central tenets of this doctrine. "The law," the earlier court had held, "leaves employer and employee to make their own contracts; and these, when made, it will enforce; beyond this it does not go. Either the employer or employee may terminate the relation at will, and the law will not interfere, except for contract broken. This secures to all civil and industrial liberty." In making the terms of contracts the strict measure of legal obligation regardless of statutory amendment, Turney's narrow decision fitted comfortably within accepted legal doctrine.[79]

Toward the end of October 1891, Judge Turney once again took advantage of an opportunity to strengthen the legal position of Tennessee's coal operators by overturning Judge Sneed's earlier granting of Warren's habeas corpus petition. Turney's opinion was brief and followed the basic outlines of Colyar's argument before the circuit court. The chief justice held that a convict confined in a legal branch prison under the supervision of a deputy warden could not file for habeas corpus. The plaintiff's complaint that the sublessee held him rather than the original lessee to the penitentiary, he explained, was a matter that only the Board of Prison Inspectors could determine; moreover, such a complaint was not germane to a habeas corpus proceeding. Following Turney's ruling, a disappointed Williams penned a brief note to Eugene Merrell, summing up the import of this defeat. "Your cause," he wrote, "has met its Waterloo."[80]

The miners' encounter with state government during the summer and early fall of 1891 provided them with some hard-nosed instruction in the realities of late-nineteenth-century politics. Widespread support for a political principle did not necessarily translate into adoption of favorable policy. Though individuals and groups throughout Tennessee society viewed the convict lease with moral disdain, politicians understood that the costs of abolishing it were high. The lease augmented the state's revenues, thereby reducing taxation; many politicians also viewed it as a crucial spur to industrial growth. The countervailing pressures of social cost and fiscal benefit left politicians hard-pressed to reach a comfortable compromise on the lease issue. As a result, nonelected officials took the lead in efforts to rid Tennessee of the penal institution.

The two officials who would take actions most favorable to the miners' cause both had discernible links to the workingmen of Anderson County. Commissioner of Labor Ford had devoted his life to the interests of the wage-earning population; Attorney General Pickle came from the same mountains as did the miners. But these men could push their authority only so far. They might publicize issues surrounding the convict lease, as Ford did in his report on the horrific conditions of TCMC's mines and stockade. They might also offer favorable but nonbinding legal interpretations of the convict lease, as when Pickle argued that the state's contract prohibited subleasing in the opinion he gave to the legislature. Neither of these officials, though, had the authority to make policy without the ratification of other governmental bodies. For a time, Ford gained the endorsement of the comparatively independent Board of Prison Inspectors in his bid to mitigate the impact of the convict lease. Yet that support itself depended on the sanction of the judiciary.

Unwilling to take a forceful position in the midst of a fragmented political environment, Governor Buchanan saw the value of increasing the authority of these appointed officials. If the prison inspectors had the power to limit the convict lease's operation to a few mines, the governor could ensure state revenue and simultaneously placate the miners. Indeed, this approach formed the basis of Buchanan's proposal to the legislature: the governor hoped that the representatives would either institute this proposal themselves or give the prison inspectors the authority to modify the lease's parameters.

Despite coming to Nashville in large part to contain the crisis in east Tennessee, legislators soon turned their attention away from the convict lease. The fiscal implications of a new penal system undercut attempts either to terminate the lease or to forge a compromise along the lines of Buchanan's proposal. A potential coalition with the Republicans never transpired, as the Alliance and regular Democratic members had too much in common to permit it.

Ultimately, Tennessee's judiciary respected the interests of mineowners against their employees and other branches of state government. If the lower courts in east Tennessee always demonstrated sympathy for the miners, Tennessee's Supreme Court consistently elevated the prerogatives of mineownership over the claims of convicts, free miners, or prison officials. As other branches of government increasingly deferred to the Board of Prison Inspectors as the appropriate agency to modify the lease (and in particular to curtail subleasing and restrict the location of work), the court both agreed with that impulse and shackled the board's ability to change the current system. In essence the court took away with one hand what it gave with the other, leaving hazy the locus of governmental responsibility for convicts and ensuring continued control by the coal companies.

The miners and their representatives did their best to influence these governmental proceedings, demonstrating that their views of citizenship and political behavior involved more than raised voices and trips to the polls come election time. They lobbied the governor and legislature, they sent representatives on speaking tours throughout the state in the hopes of drumming up public support, and they raised money to finance their appeals in the courts. In spite of all these political and legal maneuverings, October 1891 came and went, leaving the east Tennessee workingmen still confronted by a convict-lease system that threatened to ruin them. Seeing no immediate recourse in either the political or legal realm, the miners emulated the time-honored response of their revolutionary forebears. They reminded coal operators and Nashville officials that the east Tennessee mountaineers possessed the will to turn their backs on government and the law.

The miners are now criminals in
the eyes of the law, although until
recently they were regarded as
good citizens.
—*Coal Trade Journal*,
November 11, 1891

CHAPTER 6

Dilemmas
of Militance

On Friday, October 31, 1891, the miners convened their own "extra session."[1] In the quiet of the night, well over 1,000 masked east Tennesseans and southern Kentuckians laid siege to the stockade at the Tennessee Coal Mining Company's Briceville mine. The group met no resistance and proceeded to free the convicts, who changed into clothes that the attackers had brought with them. As miners and inmates left the scene, the empty stockade stood burning. Some of the convicts immediately sought to put themselves beyond Tennessee law, setting out north on the thirty-seven-mile "underground railroad" to Jellico, Kentucky; others joined the miners and their supporters in liberating the convicts stationed five miles away at Coal Creek's Knoxville Iron Company.

While the miners sacked the Coal Creek stockade and set fire to company property (though not the prison barracks), a group of convicts looted a store owned by the mine superintendent, Captain John Chumbley. Both the miners and the convicts picked their targets carefully. The miners wished to render any effort to return the convicts to the stockades inconvenient and expensive; the convicts probably thought Chumbley long overdue in receiving his just deserts. For over a decade, the elderly Virginian had served the convict lessees—first as deputy warden and later as superintendent. His front door had always been open to prison guards and agents of the convict lessees, providing them with a home, even if for a fee. Before leaving the penitentiary, a miner or an ex-convict paid final tribute to unfree labor by dressing a dead hog in convict "garb," placing an empty jug beside it and an old pipe on its belly.[2]

The actions at Briceville and Coal Creek set free approximately 300 convicts and involved no violence against persons. The following day, even the Democratic *Knoxville Tribune* conceded the decisive character of the miners' deeds, implicitly contrasting them with the do-nothingism of state government. The paper told its 1,700 subscribers that the "miners have acted for themselves and have solved the convict problem with a vengeance." Many newspapers reported that the miners went about their business with discipline and dispatch. Though clearly partial to the miners' cause, the *United Mine Workers Journal* was not atypical in suggesting that the miners had left "nothing to indicate that a great uprising had taken place," except for the remains of the stockade and convict clothes "scattered for miles along the Coal Creek Valley."[3]

In turning their attentions away from legislative halls and judicial chambers, the miners and their Anderson County supporters did not alter their fundamental goals. They still wished to restore what they perceived as a just, republican social order, one that safeguarded the legitimate rights of workingmen and handed out no special privileges. Though the miners burnt stockades and liberated convicts, they continued to demonstrate that they remained "neither of the school of the commune nor nihilist." The attackers took pains to protect company and private property not contaminated by the convict lease.

Furthermore, the miners' frustration with administrators, legislators, and judges did not lead them to ignore state officials. They continued to negotiate with Tennessee's governmental representatives, just as they maintained lines of communication with their employers. Indeed, within months of liberating the convicts, the Briceville miners formed a cooperative mine with one of the coal operators. At roughly the same time, the miners joined Tennessee's industrial workingmen and farmers in a State Labor Congress, whose main objective was to lobby the legislative assembly. This two-pronged effort—exploring cooperative ventures and pursuing new lobbying tactics—reflected the miners' continued willingness to seek solutions through both economic and political tactics. The raids of October and November, however, changed the nature of the miners' initiatives. Although temporarily rid of the convicts, Anderson County's workingmen soon faced new challenges from a still powerful coalition of government officials and coal operators. Confronting those challenges would lead the miners to rediscover the limits of political dissent in postbellum America.

The Third Revolt

The miners prepared their October 31 attacks with the same thoroughness that they had displayed in their lobbying efforts during the previous months. Considerable effort went into concealing the leadership of rebellion. Just three days before the attack, the committee that had directed the miners' campaign since July 1 resigned. In a widely publicized letter tendering their resignation, committee members insisted that the lease could be overturned only through constitutional means, especially by sending workingmen, irrespective of political party, to the legislature. As a first step in this project, they promised to publish a list of their friends and foes in the House and Senate. They concluded with an appeal to Divine Providence: "We give you as our parting advice, as the state has so willed it, and is prepared to enforce its will with the bayonet and Gatling gun, that you peaceably give up your work, your homes and sweet memories . . . and like Hagar, be driven out with your helpless ones apparently by the power that should shelter and protect you; driven out by the dictation of the penitentiary ring . . . and may you, as Hagar did, find a protection in a Divine Providence for surely you can find none elsewhere." Well-known community leaders, including Merrell, Irish, Ingraham, Hatmaker, and the one-time Tennessee miner and now Coal Creek hotelier, Tip Hightower, were joined by several prominent union men in signing this declaration.[4] The rhetoric drew on a long-standing idiom of republican thought. Since Locke's *Second Treatise of Government*, "appeals to heaven" had served as a code phrase for a revolutionary call to arms that would allow a providential God to redeem the oppressed and grant them justice through military victory.[5] While the miners and community leaders almost certainly did not have Locke's text in mind, they had ready access to the similar phrasing enshrined in the Declaration of Independence.

Only seemingly disheartened, the committee had concluded that the coal operators possessed more power than the state. The events of the fall of 1891 had greatly diminished hopes that the government would ensure the miners' rights; these east Tennesseans no longer viewed either the legislature or the courts as neutral arbiters. Like Sarah's slave Hagar, who was driven into the wilderness by her mistress, the miners, the committee suggested, could only look to God for guidance and rely on their own resources.

In addition to resigning their positions, the committee provided themselves with an alibi for the following Friday night. As the *National Labor Tribune* commented, "Suspicion at first alight [*sic*] upon the men who had been foremost in the former agitation." The paper continued, however, that "by a suspiciously happy chance all these men were in Knoxville Friday night at the theater." Fully aware of the legislature's new injunctions against the rebelling miners and especially their leaders, Merrell and Irish were too savvy to be caught within a ten-mile radius of Briceville or Coal Creek on the evening of October 31. Merrell further assured reporters that the uprising had been "spontaneous," that the committee had had no knowledge of these impending events, and that any future action "will be done in the same way."[6]

Merrell's suggestion of spontaneity masked the canny organization that preceded this revolt. In addition to the committee's absenting itself from the coal towns for the night, a variety of other seemingly isolated incidents pointed to the impending attack. Coal Creek hosted a large public dance at the same time that the miners marched on the Briceville stockade, providing alibis for many townspeople. This decoy brought a historical analogy to one miner's mind, who wittily remarked that "Nero fiddled while Rome burned, but Coal Creek danced while Briceville burned."[7] Mineworkers also accumulated suits of citizen clothing for convicts and apparently arranged for the "very plausible arrest of two guards at Briceville by a Coal Creek constable." In addition, the miners informed the convicts of their impending release prior to the event; they arranged for Kentucky miners to come and assist them; they carefully concealed their own identity by wearing masks, blackening their faces, or wearing padded clothing; and, moments before the actual assault, they cut the telegraph wires connecting the towns to the outside world. The attackers further chose an evening when Anderson County's sheriff, Rufus Rutherford, was conveniently away on business in Chattanooga.[8]

Emboldened by the events of Friday night and determined to exorcise convict labor from all of east Tennessee, miners from Briceville and Coal Creek attacked the Oliver Springs stockade of the Cumberland Coal Company late on Sunday, November 2. In doing so, they had to manage without help from their fellow miners to the north. Oliver Springs, which lay in Anderson County's southwest corner, fell beyond easy reach of the southern Kentucky miners. In order to lend a hand in Oliver Springs, they would have had to travel the roughly thirty-seven miles from the border to Coal Creek, from where they would have faced two options. They could have caught a train to the county seat of Clinton—a ten-mile journey—and then a connection for a further fifteen-mile trip to Oliver Springs. Their alternative, since Coal Creek and Oliver Springs had no direct railway link, would have been to cross the mountains by horseback, a distance of at least fifteen miles. Although Kentucky miners declined to make such an arduous journey, local Oliver Springs miners participated in what turned out to be a successful surprise attack. The governor and the state guards evidently assumed that Oliver Springs lay too far across the mountain for Coal Creek Valley miners to reach it in a night's journey. When disguised horsemen arrived in the middle of the night, the guards quickly surrendered. After looting the company store to supplement the clothes they had carried with them, the intruders dispersed the goods among the 150 to 200 convicts, directed the prisoners north, and set fire to the stockade.[9]

The liberated convicts at Oliver Springs, like those at Briceville and Coal Creek, reacted to their release in one of two ways. Some of those who had only a few months of their sentences to serve thought it wisest to give themselves up. One convict, who identified himself as "Richard Huber, Colored," sent a telegram to Buchanan asking his advice. "Me and one hundred and sixty men loose. Been working at Briceville. The miners have burned everything there last night at that place. What must I do? All loose here at Clinton." Prisoners with long sentences were less inclined to request advice on what to do with their freedom. Most donned their new suits of clothes and headed north to the Kentucky border rather than west and home.[10]

Despite widespread fears to the contrary, the freed convicts acted peaceably. No convicts attacked civilians or damaged private property. Forty years after the rebellion, Mollie Scoggins of Coal Creek remembered both the anxiety that the release of the convicts induced in the local population and the ease with which the convicts interacted with the locals. "The convicts," Scoggins recalled, "did not do any damage when they were turned loose though some people were afraid they would and when one came to my door for food and picked up my little boy I was scared and just trembled. But he petted and talked to him and I thought 'he is probably a married man with small children of his own.'"[11]

The assault on the branch prison at Oliver Springs was a natural extension of the struggle against convict labor in Briceville and Coal Creek. Located thirty-three miles southwest of Knoxville, Oliver Springs was not unlike the other two east Tennessee coal towns. Using a slew of pen names, local correspondents in the late 1880s and early 1890s evoked images of a booming town endowed with great beauty and abundant natural resources.[12] Though possessing a geography and institutional matrix similar to those of Briceville and Coal Creek, Oliver Springs had a distinctive commercial character. While Oliver Springs shared a similar emphasis on the coal industry and supplementary job opportunities in a saw-, grist-, and planing mill, it also boasted a tourist industry.

Endowed with nine different mineral springs, Oliver Springs gave east Tennessee its version of New York's Saratoga Springs. Large numbers of visitors from the South and beyond visited this watering place annually, especially during the summer months. The large hotel and baths that serviced these visitors employed roughly half the town's residents, providing employment and sustenance during the summer ebb in the coal mining industry's annual cycle. The heyday of the resort spanned the same two and a half decades (between 1880 and 1905) that the coal industry flourished. Although local Tennesseans and a Georgia industrialist controlled the coal industry, businessmen from Ohio invested heavily in the tourist trade, particularly during the early 1890s.[13] Yet Oliver Springs did not develop into a substantial town. Despite the relatively more diversified economy and puffing descriptions of local well-wishers, Oliver Springs's population was less than half that of Briceville and a third that of Coal Creek.[14]

Though Oliver Springs possessed a smaller population and less significant coal operations than Briceville or Coal Creek, the dynamics of the east Tennessee crisis made an expansion of the rebellion to the westernmost part of Anderson County likely. For the miners to eradicate competition from convict labor, they had to destroy it throughout the mining district. So long as convicts remained in the area, they would continue to depress the free miners' wages and threaten union organization. After the liberation of the Oliver Springs convicts, only two mid-Tennessee mines—Tracy City and Inman—still employed them.

Even more than the revolts in July, the assaults of October 31 and November 2 incorporated widespread popular participation. The rebellion "embraces all the mountaineers of East Tennessee," noted one C. L. Dego, a letter writer to a local newspaper, "for all . . . lent passive assistance."[15] Many surrounding farmers, local merchants, and professional men went far beyond "passive" aid. Several farmers loaned their horses to carry the Coal Creek Valley miners across the mountain to Oliver Springs, while a number of merchants and professionals took part in the Briceville assault. According to one contemporary, "Not only were the miners angry, but the business men of Coal Creek as well, for when the miner of a mining settlement has no money the merchant suffers."[16]

Most telling for C. L. Dego was the treatment of the convicts. "Humanity alone will not account for it," he observed. "Men took off their coats and gave them to the liberated prisoners. . . . When they called for food at the farm houses the answer usually was 'we cannot feed you, you are a convict, but if you will go around to the back yard maybe you can find something.'" Mrs. Mollie Scoggins was also struck by the generosity of the locals, especially in facilitating the convicts' liberation. One local widow, she recalled, "gave the convict her dead husband's clothes."[17]

In early November, with the rebellion intensifying, with more and more east Tennesseans directly involved, and with roughly 460 convicts free, the miners and other residents of Anderson County waited to see how the government, the coal operators, and the public would respond. Governor Buchanan declined to exercise his newly enlarged military authority to suppress the outbreak, largely because strategic odds were against him. The attackers had acted quickly and had disappeared into the local population, making a mobilization of the militia pointless. The governor could only offer rewards for the arrest and conviction of the leaders and participants in the attack. Though the payoff would have been substantial—$5,000 for the leaders and $250 for collaborators—no one came forward with information. The governor also announced a $25 payment for the recapture of escaped convicts.[18]

The government recaptured only 300 of the prisoners released by the miners. Eight other inmates died while making their escape; the remaining third almost certainly found their way to freedom. At least 100 of the apprehended convicts had already made their way to southeastern Kentucky. The Kentuckians who captured these men were largely unidentified, though one paper commented that "hunting Tennessee convicts had taken place of all other field sports." Prisoners were often in dismal shape when caught. Few offered resistance. After encounters with wandering inmates, William Webb, president of UMWA District 19, noted sardonically that "some of them were traveling around to save funeral expenses." Once arrested, the convicts were rerouted by state officials to the main prison at Nashville. A few groups of prisoners, however, never arrived, as east Tennessee miners, still utterly dismissive of state authority, occasionally confronted the arresting party. The inevitable result of these encounters was the liberation of the prisoners yet again.[19]

Governor Buchanan quickly blamed the latest insurrection on Anderson County's sheriff, Rufus Rutherford, and the primary lessee, the Tennessee

East Tennessee advertisement based on the reward for capturing convicts (Tatom, "Press Clippings")

Coal, Iron, and Railroad Company. According to Buchanan, Rutherford was culpable for the incidents in Coal Creek Valley because he did not inform Nashville of impending trouble; and TCIR made the extension of the revolt to Oliver Springs possible by not immediately increasing the number of guards at the stockade. Having located responsibility for the tumultuous state of affairs in east Tennessee with a local official and TCIR, the governor was initially unwilling to reestablish the preexisting order. Buchanan refused to send the convicts who had surrendered or had been recaptured back to the mines, on the grounds that Attorney General Pickle had declared subleasing invalid.[20]

Coal operators uniformly rejected Buchanan's analysis, arguing that bungling by the governor and state prison administrators had led to the successful attacks against convict labor. TCIR insisted that Buchanan had ample warning of renewed insurrection but did nothing.[21] E. J. Sanford and C. M. McGhee, directors of the Coal Creek Mining & Manufacturing Company—the company that owned and leased east Tennessee coal lands—further maintained that much of the blame for the revolt lay with the convict lease's stipulation that the government should appoint prison wardens and guards. Sanford complained bitterly that the government appointees exhibited a sympathy with the miners, which in his view only encouraged a general state of defiance in east Tennessee. He was particularly irked by the state's prerogative to select the guards even though the companies paid their salaries. "The result of this [arrangement]," Sanford argued, "has been that every guard employed and deputy warden employed by Buchanan, are *Knight of Labor*."[22]

Although coal magnates reached easy consensus about the government's responsibility for the breakdown in law and order in Anderson County's mining towns, they disagreed about how to react to the autumn revolts. The individuals in charge of TCIR's day-to-day administration, like secretary-treasurer James Bowron and the general manager of the company's Tennessee property, James Gaines, advocated that the corporation declare the lease broken. Their major concern was the financial toll that continued supervision of convict leasing might exact. Other company officials more removed from daily operations, like First Vice President Nathaniel Baxter, had a different view. The vice president, who knew far more about corporate finance than the details of coal and iron production, vigorously objected to any policy that would antagonize the state.[23] In east Tennessee C. M. McGhee and E. J. Sanford carried on a similar argument. McGhee expressed concern about the potentially "incalculable" damage that miners could inflict upon their "exposed" property. Sanford, by contrast, feared that east Tennessee's mining companies would lose the competitive edge to mid-Tennessee's TCIR if prisoners did not continue to work the local mines. Sanford also reiterated conventional business wisdom that the presence of convict laborers curbed the demands of free miners.[24]

While government officials, convict lessees, and east Tennessee landowners wrangled among themselves in an attempt to apportion culpability and plot a future strategy, most east Tennesseans celebrated. The successful attacks won the approval of citizens throughout Anderson and neighboring counties. Farmers, miners, merchants, and their wives—all of whom had conspired in the insurrection—now rejoiced at the successful liberation of the convicts. The local commercial press echoed the support that neighboring citizens extended to the miners. The papers that had long evinced sympathy for the miners' plight again took up their cause. The *Chattanooga Republican*, for example, carefully distinguished the men who had released the convicts from criminals or anarchists who had no respect for the rules of civilized society. "Four months ago," the editor declared, "the people had it in their power to release the convicts . . . , but they did not do it. They [the miners] appealed to the governor, they appealed to the legislature, and to every power possible to give them relief. Do ruffians and cut-throats pursue such a course?" Even the miners' recent unlawful activities, the paper contended, were performed with such discipline that Anderson County citizens did not feel the need to call upon the governor for help.[25] In the immediate aftermath of the convicts' liberation, labor organs from beyond Tennessee's borders also responded with admiration for the miners' intrepid stance. Both the *Alabama Sentinel* and the *United Mine Workers Journal* argued that there was a "limit to endurance" and that in the circumstances prevailing in Tennessee "patience cease[d] to be a virtue."[26]

Yet even as local commercial and some labor presses rallied behind the miners' actions, many union voices began to caution against a violent response to labor's ills. For several commentators in the labor movement, freeing convicts and destroying property went beyond the limits of reasonable redress. The *Journal of the Knights of Labor*, reflecting that organization's official opposition to strikes and other forms of militant action, responded equivocally. Its editor stressed the miners' discipline and the absence of indiscriminate violence but added a cautionary note, suggesting that such action provided a "dangerous precedent." Raising the specter of the French Revolution, the editor urged national reconciliation between labor and capital. "History," he observed, "is repeating itself in the United States. Let our rulers go forward with a flag of truce to meet and treat the vast column that is advancing. Don't wait for the earthquake as the church and aristocracy of France did." All Tennessee's big-city Central Labor Unions evinced similar sentiments, at once sympathizing with the miners of east Tennessee and urging them to replace warlike remedies with the election of sympathetic legislators.[27]

Two prominent Tennessee labor advocates added their voices to the chorus of restraint. Commissioner of Labor Ford and J. C. Roberts, the general organizer and lecturer of the Farmers' Alliance, each wrote to Grand Master Workman Terence Powderly of the Knights of Labor, imploring him to intercede with the miners. Both hoped that Powderly could persuade the miners to refrain from violating the law and to seek negotiations with the lessees. As a state official, Ford had a strong interest in encouraging discussions rather than direct action. Wishing to solidify his organization's recent success at the polls, Roberts emphasized practical political considerations. "Public sentiment," he argued, "which was largely in sympathy with the miners at the first" was now "rapidly changing" because of "their continued resistance to the law." The Farmers' Alliance official warned that continuing conflagration in east Tennessee would carry human, material, and social costs similar to those of the Civil War.[28] Roberts, like many other supporters of the miners, could not countenance armed revolt as a legitimate tool of political opposition to governmental policy.

As head of a labor movement that favored arbitration and the peaceful resolution of conflict, Powderly responded positively to the requests from Ford and Roberts. He wrote to five locals in Briceville and Coal Creek, arguing that irrespective of whether the convict laws were just, the miners ought to obey them. Powderly recommended that miners seek to make abolition of the convict lease an issue in the upcoming statewide election. Drawing on Roberts's argument, the grand master workman suggested that if the miners continued their insurrectionary course, they would alienate public opinion. Favorable public opinion, he contended, was their strongest ally.[29]

Powderly's warning, issued at the beginning of 1892, may have come too late for the miners to stem a growing tide of popular disfavor. By this time, commentators outside the mining communities had joined the cautious segments of the labor movement in turning against the miners. Respect for the miners' campaign against the convict-lease system had rested on what was perceived as the "gentlemanly," "orderly," "long-suffering," and "patient" behavior of the miners. Underpinning the use of such language was the regard that east Tennessee mineworkers had shown for private property. Although the miners had removed the convicts from the Briceville and Coal Creek stockades in July 1891, they did not destroy company assets. On the contrary, they had formed committees whose express purpose was to protect the companies' mining operations.[30] The miners also had not freed the convicts but had carefully guarded them on their journey to Knoxville, following such illicit behavior with attempts to curry public favor and carefully orchestrated negotiations with state officials.

Yet once the miners liberated state prisoners and engaged in arson, they abandoned "conservative," constitutional methods. The mainstream Democratic press responded to this shift with vigorous condemnation, while many Republican papers immediately called for a restitution of law and order. The Democratic *Knoxville Tribune* offered typical characterizations in referring to Anderson County mineworkers as "savages" and "maniacs," charging them with "rampant lawlessness" and "high-handed treason."[31] "Where is all this to stop and what will it lead to?" an editorial in the Republican *Knoxville Journal* asked in a similar vein. "It is bad enough to disregard and ignore the rights of property. . . . But this is a small matter when compared with the demoralization of society incident to the spirit of contempt in which law is held." Insurrection, the *Journal* proclaimed, was inconsistent with making Tennessee and the South an attractive place for investment.[32] Thus the fall incursions against the convict stockades prompted a transformation in sentiment toward the miners in many influential quarters. No longer viewed almost universally as upstanding citizens, the Anderson County workingmen increasingly found themselves branded as outlaws.

Nonetheless, east Tennessee coal companies did not have the luxury of treating the miners with impunity. Pressed by a backlog of orders for coal—the result of shortfalls in production during the tumultuous events of the past months, coupled with annual winter demand—company operators rehired many of the men who had so recently taken part in the destruction of company property. Reports of full employment and mines working to capacity filled the November and December newspapers. The heavy demand for coal enabled the miners to win a number of concessions from the coal operators. Companies allowed a checkweighman at all the mines that employed a sufficient number of workers to pay for such a weigher. The operators additionally abolished ironclad contracts, ended deductions for dirt and slack, and agreed to pay miners for the full amount of coal on every car rather than the standard 2,500 pounds.[33]

A strong coal market only partly accounted for these concessions. They also resulted from strong union organization. Marcena Ingraham, a stalwart of the rebellion, reported in December 1891 that "Coal Creek never was in so prosperous a condition as it is at the present time. We have five assemblies all in good working order and the sixth one ready to be organized."[34] Such work-related victories buoyed the hopes of Anderson County miners; but they did little to stem the growing concerns expressed by their supporters or the increasingly stern censure they received in mainstream newspapers.

The Reimposition of Convict Leasing in East Tennessee

However pleased the miners might have been with the return to work and the winning of concessions from their employers, they had not achieved their primary goal—the end of the convict-lease system. In the immediate aftermath of the attack at Oliver Springs, Governor Buchanan had seriously considered not sending the convicts back to the east Tennessee mines, on the legal pretext that subleasing was illegal. Within a month, however, the governor and the lessees had begun to express a similar urgency to restore and maintain the status quo ante. Both parties wished to exhibit forceful and united resolve in the face of the miners' widespread resistance, to maintain business confidence, and to avoid the expenses associated with idle prisoners.[35] To these ends, company and government officials arrived at an agreement on December 15 that sought "to produce harmonious action . . . and avoid an open breach between the state and the lessees in the face of the excited and threatening miners." The two parties realized that to send convicts back to the branch prisons without a statement of joint resolve would be unwise if not futile.[36]

Moreover, representatives of both the government and TCIR recognized the pressing need to demonstrate that blatant challenges to state authority would not be tolerated. Public confidence in the state's ability to ensure law and order, Nashville officials assumed, required that the government prevent east Tennessee miners from any further interference with convicts. Attorney General Pickle, who appears to have won Governor Buchanan's respect, advised the governor to "keep the convicts away altogether or *send them back to stay at all hazards*. There is no half-way position in this matter."[37] Yet Pickle did not advocate the "wholesale" return of the convicts. Rather, he counseled that Buchanan review conditions in each town separately—advice that the governor followed, even as he resolved in early December that "the convicts shall be returned to the mines if it takes every able-bodied man in the state to do it."[38]

Tennessee officials believed that Coal Creek was an obvious place to station at least some state inmates. The existing infrastructure and a history of reasonably amicable town-lessee relations rendered Coal Creek the most hospitable place to garrison prisoners. The survival of the barracks and the relatively harmonious relationship that the Knoxville Iron Company had with the townspeople would facilitate the convicts' peaceful stay in Coal Creek—or so Buchanan hoped. In mid-December, with these circumstances in mind, the governor ordered prison officials to return inmates to the town on January 1, 1892.[39]

The prospects for sending prisoners back to Briceville were far dimmer. As early as November 4, TCIR's management contemplated taking over TCMC's Briceville operation so as to circumvent Buchanan's initial refusal to allow convicts to return as workers for a sublessee. Since TCIR needed to find employment and shelter for the convicts, the corporation's assumption of the Briceville coal mining lease struck executives as a sensible option. The company's plan hit a snag, however, when sublessee B. A. Jenkins, still TCMC's president, requested an indemnity bond of $50,000 as insurance against losses caused by additional attacks on company property. By December 1891, Jenkins no longer wanted anything to do with prison labor. Unwilling to sign such an agreement, TCIR's managers chose not to send inmates back to the scene of the first revolt.[40]

Though conditions in Oliver Springs were similar to those in Briceville, the outcome in the former town mirrored that of Coal Creek. Like Jenkins, J. W. Renfro, the president of the Cumberland Coal Company, did not want prisoners returned to his care. In the months before the November release of convicts at Oliver Springs, Renfro had expressed great frustration at the inefficiency of the inmates working for him, variously commenting that he would "willingly give $500 to be rid of the whole gang of convicts" and that he would give any employee "a suit of clothes if he would get a mob to come and take the convicts away." Desperate to make their prison wards pay for their keep, TCIR purchased the mining lease for the coal lands surrounding Oliver Springs's Big Mountain Mine on January 22, 1892. By hastily erecting prison facilities, TCIR made possible the return of state inmates to Oliver Springs.[41]

Governor Buchanan, then, compromised his stance toward subleasing, while TCIR retreated from an initial insistence that the convicts go back to all the places from which miners had evicted them.[42] In the intervening months between the convicts' liberation and the return of recaptured inmates to the mines, the two parties had time to reflect on the constraints they faced, leading each to modify its position. Both governmental officials and the convict lessees faced pressures to work the convicts and, in the process, to remind east Tennessee miners of some basic truths—that the government made state policy and that the coal operators made company decisions.

Yet neither governmental nor company officials wished to appear to be riding roughshod over the miners' demands; such an image might stem the flow of public opinion against the miners. TCIR executives sought to avoid the appearance of corporate heavy-handedness by "negotiating" the return of the convicts with the miners themselves in mid-December. Essentially, TCIR agreed not to work convicts at Briceville; in return, the miners promised not to interfere with any inmates sent to Coal Creek and Oliver Springs. Despite his very public resignation from the affairs of east Tennessee, Eugene Merrell stood out as a key figure in these negotiations. His continued high profile confirmed that his "abdication" from a public position said more about the government measures threatening Anderson County's leaders than it did about their ongoing commitment to local mining communities.[43] The miners most likely accepted this agreement because they hoped to convince Tennesseans that they remained a responsible group concerned only for their legal rights. They may have also viewed themselves as setting a crucial precedent about the introduction of convicts into Tennessee's coalfields. If the agreement solidified into custom, any lessee of state prisoners would need the consent of a coal mine's free laborers before handing picks and shovels to their wards.

On a damp and dismal New Year's Day, Kellar Anderson, a Confederate veteran prominently connected with the elite Chickasaw Guards of Memphis, led almost 200 convicts and around 80 militiamen from mid- and west Tennessee into Coal Creek. Describing Anderson as an "ideal soldier," newspapers claimed that "no matter what circumstances may arise, no matter how thick the shot and the shell," he would perform his "duty." The soldiers under his command had the reputation of being "fighting men" who obeyed orders. During the next few days, despite cold, wet weather, the troops erected a fort dubbed Fort Anderson and settled in for a prolonged sojourn. Four weeks later, Captain W. H. Brown arrived in Oliver Springs with his troops and approximately 70 convicts.[44]

The return of the convicts to the mines required arrangements for the payment of scores of militiamen. A dispute about who would bear financial responsibility for the militia occupied representatives of the state and TCIR throughout their negotiations in late 1891. In the December 15 accord, TCIR agreed to pay for civil guards and the first twenty-five military guards, including arms and ammunition for all guards sent to Coal Creek and Oliver Springs. The company, however, reserved the right to deduct the expenses of additional armed personnel from the lease rental.[45] This compromise left only a murky line separating civilian guards and military personnel. Reflecting widespread confusion, newspaper reports did not distinguish between guards, troops, militia, and the "Army of Tennessee." Reports on the number of civilian and mili-

COLONEL KELLAR ANDERSON, THE HERO OF COAL CREEK.   FORT ANDERSON AS SEEN LOOKING UP FROM THE STOCKADE.

Fort Anderson on Militia Hill, Coal Creek (*Harper's Weekly*, August 27, 1892, Yale Collection of American Literature, Beinecke Rare Book and Manuscript Library, Yale University)

tary men accompanying the convicts back to Coal Creek and Oliver Springs ranged from 80 to 200.[46] The ambiguities surrounding the guards and militia went beyond naming or counting them. Governmental officials, TCIR directors, and military commanders did not share a clear conception about the troops' mission.

The attitude of the militia toward Coal Creek residents in 1892 differed markedly from the friendly posture adopted by the east Tennessee corps who had come to Anderson County in response to the previous July's rebellion. Many of the state guards acted as if they were part of an occupying army, almost immediately creating tensions in Coal Creek Valley. Within weeks of the soldiers' arrival, Eugene Merrell complained publicly that the soldiers "were blowing and bragging about having come here to stay" and flaunting "their authority" in an "aggravating" manner. A few days later, the community leader wrote to Governor Buchanan, protesting that militiamen were "molesting citizens on public roads." In reply, Buchanan tried to assure Merrell that the troops had come to Coal Creek not to "bring about a conflict with the law abiding peaceable citizens of Anderson Co. but to protect the state prisoners."[47] Some of the mid- and west Tennessee soldiers were obviously taken with the idea of guarding criminals. At the same time that the exchange between Merrell and Buchanan took place, a group of soldiers arranged to have their photographs taken in the act of overseeing a convict. The guards marched an inmate to an appropriate backdrop and raised their guns for the camera. One of the guns went off, killing the prisoner instantly. This macabre event contrasted visibly with the governor's reassuring words that he had sent the troops to Coal Creek to protect the state's wards. One newspaper reporter noted bitterly that "he was only a convict, a nigger at that, so it is not likely anything will be done about it and probably the matter will be hushed up."[48]

In characterizing the role of the militia, Buchanan paid close attention to legal niceties. If the soldiers had the task of protecting the convicts in east Tennessee, financial responsibility for the men would rest with the convict lessees; but that interpretation conflicted with Buchanan's constitutional authority. The extra session of the legislature had expressly limited the governor's power to call out the militia to situations in which a rebellion was imminent. Buchanan lacked the authority to use militiamen to guard prisoners. He tacitly recognized this constitutional difficulty when he later stated publicly that the troops' directive was "to keep down any mob or rebellion against the laws of the state."[49] Nonetheless, the distinction between guards and soldiers and between safeguarding convicts and preventing an imminent rebellion remained unclear as long as the militia stayed in east Tennessee. The men selected to serve at Coal Creek and Oliver Springs took the oath of the state militia and became deputies under the law passed by the legislature during its 1891 extra session; yet these troops received their paychecks from the convict lessees. Employed by TCIR, they laid claim to the full authority of the state.

The tempers of both Coal Creek miners and militiamen continued to flare for months after the incidents in mid-January reported by Eugene Merrell, with each side accusing the other of "indiscriminate shooting" and reporters repeatedly predicting "serious trouble." Locals deeply resented what they perceived as the insulting and high-handed behavior from the outsiders and showed contempt for the drunken and disorderly conduct of many troops. On several occasions, individual soldiers received fines in local court for disturbing the peace or carrying firearms illegally. Throughout the militia's stay, men,

CONVICTS GONE!

on the 20th Day of July, 1891,

— AND ON —

WED'Y, JULY 20th, 1892,

— there will be a —

Grand Picnic at Briceville, Tenn.,

near the mines of the Co-operative Mining Company.   This picnic is to celebrate the day the Convicts and State Militia were driven out of Briceville.

Orators.

The Addresses of Welcome will be delivered by EUGENE MERRILL, of Briceville, and W. C. WEBB, of Pittsburg, Ky., Also Mr. B. A. JENKINS will positively deliver an address to the crowd.

Amusements.

There will be a Grand Ball given, and a platform will be erected 30x60 feet from the lumber remaining from the destroyed stockade.

FOOT RACE BY BOYS under 15 years old will be rewarded 1 pocket knife by J. F Matthews and 1 scarf by W. B. Robbins.

SACK RACE, 100 yards, by men winner to receive a meerschaum pipe by L. N. Brown.

THREE LEGGED RACE, 100 yds., $1.00 in cash by John Simpson.

WHEELBARROW RACE, blindfolded 20 yds., by ladies premium pair of Mits by Mrs. C. Leinart.

THE YOUNG LADY who gathers 25 potatoes first will receive $1.00 by Dr. C. L. Hill.

THE YOUNG LADY, who runs 25 yds., with an egg in a spoon will receive a handsome album by H. S. Pless also $1.00 cash by Dr. Madison.

JUG BREAKING, by ladies blinded, premium 1 scarf by S. S. Burris.

TAILING THE MULE, by ladies, successful lady $1.00 by W. B. Underwood 50c by Dr. S. Petree.

HAMMER THROWING, by men 1 box cigars by G. E. Irish.

RACES RUN by men, weighing 200 pounds or more 1 pocket knife by R. M. Chapman.

RACES BY LADIES weighing 200 pounds or more pair fine slippers by M. E. Bibee.

THE HANDSOMEST young lady over 15 yrs., 1 pair silk mitts by Robt. Hart.

THE YOUNG LADY repeating the largest number of words in five minutes, Silk Handkerchief by W. H. Branscom.

SHOOTING MATCH, 27, yds., off hand, and 40 yds., with a rest premium, $2.50.   Entrance fee 50 cents.

BASE BALL TEAMS have been invited and are expected.

Music will be Furnished for the Occasion by the Famous Rockwood String Band.

REFRESHMENTS of all kinds will be served by Local Assemblies Nos. 361 and 2957.
The Railroads will give Excursion Rates from Jellico, Harriman Junction and Clinton.

Committee of Arrangements :

C. M. WOODWARD, President,
SAMUEL TAYLOR, Secretary.

Poster for celebratory picnic in Briceville, 1892 (Tatom, "Press Clippings")

Picture of a Coal Creek woman, kept as a memento by a Tennessee militiaman (Tennessee National Guard, *Souvenir of Company "C"*)

women, and children scoffed at the state guards, mocking their valor. The women and children of Coal Creek reportedly sang,

> There was a little soldier,
> And he had a little gun,
> A miner shook his fist,
> And the little soldier run.

The citizens of Coal Creek Valley vividly demonstrated their contempt for the militia's presence and mission during a community picnic on July 20, which celebrated the previous year's eviction of convict labor from the valley. Residents took special pleasure in building the dance floor for the picnic out of wood taken from previously destroyed stockades. The picnic incident and the song suggest a community wholly separated from the militiamen and unrelenting in its hostility. But matters were more complicated. Some local women entered into romantic liaisons with the occupying soldiers. These relationships led to both scorn from the labor press and an intensification of hostility between the militia and the local men.[50]

The militiamen were not content to lord it over the locals by taking their women. They also engaged in competitions to see who might be the best shot. These contests did not leave the militiamen impressed with their adversaries' character. While Coal Creek residents sang ditties questioning the soldiers' valor, the soldiers wrote disparaging letters to their superiors. The company surgeon at Fort Anderson described his new abode as "this weird desolate mountain country" and characterized the miners as "possibly the most consummate band of out laws known in the history of any country." To the surgeon, local residents were a "cowardly" and "vindictive" bunch.[51] Throughout the winter and spring of 1892, animosity between the miners and the militia structured daily life in the town.

In Oliver Springs the presence of militiamen also resulted in friction between soldiers and residents. The level of conflict, however, stayed far below that experienced in Coal Creek. By the end of February, Governor Buchanan was already predicting that state troops would soon be leaving the area, as he had received intelligence that the Oliver Springs miners had "hesitated considerably before joining in the stockade burning last fall" and were "disposed to be very peaceable." Although state guards remained in the Anderson County resort town somewhat longer than Buchanan expected, the local situation stabilized sufficiently by the end of spring to warrant the militia's withdrawal in late June.[52]

Conflict and "Cooperation" along Coal Creek

The new year brought more than the return of the convicts and militia to Coal Creek Valley. The region's economic outlook also changed dramatically with the coming of 1892. In contrast to the reports of November and December 1891, which told buoyant tales of employment opportunities and an improved work environment, newspaper accounts in the new year depicted deteriorating work schedules and reduced production figures. Such fluctuations were not completely out of the ordinary. The economic downturn partly reflected the seasonal ebbs and flows in the coal mining industry. In March 1892, for example, secretary-treasurer William Riley told *United Mine Workers Journal* readers that work was "dull" throughout District 19, attributing the slump to seasonal cycles in the coal trade.[53]

In addition to a deteriorating economy, the winter of 1892 witnessed a rise in racial tensions throughout UMWA's District 19. Harmonious race relations were always tenuous in the district's coalfields. As in the rest of central Appalachia, blacks and whites worked alongside one another as miners and received the same pay for equal work. In some respects, east Tennessee's blacks maintained a more secure social position than African Americans in the western part of the state or in the Deep South. Unlike in the Deep South, where union offices had to be reserved for blacks, Tennessee miners could voluntarily elect a black man like William Riley to high-ranking union office in preference to white candidates. Beyond the coal pit and union halls, black Anderson County residents continued to assert their political rights, voting in state and local elections throughout the 1890s despite the enactment of electoral laws that curtailed the citizenship of the illiterate and poor.[54] Unlike in the rest of the state, black voters did not challenge the political hegemony of their white east Tennessee brethren. Both voted the Republican ticket. The white miners, however, never came close to accepting a black miner as a full-fledged "brother miner."[55] Riley, for example, periodically complained about the limits of union solidarity, noting the strains that a black organizer faced in a world socially hostile to blacks. In a letter on the difficulties of organizing in the South, Riley concluded that "the readers may think that boarding houses are scarce where I have been traveling, but not so. Some were close, but they had no colored food, only what was in their kitchens, and I did not go in there after it."[56]

Once out of the union hall, relations between blacks and whites exhibited a mercurial and often violent character. At the best of times, the position of black unionists was unpredictable. White miners generally did not look to safeguard their fellow black union members on the streets of the region's coal towns. In defending the desire of black rank and file for black organizers, Riley asked rhetorically: "Can you blame them, when their white brother, so-called, will come out of the lodge room with him at 10 p.m., and if, while on his way home he meets a drunken white and the white man wants the negro to run and the negro is too lazy to run, and won't take a whipping, this drunken white man can just go to some of his brothers and tell his tale, and they will all have their Winchesters and be ready to kill the brother negro before day." Despite the centrality of racial cooperation in official union philosophy, Tennessee's mining organizations never removed racial antagonism from within their ranks. The poisonous effects of those tensions would plague the state's mining union, remaining, in the evocative phrase of William Riley, "as a grain of arsenic . . . in a glass of milk."[57]

Black workers in the mines, though, faced greater difficulties in some periods than in others. A period of heightened tensions set in during the first half of 1892, largely as the result of white responses to increased assertiveness by black miners. In the early months of the year, black miners in locations throughout District 19 demanded that they receive a fair share of choice positions at work. One incident occurred in Newcomb, north of Coal Creek. The Newcomb miners had agreed to share the position of checkweighman based on the proportionate numbers of black and white miners. But when the workforce duly elected a black man as checkweighman, whites refused to work under him. These men offered unconvincing excuses for their behavior, saying that the recently chosen checkweighman lacked competence and had not been legally elected. When Riley proposed a Solomonic compromise suggesting that the man initially chosen for the job stand down and another black man replace him, the whites balked. They simply did not want a black man to fill the coveted position of checkweighman. A kindred incident occurred just north of the Tennessee border but still within District 19. In Altamont, Kentucky, white miners objected to working under a black assistant bank boss. Such incidents infuriated Riley. As secretary-treasurer of District 19 and a former checkweighman at a mine close to Newcomb, Riley symbolized the fluidity of race relations in the coal areas of the Appalachian South. Yet, as Riley himself intimated, episodes like the ones at Newcomb and Altamont served to illustrate the precarious position of southern blacks who rose above the "pick and shovel."[58]

Race relations in the coalfields could similarly take a turn for the worse when blacks too forcefully pushed their notions of appropriate work rules in the mines, or when a community's miners faced shrinking job opportunities. Both these conditions obtained in Oliver Springs at the tail end of 1891. Sharp disagreements arose between white and black Oliver Springs miners as to the appropriate time of day to blast coal. During this period of heightened friction, Captain Renfro, the president of the Cumberland Coal Company, fired some of the white miners, probably in anticipation of the convicts' return to the mines at the beginning of the new year. The men responded to their forthcoming dismissal by refusing to work that day and getting drunk. That afternoon they attacked the black miners and chased them out of the valley. Labor newspapers quickly condemned the whites, asserted the black miners' right to work, and pointed out the difference between "miners" and "rowdies."

Here, as elsewhere, UMWA officials sharply distinguished between those who fell within the labor movement and its ideals of industrial unionism, discipline, cooperation, and interracialism and those who had not yet sufficiently imbibed union principles. But faced with the racially fraught realities of southern life, union organizers frequently had to put pragmatism before principle and mediate between "miners" and "rowdies." They did so in this case, and ten days later black and white miners were back at work.[59]

These three circumstances in east Tennessee—the renewed presence of convicts and militia, the cyclical slump in the coal trade, and the increase in racial hostility—did not provide the only context for relations between labor and capital in the first half of the year. In spite of difficult conditions, east Tennessee miners redoubled their efforts at union organizing, with substantial success. The intense politicization of social relations in the coalfields led William Riley to suggest in March 1892 that District 19 was "in better condition for organizing now than she ever has been by half." Two months later Riley boasted that "our district is gaining very fast in membership. I was out in the field about two weeks last month and I swung about 300 of the boys into our union lines." Briceville and Coal Creek were among Riley's successes, with ten local assemblies in the two towns, albeit separated along racial lines. There was virtually no one left to organize.[60]

These gains meant that the miners could call on hefty numbers during the first half of 1892 if the coal operators once again strove to reassert the prerogatives of management to set the terms of work. But union strength varied considerably in Coal Creek Valley. In January 1892, Coal Creek miners toiled in the shadow of "Militia Hill" and alongside convicts, while their counterparts in Briceville worked in mines that employed only free labor. This crucial difference shaped both the boldness of actions taken by employers and the power of union locals. In Coal Creek, the dominant theme of labor negotiations would be conflict; in Briceville, owner and workers would come to consider cooperation.

Coal Creek employers did not wait long before trying to abrogate the concessions that they made to the miners during November 1891. Mineowners sought to extend the period between paydays and eliminate independent checkweighmen; they also refused to enter districtwide negotiations to set pay scales for the following year. One Coal Creek company went even further, seeking to destroy its workers' labor union. In responding to these initiatives, the miners achieved only mixed success. They could neither force nor cajole the Coal Creek operators to join a districtwide agreement ensuring their employees regular, fortnightly wage payments. The result was a much weaker agreement enabling the signatories to withdraw from their obligations after a certain period in the event that the recalcitrant industrialists maintained their position. The same group of mine managers refused to join the annual bargaining session—a spring ritual that set wage scales for the following year. Secure in the shadow of Militia Hill, the Coal Creek operators declined to engage in talks with union representatives.[61]

Although Coal Creek's mineowners could dismiss the miners' union representatives, they could not act unilaterally or with impunity. Executives of the Black Diamond Coal Company discovered the limits of their power in February 1892. When the Black Diamond management precipitated a lockout at its Empire Mine in the hope of regaining the right to choose the checkweighman, sympathy strikes at the company's two other mines (Black Diamond and Shamrock) forced the company's executives to back away from their demand.[62] Though this offensive failed, other companies took up the charge in the late spring of 1892, going so far as to dismiss union workers.[63] Thus the relationship between Coal Creek mineowners and their free workers never strayed from mutual suspicion and antagonism.

Company executives and miners adopted different stances five miles up the valley. On February 12, 1892, B. A. Jenkins, the president of the Tennessee Coal Mining Company and nemesis of the Briceville miners, arrived in town to discuss the formation of a mine cooperative with community leaders, including Eugene Merrell and Marcena Ingraham, and Commissioner of Labor Ford. Jenkins's plan called for broadening the ownership of the company's stock and reorganizing the company's management. Under the plan, the number of TCMC shares would increase from 50,000 to 100,000. The original stockholders would retain their block of shares, allowing the Briceville miners and working people throughout the state to purchase the additional 50,000. Each new share would cost $100 and would be payable in twenty monthly installments of $5 each. The new shareholders would acquire representation on the board of directors commensurate with their investments. A ten-man board would double the size of the old directorship, with the Briceville miners electing one new director and the Central Labor Unions in Knoxville, Chattanooga, Nashville, and Memphis nominating the other four.[64]

Two weeks later, the miners unanimously endorsed the proposal at a mass meeting. They elected the financial secretary of Knights of Labor Local Assembly 2957, William F. Miller, as their representative to the board of directors and "enthusiastically endorsed" Jenkins as president. Jenkins had offered to stand down, but Merrell, Ingraham, and Ford refused to hear of it. Jenkins, in their view, had "never in any way betrayed the miners; he had kept every promise to them, whether it had been good or bad." These traits qualified Jenkins as a "trustworthy president" of the proposed company.[65]

Jenkins's decision to turn from convict labor to a cooperative scheme with free miners may seem curious in light of the antagonistic stance toward free labor that he maintained through 1891. But the TCMC president had come to find convict labor unsatisfactory and, to a degree, unprofitable. Back in October 1891, Jenkins had complained that his company was losing business in Atlanta and Asheville, North Carolina, because of the poor quality of convict-mined coal. Jenkins's annoyance and exasperation at the second-rate coal his company had shipped led him to declare rather petulantly that he "would rather have miners' troubles a thousand times over than these annoying complaints and continual loss of business." A boycott of TCMC's coal also helped Jenkins see the errors of his ways.[66]

Dissatisfaction with convict-produced coal and public pressure prodded Jenkins to eschew convict miners. Other motivations enticed him to return to free labor. By providing the miners and workingmen elsewhere in the state with a stake in TCMC through the sale of stock, company officials hoped to diminish conflict between themselves and their employees. Furthermore, by adding a very large number of small consumers to its stockholders, the company's directors anticipated a substantial growth in the demand for their coal— a naive conjecture since the railroads far outstripped domestic consumers of coal. In selling the proposal across the state, Jenkins and Merrell nonetheless called on labor solidarity to promote the purchase of TCMC coal. The cooperative plan, Jenkins reasoned, would improve production and consumption to such an extent that everyone involved would profit.[67]

Soon after the meeting with the miners, the company implemented the new stock plan. Eugene Merrell became the sales agent, drumming up orders for the company's coal. At the same time, 127 Briceville miners subscribed to shares in the company. The motivations of Merrell and the Briceville miners were multifarious. No doubt many believed that their employment prospects would improve and that participation in the cooperative scheme would guarantee them "working wages." Others feared that should they not accept Jenkins's proposal, TCIR would take over TCMC's lease and reinstate convicts in Briceville. The miners also had a wider objective in mind when they embarked on this venture—to undermine the convict-lease system. If the Briceville miners produced competitively priced coal and union men around the state pa-

Poster advertising the Briceville
Cooperative Mine, 1892 (Tatom,
"Press Clippings")

tronized TCMC, Merrell explained to a Memphis audience, the employment of convicts would become unprofitable. Such a situation would signal the death knell of convict labor in Tennessee.[68]

The existence of cooperative industries and mines elsewhere in east Tennessee and District 19 also encouraged the miners to embark on such an enterprise. "The cooperative idea is gaining ground every day," one newspaper commented during the negotiations between Jenkins and the Briceville miners.[69] These endeavors ranged from processing factories in Knoxville to coal mines in the Kentucky and Tennessee border town of Jellico. Most were initiated by or had the backing of organized labor (whether Knights of Labor or UMWA). Indeed, the first and second District 19 presidents, William Webb and S. P. Herron, took the lead in the September 1892 establishment of the district's Pioneer Co-Operative Mercantile and Manufacturing Association. Far from being an alien concept, Jenkins's proposal struck a chord with miners schooled in Knights of Labor precepts of cooperative production.[70]

Faced with the stark alternatives of convict labor or a cooperative mine, labor groups and supporters generally praised Jenkins's scheme. When Jenkins and Merrell put the plan to the Central Labor Unions in Nashville, Knoxville, Chattanooga, and Memphis, all endorsed the scheme and promised to lend their support so long as union men worked the mine on a cooperative basis. In response to Jenkins's requests for early sanction of his proposition, Robert P. Porter, superintendent of the U.S. Census, and Terence Powderly, master workman of the Knights of Labor, conveyed their approval. Drawing on the miracles of the New Testament, William Webb praised the inspiration that lay behind Jenkins's blueprint: "I am glad," he wrote, "to see the scales fall from B. A. Jenkins's eyes like Saul of old, who afterwards became the saintly Paul—may our Jenkins become the saintly Arthur and deal with labor as it deserves." Referring to the biblical Saul's conversion while on the road to Damascus, Webb expressed his hope that Barry Arthur Jenkins would embrace the cause of justice for the working man.[71]

But if Paul left the Damascus road wholeheartedly committed to Christianity, Jenkins returned from his trip around the state with less than complete faith in labor-capital cooperation. One letter writer to the *United Mine Workers Journal*, George H. Simmons, seemed incredulous that the president of UMWA's District 19 had endorsed the proposal, arguing that the new scheme only reinforced managerial prerogatives. "Brother Webb and others," Simmons observed, "have sounded [the cooperative scheme's] praises up into the heavens . . . almost tak[ing] the heavens by surprise." The correspondent had good reason to be skeptical, as TCMC's founding directors would be able to outvote the new stockholders unless workingmen bought all of the new shares and voted as a block. So long as representatives of capital maintained effective control, all talk of cooperation "amount[ed] to a hill of beans."[72]

Simmons's concern was not a lone cry in the wilderness. After a close reading of Jenkins's proposal, Powderly also expressed reservations, telling Commissioner Ford that he could not "find in the prospectus anything at all concerning cooperation, it is simply a stock company, nothing more." Powderly did admit, though, that the new plan constituted "an improvement over the convict system."[73] Perhaps the harshest criticism came from a potential TCMC competitor. In a letter soliciting Powderly's endorsement, the agent for the Jellico cooperative mine drew a sharp distinction between his operation and Jenkins's proposal. Employing a sarcastic tone, agent William T. Love argued that the TCMC proposal was a sham. The company, Love maintained, "has just doubled its capital stock (watered it) and is offering one half of it to the miners and consumers, under the name and pretense of being a cooperative enterprise." The old management, the Kentucky agent continued, retained control of the company. They could still elect the board of directors, vote themselves salaries, and mortgage and sell company property. Leveling an attack on Jenkins's integrity, Love asked: "Is a man who turns out honest miners to put convicts in their stead . . . safe to become the trustee and guardian angel of the miner?"[74]

These suspicions reflected a larger discord about political economy. In discussing the cooperative scheme's viability, Jenkins had remarked in an offhand manner that "a good citizen must be selfish."[75] His comment emanated from a social philosophy drawn far more from Adam Smith than Thomas Jefferson or Terence Powderly. The miners could never have accepted such a formulation. For them, cooperative enterprise embodied a mutualism in their particular economic activities; it also symbolized a transcendent conception of the common good, one that went beyond the simple summation of every individual's selfish desires.

The Promise of a Producer's Coalition

The east Tennessee miners' liberation of the convicts in their communities did not stop these wage earners from further efforts to lobby state government. Having ensured that the state would at least keep convicts out of Briceville, east Tennessee labor leaders looked for ways of regaining favorable public opinion and convincing state officials to do something about the convict lease. The first strategy that mine leaders pursued was a long-standing one—the attempt to purge the legislature of men who catered to the penitentiary ring.

In east Tennessee the way to send trustworthy representatives to Nashville was to stick with the Republican Party. "There is only one way that the people can rid themselves of this curse [the lease]," one east Tennessee commentator observed, "and that is by voting the republican ticket."[76] Both white and black east Tennesseans maintained their trust in the party of Lincoln. The voters of east Tennessee, however, could send only a limited number of representatives to the state legislature. The majority of Tennessee's population lived in mid- and west Tennessee, and citizens in those regions voted for legislators who, by and large, had supported the continuation of the lease. Commentators in the mountainous part of the state well understood this political arithmetic. The editor of the *Clinton Gazette*, for instance, directed his readers "not to lose sight of the fact that such legislation as is now patent in Tennessee has been put upon the statutes by and with the concurrence of a majority of the voters of the State." Mine leaders similarly recognized the popularity of the representatives who had disregarded the miners' rights and interests. To move the government at Nashville, the east Tennesseans needed a change in elected officials from the west, or changed minds among those legislators who had so recently acted against workingmen's interests.[77]

The miners eventually pursued both these goals by joining a newly created State Labor Congress. The idea for such a congress originated with the Nashville Central Labor Union. When its representatives discussed the proposal with Merrell and Ingraham in late 1891, they immediately supported the proposed umbrella group.[78] Though conceived as a means to foster understanding among Tennessee's urban and rural industrial workers, the State Labor Congress soon became a more ambitious project. Between the conceptualization of the congress in November 1891 and its first meeting in late February 1892, the Farmers' Alliance joined the trade unions in the formal establishment of the organization. Once this partnership was forged, the hopes of congress affiliates, and particularly the miners, grew. Congress members increasingly viewed the organization as an effort to unite "city and country" and assumed that it would "have an influence in the State." Expecting the congress to pay close attention to state as opposed to national issues, to eschew narrow political controversies, and to forward legislation to the state assembly, many mine leaders expressed optimism that the next legislature would repeal the convict-lease system.[79]

The Farmers' Alliance and the umbrella organizations of industrial workers had much to gain by this formal association. With the 1892 elections fast approaching, attaining political power was foremost in the minds of both the initiators and detractors of the State Labor Congress. Charges in mainstream Democratic newspapers laid bare the Alliance's interest in the partnership. "Those Alliance people are trying to drag the labor element after their car. They want their votes," a *Nashville Herald* editorial intoned. "They are dickering for a political trade." The editor harped on the Alliance's record of failure while appropriating the mantle of labor's friend for the mainstream of the Democratic Party: "Labor appealed to them [Alliance legislators] in vain in the Legislature. . . . As a Democrat we believe his [a laboring man's] appeals to that party will not be in vain." At the same time the editor cautioned against the Alliance's foolhardy embrace of the subtreasury plan, insisting that "we must draw the line at Ocalaism and all its attendant absurdities."[80] Traditional Democratic Party leaders were determined to derail an Alliance–trade union coalition.

Mainstream Democrats did not misread the Alliance's interest in promoting a strategic collaboration with the trade union movement. John H. McDowell, as state chairman of the Alliance, onetime editor of the *Weekly Toiler*, and the man most committed to Buchanan's successful reelection effort, hoped such a coalition would bring his candidate significant support. McDowell got himself elected chair of the State Labor Congress meeting, a position that provided an excellent opportunity to promote Buchanan. McDowell not only invited the governor to speak to and mingle with delegates, but he also held sessions behind closed doors so as to preclude the critical assessment of mainstream Democratic papers—a move that brought charges of Know-Nothingism upon congress proceedings.[81]

If Buchanan had cause to cultivate the miners' support, the miners had reason to give the governor a hearing, despite his actions to restore law and order in east Tennessee. Union leaders recognized that many influential voices of public opinion had turned against them after the third revolt. By returning to more traditional ways of seeking political objectives, the east Tennesseans expected to recapture some of the ground they had lost following the liberation of the convicts. Moreover, the alternative to Buchanan in the 1892 gubernatorial elections would almost certainly be Democratic Supreme Court judge Peter Turney, the man who had so effectively blunted the miners' legal forays against the policy of subleasing convicts. The east Tennesseans loathed "old Pete Turney." His political past was an anathema to the Unionists of east Tennessee. When Tennessee initially voted against secession in February 1861, Turney, a delegate to that convention, returned home hoping to lead the withdrawal of Franklin County from the Union and to orchestrate its attachment to Alabama. Turney's legal and political career also prompted a perception that he was a full-fledged member of Tennessee's penitentiary ring. Someone so closely aligned to TCIR and the other big coal interests was unlikely to regard the miners' demands as a priority.[82]

Buchanan, by comparison, seemed to the miners as much more likely to listen to their grievances. The governor had called out the militia on several occasions, and he had ordered the prison officials to return the convicts to Coal Creek and Oliver Springs. But he had also come away from the extra session of the legislature looking better to the miners than most legislators had. Buchanan had at least recognized the need to stop the spread of the convict labor to new mines. If he proved unwilling to call for the institution's immediate repeal, he was at least willing to contain it. The majority of legislators demonstrated no such inclination.

The results of the Labor Congress's first session gave the miners good reason to believe that the governor and the Alliance would redouble their efforts to address the miners' most pressing complaints. Their concerns were well represented in the list of thirteen demands that emerged from the three-day meeting in late February and early March 1892. The adoption of two demands were of paramount importance to the mining contingent—that the legislature abolish the penitentiary lease system and that it compel mining corporations to collect money from their employees to pay a checkweighman chosen by the miners. The congress readily adopted these two planks, indicating that the Coal Creek and Briceville delegation, along with the representatives from the mid-Tennessee mining town of Tracy City, served their constituents well—although in keeping with the earlier ambivalence of the Farmers' Alliance, the relevant resolution did not specify whether the legislature should immediately abrogate the lease or simply not renew it when the current contract expired at the end of 1895.[83] The mining delegates probably joined with Nashville workingmen in the formulation of three additional demands—that the government require all manufacturers to stamp prison-made articles as "convict-made goods"; that the legislature pass regulations improving the physical protection of miners and operatives; and that the government move the current penitentiary from the city limits of Nashville.[84] The congress directed its executive and legislative committee to take its demands as the baseline for lobbying and publicity. The Farmers' Alliance mouthpiece, the Weekly Toiler, steadfastly supported both congress resolutions and future activity on behalf of those resolutions. The Toiler proclaimed that the legislative committee had an important duty "to take charge of the demands of the Congress and present them to the country and press them before the next General Assembly of Tennessee."[85]

The workingmen of east Tennessee, then, continued to hold firmly to the belief that their economic woes only partly resulted from the corrupting influence of monopoly; they still viewed their difficulties as having political causes, and they still sought political solutions to economic problems. A political alliance with urban workingmen and farmers to secure economic objectives was a pragmatic extension of this philosophy. Before this coalition had much of an opportunity to flex its muscles at the polls or in legislative halls, though, the course of conflict over the convict lease would take a dramatic new turn. Once again, deteriorating economic conditions for free miners would shape the path of unfolding events. This time, however, the scene of action would shift to mid-Tennessee.

In burning the stockades and freeing the convicts, the east Tennessee miners crossed a crucial boundary in late-nineteenth-century America. Until they resorted to these actions, the miners' most potent political ally had been favorable public opinion. But once the miners exhibited disrespect for both property and the law, they laid themselves open to damaging characterizations. The mainstream commercial press had once praised the miners as "conservative" and "manly." Many papers, especially ones from mid- and west Tennessee, now vilified them as "outlaws" and "ruffians." The miners might have expected outrage from business quarters, but they failed to anticipate the vociferous condemnation that would be expressed by the organs of the two major political parties. The east Tennesseans also did not count on the level of concern that their actions would raise for some representatives of organized labor, such as the Knoxville Central Labor Union and officials of the Knights of Labor.

According to a central tenet of republican society, the miners should have directed their protest through constitutional channels. Because republican government entitled men to vote, the failure of government to express popular will lay with individual representatives or other voters. The miners, however, eventually decided to draw on another aspect of republican tradition—the revolutionary heritage of opposing entrenched injustice through force of arms.

But by the 1890s, citizens who appealed to "a long train of abuses and usurpations" as justification for taking up arms against "absolute Despotism" faced public skepticism. The Civil War loomed large in the memories of Tennesseans. As Unionists during the war, east Tennesseans had fought to uphold the Constitution against Confederates who traded electoral and legislative campaigns for military ones. This heritage placed heavy burdens on any group that picked up guns in order to defend claimed rights. The more immediate legacy of labor strife in both North and South only heightened suspicion of such behavior.

The combination of a widespread commitment to law and order and fiscal constraints on both state government and convict lessees kept the miners from achieving their ultimate goal—the abolition of the convict lease. But the miners did obtain a lesser objective. Like Republicans who opposed the expansion of slavery in the 1850s, they stopped the spread of an entrenched social and economic institution that they felt threatened the most basic foundations of liberty.

With the lease confined to its locations prior to the revolt, the miners turned once again to less militant strategies. Some of these men, particularly those in Coal Creek, concentrated on traditional labor organizing and negotiations with a hostile management. The miners in Briceville pursued, if only for the moment, the cooperative vision so central to the Knights of Labor philosophy. At the same time, representatives from both Coal Creek and Briceville joined miners, mechanics, and farmers from throughout the state in an unprecedented attempt to combine their political clout.

The situation in Tennessee's mining communities, however, would prove too volatile for any of these strategies to resolve the deepening conflicts among miners, lessees, and the state. Both the miners and governmental officials had launched their campaigns and responses to restore preexisting conditions—the miners wished to resurrect community life as it had been before the convicts' initial arrival, while the government sought to enforce the convict-lease law. In trying to achieve their objectives, both groups had resorted to the use of force. Far from serving as restorative ingredients, though, arson and armed occupation only further convulsed Tennessee's political and economic environment. Like the Civil War—a war also fought to reclaim the status quo—the Coal Creek wars transformed politics and the economy, making retreat into the past impossible.

Public opinion, which had been
somewhat divided until a gun was
fired, became as solid as a rock.
Law and order became the watch-
word when news came of the death
of popular John Walthall and
brave Butch Givens, hot indignation and deadly anger could be
seen on every face.
—*Knoxville Journal*,
August 20, 1892

CHAPTER 7

The Spread
of Rebellion

When Tennessee mineworkers massed for the fourth time, Winchesters in hand, they hailed from the middle part of the state rather than the east.
Miners in the Chattanooga region, who all worked for the Tennessee Coal,
Iron, and Railroad Company, had eschewed militant action during 1891, both
because TCIR maintained a stronger hold on its workforce than the smaller
east Tennessee mines and because the mid-Tennessee company faced less
daunting economic problems through the first two years of the decade. Nonetheless, TCIR's response to a deteriorating economy eventually pushed the
corporation's more cautious employees to rise up against the convict lease.

Once miners' brigades had destroyed the stockades at Tracy City and Inman,
the pressure on east Tennessee workingmen to follow suit grew apace. The
apparent failure of lobbying efforts such as the State Labor Congress strength-

ened the impulse among Anderson County miners to assail the local branch prison by force. Rank-and-file east Tennessee mineworkers became convinced that they would have to attack the convict lease wherever it had become established if the institution were to become a relic of Tennessee's past.

As with the 1891 revolts, representatives of the state came to the aid of mine-owners after the assaults of mid-1892, this time with far greater force and less deference to the position of the miners. The state now enjoyed increased flexibility in responding to the miners' militance, as the 1891 legislative extra session had armed Governor Buchanan with the power to call out the state militia should any popular revolt seem imminent. Buchanan was initially hesitant to exercise this power, most likely because he recognized the militia's ambivalent attitude to the task at hand and the state troops' record of incompetence.

Nonetheless, Buchanan soon called out his biggest guns. Although these guns did not always fire with the greatest accuracy—indeed, in some cases they did not fire at all—the governor's reliance on the military proved effective. So long as the miners could avoid direct engagement with state troops, they acted with impunity. But these workingmen repeatedly shied away from pitched battles with the militia, even when the miners' possessed superior military intelligence and numbers. For a people who had fought to maintain the Union—and the mining communities boasted their fair share of combatants who had rejected secession—such a step exceeded the bounds of legitimate political protest. Despite the miners' initial successes throughout the state, state troops controlled all of Tennessee's fractious mining communities within a week of the first uprising in Tracy City.

This triumph was not without irony, as the alliance between state officials and corporate executives almost immediately fell apart. Although these leading Tennesseans coalesced around the need to put the miners in their place, the two groups soon became ever more mistrustful of one another. In the wake of the 1892 revolts, both Tennessee's government and its mining operators wished to rid themselves of the convict lease. Neither state officials nor TCIR executives, however, wanted to bear the blame for the lease's demise, nor pay the costs associated with insurrection. Each sought to saddle the other with the moral, legal, and financial obligations resulting from the termination of convict leasing.

Slow Fuse in Mid-Tennessee

Until August 1892, mid-Tennessee's coal mining communities remained relatively quiet, as the approximately 450 free miners in Tracy City refrained from

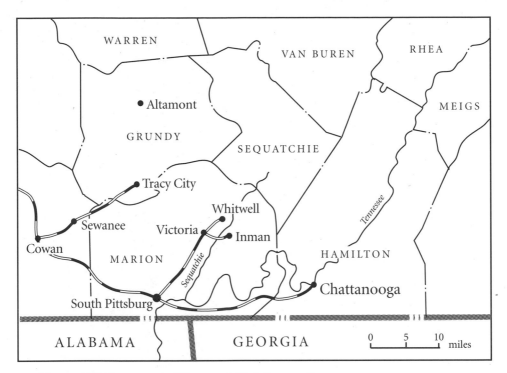

Map 7.1. Mid-Tennessee Coal Towns and Their Surroundings

direct attacks against the convict lease. This stance did not reflect approval of the 410 convict laborers in their community or of the additional 279 inmates who worked at the Inman ore mines in neighboring Marion County. From the first days of union organizing in Grundy County, convict labor served as a rallying point.

Thomas F. Carrick, the forty-year-old Tracy City miner who served as master workman of the Knights of Labor local, led that coal town's opposition to the convict lease. Carrick and his family were not new to social and political conflict. His Scotch-Irish great grandparents had been "old Indian fighter[s]" and soldiers under Andrew Jackson, while he had fought for the South during the Civil War. Carrick shared the values and attitudes of most late-nineteenth-century southern white men. He fondly recalled the days of the Confederacy, hated Yankees, and distrusted blacks. Yet in one regard Carrick was atypical of his contemporaries. He possessed a profound commitment to southern white workers, which edged toward socialism. An articulate and literate spokesman for mid-Tennessee's miners, Carrick was also a practical man. While socialism may have represented his ultimate dream, in the 1890s he settled for the Farmers' Alliance. Grundy County voters, though staunchly Democratic, opted for

Thomas F. Carrick, early 1930s
(William Ray Turner Collection)

the Alliance in the early 1890s, electing an Allianceman for both state representative and state senator.[1] With half the county's population associated with mining, these people voted the Farmers' Alliance ticket largely because of its election-time opposition to the convict lease.[2]

By the time Tracy City miners joined the east Tennesseans in lobbying at the 1891 legislative extra session, the mid-Tennessee mineworkers were already veterans of constitutional opposition to the convict lease. They regularly petitioned the Nashville government to abandon convict leasing and kept up a steady correspondence with the press, continually protesting against the use of prisoners in mining. Most of this correspondence sought both to foster a public outcry against the institution and to urge sympathizers to vote against legislators who supported the penal system.[3] Tracy City also sent a delegation to the

May 1892 State Labor Congress, vigorously supporting the proposed resolution in favor of the lease's repeal. In addition, when the east Tennesseans turned from petitions and lawsuits to military formations, their mid-Tennessee counterparts were quick to offer approving statements and monetary contributions.

Anderson County miners appreciated the mid-Tennesseans' multifaceted support, but they expressed deep frustration with the apparent limits of the Grundy County miners' solidarity. Eugene Merrell was convinced that had the mid-Tennesseans marched on the Tracy City and Inman stockades when the east Tennesseans had first launched their attacks—or in his words, if they had offered a "little lively thrusting"—state officials would have been compelled to act against the convict lease.[4] Whether or not Merrell was correct in this calculation, there is no question that coordinated action in mid- and east Tennessee would have greatly intensified the pressure on the state government. Why, then, did the mid-Tennessee miners stick to their constitutional protests in the face of the east Tennesseans' more combative example?

The answer lies in a combination of steady work, company paternalism and control, and division within the miners' rank and file. The periodic downturns in the Tennessee mining industry during the early 1890s did not affect all the operators equally. TCIR was immune to neither the shock waves that the November 1890 failure of Baring Brothers sent through the New York Stock Exchange nor the declining prices of pig iron since the beginning of that year. The company proved able, however, to draw upon its market flexibility and greater capacity to temper the repercussions of a weakening market. In 1890 TCIR's Tracy City division earned almost $100,000 in gross profits for the company. A year later, this division's contribution had increased by almost 20 percent. Throughout 1890 and 1891, the company as a whole registered consistently good profits.[5]

TCIR's solid performance continued into the early part of 1892. By the middle of that year, TCIR and the two dominant coal and iron companies in Alabama—the DeBardeleben and Sloss companies—had consolidated their operations. With TCIR's acquisition of these concerns, it virtually doubled its capital stock, landholdings, and daily coal excavation. Henceforth, TCIR would rank third in the nation's production of pig iron, following Illinois Steel and the industrial empire of Andrew Carnegie. With fierce competition from its two regional rivals a thing of the past, TCIR looked forward to a period of prosperity. Thus while the east Tennessee operators spent the first half of 1891 battling a deteriorating market and their own particular vulnerabilities—the production of a single product, high royalty rates, and small size—TCIR received sufficient orders to keep its free miners working steadily. With dependable employment and earnings of about $1.65 per day, the mid-Tennessee miners were loath to jeopardize their good fortune.[6]

The mineworkers in Grundy and Marion Counties also confronted an employer that boasted far more checks on its employees than the mining corporations in east Tennessee. TCIR constituted far and away the most important avenue for social advancement in the counties where it operated. The company provided local coal towns with schools and churches; it created loan schemes to enable its skilled workers to become homeowners; and as the owner of most local real estate, it exercised great authority over property use through deed restrictions. As a result, the company forged much closer bonds with its miners than did small mining operations like B. A. Jenkins's Tennessee Coal Mining Company or even the Knoxville Iron Company. These bonds were reflected in the warm relations between TCIR officials and labor leaders, and they helped to limit the combativeness of unions in mid-Tennessee.

The effectiveness of organized labor in Tracy City and Inman, moreover, suffered from a number of splits within the ranks of mid-Tennessee's free workers. TCIR cultivated an elite group of skilled miners, men who earned substantially more than other miners and who often developed strong company loyalty; both the company and union leaders worked to exclude blacks from mining unions; and union leaders had a habit of getting into squabbles with one another, leading Thomas Carrick to complain in December 1888 that "politics" had resulted in a schism from the then dominant local. Finally, heavy-handed tactics by TCIR constrained the capacity of its workers to act cohesively. Mine managers did not hesitate to hire informants to spy on union meetings, giving ample warning of worker sentiment and strategy.[7] Together, company paternalism, the divisiveness within TCIR's workforce, and the use of company spies all encouraged mid-Tennessee miners to stay away from the local stockades. But the most significant guarantor of peaceful industrial relations was steady, full-time employment. When the economic fortunes of TCIR worsened, the disposition of the region's miners toward the company quickly soured.

By July 1892, TCIR began to feel the effects of a nationwide industrial slump. Orders from railroads and industrial concerns plummeted, leaving TCIR workers with the task of piling iron rails and rods on top of one another. To reduce the enormous stocks of iron that the market could not absorb, TCIR cut its coal production. From a high of 36,000 tons in July 1891, TCIR decreased its monthly output to 28,000 tons a year later. As in east Tennessee, the effects of depressed production fell most heavily on free miners. Since TCIR had to feed its convicts whether they worked or not, the company chose to keep its unfree laborers on a full-time schedule. As a result, free miners bore the brunt of the slowdown, finding themselves with only half-time work.[8]

On August 13, the Tracy City miners reached the end of their tethers. As on so many other days that summer, they asked company officials for a more equitable distribution of work between the convicts and themselves. The response from superintendent Nathurst—that he would have to consult his superiors—struck the miners as disingenuous. The restive crowd grew increasingly angry and frustrated. "Slowly," one journalist recounted, "the ominous air of suppressed excitement became tinged with open threats and promises of destruction to the stockade or a battle." At 8:30 A.M., in broad daylight and without masks, the miners marched on the stockades.[9]

This action took place without the presence of long-standing leader Tom Carrick. Prudence most likely caused Carrick to desist from open insurrection. In August 1891, just after the rebellion in east Tennessee, he and his wife had taken out a mortgage on their home from the Mountain Home and Loan Association. Perhaps mindful of his repayments and the vindictive streak that TCIR officials freely exercised, he chose caution over valor. Following the rebellion, Carrick would be richly rewarded for his circumspection. In December 1893 the Democratic Cleveland administration appointed him a deputy U.S. marshal, a patronage position over which the local business and political elite would likely have had a say.[10] In Carrick's absence, three previously unknown miners came to the fore. One of the insurrection's leaders, Robert Vaughn, was a young man of twenty-one who owned a small house valued at $50. Biographical information on the other two men—Berry Simpson and Jim Frazier—remains elusive. Neither appeared in the Tracy City tax records or Grundy County's enumeration of adult men.[11] Probably both were still too young to qualify for the franchise.

The new leaders replaced the previous demand for equal work with an order that the stockade guards release their charges. The guards offered no resistance. Having grown to between 150 and 300 men, the miners proceeded to remove the supplies that TCIR had stored in the stockade. The crowd then razed the building to the ground. Once on the path of militant resistance, the Tracy City miners strove to limit the ability of outside forces to respond to their initiative. To prevent news from leaving Tracy City, the miners cut the telegraph wires. They then commandeered a Nashville, Chattanooga & St. Louis train and put the 390 convicts aboard its cars. Within two hours the train slowly left the station, carrying the convicts to Nashville's main penitentiary.[12]

The miners had begun to plot their offensive even while they appealed peacefully to the company for more work. The preparations involved both attention to timing and military training. For weeks before the assault, the miners met on Sundays in a "holler back of [a] hill" to consider their options and eventually to set the time when they would "run the convicts off the mountain." In those same weeks, the local sheriff, Captain Alec Saunders, "drilled the men," giving the miners some pointers in military comportment and discipline. Several commentators, including a *United Mine Workers Journal* reporter and Superintendent of Prisons E. B. Wade, described the attack as "well planned," suggesting that Saunders did a good job with the miners.[13]

With all this activity taking place in and around Tracy City, the attack on the stockade did not come as a surprise to TCIR officers. Indeed, TCIR's vice president Nathaniel Baxter made clear that he had more than an inkling of impending events. Three days before the miners marched on the Tracy City branch prison, Baxter informed Governor Buchanan that "the plans of the mob are becoming more and more public." Though Baxter dutifully informed Buchanan of the impending assault, he took no further steps to prevent it.[14]

Governor Buchanan responded to TCIR's warning in a limited fashion, ordering an increase in the number of Tracy City guards. "This is the only recourse under the laws of Tennessee we can avail ourselves of under existing circumstances," Buchanan replied to Baxter.[15] In retrospect, this posture seems hesitant, especially in light of the recent expansion of executive powers. The 1891 legislative extra session had specifically promulgated a law enabling the governor to call out the militia if he believed an insurrection to be in prospect. Legislators had designed this law to meet just this kind of exigency. Furthermore, Buchanan's request went nowhere. E. B. Wade thought Nathaniel Baxter was overreacting and delayed sending extra guards to Tracy City. Because of the superintendent's foot-dragging, the extra contingent was not on hand to meet the miners' attack.[16]

The relative inaction on the part of both company personnel and state officials left the initiative with the miners. News of events in Tracy City caused great excitement in neighboring Marion County, home of TCIR's Inman ore mines. On August 15 miners from Grundy and Marion Counties marched on the Inman stockade. On their way to the Marion County branch prison, about 200 miners accidentally intercepted a group of extra guards who were on their way to help those stationed at Inman. The miners, mostly from Whitwell (another TCIR coal-rich property eight miles from Inman), disarmed the reinforcements and sent them toward Jasper, a town to the south. The Whitwell men then continued their hike toward the convict stockade, facing no other challenges. Though Judge Moon of the circuit court had ordered Marion County's sheriff, J. W. Morrison, to the scene, the latter official refused to act.

The stockade at Inman (*Harper's Weekly*, August 27, 1892, Yale Collection of American Literature, Beinecke Rare Book and Manuscript Library, Yale University)

Whether he based his refusal on his inability to raise a posse, sympathy for the miners, or opposition to the convict lease remains ambiguous.[17] On the miners' arrival in Inman, the thirty guards stationed there capitulated immediately. The visitors, including around thirty blacks from Whitwell and some ex-convicts, called the 290 convicts from the mines, loaded them onto trains, and sent them to Nashville.[18]

Unlike the Tracy City men, Marion County miners did not cut the telegraph wires, choosing to control rather than stymie news coverage. To this end, the Inman miners posted at nearby Victoria an editor, who "exercised rigid censorship over every dispatch that went out." The miners additionally chose to refrain from pyrotechnics, acceding to the mine superintendent's request that they not burn the stockade for fear of damaging the nearby railroad. Instead of torching the building, the miners emulated prerevolutionary New England mobs, who had a penchant for "pulling down" the houses of lordly colonial officials—they dismantled the structure piece by piece. These events took place without great conflict. Neither miners nor guards fired a single shot during the entire episode.[19]

By their actions, the workingmen of Grundy and Marion Counties halted all of TCIR's mid-Tennessee operations, wreaking a "temporary disaster" on "commercial interests." Within three days of the August 13 release of Tracy

City's convicts, TCIR's coal mines at Tracy City and Whitwell, its coke ovens at Tracy City, Whitwell, and Victoria, its ore mine at Inman, and its blast furnaces at South Pittsburg (a town located in southern Marion County near the Alabama border) had all ceased to operate.[20]

If the miners had intended to make the continued use of convict labor increasingly and even prohibitively expensive, they set about their business with dispatch. TCIR officials immediately issued public complaints about the great cost of rebuilding destroyed property. In addition to demolished stockades, the company confronted substantial damage to its Inman ore mine. During the convicts' absence, a cave-in caused serious obstructions in the mine's entryway. TCIR also claimed injuries beyond the physical damage to its properties. Officials immediately began grumbling about the "general demoralization and the breaking down of its business." Five months after the revolt, the assistant general manager noted in his annual report that the company had "not been able to 're-establish' the standard of labor or the quality of coal and coke. Our furnaces," he continued, "are still suffering from the use of inferior coke, consequent upon this outbreak."[21]

Although TCIR may not have anticipated the long-term effects of the revolt in mid-Tennessee, company executives were not completely averse to the demise of the convict lease. Such diverse observers as the governor and a *United Mine Workers Journal* reporter intimated that TCIR officials colluded with the miners, "secretly rejoic[ing]" at the pretext the miners' assaults provided to rid the company of the convict lease.[22] But before journalists or legislators could even begin to investigate such charges, the miners of east Tennessee once again grabbed the public spotlight from their counterparts to the west.

Rebellion Reignited in East Tennessee

Miners in east Tennessee had no prior knowledge of the mid-Tennesseans' decision to march on the stockades in their communities. On the same day that Tracy City's miners attacked their local prison, a three-man committee of Coal Creek citizens delivered a petition to Governor Buchanan pleading for the removal of soldiers from their town. The delegation consisted of John Lewis, Rufus Bennett, and John A. Wilson, men who had not played a prominent role in the struggles of the previous year. Though nothing is known about Lewis, Bennett and Wilson were longtime residents of Coal Creek. Both were property owners, and Wilson was a Knights of Labor officeholder known for his advocacy of peaceful methods.[23] The men traveled to Nashville to assure the governor that if he removed the troops, the Coal Creek community would not interfere with the convicts before the next meeting of the general assembly in early 1893. By mid-summer in 1892, relations between the people of Coal Creek Valley and the troops stationed there had become so bitter that Coal Creek residents shifted their demand from the removal of the convicts to the removal of the soldiers. But before any deal could be hammered out, news arrived of the attack on the Tracy City prison.

The Coal Creek delegation was more surprised than the governor, who at least had been forewarned of impending "trouble." Suddenly confronted with this unexpected change in the course of events, the delegation beat a hasty retreat to Coal Creek. Before they left, Buchanan promised that he would soon come to the Anderson County town to confer with residents. The governor also reiterated a point he had made numerous times before—that he could do nothing about the convict lease. Perhaps in an effort to forestall a new crisis in east Tennessee, he added that he would withdraw the troops from Anderson County in the near future.[24]

Upon their return home, the committee convened a mass meeting. Bennett and Lewis addressed the gathering, urging the miners "to frown down any efforts that might be made to raise a disturbance." Invoking their rights and responsibilities as homeowners, the speakers emphasized that the success of their appeals depended more than ever on disciplined "conduct." The "late disturbances between the people and the soldiers," Bennett argued, "were brought about through the action of men who were not responsible [and who had] no interest at stake and no homes, on one side, and some men who, while they wore the uniform of a soldier, were no better . . . than those on the other side." Unwilling to rely on the better instincts of community members, he followed a well-established tradition and recommended that the Knights of Labor form a committee of Coal Creek's fifty best citizens to prevent any "unlawful demonstration[s]."[25]

Two days later, Governor Buchanan privately concluded that there was a possibility of doing what only a few days before had been "impossible"—canceling the convict lease. The governor threatened TCIR with such an action because of several decisions taken by the corporation over the proceeding twelve months. TCIR had withheld its quarterly lease payments since September 1891, leaving the company almost $100,000 in arrears to the state; it had refused to reimburse the government for incidental expenses incurred during the miners' 1891 revolts; and it remained unwilling to provide for the convicts sent to Nashville's main prison during the most recent insurrection.[26] A combination of the resolve by prominent miners to restrain militant impulses and

Buchanan's abrupt reversal would seem to auger peace in east Tennessee. But mistrust among Anderson County's rank and file and Buchanan's failure to make his stance public set the rebellion in motion once again.

There is no way of knowing what might have transpired had the governor acted decisively or had the Coal Creek miners stuck to the resolution to await his intervention. But Buchanan did not act firmly, leading east Tennessee miners to emulate their counterparts in Grundy County. Coal Creek's more moderate citizens soon discovered that they could no longer contain the "smothered excitement" in east Tennessee. Within forty-eight hours of the attack on the Inman stockade, 100 to 200 men assaulted the prison house at Oliver Springs. They first targeted the Oliver Springs stockade because the militia had departed in June, leaving behind just forty civilian guards.[27]

Much to the surprise of the coal miners who marched on the Oliver Springs stockade, the guards there refused to relinquish their charges—the first time during the revolts that an assault did not bring immediate capitulation. In anticipation of the dawn attack, the warden, Captain Ferris, placed his guards at strategic positions in the well-entrenched branch prison. He also took the precaution of readying a few men to prevent the convicts from stampeding, thereby preempting a joint assault. A half-hour shoot-out ensued, whereupon one of the miners' leaders, under a white flag, requested permission to remove their wounded. With such permission granted, the miners retired.[28]

Captain Ferris's defense of the stockade was based on a notion of honor rather than conviction—given an order, he was determined to perform his duty. Ferris had no interest in routing the miners; his sole objective was to guard the convicts. The warden could have collected a $5,000 reward had he divulged the name of the mine leader who had approached him under a flag of truce. But because the man—John Hatmaker—had requested anonymity, Ferris felt it would be dishonorable to disregard this appeal.[29]

Soon after this incident in Oliver Springs, Nathaniel Baxter pointedly complained to Governor Buchanan that only a handful of civilian guards were defending the Oliver Springs stockade. A combination of corporate and public pressure prompted the governor to take a more resolute military stand. Buchanan dispatched two companies, one under Major Chandler (of Knoxville), the other led by Colonel Woolford (of Chattanooga), to aid Captain Ferris.[30]

The miners also readied themselves for battle. This time hundreds of southern Kentucky miners traveled the extra distance to come to the assistance of their fellows at Oliver Springs. Within a day the number of miners converging on Oliver Springs swelled to 1,500. These men took control of the town and the surrounding area, cut the telegraph wires, preventing communication between

Oliver Springs and the outside world, and made free and unabashed use of the trains to transport recruits from Jellico and Clinton to Coal Creek.[31]

The miners deemed themselves ready on August 17, at which point a committee again approached Captain Ferris. The representatives proposed the same deal as had the Tracy City miners with their local warden—if Ferris handed over the convicts, the miners would not molest the guards. The delegation further promised not to damage any property except that used by convicts. Despite the arrival of Major Chandler's forces, Ferris readily bowed to the miners' stipulations. The insurgents then gathered the convicts, confiscated the militia's weaponry, and burned the stockade. The miners entrained the convicts and guards for their journey to Nashville, but forced Major Chandler and his men to "foot" their return home. (Colonel Woolford and his company never arrived.) The miners' strategy, a blend of numbers and tact, proved successful.[32]

Once Oliver Springs had surrendered, the miners left for Coal Creek, where their numbers grew to approximately 2,000 men. As late as August 17, caution still prevailed. The east Tennessee workingmen sent Buchanan a telegram, urging him to withdraw the troops at Coal Creek immediately. Instead of making known his decision to cancel the lease with TCIR, the governor imperiously directed the miners to "be orderly, be quiet." At the same time, he sent a message through both Republican congressman Houk and Commissioner of Labor Ford, promising that if the miners could "be patient for a few days, I have no doubt that matters can be satisfactorily arranged according to law." The miners were deeply divided over how to respond to these signals. While some wished to give the governor a chance, others argued that his recommendation to be patient was merely a ruse designed to buy more time, enabling more of the militia to mass.[33]

This latter interpretation was prescient. Within twenty-four hours of his telegram to the Anderson County miners, Buchanan called for volunteers to go to Coal Creek to assist Captain Kellar Anderson. He additionally ordered the sheriff of Davidson County (home to the state's capital of Nashville) to summon 1,000 men and the sheriffs of Knox, Hamilton, Morgan, Roane, Grundy, Marion, and Anderson Counties to recruit 500 men each. The recruitment of the citizen corps fell far short of the governor's expectations. Anderson County's Sheriff Rutherford did nothing, explaining that he was powerless to raise a company. Though Morgan County's Sheriff Holloway recruited his posse, he was unable to arm them with guns or ammunition and had no transportation or rations for them. Until Buchanan could somehow redress these problems, Holloway felt compelled to dismiss his troops. Many of the other sheriffs did not even bother to respond.[34] The behavior of these local law enforcement officials suggests strong independent decision making on their part. Although the governor had finally turned to the military to put down the miners, his maneuverability was limited by local public servants. These officials were in an ambiguous position. They were at once part of the repressive machinery of postbellum government and answerable to a constituency that supported a challenge to the state government's authority.

Although volunteers from rural counties were not forthcoming, those from more faraway and urban centers did offer their services. Roughly 120 men from Chattanooga, 30 from Nashville, and 80 from Knoxville volunteered and left for Coal Creek. The recruits, "comprised of men in the business walks of life," volunteered "from a deep conviction that . . . the state's honor should be redeemed at all hazards." In addition to the civilian contingents, state militia commander in chief Sam T. Carnes left for Coal Creek with 583 regular troops.[35] In ordering out these forces, Governor Buchanan exercised his executive powers to their utmost limit.

One reporter astutely noted that both Union and Confederate veterans presented themselves for duty, thus making the occasion the first time that the State of Tennessee had given blue coats and gray the opportunity to serve together. Another commentator had a deeper sense of the past, reflecting more fully on the irony that the mingling of the old blue and gray presented. Comparing the Civil War to the events in east Tennessee, the editor of the *New Orleans Daily Picayune* maintained that the former struggle "was bad enough but to a war of classes it is a tame affair. The French reign of terror in 1793 and the rise of the Paris Commune in 1871 show what a war of classes is." The editor probably linked these two events since they represented the ultimate horror of class conflict to so many Americans. Yet he need not have looked abroad for a precedent of Civil War veterans intervening on the side of corporations to put down labor strife. The massive nationwide railroad strikes of 1877 should have come readily to mind. These momentous events, together with the compromise election of President Hayes, had symbolized the burial of sectional conflict. Henceforth, northern and southern business elites joined forces to stymie the efforts of workers to imbue the post–Civil War era with their ideas of a just industrial order.[36]

As more and more state troops mobilized, calls for militant action grew louder and more insistent in Coal Creek. Tensions in the town rose considerably. On August 18 the business community suspended trade. Early that same day, citizens gathered in the streets to discuss the situation. Everyone knew of the long-standing animosity between the miners and the 150 soldiers now encamped in Fort Anderson. "They are on the brink of a volcano," one informant told a *Knoxville Journal* reporter. In the early afternoon, a number of relatively minor events tipped the balance in favor of the hardliners. At the request of John Hatmaker and another miners' representative, D. B. Monroe, Captain Anderson left the fort overlooking the Coal Creek stockade. Anderson came to town in the hope of defusing the explosive situation. The mission, however, went horribly wrong. Some reports claimed that Anderson got drunk; others maintained that militant miners threatened to kill him after he refused to release the convicts. In either case, Anderson ended up as a hostage, in the views of some, and in protective custody, in the views of others. The press capitalized on this incident, extolling Captain Anderson's heroism and lambasting the miners.[37] Whatever the precise circumstances surrounding Anderson's internment, the action removed him from the immediate scene.

Later that afternoon, Superintendent John Chumbley and a warden named Gammon agreed to surrender the Knoxville Iron Company stockade and dispatch its 140 convicts to Nashville. The combined absence of the militia's commanding officer and the guards' growing resentment at irregular payment of wages by the convict lessees—their erstwhile paymasters—led Chumbley and Gammon to succumb to the miners' demands.[38] When the pair notified Lieutenant Perry Fyffe, the acting commander of the fort, of their decision, he retorted that if they brought the convicts out of the stockades, he would turn his Gatling gun on them and their demoralized guards without hesitation. Once Fyffe's threat became known, the period of cautious waiting came to an end. Scores of miners began firing on Fort Anderson from positions in the surrounding hills. The miners then charged the fort, giving violent expression to the hatred they had developed for the occupying soldiers. During the attack, two militiamen, Privates Frank Smith and S. L. Waterman, received mortal injuries, and a number of other men were wounded.[39] Press reports leave unclear whether any miners died during the fracas.

The fight was over before any reinforcements could arrive in Coal Creek, with the attackers ceding the field in the late afternoon. For fear that the miners had dynamited the railroad, General Carnes and his regular troops had alighted the train three miles outside of Clinton, the Anderson County seat, and hiked the remainder of the way. Unfamiliar with the country roads, the troops took a wrong turn and ended up close to where they had begun their march. The general finally loaded his men onto a train for the final journey to Coal Creek; but the "walk-about" delayed his arrival. Once again, Woolford's company failed to arrive. While crossing a series of hills near Coal Creek, the commander and his Knoxville volunteers encountered a group of miners. A

Miners in the hills surrounding Coal Creek during the August 18, 1892, assault (*Harper's Weekly*, August 27, 1892, Yale Collection of American Literature, Beinecke Rare Book and Manuscript Library, Yale University)

skirmish ensued, during which two state recruits, Butch Givens (a fifty-year-old Knoxville constable) and John Walthall (a twenty-three-year-old railroad clerk), received fatal wounds. Exhausted and lacking food, water, blankets, or a clear sense of direction, the contingent retreated to Clinton.[40]

Immediately following the rebellion, rumors began to circulate about the questionable competence of the militia, particularly its citizen corps. The skirmish on the hills close to Coal Creek would be revisited in a court martial of Colonel Woolford, whose superior, General Carnes, charged him with cowardice and incompetence. During this inquiry into the state's military offensive, at least three militiamen directly or indirectly suggested that Givens and Walthall lost their lives at the hands of their fellow troops—an opinion shared by General Carnes. The military court learned that the miners were "across a cornfield west of the ridge" and thus too far away to have caused these deaths. More damning testimony came when one witness described the formation that the men had assumed—"all the men . . . were very much mixed . . . [they were] something in the shape of a hollow square." Thus Woolford had arranged his men in such a way as to place many of them in the firing line of their compatriots.[41]

The regular troops also demonstrated considerable incompetence. Again Carnes took the lead in casting aspersions on the capabilities of a lower-ranking officer—this time his second in command, Major Chandler. The commander in chief admonished what he perceived as Chandler's skittish behavior, claiming that a junior officer had to assume command when Chandler became "wild" and "scared." The major, Carnes maintained, had made a "fool" of himself. Had the junior officer's levelheadedness not prevailed, the militia "would have had a desperate engagement with the trees and rocks on the opposite mountain."[42] The two deaths within Fyffe's ranks—those of Waterman and Smith—were shrouded in mystery. Initial newspaper coverage suggested that these men were fatally injured by the premature and accidental discharge of their own weaponry. Though Smith's death would be revisited in D. B. Monroe's trial following the rebellion and attributed to Monroe, early press reports ascribed all the militiamen's deaths to the "carelessness or frightened condition of the militia themselves."[43]

The individuals who led the east Tennessee revolts remain somewhat shrouded in mystery. Throughout the 1892 rebellion, the press did not mention the whereabouts of the men in charge of the 1891 campaigns—Eugene Merrell, Marcena Ingraham, or George Irish; nor, for the most part, did they single out other persons as directing the miners' actions. After the rebellion, when the wheels of the legal system began to grind, state officials did identity some leaders. The man who became most visible was a relative newcomer to east Tennessee, D. B. Monroe. Born in Ohio, Monroe first moved with his family to Michigan. After serving a four-year stint in the Union army, Monroe returned to Michigan where he lived until 1885. Thereafter he traveled south, settling in Chattanooga for two years and then Alabama for five. He arrived in Coal Creek in February 1892. Journalists described the fifty-two-year-old Monroe as "far above the average miner in point of intelligence and . . . very cunning." They also pointed to his compelling presence. "He makes a very agreeable companion and an excellent story teller. He [is] a man of remarkable physical powers and is in every way well qualified for a leader of outlaws."[44]

Another name that participants reluctantly mentioned in connection with the rebellion was that of John Hatmaker—the individual who approached Captain Ferris on August 16 to ask for a truce. Thirty-seven years old in 1892, Hatmaker had lived in Coal Creek for at least twelve years. One newspaperman described him as a "small man of dark complexion." If he had ever owned any property, he no longer did by the 1890s. The absence of assets to his name, however, did not mark him as a person with few commitments. A married man, Hatmaker took his civic duties seriously, consistently paying his poll taxes, presumably in the belief that the economic troubles of east Tennessee's miners could still find a solution in the political arena.[45]

Instead of concentrating on the identification of the insurrection's leaders, newspapers primarily conveyed images of an unrestrained and reckless "mob" that tore down telegraph wires and dynamited railroads. The *Knoxville Journal*, owned by land and railroad mogul E. J. Sanford, adopted a now familiar tactic of denigrating the miners' independent organizations as lawless threats to justice and order. Sanford's paper, the largest east Tennessee publication and a Republican broadsheet, dubbed the men "a society of anarchists."[46] As evidence of a secret association, the *Journal* pointed to an oath taken by the miners, which allegedly bound them to a "covenant" made before "Almighty God" and which committed them to abide by the orders of the organization's leaders.[47]

Description of the miners in most commercial papers as an immoral and aimless mob moved labor spokesmen to criticize press coverage. Indeed, the *United Mine Workers Journal*'s editor went so far as to lament the inequities engendered by the concentration of the media in the hands of private corporations. "In this Tennessee trouble," the editor bemoaned, "we have again presented to us an illustration of the stupendous advantage capital wields in the possession of the channels of news of the country. . . . From the beginning to end of this turmoil not a sentence has appeared in the daily press which gave square and honest facts, but instead have contained a sinister twist prejudicial to the side of the miners."[48] One of the long-term effects of the rebellion would be George Ford's establishment of the *Knoxville Independent* as a voice for labor in 1894. More immediately, though, east Tennessee's residents faced a barrage of "bad" press. Whether emanating from more sinister motives or from a simple desire to sell newspapers, reporters embellished their stories. Although militants did commandeer trains, they never laid dynamite on railroad tracks or sabotaged the railways in other ways, as several papers asserted. Similarly, journalistic predictions that the miners would go on a rampage, indiscriminately destroying property, never came to fruition.[49]

The Watchwords of Law and Order

Though some political commentators and labor activists tried to keep the convict-lease system at the center of public debate after the 1892 rebellion, most Tennesseans focused on the consequences of the miners' insurrectionary tactics, and especially on the deaths of the four militiamen. Responses generally derived from a visceral anger at what people assumed was the miners' handiwork. The public took for granted that the miners had killed these men; popular outrage quickly followed. The *Knoxville Journal*, which had long touted law and order as the most fundamental prerequisite of securing investment for the New South, helped to crystallize this transformation in attitude. Its reporters constantly referred to the "red handed anarchism" of the miners, contrasting it to the "lofty patriotism" of John Walthall.[50] Thousands of men now offered their services to volunteer posses, where before only dozens or at best hundreds had done so. Journalists frequently counted the "best men" in the numbers of these would-be militiamen.[51]

But extra civilian volunteers turned out not to be needed to suppress the Coal Creek miners. As soon as General Carnes arrived in Coal Creek on August 19, he demanded the return of Captain Anderson and the surrender of the town, vowing that a refusal would be met by the full complement of his troops and all of the weapons at their disposal. No one offered resistance; the men holding Captain Anderson handed him over unhurt. Carnes then ordered his troops to arrest the miners and their supporters. A couple of days later the general sent all volunteer troops home.[52] During the next two weeks, soldiers scoured the countryside smoking out abandoned mines in search of insurrectionaries. The militiamen traveled north to the Kentucky-Tennessee border town of Jellico, arresting all whom they considered rebels.[53]

Reports of the militia's ineptitude contrasted markedly with several accounts of the miners' behavior. Observers as prominent as Congressman Houk praised the miners for their military discipline and organization.[54] The absence of indiscriminate violence and the efficiency of the miners' military endeavors both support Houk's characterization. With over 150 Civil War veterans living in the mining towns of Briceville, Coal Creek, and Oliver Springs, such discipline and organization came relatively easily to these men.[55]

Given the abilities of the miners and the weaknesses of the militia, the quick capitulation of the former is puzzling. In spite of clear advantage in numbers and organization, the miners offered absolutely no resistance to General Carnes. In the absence of evidence that directly indicates why the miners chose to back off, two possibilities suggest themselves. Throughout the miners' struggle to free themselves from convict labor—whether in their direct appeals to government or in their militant actions—the Anderson County men had sought to right an injustice and to gain a voice in government. They voiced no intention of overcoming governmental authority. During the past fifteen months, they had argued that public officials were behaving improperly or that outside forces (such as monopolists) were corrupting the accountability of their republican government. This world view—one that easily jelled with their defense of the Union some thirty years previously—encouraged the miners to refrain from directly engaging state troops.

Yet this same worldview also allowed that long-standing usurpations might justify armed resistance; such resistance offered the ultimate protection of infringed rights. Hundreds of miners, moreover, had clearly lost both faith and trust in their government and governor. Restraint in opposition to perceived subversion of liberty almost certainly received a boost from considerations of prudence. Though Governor Buchanan had not requested assistance from federal troops, he had requisitioned Tennessee's quota of arms and ammunition that Washington set aside for support of the individual state militia.[56] In addition to knowing about this limited federal aid, east Tennesseans were acutely aware of the recent use of federal army regulars in the Buffalo switchmen's strike and of the overwhelming use of state troops in the showdown between the Carnegie Steel Company and the Homestead steelworkers. The outcome of these conflicts surely contributed to the miners' refusal to engage in pitched battle.[57]

Carnes's troops continued to encounter little or no resistance in their "mopping up" operations. The general nonetheless sought to augment his powers to deal summarily with those whom he believed had transgressed the authority of the state. On August 22 he asked the governor to call another special session of the general assembly, this time to declare martial law in east Tennessee's Anderson, Morgan, and Campbell Counties as well as in mid-Tennessee's Grundy and Marion Counties. Carnes sought such a declaration, even though "all was quiet and arrests go on at a rapid rate," because he did not trust local authorities to reestablish control of the mining towns or mete out rebellion-related punishments. The general doubted that local sheriffs' offices, courts, and juries would deliver indictments and convictions against those who had flaunted governmental authority and overturned managerial prerogatives.[58]

Carnes was thwarted in his appeal, as John A. Pitts, the governor's legal counsel, quickly squelched his call for military rule. Invoking the 1870 constitution, which prohibited "unrestricted power of military officers or others, to dispose of the persons, liberties or property of the citizens," Pitts informed Buchanan that conditions in the coal towns did not justify a suspension of civil law. "Smarting under the abuses of the executive prerogative during and succeeding the late war," Pitts explained, the constitution's framers went to "an extreme on this question which now, unfortunately, most seriously cripples the power of the State to deal with crises of this kind." Little more than two decades after Democrats had written the 1870 constitution to restrict Republican authority, that document repeatedly constrained the ability of Democrats to squash a rebellion in Republican east Tennessee.

The governor's attorney, however, was not unsympathetic to Carnes's desire to prosecute the miners vigorously. Aware that local juries might be lenient with individuals whom the state arrested, Pitts advised Carnes to send the accused to jails in Knoxville, Chattanooga, and Nashville. Once they were ensconced in these major urban centers, prosecutors could charge them with any one of a number of crimes. Shrewdly playing on the social tension between city and countryside, Pitts counseled the general that "plenty of persons willing to prosecute will be found at these places."[59]

Although General Carnes could not remake the 1870 constitution, his behavior indicated slight regard for that document. When Anderson County's sheriff refused to get involved in what he perceived as illegal detentions, Carnes assumed control. The general felt compelled, according to his own testimony, "to practically establish martial law."[60] Relying on the testimony of informants such as the notorious Bony Craig, a Knoxville Iron Company guard and nemesis of the miners, Carnes's troops arrested between 200 and 500 men within a week. Most arraignments were held in local churches and schools. The state regulars singled out members of the Knights of Labor and UMWA for particular punishment, ransacking their homes and destroying whatever they found that belonged to the two organizations. Devoid of public support following the deaths of the four militiamen, the miners could do little more than make these iniquities known to the national offices of their unions.[61]

The state militia vigorously attacked the miners and their supporters in their public commentary as well as in their official duties. Carnes, now hailed as a "Napoleonic genius" by the South's elite, took the lead in this effort. He adopted one of several age-old techniques for impugning the character of Americans who bucked authority. Eschewing the more common postbellum references to the intrigues of foreign radicals, the slavishness of European immigrants, or the cabals of domestic secret societies, Carnes chose the "uncivilized" Indian as his bogey. He characterized the miners as "mean, cowardly, bullying outlaws, narrow-minded and intensely prejudiced against anything that smatters of authority, and without the manhood to back their opinions save when they possess every advantage. They are more treacherous than Indians and nearly as shiftless."[62] In this commentary, the general strove to wrest Tennessee's frontier heritage from the miners, placing them outside its confines. For Carnes, the free laborers of east Tennessee's mining communities were not just Indians; lacking any attributes of nobility, courage, or "man-

General Samuel T. Carnes
(Tatom, "Press Clippings")

hood," the miners resembled only "treacherous," "shiftless" Indians. In other words, the miners possessed only the negative characteristics of the white Tennessean's savage.

By the end of the summer in 1892, Tennessee miners had pursued several routes in their quest to rid themselves of the convict lease. Initially, they had pressed their employers to redress their economic grievances. When those entreaties received scant attention, they lobbied the state legislature and its executive, urging them to bring the miners justice and secure their constitutional rights. Where appropriate, these workingmen took their case to the courts of their state. After political and legal avenues seemed closed, some of the miners tried to solve their problems through cooperative ventures. None of these efforts, however, gave the miners satisfaction. Committed to the destruction of the convict lease, the free laborers in Tennessee's mines periodically determined that armed rebellion would provide the only way that they could achieve their objectives.

Despite the fears of the popular press, the miners never ceased to display considerable discipline in their attacks on the convict lease. Though Tennessean and southern Kentucky miners commandeered trains and demolished stockades used to house convicts, they never went on a rampage, indiscriminately destroying company or private property. Throughout the revolts, many of the residents of Tennessee's mining communities were guided by an image of themselves as homeowners and citizens. Implicit in both labels were rights and responsibilities. Rights included work, a decent community life, and a responsive government. Responsibilities entailed a respect for private property and for the ultimate authority of legitimate government. For the miners, political dissent was circumscribed. The mining communities could not conceive of themselves in full-fledged rebellion; they could not engage state troops in battle.

Like Buffalo's railwaymen or Homestead's steelworkers, who also tried to control their destiny through collective action, the miners of Tennessee soon faced grave consequences for their militance, even though that militance stopped short of outright war. Governmental officials readily answered the call of corporate leaders to silence their fractious workers. Neither the men at the helm of government nor those who ran Tennessee's coal mines could abide the challenges that these workingmen posed. The former could not accept such defiance of legal authority; the latter could not accept such encroachment on the prerogatives of ownership. Local labor leaders came to understand that the mineowners could count the state militia in their corner. Three and a half months after the rebellion, the second president of the UMWA's District 19, S. P. Herron, remarked that "if the militia are the tools of corporations to overawe and keep in subjection the laboring people—and it seems they are— we must learn the fact and prepare ourselves for the coming danger."[63] Only the passage of time would show how well Herron's fellow workers absorbed his message and adapted to the new conditions in Tennessee.

There was an important difference, though, between this latest rebellion and most labor conflicts in the late-nineteenth-century United States, including the previous uprisings in Tennessee's coalfields. The 1892 coalition between Tennessee's government and its coal operators came about in spite of a growing disenchantment that each of these allies felt for the other. The previous two years had lessened TCIR's commitment to the convict lease. Many company officials no longer viewed this contractual arrangement with the state as a panacea for its labor problems, especially since the state proved unwilling to provide what company executives viewed as adequate protection for mining property and convicts. The destruction of stockades, the disruption of mining operations, and the need for extra guards all contributed to the perceived unprofitability of the convict lease. The depressed state of the U.S. economy made the commitment to convict labor more of an albatross for TCIR. The company could always lay off free workers or put them on reduced time; but the care and feeding of the convicts constituted an essentially fixed cost.

Motive, then, certainly existed for TCIR to find a way out of its contract with the state. Indeed, for over half a year the company had refused to pay the state its quarterly rental fees for the convicts. This refusal did not sit well with Governor Buchanan, who had to worry about both fiscal realities and political pressures. Buchanan's estimation of the company took a further turn for the worse in the weeks leading up to and following the rebellion; the governor came to suspect the company of intentionally provoking the miners and doing little to contain what had become an explosive situation. Whether or not TCIR engaged in a conscious attempt to foster rebellion, Buchanan no longer viewed the company as acting in good faith. These tensions would continue for years to come, contributing to a transformation in Tennessee's approach to penal administration.

The revolt exposed more than the strains between Tennessee's government and its largest coal company; it also revealed fundamental shortcomings in the government at Nashville. Buchanan encountered substantial impediments when he tried to resolve the conflict militarily. Local law enforcement officers, whether from Republican east Tennessee or Democratic mid-Tennessee, demonstrated considerable reluctance to carry out the governor's orders. These sheriffs owed their positions to electoral victories in the communities that they served and saw no reason to jeopardize their chances of future success. Some acted from narrow self-interest; most understood the plight of the miners and sympathized with them.

Difficulty in marshaling troops and ensuring the compliance of the sheriffs, if not their loyalty, was only one of Buchanan's military problems. The state militia was supposed to serve as the government's ultimate guarantor of its authority, but it performed at a level well below the mythic standard of southern military prowess. This problematic implementation of executive policy was coupled with scant regard for constitutional limitations on the exercise of military force. General Carnes acted with impunity on his arrival in Coal Creek. The general set up a virtual state of martial law, destroyed private property belonging to the miners' organizations, and pursued suspected participants of the rebellion across the state line, theoretically beyond the limits of his authority. Carnes rode roughshod over the law because he had no faith that local courts would deliver justice, or at least his version of justice.

The late-nineteenth-century Tennessee state was weak and fractured. Able to enact one repressive law after another, officials in Nashville could not always ensure that legislation or executive orders would be enforced. As the growing tensions between the state and TCIR would mold events following the 1892 rebellions, so too would the weaknesses of a government often divided against itself.

Alias Capias [not to be found]
—Docket entry for Cal Disney
    and scores of other individuals
    charged with insurrection in
    east Tennessee, Anderson
    County Execution Dockets,
    1892–97

[This company] denies that it
alone should be made to bear the
expense of putting down an insurrection so formidable . . . that the
complainants themselves admit it
humiliated the State.
—Answer to Original Bill,
    October 1, 1892, Trial Record,
    51, *Buchanan v. TCIR* (1897)

CHAPTER 8

Aftermath

General Carnes's success in suppressing the August 1892 revolts left Tennessee once again free from overt challenges to state authority. But the peace that obtained in the state's mining communities did not resolve the conflicts among free miners, their employers, and governmental officials. The problem that persuaded thousands of workingmen to take up arms against state and corporate authority continued to afflict Tennessee's free miners. These men still faced ruinous competition from convict laborers.

Fresh disputes joined long-standing areas of contention in post-rebellion Tennessee. The attempt to settle complex economic and political controversies through resort to arms only created additional dilemmas. The miners' latest marches on the stockades and the military reaction to them saddled Tennessee officials and mining operators with two crucial problems. The first concerned the individuals who had flouted state law. Convinced that indulgence toward lawbreakers would only foster new outbreaks, governmental leaders sought to punish the lawless and bring the miners to heel. With the November state elections around the corner, calls for the restoration of law and order in east Tennessee acquired a special urgency. All three gubernatorial hopefuls— Buchanan, who announced his independent candidacy in mid-August; Peter Turney, the Supreme Court judge who consistently ruled against the miners and who owed his selection by the Democratic Party to dissatisfaction with Buchanan's handling of the mining crisis; and George W. Winstead, the Republican nominee—presented themselves as the man to restore Tennessee's honor through vigorous prosecution of insurrectionaries. The second problem involved the enormous expenses and losses generated by the miners' revolts. Someone had to pay for razed buildings and militia paychecks, while the Tennessee Coal, Iron, and Railroad Company wanted recompense for lost workdays and the diminished value of the convict lease.

In addition to new areas of discord, the aftermath of the 1892 rebellions witnessed a dramatic diminution in the miners' ability to set the direction and pace of events. Through August of that year, the miners had frequently compelled Nashville officials and company managers to respond to their initiatives. When the miners capitulated to General Carnes's troops, they allowed the state government to seize control of the situation in mid- and east Tennessee. Governmental officials took advantage of the opening, assigning immediate priority to the punishment of the rebellious and the extraction of payment for the havoc they had created. The fate of the convict lease would not disappear from Tennessee politics, but resolution of that issue would take a backseat to these other concerns.

The miners did not wholly lose their ability to shape the course of Tennessee's industrial future. Indeed, worsening relations between TCIR and the state after the 1892 revolts offered these workingmen some opportunity to further their interests. What they made of this opportunity would turn on age-old determinants of union effectiveness—the extent of the miners' organization, the quality of their leadership, and the degree of solidarity within their ranks.

Crimes of Rebellion

Immediately following the August revolts, pressure began to build to end the convict lease and to punish the miners who had flouted the law. Each of the three gubernatorial candidates promised the abolition of the lease system. With the repercussions of the miners' rebellions costing Tennesseans sums of money far in excess of the rental fees paid by TCIR, such promises came cheaply. None of the nominees, however, wished to be seen as "soft" on those

TENNESSEE'S SHAME!

Convicts in the Coal Creek Mines.

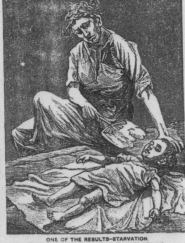

CONVICTS AT WORK.

ONE OF THE RESULTS—STARVATION.
The father and husband has gone to a distant State for work.

Vote for TURNEY for Governor and WELCKER for Congress, if you wish this to continue.

Vote for WINSTEAD for Governor and HOUK for Congress, if you wish to abolish this great crime, which has so long been committed in order to raise Democratic campaign funds from the lessees

1892 Republican campaign poster ("Ephemera," McClung Collection)

who had recently challenged the state's authority.[1] Buchanan, who launched his independent bid to retain the governor's mansion after losing the Democratic nomination to Peter Turney, was particularly intent on taking a tough stance against those who had engaged in the rebellion. Although the governor needed the votes of Tennessee's working people, he feared the political implications of the miners' rebellions, which were portrayed as a "disgrace" in the Democratic dailies. Decisiveness and firm results were needed to counter his growing reputation as a "blundering politician."[2]

East Tennessee's Republican politicians similarly offered paeans to law and order, even as they lambasted the Democrats as a party beholden to the penitentiary ring and responsible for "Tennessee's Shame," the convict lease. Republican bosses had long grown impatient with their constituents in Anderson County's mining communities, believing that they were ruining regional economic prospects. Business interests now coalesced with political concerns. As the election approached, the largest Republican paper in east Tennessee tried to dispel any notion that politics entered the predominantly Republican courts in the region. "If any man wished the greatest, deepest, most diabolical harm to the republican party," the *Knoxville Journal* editorialized, "he could do no more than make it appear that republicans sympathized with miners in their wild, reckless, rebellion against the state."[3]

As Republicans carefully distanced themselves from the recent acts of insurrection, Democratic publicists argued that the miners' revolts served as an extremely dangerous model for Tennessee's African American minority. According to the editor of the *Nashville American*, the Briceville miners' example was prompting the state's Colored Farmers' Alliance to contemplate militant strikes and boycotts. The implication was that Tennessee's racial hierarchy depended both on a Democratic victory in November and stern treatment of the miners. Turney won the election in November, but the tenor of the campaign ensured that the state government would continue to take a hard line regardless of who won the governorship.[4]

With political pressure mounting and Carnes's state guards on standby in east Tennessee, Anderson County's grand jury began to indict participants in the rebellion. Local judges took the *Knoxville Journal*'s admonishments to heart, using their courtrooms to teach the miners a lesson about the requirements of Tennessee law. In so doing, they indicated their hostility to labor organizations. The courts refused to accept the testimony of any member of the Knights of Labor. Every potential witness, one Knight complained, was "told that he belongs to an oath-bound organization sworn to defend each other and his evidence is not accepted."[5] This ruling essentially held that the miners' organizations were illicit and outside the bounds of republican thought and practice; it also heralded that Anderson County was once again ready for business.

Throughout the final four months of 1892 and the whole of 1893, the local grand jury handed down scores of indictments against alleged insurrectionaries. The judges' hostility toward the Knights of Labor and the avalanche of indictments, however, tell only a partial story. Of the roughly 2,000 men who picked up their Winchesters and confronted the state at Oliver Springs and Coal Creek, fewer than 300 ever faced criminal indictments. The vast majority of miners who took part in the revolts never faced the possibility of a conviction.

While most miners avoided legal thickets, the 294 who found themselves enmeshed in them—including seven blacks—faced curiously similar treatment from the grand jury. The indictments themselves seem to indicate that the grand jury carefully differentiated among the crimes that these miners allegedly committed. The charges faced by the miners included "felony," "treason," "conspiracy," and "riot." The few accused of treason were charged with enlisting or persuading others to join in the battle against the state militia. A close reading of the other indictments, however, suggests an essential uniformity to them. The grand jury universally accused the miners of "hindering, interrupting and interfering with the workings of the penitentiary convicts . . . against the peace and dignity of the State." Without any obvious rationale, the grand jury members then characterized such behavior as "felonious," or as constituting "conspiracy" or "riot."[6]

In September 1892, the circuit court convened in the Anderson County seat of Clinton to begin the process of pursuing the 294 indictments, with Judge W. R. Hicks presiding. The forty-nine-year-old judge came from a modest farming family in Anderson County and had fought for the Union army. At the end of the war, he embarked on a career in law. In 1886 Hicks achieved one of the highest honors that his east Tennessee compatriots could bestow upon him, gaining election as circuit court judge for seven counties.[7]

Hicks's charge to the jury did not reveal any special sympathy with the electorate who had time and again returned him to the bench. On the contrary, he took special care not to allow "passion, party, or creed" to color his instructions. He reminded jurors that the lessees had lawfully confined the state convicts in a number of the county's mines, as the legality of subleasing convicts had been settled by Tennessee's highest court. In addition, he told the citizens seated in the jury box that since September 1891 the obstruction of convict work was illegal. (The 1891 extra legislative session had specifically enacted this law to prevent the miners from attacking the stockades.) If the accused had violated this law, the judge continued, the jurors were oath-bound to find the lawbreakers guilty. From the bench, Hicks confidently maintained that his lengthy instructions would settle "that almost infamous and yet oft repeated question, 'What will the courts and jurors of Anderson county do?' "[8] The implication was that Anderson County's judges and citizen-jurors would uphold the sanctity of law against the miners' assaults.

Judge Hicks, however, spoke too confidently. A large number of miners accused of interfering with the convicts managed to slip through Anderson County's legal dragnet. The miners' trials began in September 1892, while parts of Anderson County were still under military occupation, and dragged on for four years. The major reason that the cases remained on the docket so long was that many miners simply failed to appear in court. Literally hundreds of Coal Creek, Briceville, and Oliver Springs residents left town following the 1892 rebellion. The vast majority of those who picked up and left were not property owners, though they had been assiduous about paying their poll taxes.[9] Choosing to skip town or simply to avoid an appearance in court proved to be a wise

Militia Company C at Coal Creek after the August 1892 rebellion (Tennessee National Guard, *Souvenir of Company "C"*)

strategy. Once the militia left Coal Creek in late 1893, the zealousness of court officials to pursue the miners dropped precipitously. In 1896 Judge Hicks finally agreed to drop the charges against any miner who had disregarded his court summons, so long as that individual agreed to pay court costs.[10] For scores of other miners who did answer their indictments in court, the punishments for their actions were slight. In the six to nine months after the rebellion, these miners submitted a guilty plea to the charge of rioting. Their punishment consisted merely of having to pay court costs and a fine.[11] The legal treatment of the miners' leadership largely paralleled that of the rank and file. The grand jury dubbed several miners as "leaders" when handing down indictments. But for the most part, this designation seems to have been as random as the characterization of criminal activity had been; and being characterized as a leader generally had no implications for a defendant's ability to ignore his summons or successfully offer a guilty plea.

Four men received closer scrutiny as possible masterminds of the rebellion. Two of the four—John Hatmaker and George Irish—were well known, both having assumed public roles in community affairs the previous year and both having conspicuously "resigned" from their leadership positions the evening before the October 1891 revolt. Hatmaker had undoubtedly participated in the 1892 attack at Coal Creek, as he had sought permission from Captain Ferris to remove the wounded under a white flag and, along with D. B. Monroe, had later persuaded Captain Anderson to leave the fort to come and discuss the crisis with the Coal Creek community. Hatmaker's resignation in October 1891 had plainly been a ruse to disguise his ongoing activism and avoid arrest for interference with convict miners. While Hatmaker's prosecution resulted from continued public prominence, that of George Irish's did not. Throughout 1892, his name was consistently absent from press reports.

Despite their apparently very different roles in the 1892 rebellion, both men joined the ranks of those who escaped censure from the legal system. In September 1892 Hatmaker was designated a leader and indicted for felony. Though he posted a $1,000 bond in January 1893, he repeatedly failed to appear in court. Six times his case was delayed; yet he never forfeited his bond. Only in June 1894 did he admit guilt. With the public glare long faded and the militia long gone, the court merely insisted that he pay the costs of his case.[12] Irish's case similarly dragged on until 1894. Throughout the year and a half following the rebellion, he remained free on a bond of $2,000. When his case came to trial in September 1893, he entered a plea of not guilty. The jury failed to reach a verdict. A second trial, in early February 1894, found him not guilty.[13]

The other two men charged as ringleaders—S. D. Moore and D. B. Monroe—were not so lucky. Moore, a Baptist minister from Briceville, had served on several miners' committees during 1891 and 1892 and faced a jury trial for conspiracy and felony. Prosecutors offered two major pieces of evidence against him—that he had made comments expressing the legitimacy of the miners' taking the law into their own hands and that witnesses had seen him carrying a Winchester at the town depot just before the actual revolt. At the end of Moore's trial, Judge Hicks gave a jury charge that strongly implied the minister's guilt.[14] The jury returned a guilty verdict, and Hicks sentenced him to one year's imprisonment.

Why the jury and Judge Hicks singled Moore out of the thousands of people arrested and the hundreds indicted remains a mystery. He appears to have been a settled family man and respected member of the Briceville community. Far from being an itinerant preacher, he owned a 243-acre farm in the Briceville district, which remained in his name at least until 1909. During his indictment he had had the support of at least two relatively substantial Coal Creek property owners, both of whom helped him post his bond. Perhaps Moore suffered simply because witnesses were willing to come forward against him.[15]

Moore's trial received little public attention. By contrast, the prosecution of Monroe generated substantial excitement throughout Tennessee. Soon after Monroe was arrested, the press dubbed him "anarchist Monroe," "leader Monroe," and "big chief Monroe." Within a couple of days of beginning its work, the grand jury handed down an indictment against him, alleging that he had led a "mob" who had "feloniously" interfered with the workings of the state convicts. A second indictment charged Monroe with the murder of Frank Smith, one of the two militiamen killed at Fort Anderson. The court held Monroe without bail.[16]

The state's prosecutor brought the same evidence against Monroe before the grand jury and at his trials. The state showed that Monroe had gone to Oliver Springs with a Coal Creek contingent that sought to release the convicts; that he had ridden back on the commandeered train's engine (an action that the prosecution portrayed as signifying his elevated status); and that during the crisis he had visited Captain Anderson at the fort and met with Captain Chumbley, the superintendent of the convicts. In addition, trial evidence demonstrated that Monroe had conferred with Congressman Houk, that he signed a note easing the passage of a number of men through the miners' pickets, and, most damning, that he had included the word "chief" after his name when he signed the pass.[17]

Over the course of his defense Monroe depicted himself as a peacemaker. The onetime northerner explained that he had gone to Oliver Springs with the express purpose of preventing any loss of life or destruction of property. Monroe acknowledged having been in good spirits on the return journey; he felt as if he and others had held some of the more militant miners in check. Monroe also had explanations for the other allegations. He testified that he had visited Captain Anderson to find out whether Governor Buchanan had ordered the troops to withdraw. This claim does not seem unreasonable. A three-man committee from the miners had met with Buchanan to discuss the militia's departure just a week prior to the east Tennessee revolt. Indeed, Buchanan had been favorably disposed to the request, though the Tracy City rebellion had intervened before he could act. Newspapers had reported at the time of the visit that Anderson and Monroe had had a very amicable discussion. After discussing the business at hand, they had drunk "corn juice" together.[18]

Monroe also readily explained the Chumbley and Houk meetings. The first encounter had taken place at Chumbley's request after the superintendent of the convicts had asked for "good men" to come and discuss the terms on which he would hand over the convicts. Monroe and John Hightower, the proprietor of a Coal Creek hotel and a resident of the community for the past twenty-three years, had served as the community's representatives. As with his other meetings, Monroe swore that he had met with Congressman Houk solely to seek a peaceful resolution to the tense situation in east Tennessee. The most incriminating evidence the prosecutors brought against Monroe was the pass he had signed, calling himself "chief." Monroe strenuously denied that he was the overall leader of the miners. He testified that he had signed the note in his capacity as head of a group of thirty to forty men whose objective was to "suppress promiscuous shooting." Monroe added that he made his rounds in that capacity unarmed.[19]

Monroe did not solely base his defense on his answers to specific allegations. His lawyers further challenged the legality of the indictment itself. In so doing, the defense appealed to one of the most fundamental principles of the common law—that any criminal charges must be clear and specific in nature. Monroe's attorneys emphasized that the indictment could hardly have been more vague. It did not name the convicts whose work Monroe allegedly interrupted. It made no reference to the name of the branch prisons where the avowed events occurred, or to the manner in which Monroe interfered with the convicts' work, or to the names of people Monroe apparently led. In short, the indictment did not make sufficiently clear of what Monroe stood accused. Monroe was not alone in his invocation of the common law. S. D. Moore attempted a similar defense.[20] Neither man, though, achieved any success with this line of argument.

Monroe's first trial for "feloniously" interfering with the convicts ended in a mistrial; ten jurors voted for acquittal and two for conviction. Unlike George Irish, whose experience of a hung jury signaled the end of his troubles, Monroe would see much more of Anderson County's courtrooms. The state retried Monroe in February 1893 for obstructing the convicts' work and six months later for murdering Frank Smith. Both times the juries convicted him, though the second set of jurors reduced Monroe's conviction to involuntary manslaughter. Monroe received sentences of two and five years respectively.[21]

The grossly different treatment that befell the men accused of being leaders in the rebellion raises the possibility that an unspoken understanding obtained among the miners, the county's law enforcement officers, and the prosecutors. The county and state had strong motivations to find a scapegoat, someone who would take the blame for the recent troubles and thereby expunge the blot of lawlessness from the region. As a newcomer to east Tennessee, Monroe served admirably in such a role. This man, who quickly made a strong impression on the miners and townspeople of Coal Creek, had arrived in the town only six months before the revolt. He had also never mined coal prior to taking up residence in George Black's Coal Creek boardinghouse. The fact that Monroe did not have deep roots in Anderson County either through relatives or homeownership rendered him vulnerable. Indeed, these blemishes on his character formed the basis of the closing remarks by state prosecutors in his second felony trial. Rather than tackle the evidence, both Judge Young and J. A. Fowler played on this theme of the outsider. Judge Young denounced Monroe as an anarchist. He observed that the defendant "had been everywhere but no where long," implying that Monroe was a "bird of passage," "a foreign substance brought to Coal Creek to stir up strife." Young finally appealed to the jury as "Anderson County men," urging them "to punish this man for coming into Anderson County and getting Anderson County boys into trouble."[22]

J. A. Fowler's argument was a little more wide-ranging in its accusations and even more full of innuendo, half-truths, and outright falsehoods. Following Young's central theme, Fowler urged the jury to let Monroe know that "a man from Michigan can't rule in east Tennessee." In addition, Fowler painted two images that opponents would invoke to undermine labor leaders for generations to come. He first raised the issue of patriotism, asserting that Monroe, as leader of a "mob," had ordered the miners to "fire on the United States flag which floated at Camp Anderson." Monroe, in the prosecuting attorney's mind, was a traitor, a "Benedict Arnold." Second, Fowler created a picture of Monroe as a man who had taken money from the poor miners and "had bought fine whisky and cigars for himself." The jurors concurred that they could not let this whisky-guzzling, corrupt, and unpatriotic outsider go free.[23]

Monroe's seven-year sentence, then, may not have been unrelated to the limited prosecution of the rank-and-file miners of east Tennessee. The imposition of the former may have eased the way for a more casual treatment of the latter.[24] Partially as a result of that more casual treatment, the legal repercussions of rebellion did not turn out to be a devastating affair for the vast majority of miners. The endless entries of *nolle prosequi* and *alias capias* into the docket books suggested that the prosecutors either withdrew cases or that the alleged perpetrator could not be found. Local government in east Tennessee simply proved unable or unwilling to bring most indicted miners to account. Whether or not the state government wished to prosecute the miners to the law's fullest extent mattered little. The miners could simply evade legal proceedings, especially if local courts and sheriffs felt sympathetic to the individuals concerned.[25]

Although the legal ramifications of the revolt primarily forced miners into the dock, one other participant in the rebellion found himself indicted for actions during the uprising. The state accused T. L. Craig, nicknamed Bony Craig, of killing a black miner, Jake Whitson. The animosity that led to Craig's indictment had a long history. Shortly after his arrival in Coal Creek in 1881, the Knoxville Iron Company employed Craig as an assistant mine boss. He remained with the company until June 1892, when he became a prison guard at the Coal Creek stockade. Prior to his formal employment by the State of Tennessee, Craig had engaged in "detective" work for Captain Kellar Anderson and Lieutenant Perry Fyffe. Fyffe eventually mustered the Coal Creek guard into the state troops to protect him should he run afoul of civilian law. Craig was "outspoken" in his disapproval of the miners' rebelliousness and was known as one of the few citizens in the Coal Creek vicinity to espouse the militia's cause.

The bitterness that the Coal Creek community already felt toward Bony Craig only intensified after the miners' surrender to General Carnes. Craig joined Carnes on a trip to Briceville to identify insurrectionaries after the general had specifically asked him for assistance in capturing miners who had joined in rebellion. From Carnes's point of view, the excursion was successful; between 80 and 100 men were arrested.[26] The August 20 trip, however, marked the beginning of a stressful period in Craig's life.

As the train carrying the troops from Coal Creek pulled into the Briceville station, Craig spotted Jake Whitson, who had consistently evinced contempt for the militia, and called for him to advance. Whether Whitson obeyed this order remains unclear. Three shots rang out, including one fired by Craig, and the black miner fell dead. Many decades after the rebellion, W. M. Scoggins recalled the widely held belief of many Anderson County citizens about this incident—the troops did not order Whitson to halt; they simply shot him in "cold blood." A number of soldiers maintained to the contrary that Whitson had hesitated and then turned as though he intended to flee. Captain Kellar Anderson, the man in command of Militia Hill, additionally observed that the bullet which killed Whitson came from a Springfield rifle whereas Craig carried a Winchester. The bullet that the prison guard had fired lodged in the deceased's leg and was not the cause of death.[27]

Despite the ambiguities surrounding Whitson's demise, Anderson County officials prosecuted Bony Craig for murder in the first degree. Initially indicted in October 1892, Craig was convicted of murder in the second degree in February 1894. His conviction carried an eleven-year sentence in the state penitentiary—a sentence far in excess of that given D. B. Monroe.[28] No sooner had the jury returned its verdict than appeals for pardon flooded into Governor Turney's office, including requests from General Carnes, Kellar Anderson, John Chumbley, Coal Creek's justice of the peace, its prison chaplain and prison doctor, the guards and soldiers who had been on duty in Coal Creek during the rebellion, and J. C. J. Williams, the Knoxville lawyer and Democrat who had acted on the miners' behalf in challenging the legality of subleasing in

August 1891. Williams had taken on the miners' case free of charge and now did the same for Bony Craig. In addition to disputing whether Craig's gun actually killed Jake Whitson, Williams raised the specter of politics. The jurors and court officials were Republicans, which, according to the Knoxville attorney, meant that no Democrat could receive a fair trial.[29]

The appeals from Democrats and militiamen moved Governor Turney to swift action. Clemency for Craig came so quickly that he never had to don prison stripes. The governor claimed that he pardoned Craig in recognition of the service he had rendered to Captain Anderson during the miners' revolts in 1892. In an angry editorial, the *Clinton Gazette* told its readers that the judge's ink had hardly time to dry before Governor Turney extended clemency to the erstwhile prison guard.[30]

The response of Anderson County commentators to Craig's trial and pardon suggests the complexities of race relations in postbellum Tennessee. Those individuals who made their voices public thoroughly condemned Craig. Although Anderson County citizens may have viewed Whitson in paternalistic terms—Scoggins remembered him as a "good old darkey"—they nonetheless saw him as a fellow miner and a county resident. Despite his color, Whitson became an insider, at least in death. His neighbors were more than willing to imprison a white man for his murder, particularly one who had betrayed their community.

On the whole, the officials of Tennessee's legal system encountered great difficulty in visiting justice upon those individuals who had violated the state's criminal code during the 1892 revolts. The legal system further demonstrated a tendency to soften the punishment of individuals who did not escape adverse judgment. Yet one should not draw the conclusion that the post-rebellion activities of Tennessee's courts lacked important consequences and, especially, that the miners' brush with the law did not mean much because the rank and file largely avoided either imprisonment or fines. Criminal proceedings took their toll on the miners' organizations. When the defendants who chose to ignore their summonses left their coal communities "for parts unknown," union locals lost valuable members.[31] Those individuals who did show up in court often found themselves occupied with seemingly unending hearings and continuances. Defendants also lost more than time and energy to the criminal trials; they had to pay for their legal representation and court costs. The fines owed by those who pleaded guilty, while not as onerous as prison sentences, took scarce dollars from individual pockets and organizational coffers. Indeed, the fines that Oliver Springs miners paid alone amounted to over $3,000.[32]

These blows to individual and collective resources significantly compounded the damage that miners' organizations suffered during the rebellion itself. The criminal complaints arising from the rebellion continued to sap the state's mining unions through the mid-1890s.

The Nashville Compromise of 1893

As Tennessee's courts presided over the trial of the rebellious and the over-zealous, other institutions of state government and TCIR struggled with the convict lease. The August 1892 revolts had uprooted most of Tennessee's prison population; Tennessee miners had removed the convicts from Tracy City, Inman, and Oliver Springs, sending them to the main penitentiary in Nashville. These actions placed the "putting out" system of convicts under enormous strain. The central penitentiary was no more adequate in the summer of 1892 than it was when its warden had described it in 1881. It remained unrenovated, poorly ventilated, porous to the elements, and barely large enough to accommodate its normal contingent of 400 prisoners. Nonetheless, the number of inmates housed in the prison had swelled to almost 1,200 men by August 17. Hot weather exacerbated the overcrowded conditions. "With the oppressive weather," one prison official told a reporter, "they [the convicts] will be dying like sheep within less than a week."[33]

TCIR's response to these shipments of prisoners precipitated a standoff with Governor Buchanan. As early as August 15, company vice president Nathaniel Baxter proclaimed his company's unwillingness to maintain or support any convicts from the branch prisons sent to Nashville. Baxter insisted that TCIR had an obligation only to clothe and feed convicts who labored on the company's behalf.[34] Though TCIR's uncompromising attitude had prompted Buchanan's threat to cancel the convict lease, subsequent events persuaded the governor to postpone such a proclamation. The miners' defiance overshadowed that of the company, at least for a time. Within two weeks of the August 1892 rebellion, prison authorities had sent convicts back to Tracy City, Inman, and Oliver Springs.[35]

The return of state inmates to the branch prisons did not resolve the brewing conflict between TCIR and the government in Nashville. A full understanding of this conflict requires consideration of some legal maneuverings just prior to the August uprisings. A month before Tracy City miners rekindled the flames of insurrection, the State of Tennessee sued TCIR over a variety of issues relating to the convict lease. Filing the suit in Nashville's chancery court, the solicitor general alleged that TCIR owed $147,000 for back rental, the arrest and return of the convicts the miners liberated in the fall of 1891, and the expenses the state incurred in maintaining military guards and escorts.[36]

Company officials reacted to the suit with strong emotions. To the horror of James Bowron, TCIR's secretary-treasurer, the state's brief made no allowances for the losses incurred by the company when miners had turned convicts loose. This omission, though, was not as troubling to Bowron as several other aspects of the state's lawsuit. In presenting Tennessee's case, the solicitor general, John A. Pitts, adopted a number of legal interpretations that the miners had put forth four years previously. Following the basic outlines of Attorney General Pickle's reasoning in his 1891 submission to the legislature, Pitts maintained that subleasing was illegal, as the responsibilities and obligations embedded in the contract were of a nature that precluded any form of "substitution." The Board of Prison Inspectors, Pitts emphasized, had assessed potential lessees for their "fitness, competency, and trustworthiness." TCIR met these criteria, since "it was believed to be one of the strongest and wealthiest corporations of the State, officered and managed by prominent and influential citizens . . . of known responsibility, fairness, competency and humanity."[37] In essence, the state implied that the paternalistic aspects of the lease set crucial limits on its economic character; the lessee's duties to the convicts, like a feudal baron's duties to his land or to his serfs, made the convict inalienable.

Bowron, who would become increasingly hostile to what he perceived as unnecessary interference by government in the affairs of business, vehemently objected to this legalistic shackling of the convict lessee. The TCIR official interpreted Pitts's argument as an affront to settled law. With Judge Hicks, he believed that the state Supreme Court had unambiguously found the sublease legal when it had upheld the confinement of prisoner Warren in the Coal Creek branch prison.[38]

Bowron and other TCIR executives were further angered by another contention in the state's lawsuit—that the company's subleasing policy had precipitated the crisis over convict labor. Pitts's brief enumerated many of the alleged legal infractions committed by B. A. Jenkins and the Tennessee Coal Mining Company, such as the refusal to allow the miners a checkweighman, the payment of wages in scrip, and the imposition of an ironclad contract. Pitts further intimated that these actions were far from being out of character for Jenkins, as he "was known by the defendant, the lessee of the penitentiary, to be obstinate, overbearing, dictatorial, and exceedingly obnoxious to the free miners of that section." In sum, the state government held TCIR responsible for an illegal sublease to a man with no scruples, who lacked all the attributes necessary to serve as a watchful guardian of unfree workers. E. J. Sanford had once placed the origin of Tennessee's mining revolts in the "fool contract" that William Morrow made with Jenkins and in Jenkins's proclivity to boast about it all over east Tennessee. The solicitor general now made this private accusation public.[39]

TCIR's legal representatives responded to the state's suit with an extensive brief filed in early October 1892, which contested each of the assertions in Pitts's original bill. Company attorneys first contended that subleasing had been "open and notorious" for many years. Surely, they suggested, an institution tacitly recognized for years by "the State, the Prison Inspectors, the Superintendent, the Wardens, the governor, the Legislature, and the people of Tennessee" could not have been for all that time outside the law. Anticipating a potential objection that branch prisons might be legal while subleasing was not, the lawyers further observed that every branch prison was built, operated, and initially owned by sublessees.[40]

After canvassing the state's position on the illegality of subleasing, the company's lawyers turned their attention to the issue of fiduciary responsibility. The state had argued that the convict lease reflected a unique faith in the competence and moral stature of TCIR's managers and precluded any transfer of the weighty trust placed in the hands of the lessee. In reply, TCIR's counsel argued that such a position reflected a hopelessly flawed understanding of the modern corporation. For state officials to have had a unique faith in the company's leaders, those public servants must have been able to identify some group of men who would stay at the company's helm. But, TCIR's brief observed, "the stock of this company, like that of all great companies, constantly changes hands. There have been times when the entire stock was held by less than a dozen persons, and other times when the stockholders numbered more than four hundred." The brief then noted that according to the terms of the company charter, a "charter granted by the State of Tennessee, its directors were elected every two years, and its executive officers were then chosen by every board of directors." The attorneys drew what to them seemed an ineluctable inference—it was "impossible that the lease to the Coal Company involved a personal confidence and trust upon moral grounds." If the convict lease never created such a special obligation, counsel concluded, then the question of its transferability became moot.[41]

Finally, TCIR's answer to the state's suit unreservedly denied that the company was in any way culpable for the various revolts against convict labor in Tennessee. The corporation refused to accept responsibility for the lawless behavior of the state's miners. Instead, TCIR's brief repeated allegations that

Nashville officials had consistently failed to improve security at the branch prisons, even though they had received evidence about likely attacks.[42]

The state's filing of the chancery suit, the August revolts, and TCIR's initial answer to the suit in October set the stage for almost a year and a half of constant and always fruitless negotiations. While the state bureaucracy and many of the corporation's executives had grave reservations about continuing the lease, neither group wished to accept public or financial responsibility for its termination. So they bickered on, each side trying to ensure the most advantageous outcome. TCIR pressed for recognition of the costs it had incurred through destruction of property and lost workdays; company officials further saw no reason to pay for military protection, since the upholding of law and order was the most fundamental purpose of state government. For its part, the government pushed for payment of back rental of prisoners, military expenses, and reimbursement for the convicts' capture; state officials saw no reason to take the losses suffered by TCIR into account.[43]

Before TCIR and the state government eventually reached a final settlement, pressure on each had to grow precipitously. TCIR encountered one significant prod five months after the August 1892 insurrection. In December of that year, William Morrow reneged on his sublease of 500 convicts, most of whom were in the main penitentiary. Following the 1890 prison fire, the Cherry-Morrow Manufacturing Company had stopped manufacturing wagons within the penitentiary; but for the next two years, it was able to find alternative employment for its wards. By the end of 1892, though, Morrow had no means of putting his charges to work. Idle convicts offered scant prospects for covering their own upkeep, let alone yielding a profit for Morrow. So the manufacturer broke his contract, returning the prisoners to TCIR's care and control. The mining conglomerate was left with an additional third of the state's convicts to feed, clothe, and guard.[44]

This extra stress on TCIR's finances came at a time when its Tennessee division showed declining profits. Both Cowan and South Pittsburg registered in the red on TCIR's account books at the end of 1892. Tracy City remained lucrative, but gross profits for that operation fell almost 20 percent between 1891 and 1892. TCIR's continued overall financial well-being largely emanated from its holdings in and around Birmingham, Alabama. Even that situation changed dramatically in 1893, when TCIR's net profits declined by 92 percent. The following year the company only broke even.[45]

As the depression of the 1890s bit deeper, TCIR found that it had no better luck employing the convicts than Morrow had had. Hostile public opinion increasingly impeded the company's ability to make the lease a going proposition. In April 1893 recently inaugurated Governor Peter Turney fulfilled an election promise, signing legislation that provided for the building of a new penitentiary and for the government's purchase of farm and coal lands. The legislature explicitly characterized this measure as preparatory for the "abolition of the convict-lease system in Tennessee." After Tennessee's contract with TCIR expired on December 31, 1895, the government committed itself to reclaim direct control over the state's inmates, using them primarily to work state-owned coal mines.[46]

The act providing for a new penitentiary was not the only law that signaled a turnabout in governmental policy concerning the "convict question." In the same month, the state legislature passed a second statute that gave Tennessee's four largest cities greater latitude to set the terms of city contracts. This law enabled Nashville, Memphis, Chattanooga, and Knoxville to reject the lowest bid for a city contract if that bid were predicated on the use of convict labor.[47] The measure had gained passage largely at the behest of Nashville's workingmen, who had sought to prohibit city authorities from giving a major sewer contract to TCIR. Without the ability to use convict labor, TCIR had no hope of fulfilling its winning $273,000 bid to build a new Nashville sewer line. The company had no choice but to withdraw its offer from consideration.[48]

TCIR, which had been the primary convict lessee for over a decade and had successfully employed convict miners for over twenty years, increasingly found reliance on unfree labor onerous. The convict lease now came more and more to confine those responsible for the legally confined. Company officials faced an ever-shrinking range of possible employment for the convicts, while the obligations of providing for those prisoners remained constant. Despite the best efforts of company executives, TCIR henceforth kept between 500 and 700 convicts in a state of "enforced idleness."[49]

After the 1892 rebellion, then, TCIR confronted dilemmas not unlike those faced by many postbellum northern railroads. The rail lines had expended enormous amounts of capital to make their operations possible; they had to maintain those facilities regardless of the demand for their services. TCIR's difficulties did not attain such great proportions. Nonetheless, convicts represented fixed costs. Getting something for that expenditure beat getting nothing, even when the "something" was a pittance.

The shortage of companies willing to sublease portions of TCIR's unfree labor force led the company to accept a number of financially undesirable alternatives. Two examples stand out. First, TCIR kept its Inman iron mine and South Pittsburg furnaces running even though the depressed iron market rendered such operations unprofitable.[50] Second, in the fall of 1893, TCIR loaned large numbers of convicts to Jere Baxter, Nathaniel Baxter's brother and a railroad entrepreneur. Jere headed a consortium set up to build the Tennessee Central Railroad, in which Nathaniel shared a pecuniary interest.[51] TCIR executives did not expect payment for the loan, hoping only that the railroad would house and clothe the inmates under its responsibility. Unfortunately for the convict lessee, the Tennessee Central proved unable to provide the convicts with even a minimum of care. Nathaniel, who was by then TCIR's president, took additional steps, ordering Bowron to provide his brother with loans that would "help keep up the convicts." The prudent secretary-treasurer was dismayed by this development, for he knew that TCIR was simply "piling up bad debt."[52]

The state of the coal industry and the economy in general exacerbated TCIR's situation. In late 1893 a newly installed commissioner of labor estimated Tennessee's adult male unemployment at around 25,000, a figure that led him to characterize the past year as "one of the most disastrous years in the history of our State and country in all branches of business and trades." The precipitous drop in Tennessee's coal production mirrored the depressed labor market. Output plummeted in all four counties directly affected by the miners' rebellion.[53]

TCIR officials responded to the sagging demand for their products with genuine anguish. A. M. Shook's letters and Bowron's diaries between late 1892 and late 1894 tell vivid tales of hard times and economic stringency. In November 1892 Shook complained that TCIR's Tennessee division was not earning sufficient money to cover the company's fixed costs. Almost a year later, he noted that economic conditions were giving him "the blues." Shook had good cause to feel depressed; in August 1893 a fate befell his corporation only slightly less daunting to a corporate leader than bankruptcy—TCIR lacked the cash flow to pay the salaries of its managers and executives. In October the company still did not have sufficient resources to meet the payroll for the previous three months. The new year did not bring much improvement. Only in December 1895 did TCIR officials finally regain their optimism about the economy, as Bowron noted laconically that "business was picking up."[54]

The mines in east Tennessee fared no better. During the depression, TCIR, which had taken over the Cumberland Coal Company's lease in Oliver Springs, found it impossible to mine coal profitably under the conditions imposed by its landlord, the Coal Creek Mining & Manufacturing Company. As the primary convict lessee, TCIR also had difficulty obtaining its sublease payments from the Knoxville Iron Company. The financial difficulties that the coal companies experienced were reflected in the numerous complaints issued by their employees. East Tennessee miners reported that there was no work to be had for most of 1893. In 1894 one man observed that east Tennessee miners were not earning enough to "purchase cornmeal and molasses." Conditions in east Tennessee improved at much the same time as they did in the middle section of the state. By February 1896, miners began filing reports that Oliver Springs and Coal Creek were shipping all the coal they could handle.[55]

Changes in governmental policy toward the use of convict labor on state projects, TCIR's growing difficulty in finding new subleases, and the worsening economy all combined to push the company toward an accommodation with the state. But somehow the numerous rounds of negotiations over the course of 1893 always ended in stalemate. Finally, government officials turned once again to legal tactics to concentrate the minds of TCIR's executives and lawyers. The solicitor general filed a suit on behalf of the State of Tennessee and Grundy County for back taxes allegedly owed by TCIR. In an effort to make TCIR's executives sit up and take notice, government lawyers made the assessment so large—$250,000—that a successful claim against the company would threaten it with bankruptcy. Bowron recognized this gambit for what it was—a thinly veiled effort to force TCIR to come to an agreement on the disputed issues pertaining to the convict lease.[56]

The Nashville government's turn to such hard-nosed measures reflected its own set of imperatives. The drain that the miners' rebellion put on the state's coffers, together with its need to pay creditors, compelled government officials to seek a settlement with TCIR. By late December 1893, government expenditures related to "the mining troubles" had skyrocketed. Arrears in rental fees continued to accumulate even as military expenses escalated enormously following the August 1892 uprisings. The cost of maintaining the militia would eventually reach $200,000.[57] Sometime after 1893 the state's attorney estimated the combined cost to the government at $372,477. Excluding the government's military bill from the August 1892 revolts and the price of maintaining an armed presence in Anderson County, Tennessee's solicitors still claimed almost $250,000 from TCIR.[58]

The government needed this money desperately. Tennessee's bond coupons fell due on January 1, 1894, and the state did not have much hope of tapping additional sources of credit in order to meet these payments. In light of the national depression and Tennessee's burgeoning expenses, the State of Tennessee could not, in James Bowron's estimation, "borrow money except on such terms or conditions as might not have been compatible with its dignity."[59] To avoid a total collapse of state credit, the government in Nashville had to collect a substantial sum from TCIR—and collect it sooner rather than later.

The need to improve balance sheets was complemented by other shared impulses to compromise. Conflict between the militia stationed at Coal Creek and local residents erupted in mid-August 1893, leaving representatives of both capital and the state concerned once again about peace in east Tennessee. In circumstances that remain opaque, a militiaman, Private William Laugherty of Knox County, died during a fracas in a bawdy house. In retaliation for Laugherty's death, a group of soldiers forcibly entered the boardinghouse where a twenty-five-year-old miner named Richard Drummond lived. They dragged him to a railroad trestle near Coal Creek and hanged him. Conditions in Anderson County became explosive following these two deaths. To defuse local tensions, Governor Turney publicly denounced both murders, promised an inquiry into them, and announced that he would withdraw the troops stationed in Coal Creek.[60]

This series of events brought renewed fears of civil unrest to TCIR's executives and state officials. Having experienced the dreadful cost of rebellion so recently, both sides had no desire to find themselves embroiled in similar circumstances. In addition, company leaders and state representatives also worried about the possible implications that their continued bickering might have for union organization and behavior. These men knew that as long as the state of Tennessee and one of its largest corporations remained resolutely and publicly opposed, their quarrel might offer the miners a strategic opening. So long as the lease remained in effect, both TCIR and state officials realized that their best interests were served by presenting a united front.[61]

Mindful of both looming financial disaster and potential labor resurgence, TCIR and government officials reached an out-of-court settlement on December 14, 1893. The government agreed to scale back its original claim from $250,000 to $150,000 and forswore "all claims and demands for back taxes" prior to and including 1893, implicitly confirming Bowron's hunch that the state's tax suit was directly related to the unsettled dispute over the convict lease. TCIR made several concessions in turn. The company both promised to resume rental payments of the convict lease and accepted the state's refusal to consider the company's counterclaims for property damage and loss of convict labor during the revolts. TCIR additionally agreed to pay half of the $150,000 settlement immediately upon the state's withdrawal of the lawsuit still pending in the chancery court.[62]

Arrangements regarding the payment of the remaining $75,000 were at once more complicated and more ambiguous. TCIR could discharge this latter sum by leasing convict labor back to the state. Company and government officials entered into this agreement knowing that the state would soon construct a new penitentiary and open a coal mine in anticipation of the convict lease's demise. Although no provision expressly mentioned the state's need for construction crews, both parties assumed that the government would use convict labor, at least in part, to build the new prison and establish its mine. And since TCIR had the rights to the labor of all state prisoners until the end of 1895, the Nashville government would have to sublease convicts from the coal company if it desired to build the state's correctional facility and open its mine with unfree bricklayers and miners. To the extent that the state relied on convict workers, it would reduce the sum of TCIR's remaining debt.[63]

The cordial relations that followed this entente between the representatives of the state and TCIR did not last long. Fiscal stringency and wrangling within Tennessee's government departments delayed the state's new project. By the time Tennessee officials were ready to build the new prison and open the mine, the end of the convict lease beckoned. As a result, the government had no hope of employing convicts for a long enough time to wipe out TCIR's debt to the State of Tennessee.[64]

TCIR's post-compromise difficulties with the state extended beyond the tarnished prospects of extinguishing the company's debt though contracts for prison labor, as the mining conglomerate had to deal with increasingly stringent oversight of the convict lease. Beginning in mid-1894, the Board of Prison Inspectors sent out a number of memoranda to the corporation, reminding company officials about admissible forms of punishment and legally stipulated levels of care.[65] With their potential revenues for the convict lease reduced and their obligations to the convicts more vigorously checked, TCIR officials soon viewed the state government with renewed distaste.

TCIR's conduct in turn alienated officials in Nashville. Whether as a form of retaliation or simply as a result of economic necessity, TCIR annoyed the state comptroller's office by failing to pay its quarterly rental fees either in full or on time. The company also billed the state far more for the hire of its convicts than it did other sublessees, charging Nashville more than double the price it billed the Knoxville Iron Company for an unskilled laborer. As a result of the increased fees, state officials cut back on their request for prison labor.[66]

Even after the convict lease expired, the State of Tennessee would not let matters rest, eventually turning to the courts to recover TCIR's remaining debt. Early in 1896 Tennessee's attorney general revived the 1892 chancery suit against the convict lessee, arguing that TCIR had broken the terms of the 1893 settlement and consent decree. The state asked the court to order TCIR to pay $44,000 to the Tennessee treasury—the amount that the corporation had not discharged through cash payments or subleasing of convicts—plus interest.[67]

TCIR vigorously defended itself against this legal salvo. The corporation's lawyers took hundreds of pages of depositions in an attempt to show that the state, rather than TCIR, had violated the Nashville accord. In building their case, TCIR's counsel stressed the political context in which the two sides negotiated and the private understandings that supplemented the written agreement. Several TCIR officials testified about assurances they had received from state officials at the time of the compromise and afterward. Bowron, Baxter, and Shook all recollected that key state negotiators had promised that the company would be able to pay off half of this agreed-upon debt through the lease of convicts back to the state. This promise, TCIR's attorneys contended, came without any conditions attached. The lawyers conceded that the agreement nowhere included an explicit clause ratifying this arrangement—the political environment at the time made such a clause unseemly. Nonetheless, that verbal understanding had created settled expectations that the state had failed to meet. Unwritten understanding, TCIR's brief argued, had to govern written contract; the spirit of the settlement was more important than its letter.[68]

In addition, TCIR's lawyers once again catalogued the great expense that TCIR had incurred because of the miners' rebellions against the convict lease. Particularly through depositions, counsel revisited each of the calamities that had befallen the company: ravaged property, lost manhours of convict labor, inability to operate mines and furnaces, diminished ability to sublease convicts, and the obligation to provide between two and three years' worth of board and lodging to several hundred idle convicts. Rather than the corporation owing money to the state, TCIR's attorneys suggested that Tennessee should pay damages to its convict lessee.[69]

Tennessee's legal representatives replied by introducing testimony from several state officials who recalled no verbal promises about a specified reliance by the state on convict labor leased from TCIR. The December 1893 agreement, state lawyers maintained, only created the possibility of TCIR's extinguishing half of its $150,000 debt by leasing convicts back to the state. Such an arrangement depended on continual findings by legislators and prison administrators that public use of the convicts would serve the public interest. The state, therefore, had no legal obligation to expunge TCIR's debt via convict labor.[70]

On June 26, 1896, Davidson County's chancery master found for the state, declaring that TCIR owed the Tennessee treasury an additional $44,000. The company immediately objected to the master's finding and appealed the case to the Davidson County chancellor, who rendered a similar judgment. TCIR appealed once more to the Tennessee Supreme Court. In February 1897 that body of jurists provided the company with their answer. The court's opinion observed that the case presented a special difficulty—"a number of honorable men" had testified on both sides of the matter, with the recollections of those on one side diverging markedly from those on the other.[71] The justices managed to reach their decision, though, without impeaching the character of any witness.

The Supreme Court's determination hinged on its reading of the 1893 act concerning the new state prison. That legislation, which became law eight months before the December 1893 settlement, provided that the state could be bound to agreements about the use of convicts only through a written contract signed by the general assembly's Penitentiary Committee. Since the committee had consented to no such written agreement, the court had no choice but to confine itself to the express terms of the 1893 compromise. Under those terms, the state's representatives had an obligation to take only as many convicts as "could be used to best advantage." Agreeing with the Davidson County chancery master that the state had reasonably followed this prescription, the court upheld the ruling below.[72]

TCIR's misfortune in Tennessee's courts extended beyond this case. When the Nashville government agreed in December 1893 to forswear any claims on TCIR for back taxes, the concession in no way constrained Grundy County. County officials continued to seek $25,000 in back taxes from the company, pursuing their suit against TCIR to its conclusion. These officials particularly sought back-assessment on TCIR's intangible property—its cash on hand, commercial paper, and account debts. Company lawyers attempted to fend off this potential drain on the company treasury by arguing that such intangible property derived mostly from operations outside Grundy County boundaries. In effect, the company's attorneys argued that TCIR was everywhere but nowhere for the purposes of taxation. Tennessee's Supreme Court rejected this contention in 1894. Its justices observed that Grundy County housed the company's headquarters and that company executives directed and accounted for all corporate property from those headquarters. Drawing on relevant precedents from both Tennessee and federal cases, the court ruled that TCIR had to pay Grundy County its due.[73]

By the lights of Tennessee's jurists, then, TCIR was a corporate citizen of Grundy County and the state of Tennessee. This status conferred weighty obligations as well as rights. The company had to pay its fair share of taxes; it further had to exercise great care in its supervision of the convict lease. Soured by its experience in Tennessee and enticed by opportunities in Alabama, TCIR soon exhibited the rootless character of many modern corporations. By 1897,

TCIR's holdings in mid-Tennessee no longer boasted the plentiful and easily mined coal seams that abounded in past decades. The demise of the convict lease additionally reduced Tennessee's attractiveness.

While the virtues of Tennessee waned in the eyes of TCIR's executives, those of Alabama waxed. Since the mid-1880s, Birmingham had beckoned as a far more lucrative field of operation, with the rich coal seams in the Birmingham area encouraging corporate management to direct more and more investment to the southwest. As early as 1893, TCIR officials ratified this geographic shift, initiating the removal of offices and headquarters to the state that had become home to most of the corporation's capital. In 1904 the Tennessee Coal, Iron, and Railroad Company would still own a handful of coal mines in Tennessee.[74] But by that time, the company's most significant link to the state would lie in its name.

The Fraying of Labor Solidarity

Throughout the years following the 1892 rebellion, Tennessee's coal operators expended considerable energy wrangling with the state. As a consequence, they no longer enjoyed the united front with governmental officials that so crucially influenced the course of the early revolts. Following the October 1891 rebellion, mineowners could rely on state officials to close ranks with them. Despite some initial hesitancy, Governor Buchanan sent the state's convicts back to the communities from whence the miners had so recently banished them. In late 1892 and early 1893, mineowners could not so readily count on the state's cooperation. Moreover, this last rebellion left labor relations in Tennessee's mines in a state of flux. By April 1893, the cost associated with the rebellion had become so prohibitive that the State of Tennessee clearly signaled its intention not to renew the convict lease when it expired in January 1896. Thus the questions of who would work in Tennessee's mines and what relationship they would have with coal management lacked obvious answers.

With the state no longer a reliable ally of mineowners, labor arrangements in Tennessee's mines uncertain, and the mineowners less and less happy about serving as convict lessees, one might presume that a significant opportunity existed for Tennessee's free miners. These men had demonstrated trenchant organization and considerable savvy during the previous two years of struggle with their employers and the state. They would seem well positioned to shape the eventual redefinition of labor in the mines. But the miners were largely unable to capitalize on the fissures engendered by the most recent revolt.

The strength of organized labor in Tennessee's mining communities plummeted after the 1892 uprisings. Mining unions did not completely wither, nor did they completely turn away from militant collective action. But Tennessee's miners could no longer muster the sustained, coordinated offensives of 1891 and 1892. Union membership in UMWA District 19 dropped from 1,200 to 500 in the year after the 1892 revolts, a decrease that reflected both the strain experienced by union locals in fending off criminal charges and the dramatic exodus of rebellion participants from Coal Creek Valley. District 19 never achieved more than two-thirds of its pre-revolt strength during the decade following the uprising, with Tennessee absorbing the bulk of the reduction in membership. In the wake of the August 1892 attacks, UMWA official William Riley lamented that after he and William Webb spent much of 1891 and 1892 "getting the lower part of the district into the union," the trouble at Coal Creek caused the union to "lose the greater part of our year's work."[75]

Diminished membership was coupled with less militant and less effective union leadership. In 1893 miners in Grundy and Anderson Counties each engaged in one major act of resistance. The Tracy City miners' efforts failed completely, while the Coal Creek miners proved only partially successful. Perhaps emboldened by the legislative declaration in early April 1893 that the convict lease would not be renewed after the current contract's expiration, between 40 and 100 TCIR employees once again attacked the Tracy City stockade on the evening of April 19. A combination of inclement weather and a lack of widespread support led to their quick defeat. Heavy rain that night prevented the dynamite the miners had placed next to the stockade from exploding, easing the task of guards in repulsing the small gathering of workingmen. By the time a group of 125 militiamen arrived the following day, all was quiet. A minor episode compared to the revolts of the previous two years, this outbreak received considerably less attention. The only repercussion of the abortive attack was felt by the miners themselves. TCIR refused to reemploy those implicated in the raid.[76]

The Coal Creek and Briceville miners eschewed tactics akin to the abortive attack in mid-Tennessee. Later in the year, however, over 1,000 miners engaged in an eleven-week strike against a 20 percent reduction in the wage scale. Their efforts did not go wholly for naught. Having laid down their picks and shovels in August, the men reached a compromise with the coal companies two months later. Mineworkers agreed to a 10 percent reduction in their wages, but secured a one-dollar decrease in company house rents. The Anderson County miners, though, were unable to sustain this fortitude. Four months later, the men accepted a demand by the local companies that they receive wages only once every five months. Since the miners were only working two days a week at the time, they perceived this maneuver as adding insult to injury.[77] Aside from organizing the 1893 strike, the union locals that survived the 1892 revolts did not keep much of a focus on the pressing issues of labor arrangements in the mines. Instead, they busied themselves with appeals for contributions toward the legal defense of those who had rebelled the previous year and with trivial matters pertaining to Knights of Labor rituals.[78]

The 1894 nationwide miners' strike of over 100,000 men served as the best post-rebellion litmus test of union organization in Grundy and Anderson Counties. Tracy City miners failed that test miserably. Seventeen days before this widespread strike to restore pay scales to pre-depression levels, TCIR's employees accepted a ten-cent reduction in wages. Company secretary James Bowron noted that they had done so "without [a] strike." A few weeks after the beginning of the national labor action on April 21, Tracy City mineworkers rejected the appeals of striking miners at Whitwell to join them in battle against TCIR.[79] A Grundy County newspaper praised the miners for refusing to join the strike, extolling them as "a fine body of men [who] will not be influenced by any demagogical pleas for sympathy with northern miners." The Tracy City miners got more out of their willingness to continue working than the approval of their employers and of the local business community. Throughout a large part of 1894, miners worked at full stretch, trying to "meet the unusually heavy demand for coal because of the strike." While miners nationwide were trying to better their long-term working conditions, Tracy City's miners settled for short-term full employment. Just as the miners of the town could boast of "improved conditions," so could company managers. TCIR's balance sheet for Tracy City brightened considerably because the mine stayed open. Profitability at TCIR's Alabama mines, where workers struck for months, suffered enormously.[80]

The east Tennessee miners ultimately joined their northern brethren, but not without considerable ambivalence and hesitation. In Anderson County mineworkers initially voted not to strike. Ten days into the national walkout, the Coal Creek miners changed their minds. From the beginning of the strike, there had been a great deal of tension in the mining district. To the north of Coal Creek, on the Kentucky border, about 3,000 Jellico miners had struck. During the 1891–92 east Tennessee revolts, these Kentuckians had closely allied themselves with their fellow miners to the south, joining the Tennesseans' military formations. Now the miners from Jellico wanted the men of Coal Creek to unite with them in their struggle for better pay. Though the Coal

Creek miners finally yielded to this demand on April 30, they did not have much staying power. Within two weeks they had returned to work. They came out on strike again in early June; this time for only four days. The Jellico miners, by contrast, remained on strike for three full months.[81]

Much of the organization and discipline that characterized Tennessee mining communities in the early part of the decade had dissipated. Richard Alston, a staunch Populist, offered vivid testimony to the transformation of Tennessee's mining unions in 1896, comparing Coal Creek's pre- and post-rebellion standing among union miners. "Coal Creek has been a stench in the nostrils of all honest miners ever since the convict troubles there some years ago," Alston told readers of the *United Mine Workers Journal*. "A miner going from there to any organized camp," he continued, "was looked on with suspicion, if he was allowed to work at all—usually he was invited to travel on."[82]

Documenting the demise of once stalwart labor organization does not by itself account for the decline. Alston also hazarded an explanation for the declension among east Tennessee miners, arguing that the coal operators purposefully instigated the rebellion to destroy the town's powerful leadership and strong organization. Having succeeded in their objectives, mine managers remained intent on preventing the union's resurrection.[83] Even if coal operators did not conspire to provoke the 1892 rebellions, their outcome significantly hindered later union activity. These uprisings left destroyed union offices and depleted union coffers in their wake. In spite of the limited ability of Tennessee's legal system to call insurrectionary miners to account, the revolts left hundreds of miners with legal headaches, fines, and lawyers' bills.

Yet the actions of Tennessee's militia and legal system were not wholly to blame for the union's post-1892 woes. In seeking to enrich Alston's explanation, one might reasonably turn first to the dreadfully weak economy that followed the Panic of 1893. If TCIR's executives had difficulty paying themselves, the state's miners did not always know where they would find the cornmeal and molasses for their families' next meal. Great economic hardship, however, did not inevitably lead to a deterioration in the collective activities of nineteenth-century workers. Economic depression in the late 1830s and early 1840s almost universally squelched the campaigns of organized labor. But by the 1890s, a fundamental shift had occurred in the response of workers to hard times. In the latter decades of the nineteenth century, unions often grew stronger and more resolute in the face of adversity, as the ability of the UMWA to organize its 1894 nationwide strike indicates.[84] Thus the impact of a military crackdown and the onset of a depressed economy cannot fully account for the difficulties of Tennessee's miners. Internecine conflicts within UMWA District

19 and the Knights of Labor, discontinuities in leadership, and a resurgence of racially charged incidents additionally hampered efforts by the miners and their organizations to press their interests.

Internal dissension constituted a crucial impediment to the recovery of strong mining unions in Tennessee. The sources of conflict lay in turf battles and disputes over organizational affiliation. In 1890 the National Federation of Miners and Mine Laborers and the Knights of Labor National Trade Assembly 135 had merged to form the UMWA.[85] Initially, many miners retained their association with the Knights of Labor even as they signed up with the new mining union. In the first couple of years, the affiliation of Tennessee's rank-and-file miners to both unions remained unproblematic. Local and district leaders and organizers successfully incorporated the structures of both unions and the ideological emphases of each into their daily lives. Although there were a few isolated reports of discord as the two organizations worked out their relationship to each other, the disharmony that existed—called "factionalism" in contemporary parlance—did not significantly affect the representation that the Knights and UMWA afforded their members.[86]

By late 1892 and early 1893, though, factionalism had intensified. Leadership among Tennessee's miners fragmented, as several former spokesmen, such as Eugene Merrell and Marcena Ingraham, left their communities after the arrival of General Carnes's troops. In UMWA District 19, the successful partnership of William Riley and William Webb broke up with Webb's resignation as district president. His two successors soon fell out with Riley. Webb, who stayed in the area, and the second president of District 19, S. P. Herron, also engaged in a bitter war of words. Though part of the acrimony between the men can be traced to a clash of temperaments, more than personality was involved.

In November 1892 newly elected district president Herron and several other leaders began to lobby for the formation of a new National Trade Association of southern miners. They wished to change the relationship between the Knights' NTA 135 and the UMWA, as well as the manner in which the two unions allocated funds. Many members wished to establish a separate southern NTA for financial reasons; they resented what they perceived as an "extra tax" levied on southern miners by the national union for the benefit of men in the North.[87]

Webb, Riley, and a number of rank and filers opposed a new National Trade Association, which would in reality constitute merely a regional body. Webb accused Herron of "writing for a Mason and Dixon line for the South," while

Riley lampooned the proposal's champions. "If I could only buy these men according to what they actually do know, and sell them for what they think they know," the union secretary-treasurer mocked the proponents of a southern National Trade Association, "why, I could furnish enough money to organize the United States." Ordinary miners did not leave the fight to their leaders. They argued in letters to union journals that the demand for lower levies in the immediate term was shortsighted, pointing out that wages paid to miners in the North directly affected those secured by their southern counterparts and that union dues from the North had paid for southern organizers. Yet other Tennessee miners simply reminded their fellow workers that "together we stand divided we fall." Despite these misgivings, Herron's initiative quickly won converts. As a result, District 19 soon faced a serious cleavage in its ranks. "The men are divided," William Riley reported in October 1893, "some [are] for district 19 and 135, some for a new district and some for no district at all."[88]

Although disagreement over finances and affiliation with northern miners initially kindled the controversy among Tennessee's miners, personal animosity soon fanned its flames. The conflict engendered attacks by various leaders on one another. The most serious hostility flared up between William Webb and S. P. Herron. Webb publicly accused Herron of being a "mogul with a giant character" and of being an agnostic, a state of mind that Webb viewed as precluding effective union leadership. Herron, by contrast, charged that Webb had lobbied on behalf of a railroad before the Kentucky legislature. In consideration for these services, Herron alleged that Webb received a "free pass" for a year. This activity, the former maintained, had taken place while Webb held the office of District 19 president. Herron was horrified that Webb could align himself so intimately with corporate interests.[89]

Neither the conflicts over affiliation nor the personal animosity between District 19's leaders found easy resolutions. Both persisted from late 1892 until mid-1895. If the parties concerned had confined themselves to mudslinging, their exchanges might have only made for interesting reading in the columns of the *United Mine Workers Journal* and the *Journal of the Knights of Labor*. The spat, however, wreaked havoc on the miners' organizations, as locals or factions within a local took up one side or the other. Moreover, the dispute weakened the stability of district leadership. Frustrated with the desultory character of internal bickering, Herron resigned early from his term as president of the district. Following Herron's lead, Riley refused to stand for reelection after his term as secretary-treasurer ended in August 1893. Both men stayed active in the union, each engaging in public discussions about the district's future—Herron pushing for a new regional affiliation and Riley opposing it. Their resignations only added to the vacuum in local leadership brought on by the miners' revolts and the state's crackdown on armed revolt.[90]

The discord in the middle and upper echelons of Tennessee's union leadership did not go unnoticed, with rank-and-file members bemoaning its presence and coal operators delighting in the wrangling. As Riley noted in the fall of 1893, "The operators can see the division in the men and they are now working to get things their way, and can you blame them?"[91] After at least two years of debating, bickering, and sniping, Herron took it upon himself to sum up the condition of the district, observing that "our organization is like a ship in the open sea, without sail, rudder, pilot or captain." As though unable to help himself, he added that "those who mutinied are still on board with their load of treachery and slime."[92] This final comment encapsulated the self-destructive infighting within Tennessee's mining unions.

A worsening relationship between black and white miners exacerbated the deterioration in District 19's solidarity. In July 1892, the month that district membership reached a high of 1,200 miners, Riley celebrated what he perceived as a decrease in racism throughout the Kentucky and Tennessee coalfields. Linking the two phenomena, the secretary-treasurer informed UMWA members across the country that "the question of color is vanishing as fast as anything I have ever seen."[93] By March 1893, seven months after the last series of revolts, Riley's letters had taken on a much less optimistic tone. At the same time that union membership plummeted, racial attitudes hardened.

Riley's March report came directly from Coal Creek and Briceville. He told his readers that he had traveled to Coal Creek, where he had seen the district vice president, J. J. Jones, standing in a small crowd. Jones pretended not to see Riley and so the latter called the vice president aside. Riley asked Jones to bring the town's miners together for a meeting. Jones turned down this request, saying that the Odd Fellows would be gathering that night. He added that the local union had a committee to look after the "colored people," implying that Riley's efforts were unnecessary and unwelcome. If this committee proved unable to organize the black miners, Jones asserted, local leaders would call for Riley's assistance.

The secretary-treasurer, understandably put off by his conversation with Jones, went ahead and met with Coal Creek's black miners. Riley ended his narration of the visit with a reflection on the racial dynamics he had encountered. "These colored men," the secretary-treasurer observed, "have always shown . . . they wanted to be organized men, but are treated so bad by their so-called white brothers that they don't feel like they are recognized in the order as

Knights." Though Riley faced racial prejudice in good economic times as well as bad, he nonetheless maintained his faith in the potential of unionization to constrain racial hostility. He concluded that black miners "are willing to try the order again, thinking that the white men of Coal Creek will yet recognize the importance of treating them as brother miners."[94] When District 19 was strong organizationally, the "question of color" receded; now that the Coal Creek local had but two dozen members in good standing, the whites treated local blacks as anything but "brother miners."

Thus the post-rebellion era witnessed a decrease in union strength, a drop in labor militance, growing dissension within the UMWA and the Knights, and a resurgence of racial animosity. These latter two developments were related, as the dispute within District 19 over national affiliation turned on more than financial considerations. As long as Tennessee's miners belonged to the UMWA, they faced national authority on matters beyond those pertaining to dues— such as racial issues. Late-nineteenth-century southern black trade unionists frequently appealed to northern-based national officers in attempts to set limits on abuse by their white brethren. No black miner from Tennessee seems to have sent such an appeal to either Terence Powderly or the UMWA president, John Rae. Nonetheless, the vehemence with which William Riley opposed the creation of an autonomous southern mineworkers' association suggests that he did not want to lose the ability to call on the aid of northern labor leaders. When Riley looked about his district in 1893, he saw white miners with decreased regard for black miners as well as white mine leaders with less and less regard for him. When he looked about the state of Tennessee and the South in general, he saw Jim Crow ever more on the rise. He almost certainly feared that once southern miners owed their allegiance only to a southern federation, black miners would find few champions.

Even as the events of 1892–93 led to more turbulent, less tolerant, and weaker labor organizations in Tennessee's mines, those events also prompted a relative shift in the miners' ideology—a subtle transformation in the way that the leaders of these workingmen made sense of their situation and discussed it among themselves. This shift was most fully apparent in the public statements of S. P. Herron around the time of and following the August 1892 revolts. Early mine leaders, such as Eugene Merrell, had espoused an ideology that took as its starting point notions of a commonwealth and a republic. A healthy American republic, including the world within Coal Creek Valley, required independent citizens and a responsive and just government. The miners' independence was to be based on fair economic relations with their employers, respect for their rights as workingmen, and their stature as homeowning citizens with a stake in a stable society. In Merrell's eyes, these free laborers represented the figurative opposite of the "proletarian"—the person who roamed from place to place. An equitable government would secure the rights of such citizens, eschewing "class legislation" and retaining its independence from "monopolists." During their 1891 campaigns, any class analysis in which the miners engaged fell primarily within the context of republican categories—the need to maintain independence among the commonwealth's adult males, the need to safeguard government from the influence of aristocratic owners and managers of capital, and the need to keep the society's governors accountable to its autonomous citizenry.

Just before and after the 1892 revolt, union leaders changed the emphasis of their public rhetoric. By this time, Herron and other letter writers to union journals showed a greater willingness to understand their predicament through the lens of class conflict. "Here let me say that I think there is too much of that silly twaddle, even among workingmen, about the relationship of capital and labor," Herron told *United Mine Workers Journal* readers just before the August 1892 revolt. The mine leader then predicted that class conflict would carry on for generations. "True there is a relationship," he observed, "but it is that of master and slave, and not that of friend and fellow worker. Our labor will create wealth for the capitalist of the coming generations to oppress our children with."[95] Here Herron provided an uncanny corollary to the private proclamation of E. J. Sanford, the CCM&MC executive. Sanford had told a business partner that the land that they owned in east Tennessee would provide an indispensable investment for their children and their children's children, a means of ensuring their class position for decades. For Herron, as for Sanford, economic struggles had profound implications for the future of Tennessee society. Each man bore witness to the dynamic of social reproduction, the mechanism whereby owner begat owner—and worker, worker.

Herron's formulation of society in class terms did not stop with this plea for the miners to contemplate the wealth of those he perceived as the idle rich; he further encouraged his fellow workers to consider the origins and conditions of the convicts as well. What came out of his meditation was a radical interpretation of the miners' relationship to the state inmates, over whose presence the crisis in east Tennessee had revolved. Tennessee mineworkers, Herron proclaimed, "must think of the poor convict—driven to crime perhaps by poverty and the dread of poverty; driven by the lash of the task masters to do double the work they are able to do. They ought and must think of the crimes against the criminals and the crimes against the citizens perpetrated by the state."[96] Union leaders, who had fought to remove the convicts from their midst, had now begun to see themselves in a position not very different from that of the state's prisoners. These workingmen had once begun their interpretation of their situation with the axiom "In the beginning, there was the commonwealth"; now they tended to start with the premise "In the beginning, there was labor arrayed against capital."

To complete his analysis of two classes positioned in an antagonistic relationship to each other, Herron also explored the structural role that the government had assumed as a lackey of corporate Tennessee. He portrayed government officials as nihilists, since they had acted against the best interests of the people and made laws "contrary to natural rights." Inquiring into the responsibilities of government, he wondered whether "the state [is] accountable for its acts such as making a wrong law" and whether "the state [has] got any conscience?"[97] These acerbic questions were a far cry from the rallying call of Chancellor Gibson, who in the early months of the Coal Creek rebellion had chastised a string of governors for having "corporation cotton" in their ears. Gibson's point had been that elected officials could remove the cotton and heed the miners' demands. While Herron's barb retained the traditional republican complaint against the corrupt politician, it was less personally directed than Gibson's remark. Herron's commentary also focused more on a seemingly intractable antagonism between the state and working people. The UMWA leadership had begun to focus less on government as they thought it should be—a neutral, responsive arbiter—and more as it seemed to them actually to be—a tool of the corporations, dedicated to the accumulation of private wealth.[98]

The relative shift in the language of union leaders did not represent an exchange of one set of perfectly coherent ideas for another. The miners always drew on a variety of ideas to understand their place in the world. They similarly turned to disparate traditions when pressing their interests with employers, governmental officials, or the public. When these workingmen negotiated with employers, they emphasized the rights of free laborers; when they lobbied the state government or sought public support for an end to the convict lease, they stressed the dangers of monopolists and the imperative of upholding republican liberty; and when these Tennesseans needed to justify rebellion, they relied on America's revolutionary and frontier heritages. The use of class-conscious metaphors reflected a widening of the mining leaders' ideological arsenal.

While Tennessee's free miners did not absorb one all-encompassing ideology, neither did they just borrow from someone else's as the situation required. Their mental worlds incorporated many ideas and traditions, which did not always coexist easily. The extent to which multifarious conceptions and attitudes commingled in the minds of the miners, and particularly their leaders, is suggested once again by S. P. Herron. Over the course of the early 1890s, the president of UMWA District 19 espoused the industrial unionism of the mining organization he represented; promoted Knights of Labor notions of a brotherhood of producers; relied on the class-conscious analysis of the Socialists; ran for office as a Populist who saw the origins of workingmen's woes in tight financial credit markets; and supported Henry George, who viewed land speculation as the source of inequality in America. The common feature of these actions was their link to broad-based movements rooted in the aspirations of working Americans. But Herron's commitment to the inclusion of all working people was suspect. His support of an autonomous association of southern mineworkers belied dedication to the full and equal incorporation of southern black workers into unionized workplaces.

Although Herron and E. J. Sanford had shared an interpretation of their and their children's respective places in the world, miners and mineowners parted ways in their estimation of how state government had responded to the mining crises in Tennessee. From the miners' view of things, state government had come to rest comfortably within the realm of corporate influence. Coal operators, especially TCIR's executives, saw matters differently. The mining magnates believed that the Nashville government had a basic obligation to corporate enterprise and special obligations to its convict lessees. State officials were to protect corporate property and maintain law and order. These services provided the essential prerequisites for business operations. As a lessor of convict labor, the state incurred still other responsibilities. Its representatives, coal operators felt, had to ensure a fair return for the lessee's investment. If any group of persons threatened the profitable use of convicts, the state had a duty to protect that use with every means at its disposal.

As far as TCIR's management was concerned, officials in Nashville fell far short of these ideals. The government had been largely unable to prevent the destruction of corporate property in both mid- and east Tennessee. It had not proved particularly efficient in punishing those individuals who had set fire to company buildings or interfered with company convicts. Perhaps most galling, it had the audacity to demand that TCIR pay for the costs of responding to insurrection without any consideration of TCIR's losses.

That workers and mineowners each had frustrations with the government in Nashville should not mislead one into considering state officials as neutral arbiters between contending social interests. Over the course of the early 1890s, state policymaking did seek to address the concerns of both the mineowners and their employees. But Tennessee's representatives never wished to take any action that might fundamentally damage industrialization and capital accumulation in their state. Furthermore, when presented with the most significant questions of public policy—as when the miners marched on the stockades—the most powerful governmental officers universally sided with the owners and managers of capital. At the point where political dissent led to attacks on property, state officials marshaled all the force at their disposal.

Nonetheless, the government could not sustain reliance on thousands of troops and mass arrests. State officials lacked both the financial resources and the political will to wage such a campaign indefinitely. The miners' actions had raised the costs of the convict lease to prohibitive levels. These costs ensured that legislators would not vote to renew the institution after the contract with TCIR lapsed on December 31, 1895.

CHAPTER 9

The Boundaries
of Dissent

The Tennessee coal miners' rebellion constituted one of the most far-reaching challenges to governmental and industrial authority in the New South. In striving to free themselves from the competition of convict laborers, the coal miners of Anderson and Grundy Counties adopted remarkably militant tactics. These workingmen and their allies did not hesitate to threaten the use of collective force as they confronted state and corporate power or to back up those threats with swift and well-coordinated action. During their sustained battles against the scourge of the convict lease, the citizenry of east and mid-Tennessee destroyed property belonging to coal companies that employed convict laborers; they freed black and white convicts; and they commandeered railroad cars and telegraph offices.

The magnitude of this resistance becomes clearer when compared with other instances in which southerners militantly resisted aspects of the region's new industrial order. In both the 1892 New Orleans general strike and the 1894 strike by coal miners in Alabama's Birmingham district, thousands of workers vigorously pressed grievances about such issues as wages, union recognition, and the distribution of available work. In each of these conflicts black and white wage earners joined together in massive withdrawals of labor, simultaneously contesting managerial prerogatives and the hardening culture of racial segregation. Yet in duration, in the willingness of participants to take up arms, and in the destruction of public and corporate property, neither of these strikes matched the coal mining rebellion in the Volunteer State. The general strike in New Orleans lasted only eleven days in November 1892; strikers did not threaten coordinated violence, and they took care not to gainsay the authority of state officials. The 1894 Birmingham coal miners' strike lasted longer, extending from mid-April to mid-August, and involved greater reliance on force. Striking miners dynamited a coal shaft, attacked some railroad property, and intimidated scabs, killing three during one confrontation.[1]

But even the actions of the Alabama coal miners fell short of the tactics adopted by the Tennessee miners in 1891 and 1892. The Tennesseans used force in a far more concerted fashion, undertaking military training as preparation for their repeated marches on the convict stockades. Their resort to arms also included blatant challenges to state officials and to other individuals clothed in the authority of the state, as the miners repeatedly threatened to shoot convict guards and militiamen if the government did not accede to their demands. Finally, the citizens of Anderson and Grundy Counties engaged in far more extensive attacks on public and corporate property. In Alabama strikers damaged one mine shaft and dynamited the odd railway trestle; in Tennessee free coal miners destroyed several stockades, deprived mining corporations of their unfree labor force, indirectly subverted the payment of lease installments to the state government, and compelled that same government to post militia units in the region for well over a year. Together, these consequences of rebellion cost mining companies and the state of Tennessee several hundred thousand dollars.

Fifteen years after the Tennessee revolts had come to a close, the Upper South witnessed another sustained challenge to the new industrial order. Between late 1905 and 1909, tobacco growers in the Black Patch region of western Kentucky and Tennessee waged a war against the American Tobacco Company, the corporation that had essentially monopolized the buying and selling of American tobacco. This conflict suggests several instructive parallels to the cause of Coal Creek, Briceville, and Tracy City miners. A comparison of the two campaigns brings the socioeconomic, ideological, and political underpinnings of the Tennessee miners' rebellion into sharper relief.

The growers' fight against the American Tobacco Company (ATC) did not emerge spontaneously. The Black Patch—so called for the particular type of dark tobacco that grew in the western sections of Kentucky and Tennessee—had a legacy of dissent that dated back to the Greenbackers of the 1870s, the Grangers of the 1880s, and the Alliancemen of the 1890s. Thorough organization brought 5,000 farmers together in September 1904 to create the Planters' Protective Association (PPA). Their goal was to create an autonomous marketing channel through which they hoped to gain higher prices for their crops. Over the next year, PPA members sent their tobacco to PPA warehouses rather than to ATC buyers, worked to bring additional tobacco growers into their fold, and successfully sought credit lines from local banks.[2]

By December 1905, however, these efforts had not appreciably improved the price of tobacco, except for nonpoolers who received higher prices from ATC buyers. Eager to increase their clout, PPA members adopted more vigorous measures. Delegations of cooperative participants visited area farmers, threatening them with dire consequences if they did not join the PPA. Soon bands of PPA growers began to burn the crops and buildings of farmers who ignored these warnings, similarly attacking the warehouses and factories directly owned by the tobacco trust and the property of individuals who worked as ATC agents. On occasion, these bands went so far as to whip or shoot individuals who refused to accept the authority of the cooperative. Most of the attacks occurred under the cover of darkness and were carried out by hooded nightriders. Although acts of outright violence were initially infrequent, incidents became increasingly common, with scores of attacks occurring in 1907 and 1908. This escalation of pressure succeeded in driving hundreds of local growers into the PPA. But the organization was badly weakened by the Panic of 1907, which sharply curtailed access to credit throughout the region, and by allegations that its president was engaged in graft. Equally important, thousands of tobacco growers continued to ignore the cooperative, lured by the ATC's temporary offers of higher prices. After 1908 the PPA went into decline.[3]

Despite the PPA's eventual defeat, the Black Patch war rivaled the Tennessee coal miners' revolts in the breadth of popular organization, the length of the struggle, and the widespread destruction of property. The participants in the tobacco war also justified their course in a manner highly reminiscent of the insurrectionary Tennessee coal miners. Members of the PPA, like the miners of Anderson and Grundy Counties, embraced classic tenets of a Jacksonian worldview. The tobacco growers emphasized the central importance of small-scale producers in American society and greatly feared the encroaching power and greed of monopolists such as the American Tobacco Company. PPA farmers, like east and mid-Tennessee miners, believed that corporate monopolies exerted undue influence in the marketplace and that they corrupted America's democratic institutions.[4]

Similar demographic, economic, and political conditions obtained in the Black Patch and in the mining areas of mid- and, especially, east Tennessee, laying the foundation for militance. In each of these regions whites predominated; and in both the tobacco wars and the Tennessee rebellion against convict labor, aggrieved whites constituted both the leadership of insurgency and the great majority of its rank and file.[5] It would have been inconceivable in the New South for blacks to mount such activities without immediately confronting overwhelming military force. To be sure, Governor Buchanan called out the state militia as soon as the miners had returned the Briceville convicts to the main penitentiary in Nashville in July 1891. But initially the troops showed sympathy for the miners, claiming that the east Tennesseans were white workingmen just like them. Such sufferance would not have been accorded African American protesters.

A substantial proportion of the tobacco farmers who lived in the Black Patch and the miners who worked in the Tennessee coalfields also counted themselves as property owners. Although property ownership in these areas was by no means universal, it was sufficiently common to foster widely held expectations that most white men would be able, even in the midst of industrialization, to gain title to either a farmstead or a house. Tobacco farmers who owned their own lands, moreover, were especially well represented among PPA members and activists.[6]

PPA members and east Tennessee's free miners additionally enjoyed relative independence during their working hours. No foreman stood over these men telling them how to plant their tobacco beds or excavate a stope. Self-direction at work was complemented by relative autonomy in community life, especially in the Black Patch and the east Tennessee coal counties. Propertied tobacco growers in western Kentucky and Tennessee and Anderson County miners both took leading roles in building local institutions, and both participated avidly in local politics.[7]

When Tennessee's convict lessees sent prisoners to work in Briceville mines or the American Tobacco Company drove down the price of Black Patch leaf, these corporations threatened the image that Anderson County miners and propertied tobacco growers had of themselves as independent, free men. The

PPA farmers' and east Tennesseans' whiteness, their title to farms or homes, and their relative autonomy all led these men to view themselves as political and social insiders. This self-perception led the Kentucky and Tennessee growers, like the Tennessee miners, to seek constitutional redress in the form of petitions, appeals to elected officials, and legal challenges.

In the Black Patch, growers sought a range of constitutional remedies to their economic problems. At the national level, they advocated the repeal of the national excise tax on tobacco and pushed the U.S. Department of Justice to bring an antitrust prosecution against the American Tobacco Company. Closer to home, growers appealed to the Kentucky and Tennessee legislatures to sanction their efforts at pooling their crops. As in the case of Tennessee's miners, Black Patch farmers had good reason to believe that democratically elected representatives and their appointed officials sympathized with their plight. A repeal of the excise tax passed the House of Representatives in 1904, only to be killed in the Senate. The Department of Justice did not ignore the allegations of antitrust violations by the American Tobacco Company, though its investigations took years and provided no immediate redress. Perhaps most important, the Kentucky and Tennessee legislatures both affirmed that farmers who entered into pooling associations were bound to abide by their contracts.[8]

Thus in the tobacco districts of western Kentucky and Tennessee during the 1900s, as in the Tennessee coal region during the early 1890s, disgruntled citizens received political recognition that their cause was just without gaining much in the way of tangible victories. When political and legal efforts failed to bring immediate results, the vision these two groups had of themselves as inheritors of America's democratic tradition strengthened the resolve to organize in the hope of vanquishing their respective foes. That vision also justified the turn to arms—a method of redress that had honorable precedents.

Identifying the contexts that nurtured rebelliousness in the Tennessee coalfields and the Black Patch tobacco region enhances comprehension of the relative quiescence of many other places in the industrial New South. In almost every other southern state, for example, opposition to the convict lease was much tamer than in Tennessee. Elsewhere below the Mason-Dixon line, workers who most keenly felt the sting of competition from prison labor generally lacked some or all of the attributes that encouraged militance among Tennessee miners and Black Patch farmers.

Free miners in Georgia and Alabama, like those in Tennessee, faced competition from convict laborers and viewed such competition as illegitimate in a democratic society. But in neither state did resistance to the use of prison labor in mines extend beyond legislative petitions. In Georgia the number of free miners was simply insufficient to spearhead outright rebellion against state authority. The state's comparatively few coal mines were worked almost exclusively by convicts. With only one Georgia miner in seven earning a wage and with the total number of free miners rarely exceeding 130 throughout the 1880s and 1890s, the state possessed no independent mining communities of any significance and had no critical mass of disaffected workingmen.[9]

If there were too few free miners to mount any serious attack on the use of convicts to excavate Georgia's coal, this constraint did not obtain in Alabama. Thousands of postbellum miners earned a living in the rich coalfields surrounding the "Magic City" of Birmingham. But by the 1890s, roughly half of Alabama's free coal miners were black; in the Tennessee coal mines that employed convict labor, free blacks never exceeded one-sixth of the labor force.[10] A large percentage of black miners militated against a frontal assault on convict labor. For African Americans to threaten state authority through a collective appeal to arms in the decades after Redemption was to court disaster.

Where convict lessees hired prisoners to work in agriculture, as they did in Louisiana, direct action against the presence of convict labor was just as infrequent. Louisiana's convicts picked cotton, cut sugarcane, and tended fruit and vegetable gardens. As a result, they most directly affected the interests of black sharecroppers, sugarcane cutters, and farmworkers. Not surprisingly, Louisiana's African American workers were hostile to convict labor, voicing complaints similar to those offered by Tennessee's coal miners: the institution robbed them of employment and depressed wages or share arrangements. The postbellum Louisianians hurt by the state's convict lease registered their objections repeatedly, most often through the voices of black legislators, but to no avail. The state legislature maintained its commitment to convict leasing in agriculture throughout the nineteenth century.[11] More aggressive resistance would have been foolhardy. If any black agricultural workers contemplated collective force as a means of removing competition from convict labor, the outcome of the short-lived 1887 Louisiana sugar strike would have suggested the inadvisability of such a course. This strike by 9,000 black and 1,000 white cutters was quickly crushed by companies of the state militia, who systematically placed leaders under arrest and evicted strikers from their homes. Toward the end of the strike, militiamen and local elites responded to the shooting of two white pickets in the town of Thibodaux by massacring over thirty black sugar workers who had moved to town after suffering eviction.[12]

One southern state other than Tennessee witnessed an armed challenge to convict leasing. In March 1886 hundreds of coal miners in eastern Kentucky responded to a Pulaski County mine's introduction of convicts as strikebreakers by arming themselves and marching on the convict camp. The crowd demanded that camp officials send the prisoners back to Frankfort, the state capital. The miners further vowed to destroy the stockade, an intention that was thwarted by the arrival of a militia company that successfully upheld the "majesty of the law." For the next two months, Kentucky legislators wrangled over proposals to ban the use of convicts in the state's mines, eventually agreeing to prohibit convict labor outside prison walls as soon as the construction of a new state penitentiary was complete.[13]

This brief Kentucky revolt sprang from a social and political context akin to that which fostered the Tennessee uprisings. The Pulaski County mining community was well established and predominantly white; shopkeepers and professionals identified their interests with those of the town's free miners; and the miners had built a strong Knights of Labor local, which was instrumental in channeling discontent into action. In addition, many state politicians from both parties had placed themselves on record as opposing the convict lease in an attempt to attract the votes of workingmen. The Pulaski County incident, moreover, served as an explicit model for east Tennessee miners in 1891. Anderson County miners were in close contact with their Kentucky counterparts during the latter's attack on convict labor during 1886. They held joint meetings to discuss demands and tactics, and some key actors in the Kentucky revolt, such as union leader William Webb, reappeared as participants in Tennessee's rebellion.[14]

Although the coal miners' revolts in Kentucky and Tennessee and the tobacco war in the Black Patch shared remarkably similar socioeconomic origins, they eventually diverged significantly in their tactics; these differences highlight the crucial importance of labor unions, and especially unions linked to national federations, in restraining the racist impulses of southern white producers. Throughout the Tennessee rebellion and during the early stages of the Black Patch war, both the miners and farmers carefully limited militant action. In their assaults on the convict-lease system, the miners focused on a small number of convict stockades; in seeking to strengthen the PPA, the farmers of western Kentucky and Tennessee initially restricted attacks to American Tobacco Company warehouses and the property of farmers who refused to withhold their tobacco from the ATC's buying merchants.

But as the two campaigns dragged on, they took very different courses. The Tennessee miners continued to act with restraint, only destroying property that had a direct bearing on convict labor and never resorting to wanton attacks on their opponents. By contrast, Black Patch farmers were unable to contain the impulse to lash out against a wider set of targets. As time passed without measurable success, the Black Patch farmers began to take out their frustrations on black neighbors, pressuring white landlords to evict black tenants and attacking the homes, crops, and families of local black farmers. In the worst incident, nightriders set the home of a black farmer on fire and then shot the occupants as they fled the burning building. This Klanlike violence against African Americans—known as whitecapping—expressed both a racial hatred and a desire to protect or improve opportunities for white farmers and laborers.[15] By channeling their disappointments into attacks on local African Americans, the PPA growers displaced their anger from a monopolistic economic system seemingly beyond their control to the one group of neighbors upon whom they could most easily stamp their authority.

Much of the explanation for these different trajectories lies in the dissimilar character of organization and leadership evident in the mining unions and the tobacco growers' cooperative. Tennessee's rank-and-file miners were subject to the oversight of two national labor organizations—the United Mine Workers of America and the Knights of Labor. Both these organizations emphasized disciplined action and expressly rejected racism. While neither organization wholly eliminated the racist inclinations of its southern members, both could, during specific strikes or organizing drives, curb those inclinations.[16] Local unions also operated on a strong base of democratic principles, which simultaneously ensured widespread support for union policies and respect for the outcomes of collective deliberations. Throughout 1891 and 1892, union and community leaders in the coal towns consistently sought the views of ordinary miners before embarking on a particular strategy, and these leaders habitually set up structures that enforced disciplined behavior.

In contrast to the Knights and the UMWA, the Planters' Protective Association was a regional organization that lacked any concern about the rights or interests of black Americans. Checks on indiscriminate violence and attacks against African Americans could only have come from the local leadership, but that leadership quickly lost influence with PPA members. The PPA's leader, Felix Ewing, became renowned for high-handed and autocratic behavior and soon alienated vast numbers of Black Patch farmers. Intimations that Ewing was embezzling PPA funds did nothing to bolster his authority. Perhaps most important, Ewing and other PPA leaders, who tended to be well-off landowners or local bankers, had no real commitment to the protection of African Americans. The ineffectiveness and indifference of the tobacco cooperative's leaders permitted the reign of terror that white farmers in the Black Patch imposed on their black neighbors.

The miners' revolts succeeded in bringing an end to the convict lease in Tennessee. By inflicting grievous costs on coal companies and the state, the miners of Coal Creek, Briceville, Oliver Springs, and Tracy City ensured that no lease contract would replace the one that expired in December 1895.[17] The destruction of convict leasing, though, came at a high price. The willingness of Tennessee miners to rebel against state authority derived partially from strong labor organization and the encouraging political environment created by the Farmers' Alliance electoral victory in 1890; yet rebellion eventually weakened both Tennessee mining unions and the electoral appeal of Populism. The combination of extended military occupation and state prosecutions crippled union locals in Anderson and Grundy Counties. At the same time, popular dissatisfaction engendered by Buchanan's inability to maintain law and order in the mining communities played a major role in the governor's crushing electoral defeat in 1892.

There were additional ironies in the outcome of the miners' assaults on unfree labor. When convict leasing died in Tennessee, the man who presided over its demise was Governor Peter Turney, the former state Supreme Court justice who had so consistently thwarted the miners' legal maneuvers and who had first won election to the governor's mansion by promising vigorous action against those who had defied state authority. Despite these stances, Turney moved quickly after assuming office to achieve a legislative repudiation of leasing convicts to private companies.

The most long-lasting irony, however, concerned the decision about what to do with all the convicts leased out by the state after New Year's Day, 1896. Almost from the moment that miners attacked the Briceville stockade in July 1891, Tennessee's legislators spent a great deal of time debating alternatives to the convict-lease system. Representatives put forward many proposals, virtually none of which found their way into the statute books. These ideas included setting up a whipping post for petty criminals, sending petty criminals to county jails to work on public highways, and amending the criminal law to lessen the number of misdemeanor prisoners who found themselves in the central prison system. Only one proposal received serious consideration— the purchase of coal lands on which the state could build a new prison and then put the inmates to work as coal miners. It was this last suggestion that ultimately found favor with Governor Turney and his new administration.

On April 4, 1893, Turney approved a bill that pursued a three-pronged strategy to reform penal administration. The bill provided for the building of a new penitentiary, the purchase of a farm, and the acquisition of coal lands in order "to provide for the abolition of the convict lease system in Tennessee." The purpose of the act was explicitly to enable the state "to relieve its citizens from the financial burdens of crime [and] to remove, as far as possible, convict labor from competition with free labor."[18] Helped by the depressed real estate market, the state government made a profitable purchase of coal-rich land in east Tennessee's Morgan County, just west of Anderson County. In 1895 the state began to construct the Brushy Mountain Mine.[19]

The development of a state-owned mine did not initially provoke serious opposition. Coal operators did not object to this venture, making no public remonstrations and privately expressing doubts about the state's ability to manage such an extensive business enterprise. In an 1893 letter TCIR's vice president, A. M. Shook, counseled a friend not to take a position at the state's proposed mine. Shook evinced skepticism as to "whether the mine will ever be opened by the State to the point where coal will be shipped." He further predicted that it was "doomed to failure on account of the management it will necessarily receive from the State officials."[20] Tennessee's miners similarly organized no opposition. Indeed, their leaders had supported such an initiative after Governor Buchanan had first mooted the idea in late 1891.[21]

The coal mine at Brushy Mountain opened in 1896. After a difficult transitional year, production and profitability soared. Between 1896 and 1900 the mine produced more than a million tons of coal, bringing steady revenue into the state's coffers. By 1898, Governor Robert Taylor could "congratulate the people of Tennessee" since "the penitentiary system, so long a source of perplexity and expense is at last a self-supporting and profit-paying institution." This venture remained highly profitable well into the twentieth century. For the fourteen years between 1903 and 1917, Tennessee realized a handsome net profit of almost $1.7 million from Brushy Mountain.[22]

The secret of Brushy Mountain's profitability lay in its emulation of the vertical integration engineered so successfully by many late-nineteenth-century industrialists. Like the Grundy County miners of the Tennessee Coal, Iron, and Railroad Company, the state prisoners in Morgan County did not simply mine bituminous coal. Rather, Brushy Mountain's management built over 140 ovens to enable convicts to process slack into coke, thereby diversifying output and adding value to the mine's product. The penitentiary further established extensive gardens, putting prisoners to work in raising food for themselves and their fellow inmates. At the same time, Brushy Mountain's general manager throughout the latter 1890s and early 1900s, J. T. Hill, implemented strict control over the labor of convicts while simultaneously introducing a detailed system of rewards for prisoners who worked efficiently. Hill divided inmates into squads of eighty men, each supervised by a mine boss, with every convict assigned a set number of tasks per day. Task levels varied from person to person, depending on fitness and skill. In order to create incentives for prisoners not to shirk labor or work badly, the general manager instituted bonuses for individuals who exceeded their allotted tasks. In concert with the state's legislators and penal administrators, he also linked privileges and eligibility for parole to work performance. Finally, Hill carefully selected the convicts who would come to Brushy Mountain, showing a strong preference for individuals with mining experience.[23]

By extending production forward into the manufacture of coke and backward into the growing of foodstuffs and by instituting effective and rigorous labor management, the state officials who ran Brushy Mountain achieved consistently impressive output of high-quality coal. Those officials additionally ensured that the sale of Brushy Mountain coal and coke would bring handsome returns to the state's coffers. From the earliest days of the state-owned mine, prison officials embarked on savvy marketing strategies, rejecting reliance on wholesale buyers. By cutting out middlemen and marketing the coal themselves, Brushy Mountain's administrators often saved expenditure of well over $1,000 dollars a month. Through the efforts of Tennessee's prison officials, coal from the state's mine found its way into markets from Cincinnati to Charleston.[24]

The successful operation of the Brushy Mountain mine led to the emergence of an uneasy coalition between the state's free miners and their employers. Tennessee's mineworkers soon soured on the new mining penitentiary. They threatened to launch an armed attack on Brushy Mountain in late winter 1895, though their opposition remained limited to verbal denunciations.[25] The state's coal operators undertook a more substantial challenge to the government's new moneymaker, with the full support and backing of their employees. In 1896 Kentucky and Tennessee mineowners organized a boycott of Brushy Mountain coal and agreed to put pressure on regional railroads to raise their freight rates for government-mined coal. By these actions, the operators hoped to confine Brushy Mountain's trade to Chattanooga and Atlanta.

Mine operators were able to place considerable pressure on the new mine, especially when its representatives convinced the new owners of the Harriman Railroad to ignore the terms of a contract that the previous management had reached with the state to haul Brushy Mountain coal. The Nashville government, however, took the railroad to federal court, soon gaining a judgment that required the corporation to stand by its promise of competitive transport rates. Attempts to dissuade corporate consumers of coal and coke from considering the output of the state's new mining enterprise were even less successful, as the high quality of Brushy Mountain's products attracted keen interest from potential purchasers.[26] With the mineowners unable to enforce the boycott of state-mined coal, Brushy Mountain became one of Tennessee's most important producers of coal and coke. The penitentiary retained that status for almost fifty years, only ceasing to sell coal on the open market in 1938.[27]

Brushy Mountain symbolized the growth of the modern, bureaucratic American state. The penitentiary in Morgan County was a complex economic institution, owned by the Nashville government, competing with mining corporations, and run for profit. Tennessee's militant miners should not have been completely surprised by Brushy Mountain. As solid members of the Knights of Labor, they stood foursquare behind the nationalization of natural monopolies like the railroads and thus for a dramatic expansion of government intervention in the economy. Some of the miners' leaders even endorsed a state-owned coal mine in late 1891 as a way to provide employment for convicts, explicitly suggesting that if the "state ran the convicts herself," it could "make a big profit."[28]

Nonetheless, Tennessee's miners did not rebel against their state government in order to secure the establishment and enduring success of a state-owned mine, which took jobs away from free miners. Instead, the men who repeatedly attacked the institution of convict leasing wished to protect elements of a Jacksonian world—a meaningful degree of social and economic equality, as well as the likelihood that workingmen would attain the status of independent property owners. These mineworkers did not pine for a preindustrial America populated by yeomen and artisans. They accepted and even embraced industrialization, according a legitimate place to corporate enterprise. But they also fervently believed that government had a solemn responsibility to maintain fairness in the industrial economy. To those Tennesseans, the state had no business in granting privileges to corporations like TCIR; rather, the state was obligated to ensure fair competition among producers and honest relations between capital and labor. These convictions lay behind the miners' demands that the state withdraw the assistance to capitalists provided by the convict lease, and that it guarantee the rights of mineworkers to an independent checkweighman and to payment in legal tender.

In attacking the convict stockades during 1891 and 1892, the men of Anderson and Grundy Counties had distinctly limited aims. They desired the vindication of their rights as upstanding Americans, not the wholesale transformation of America's economic and political institutions. Indeed, their ability to challenge the state so directly and for such an extended period depended precisely on the degree to which they were prototypical citizens of the New South. Ultimately the war against convict labor drove home the realization that industrial society would not easily accommodate the miners' updated philosophy of equal rights. S. P. Herron's embrace of the language of class conflict reflected this lesson, as did the choice of so many participants in the revolts to leave the Tennessee coalfields. For these working people, the promise of southern industrialization remained very much unfulfilled.

APPENDIXES

Appendix 1. Genealogy of the Tennessee Coal, Iron, and Railroad Company

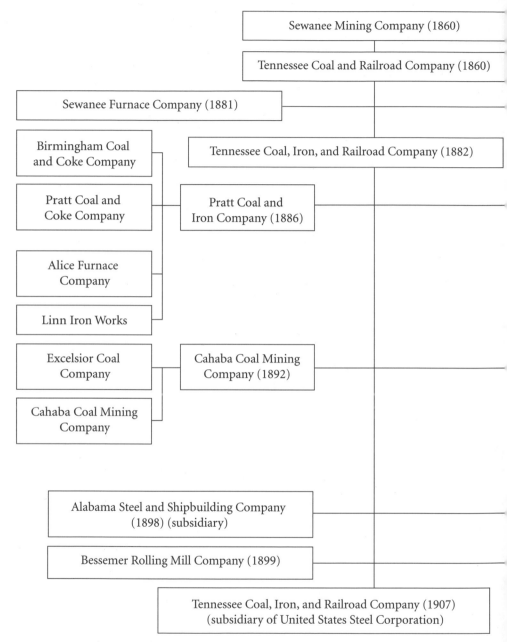

Sewanee Mining Company (1860)

Tennessee Coal and Railroad Company (1860)

Sewanee Furnace Company (1881)

Tennessee Coal, Iron, and Railroad Company (1882)

Birmingham Coal and Coke Company

Pratt Coal and Coke Company

Pratt Coal and Iron Company (1886)

Alice Furnace Company

Linn Iron Works

Excelsior Coal Company

Cahaba Coal Mining Company (1892)

Cahaba Coal Mining Company

Alabama Steel and Shipbuilding Company (1898) (subsidiary)

Bessemer Rolling Mill Company (1899)

Tennessee Coal, Iron, and Railroad Company (1907) (subsidiary of United States Steel Corporation)

Source: Fuller, "History of the Tennessee Coal, Iron, and Railroad Company," 389.

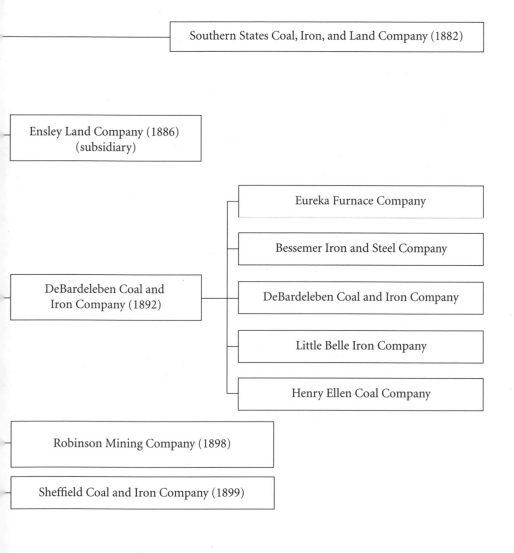

Southern States Coal, Iron, and Land Company (1882)

Ensley Land Company (1886)
(subsidiary)

Eureka Furnace Company

Bessemer Iron and Steel Company

DeBardeleben Coal and
Iron Company (1892)

DeBardeleben Coal and Iron Company

Little Belle Iron Company

Henry Ellen Coal Company

Robinson Mining Company (1898)

Sheffield Coal and Iron Company (1899)

Appendix 2. Race of Male Tennessee Convicts, 1865–1892

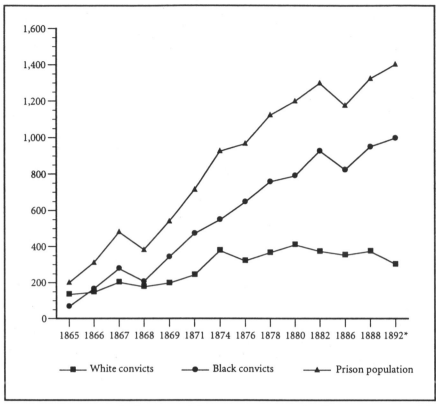

Sources: 1865–1888: Nicely, "History of the Tennessee Penitentiary," 30; 1892: *Report of the Warden, Superintendent, and Other Officers of the Tennessee Penitentiary*, 1893, 13–61.
*Race not provided for 102 convicts.

Appendix 3. Crimes of Tennessee Convicts, 1866–1892

Crime	1866	1867	1868	1869	1871	1874	1876	1878	1880	1884	1886	1888	1892
Petit larceny	205	369	216	254	349	—	—	—	444	356	304	—	67
Grand larceny	28	113	26	73	80	—	—	—	—	216	252	—	43
Larceny (combined)	—	—	—	—	—	519	379	407	—	—	—	580	516
Larceny from person	—	—	—	—	—	20	29	32	31	—	9	22	2
Burglary and larceny	—	—	—	—	—	—	—	24	28	95	21	18	17
Burglary	1	—	11	14	12	22	22	17	18	82	25	28	78
Robbery	14	41	21	28	19	20	24	28	18	27	30	41	51
Attempt to rob	—	—	—	—	7	3	—	3	2	—	—	3	2
Murder	18	47	32	48	66	85	94	106	133	139	162	150	151
Attempt to murder	—	—	—	8	13	14	21	31	27	72	73	87	70
Manslaughter	—	—	1	—	2	4	10	7	18	28	18	30	21
Malicious shooting	—	9	1	3	8	12	16	26	14	20	9	6	6
Malicious stabbing	2	—	—	—	4	13	23	19	14	—	9	9	2
Arson	1	1	3	3	5	11	9	6	15	19	17	21	25
False pretense	1	6	1	6	2	14	16	15	13	15	17	13	22
Rape	1	10	7	7	12	13	20	17	25	29	34	29	32
Attempt to rape	2	—	—	3	—	5	11	11	13	22	23	34	24
Horse stealing	—	58	45	57	73	87	114	128	124	66	42	29	13
Mule stealing	—	—	3	3	6	13	17	20	17	—	4	2	1
Felonious assault	2	6	1	3	5	—	—	6	10	17	17	28	30
Housebreaking	—	6	9	21	20	—	62	69	85	—	56	38	38
Housebreaking and larceny	—	—	—	—	6	—	15	33	—	21	46	53	67
Forgery	1	1	1	2	11	17	17	18	14	26	43	34	41
Perjury	1	9	—	1	3	—	—	—	7	17	7	4	5
Bigamy	—	—	2	3	2	3	3	3	—	6	9	6	11
Other crimes	34	19	18	12	35	88	95	127	171	50	55	98	63

Sources: 1866–1888: Nicely, "History of the Tennessee Penitentiary," 39; 1892: *Report of the Warden, Superintendent, and Other Officers of the Tennessee Penitentiary*, 1893.

Appendix 4. Numbers of Prisoners Leaving Tennessee Penitentiary, 1863–1892, by Means of Exit

Period	Sentence Remission for Good Behavior	Served Full Term	Pardon	Escape	Died	Transfer, etc.	Released and Not Recaptured	Commuted
					Method			
Oct. 1, 1863–Feb. 1, 1865	56	—	22	18	9	1	—	—
Nov. 1, 1868–Oct. 1, 1869	—	36	55	11	18	—	—	—
Mar. 1, 1870–Nov. 30, 1871	95	26	92	79	31	8	—	—
Dec. 1, 1876–Dec. 1, 1878	373	110	55	108	100	2	—	—
Dec. 1, 1878–Dec. 1, 1880	651	85	81	86	135	7	—	—
Dec. 1, 1880–Dec. 1, 1882	683	46	78	125	89	3	—	—
Dec. 1, 1882–Dec. 1, 1884	801	24	55	93	205	6	—	—
Dec. 1, 1884–Dec. 1, 1886	866	13	99	78	156	6	—	—
Dec. 1, 1886–Dec. 1, 1888	826	9	122	121	92	—	—	—
Dec. 1, 1890–Dec. 1, 1892	913	—	187	153	133	—	148	32

Sources: Oct. 1863–Dec. 1888: Nicely, "History of the Tennessee Penitentiary," 47; Dec. 1890–Dec. 1892: Report of the Warden, Superintendent, and Other Officers of the Tennessee Penitentiary, 1893.

Appendix 5. Lone Rock Song

[Sung by convicts in Tracy City, ca. 1890]

See a man a-goin',
'Cross the little hill,
Made me think of a little boy
Goin' to a mill.

Chorus:
    Buddy won't you roll down the mountain,
    Buddy won't you roll down the line,
    Yonder come my darlin'
    Comin' down the line.

He'll come down to the mine,
He'll poke his head in the hole,
The very first word you'll hear him say,
Nigger gimme that coal.

See them guards a-clusterin',
Pullin' for the shore,
Their shotguns on their shoulders,
The convicts on before.

Rovin' round the mountain,
Their guns loaded with lead,
All the guards was a-guardin' fo'
Was his fat meat and his bread.

There was a cross entry in Lone Rock,
Charlie Medlick drove it through,
News came that Charlie was dead,
And his friends was grievin' too.

They took him to the stockade,
And there three hours lay,
Walker a-takin' him in his cart,
And they hauled him to his grave.

I can't go back to Georgia,
I can't go back to France,
I'll go back to New Orleans,
To give my girl a chance.

I wish I was in Ireland,
Seated in my chair,
Mornin' paper in my hand
And by my side my dear.

The foreman he was a bank boss,
And he knows the rule,
If you don't get your task,
He's sure to report you.

And when he does report you,
The warden with a squall,
Bend your knees
Across that door piece fall.

And after you are counted,
Then they'll ring a bell,
And from that to eight o'clock
That Nigger catches hell.

Source: Dombrowski, "Fire in the Hole," 64–65.

Appendix 6. Coal Creek Troubles

My song is founded on the truth, in poverty we stand;
How hard a millionaire will crush upon a laboring man.
The miner toiling underground to earn his daily bread,
To clothe his wife and children, and see that they are fed.
Some are from Kentucky, the place known as my birth,
As true and honest-hearted men as ever trod this earth.
The governor sent the convicts here and works them in the bank;
The captain and his soldiers are leading by in rank.
Although the mines are guarded, the miners true and fair,
They mean to deal out justice, a living they declare.
The corruption of Buchanan brought the convicts here,
Just to please the rich man and take the miner's share.
The miners acted manly when they turned the convicts loose;
You see, they did not kill them and gave them no abuse.
But when they brought the convicts here they boldly marched them forward;
The miners soon were gathered and placed them under guard.

Soon the miners did agree to let them take their place,
And wait for the legislature to act upon the case.
The law has made no effort to lend a helping hand,
To help the struggling miner or move the convict band.
Buchanan acted cruelly, to put them out to toil.
He says he has not room enough for convicts in the wall.
He has no law to work them, only in the pen.
Why should they be on public work, to rob the laboring man?
I am in sympathy with the miners, as every man should be.
In other states they work free labor and why not Tennessee?
The miners true and generous in many works and ways,
We all should treat them kindly, their platform we should praise.
The Lord in all His wisdom will lend a helping hand,
And if we hold out faithful, god will strive with man.
He gives us happy sunshine, a great and glorious light,
He gives us food and raiment if we'll only serve him right.

[Alvin Vowell added from memory the following verse:]

God bless the Knights of Labor with all their wits and skill
Their efforts to accomplish intentions to fulfill.

Sources: White, *Briceville through the Years*, 80; Green, *Only a Miner,* 176–77.

NOTES

Abbreviations Used in the Notes

CCM&MC	Coal Creek Mining & Manufacturing Company
EMJ	*Engineering and Mining Journal*
SCEF Papers	Southern Conference Education Fund Papers
TCIR	Tennessee Coal, Iron, and Railroad Company
TCR	Tennessee Coal and Railroad Company
TPC	W. Tatom, "Press Clippings," 2 vols.*
UMWJ	*United Mine Workers Journal*

*In 1891, William Tatom was editor of the Democratic *Knoxville Tribune* and president of the Tennessee Press Association. During the miners' rebellion, Tatom collected two volumes of newspaper clippings from a wide variety of commercial and labor newspapers. Unfortunately, he did not always note the clipping's source. In cases of ambiguity, I have placed a question mark after the reference.

Chapter 1

1. Convicts told reporters that the miners "were not noisy or riotous . . . [nor] under the influence of whiskey either, but . . . very determined." *Knoxville Tribune*, July 16, 1891; *New York Times*, July 16, 1891.

2. For a discussion of the literature informing these generalizations, see Chapter 2.

3. In four of the five coal towns in which outright rebellion occurred—Coal Creek, Briceville, and Oliver Springs in east Tennessee's Anderson County and Tracy City in mid-Tennessee's Grundy County—migrants quickly claimed a stake in their community. The fifth town in which the rebellion took place was Inman, a small hamlet southeast of Tracy City in Marion County. Inman was dedicated primarily to mining hard red ore for the Tennessee Coal, Iron, and Railroad Company's iron furnaces in South Pittsburg. The vast majority of the men who worked in the ore pits were convicts, with a small contingent of free miners in positions of authority. Because of the overwhelming reliance on prison labor, Inman boasted very little in the way of a free community.

4. My analysis of the economic and social consequences of the convict lease largely parallels that of Edward Ayers. See his *Vengeance and Justice*, 185–222.

5. During tough economic times, convict labor could be both an asset and a liability to the lessees. When coal operators successfully used unfree labor to discipline their free miners, they viewed the use of prisoners positively. But when coal markets slumped, operators complained bitterly about the fixed costs associated with prison labor.

6. On the 1877 railroad strike, see Foner, *The Great Labor Uprising of 1877*; on the Haymarket massacre, see Avrich, *The Haymarket Tragedy*; on the Homestead strike, see Krausse, *The Battle for Homestead*; and on the Pullman strike, see Lindsey, *The Pullman Strike*.

7. Thus the miners in Tennessee had a more conservative outlook than the steelworkers in Homestead, Pennsylvania, at least according to the interpretation in Krausse's *The Battle for Homestead*.

8. On the American Federation of Labor's turn to business unionism, see Laurie, *Artisans into Workers*, 176–210.

9. Aurand, *From the Molly Maguires to the UMW*; Avrich, *The Haymarket Tragedy*.

10. On the labor struggles on the docks of New Orleans, see Arnesen, *Waterfront Workers of New Orleans*; on labor conflict and interracial cooperation in the Birmingham district, see Worthman, "Black Workers and Labor Unions in Birmingham, Alabama"; Letwin, "Race, Class, and Industrialization in the New South"; and Lichtenstein, "Racial Conflict and Racial Solidarity in the Alabama Coal Strike of 1894," 63–76. For an example of analogous interracial working-class cooperation in the east Texas timber region during the 1910s, see Greene, "The Brotherhood of Timber Workers."

Chapter 2

1. Eller, *Miners, Millhands, and Mountaineers*, 162–63.

2. Tennessee Commissioner of Labor, *Annual Report*, 1893, 29; U.S. Senate, *Report on Relations between Labor and Capital*, 1885, 4:128; Census Office, *Report on Mineral Industries, 1890*, 345; Shifflet, *Coal Towns*, 27–30.

3. Census Office, *Report on Mineral Industries, 1890*, 345, 409; Tennessee Commissioner of Labor, *Annual Report*, 1893, 27.

4. Lawrence, "Appalachian Metamorphosis," 7–18; *Coal Creek/Lake City*; *Goodspeed's History of Tennessee*, 835; McWhirter, *Revised Hand-Book of Tennessee*, 7–23; Justus, "Grundy County History"; Nicholson, *Grundy County*, 1–3.

5. Hersh, "The Development of the Iron Industry in East Tennessee," 18–21; *Goodspeed's History of Tennessee*, 260–67.

6. Eller, *Miners, Millhands, and Mountaineers*, 65–86; Nicholson, *Grundy County*, 30–31; McWhirter, *Revised Hand-Book of Tennessee*, 56–61; Census Office, *Report on Transportation Business, 1890*, pt. 1, 38, 84–89.

7. Tennessee Commissioner of Labor, *Annual Report*, 1893, 27; Armes, *The Story of Coal and Iron in Alabama*, 365.

8. Norrell provides an excellent sketch of the ebbs and flows of the iron and coal industry between the 1860s and 1900 in his *James Bowron*, xxi–xxix. For Anderson County's tax exemption, see "Historical Sketch," 9. Short or net tons should be distinguished from gross tons. The former constituted only coal bought by large-scale consumers and so excluded several hundred thousand tons purchased by local manufacturers, farmers, and residents. *The Coal Trade*, 1890, 1. For the growth in Tennessee's annual coal output between 1873 and 1891, see Tennessee Department of Agriculture, "Tennessee," 17. Also see *EMJ*, Aug. 8, 1891; Tennessee Commissioner of Labor, *Annual Report*, 1893, 27; *The Coal Trade*, 1894, 94.

9. Census Office, *Report on Transportation Business, 1890*, pt. 1, 36–38, 505–12; *Report on Mineral Industries, 1890*, xi; Belissary, "The Rise of the Industrial Spirit in Tennessee," iii, 290–91; Smith, "Joseph Buckner Killebrew," 20. Despite the emphasis that New South boosters placed on industry and manufacturing, agriculture continued to occupy the energies of most Tennesseans. In 1890, 64 percent of adult males continued to labor in agriculture, while approximately 11 percent held manufacturing jobs and only 2 percent worked in mines. Census Office, *Report on Population, 1890*, pt. 2, cxi, 610–11.

10. Quoted in Howell, "Editorials of Arthur S. Colyar," 265.

11. This biographical sketch of Colyar was drawn from newspaper clippings in the folder "Arthur St. Clair Colyar," McClung Collection.

12. Armes, *The Story of Coal and Iron in Alabama*, 373–74; Robison, *Bob Taylor and the Agrarian Revolt in Tennessee*, 5–22.

13. Quoted in Fuller, "History of the Tennessee Coal, Iron, and Railroad Company," 322.

14. Other Tennessee newspapers that advocated a New South ideology included the *Knoxville Chronicle*, the *Chattanooga Times*, the *Nashville Banner*, and the *Weekly Negro World*.

15. For sketches of O'Connor, see Armes, *The Story of Coal and Iron in Alabama*, 382; Fuller, "History of the Tennessee Coal, Iron, and Railroad Company," 38–39. For a brief biography of Cherry, see Armes, *The Story of Coal and Iron in Alabama*, 382; for Morrow, see *EMJ*, Feb. 21, 1891. For a discussion of Inman, see *New York Sun*, Mar. 7, 1896, in Bowron Scrapbook, 1895–1928; *Clinton Gazette*, Nov. 11, 1896; Armes, *The Story of Coal and Iron in Alabama*, 383; Fuller, "History of the Tennessee Coal, Iron, and Railroad Company," 44–49. For brief accounts of McGhee, see Shook to J. E. Simmons, Dec. 15, 1894, Shook Papers; *Knoxville Chronicle*, n.d., Letterbook, 1894–97, McGhee Papers. For treatments of Baxter, see Bowron Scrapbook, 1877–95; Baxter Deposition, Trial Record, 75, *Buchanan v. TCIR* (1897); Armes, *The Story of Coal and Iron in Alabama*, 383; Fuller, "History of the Tennessee Coal, Iron, and Railroad Company," 47. For evidence about Shook's background, see Shook to Sarah Shook, Jan. 26, 1893, Shook Papers; Bowron to Shook, Aug. 3, 1893, Bowron Papers; Shook Deposition, Trial Record, 127, *Buchanan v. TCIR* (1897); *Grundy County Herald*, Sept. 2, 1976; Fuller, "History of the Tennessee Coal, Iron, and Railroad Company," 47–48.

16. These phrases referred to O'Connor, Inman, and McGhee respectively. See Fuller, "History of the Tennessee Coal, Iron, and Railroad Company," 38; Armes, *The Story of Coal and Iron in Alabama*, 382; *Knoxville Chronicle*, n.d., Letterbook, 1894–97, McGhee Papers. In *New Men, New Cities, New South*, Don Doyle argues that the majority of Nashville's business elite came from modest circumstances. Doyle's broader focus on manufacturing and retailing may account for the difference in our findings.

17. Bowron Scrapbook, 1877–95; Bowron Deposition, Trial Record, 192, *Buchanan v. TCIR* (1897); Armes, *The Story of Coal and Iron in Alabama*, 386–90. The consortium was initially led by James Bowron Sr. and Thomas Whitwell and lost the support of its English backers after the deaths of these two men in 1877 and 1878 respectively.

18. Norrell, *James Bowron*, xiv.

19. The other men who held directorships in both companies were McGhee, Brice, Inman, and Samuel Thomas. *Poor's Manual*, 1891, 199; "Minutes of Board of Directors," 1891, CCM&MC Papers; *Cullen v. CCM&MC* (1897).

20. Sanford to McGhee, Oct. 10, 1891, McGhee Papers.

21. TCMC Brief, n.d., 3, *Jenkins v. TCMC* (1896); Original Bill, Trial Record, 9, *Buchanan v. TCIR* (1897).

22. *Chattanooga Times*, May 8, 1890, quoted in Sprague, "The Great Appalachian Iron and Coal Town Boom," 221. For general discussions of the New South ideologues, see Woodward, *Origins of the New South*, 142–74; Cobb, *Industrialization and Southern Society*, 1–26; Gaston, *The New South Creed*; Eller, *Miners, Millhands, and Mountaineers*, 199–225; Corbin, *Life, Work, and Rebellion in the Coal Fields*, 3–4.

23. *Memorial and Biographical Record*, 238–511. In 1891 the Tracy City miners swore an affidavit promising that all but one miner were citizens of the state and that all but six or seven men were Tennessee born. TPC, 1:71 (*Knoxville Tribune*, July 17, 1891).

24. Calculations for 1880 are based on Byron and Barbara Sistler, "1880 Census—Tennes-

see: Transcription for Anderson County." The 1900 census material is taken from the 1900 Federal Population Census, reel 1557. This distribution contrasts with national mining population statistics. Almost half of American miners and quarrymen in 1890 were foreign born, and an additional 16 percent had parents who were born abroad. Census Office, *Report on Population, 1890*, pt. 2, 610–11, 759. The local origin of the miners is also suggested by the propensity of Civil War veterans to return to their home counties and stay there after the war. See Bailey, *Class and Tennessee's Confederate Generation*, 124, 162. For a discussion of Tennessee's efforts and failure to attract immigrants, see Belissary, "The Rise of the Industrial Spirit in Tennessee," 163–95, 269–70; Donovan, "The Growth of the Industrial Spirit in Tennessee," 158–73.

25. In 1900, 60 percent of black miners in Coal Creek were native Tennesseans; the rest came from elsewhere in the South. 1900 Federal Population Census, reel 1557. See also U.S. Senate, *Report on Relations between Labor and Capital*, 1885, 134; Lawrence, "Appalachian Metamorphosis," 133; Lewis, "From Peasant to Proletarian," 77–87.

26. These statistics are derived from Census Office, *Report of the Production of Agriculture, 1880*, 84–89, 132–33; *Report on the Statistics of Agriculture, 1890*, 180–83, 227–28; *Report on the Statistics of Agriculture, 1900*, pt. 1, 39–40. The sixteen counties included Anderson, Bledsoe, Campbell, Coffee, Cumberland, Franklin, Grundy, Loudon, Marion, Morgan, Roane, Scott, Sequatchie, Union, Van Buren, and Warren. The value of farm products in Roane County dropped precipitously in this decade; the value of farm products for the remaining counties increased by 11 percent. East Tennessee community leaders openly acknowledged the work opportunities that the mines provided for the young men from counties surrounding the coalfields. See, for example, TPC, 1:65 (*Memphis Commercial*, Aug. 16, 1891).

27. Census Office, *Report on the Production of Agriculture, 1880*, 84–89, 132–33; *Report on the Statistics of Agriculture, 1890*, 180–83, 227–28. The historians Crandall Shifflet and Robert McKenzie similarly stress the tremendous effect that population pressure had on Tennessee's agricultural world. Shifflet, *Coal Towns*, 12–26; McKenzie, *One South or Many?*, 150–89. Their analyses of demographic pressures challenge the earlier interpretations of Steven Hahn, Robert McMath Jr., and Ronald Eller. In his study on upcountry Georgia, *The Roots of Southern Populism*, Hahn pays particular attention to the destruction wrought by the Civil War, the spread of the railroads in the 1860s and 1870s, and the enactment of stock or fence laws in the 1870s and 1880s. According to Hahn, these developments combined to quicken commercialization and weaken the independence of small-scale and tenant farmers. For a similar discussion of late-nineteenth-century rural Texas, see McMath's "Sandy Land and Hogs in the Timber." Ronald Eller's treatment of Appalachian industrialization and proletarianization, *Miners, Millhands, and Mountaineers*, portrays the consolidation of landownership, the intrusion of the railroads, and the emergence of the timber industry as setting the stage for the ascendancy of the coal industry.

28. Anderson County Tax Books, 1889–93, for Coal Creek (District 5), Briceville (District 13), and Oliver Springs (District 7); Grundy County Tax Book, 1892, for Tracy City (District 11). In east Tennessee the proportion of propertied residents varied from hamlet to hamlet, with the greatest number of owners living in and around Oliver Springs (65 percent), and the smallest number in Briceville (35–40 percent). In Coal Creek half of the inhabitants had purchased either a town lot or land bordering the town. In all these communities, the value of town lots began at $50, with the majority of homes receiving a valuation between $100 and $300.

29. For a discussion of how the east Tennessee towns came to be located on private land, see Shapiro, "The Tennessee Coal Miners' Revolts of 1891–92," 90–91. Coal Creek was

incorporated in 1874 but lost this status in 1879. Shortly before the convict wars, town residents discussed reincorporating Coal Creek, but the rebellion rendered it a secondary issue. *Tennessee State Gazetter and Business Directory, 1876–1877,* 105–6; TPC, 1:6 (*Knoxville Journal,* July 18/19, 1891?); *Clinton Gazette,* Dec. 18, 1891; Crowe, "Agitation for Penal Reform in Tennessee," 107.

30. *Oliver Springs News,* 1887–88; *Clinton Gazette,* 1889–92; *Tennessee State Gazetter and Business Directory, 1890–1891,* 93, 197; *Nashville American,* Sept. 19, 1890; *Chattanooga Republican,* 1889–92; *Tracy City News,* 1889–92; Anderson County Deeds, 1889–92, roll 41, 139, 141; Anderson County Deeds, 1889–92, roll 45, 140–43; Anderson County Deeds, 1892–96, roll 42, 106–7; *Grundy County Herald,* Sept. 2, 1976.

31. Precise union membership figures remain elusive, with membership numbers for 1884–85 ranging between 45–58 for Coal Creek and 65–76 for Tracy City. Garlock, *Guide to the Local Assemblies of the Knights of Labor,* 484–90; "Proceedings of the General Assembly, 1878–96"; "Quarterly Reports and Resolutions sent to the General Assemblies, 1885–90," Powderly Papers. On the philosophy of the Knights, see Laurie, *Artisans into Workers,* 141–75.

32. Coal Creek and Briceville boasted five locals between them; Tracy City and Inman had at least two apiece; and Oliver Springs had one. *Republican Chronicle,* Apr. 30, 1884; *Journal of United Labor,* Jan. 10, Apr. 25, 1885; Dec. 31, 1887; Jan. 14, June 9, June 30, Aug. 2, 1888; *Alabama Sentinel,* May 5, 1888; *EMJ,* Dec. 15, 1888, June 13, 1889; "Minutes of Annual Meeting of Stockholders," 1889, CCM&MC Papers; *Clinton Gazette,* Mar. 20, Oct. 16, Oct. 30, 1890; Nov. 26, 1891; *National Labor Tribune,* May 3, Aug. 2, 1890; "Quarterly Reports and Resolutions sent to the General Assembly, 1885–90," Powderly Papers; U.S. Commissioner of Labor, *Strikes and Lockouts,* 1894, 1:1150–61; Garlock, *Guide to the Local Assemblies of the Knights of Labor,* 484–87; Roy, *A History of the Coal Miners of the United States,* 262–82; Brier, " 'The Most Persistent Unionists,' " 53–56.

33. *UMWJ,* July 6, 1893. UMWA District 19 included east Tennessee and southeastern and northeastern Kentucky. The town of Jellico on the Kentucky-Tennessee border was its headquarters. *UMWJ,* Apr. 16, July 30, 1891. Until 1895, the UMWA allowed its locals to affiliate with the Knights of Labor.

34. For the views of R. L. Davis, a black organizer from Ohio, see *UMWJ,* May 25, 1892; for "Willing Hands" of Indiana, see *UMWJ,* May 12, 1892; and for Riley's assertion on the importance of the UMWA, see *UMWJ,* May 5, 1892. See also Gutman, "The Negro and the United Mine Workers of America," and Lewis, "Race and the United Mine Workers' Union in Tennessee," 524–36. For a critique of Gutman's analysis, see Hill, "Myth-Making as Labor History," 132–200.

35. *UMWJ,* Apr. 7, 1892.

36. The destruction of the 1890 census makes it impossible to quantify job opportunities in Coal Creek and Briceville during the convict wars. For general discussions of employment in Anderson County's coal towns, see *Clinton Gazette,* 1890–96; *Tennessee State Gazetter and Business Directory, 1890–1891,* 197; Hoskins, *Anderson County: Historical Sketches,* 108.

37. Tennessee Commissioner of Labor, *Special Report,* 1891, 16.

38. For an explanation of the Four Mile Law, see Bergeron, *Paths of the Past,* 75. On the sale of alcohol and the existence of gambling and prostitution in these towns, see TPC, 1:69; *Chattanooga Republican,* Nov. 24, 1889; *Clinton Gazette,* Feb. 20, Apr. 24, May 29, 1890; Mar. 5, 1891; Tennessee Comptroller, *Biennial Report,* 1892, 48–49; *Tracy City News,* Oct. 12, 1893; May 16, 1895; Dombrowski interview with Henry Thompson's father (July 1938), SCEF Papers.

39. Cobb, *Industrialization and Southern Society,* 7–9; Wright, *Old South, New South.* James Bowron Jr. strongly believed that the inability of southern manufacturers to make full

use of the region's mineral wealth substantially slowed the South's industrialization, contributing to its status as an outpost of the North's economy. Norrell, *James Bowron*, xiv–xxxii.

40. Killebrew, *Iron and Coal of Tennessee*, 178.

41. *Weekly Toiler*, June 3, 1891; Shook to E. S. Stahlman, Sept. 16, 1893, Shook Papers; Census Office, *Report on Transportation Business, 1890*, 262–63; Fuller, "History of the Tennessee Coal, Iron, and Railroad Company," 352–53.

42. The failure of B. A. Jenkins's Tennessee Coal Mining Company illustrates this point, as does the insolvency of the Cumberland Coal Mining Company at Oliver Springs. *Jenkins v. TCMC* (1896); *CCM&MC v. TCIR* (1900).

43. The number of mines operating in the region fluctuated in this era. Sanford to Shook, Oct. 19, 1891, McGhee Papers; Tennessee Commissioner of Labor, *Annual Report*, 1893, 37; Tennessee Department of Agriculture, "Tennessee," 16. The other two land companies were the Poplar Creek Coal & Iron Company and the Winters' Gap Coal & Land Company. "Miscellaneous File," CCM&MC Papers; *CCM&MC v. TCIR*, 16 (1900).

44. "Lease with Knoxville Iron Company," July 27, 1888, CCM&MC Papers.

45. TCIR Prospectus, 1885, Bowron Scrapbook, 1877–95; TCIR, *Annual Report*, 1893; TCIR, *Annual Report*, 1897. For a chronology of TCIR's growth from 1858 to the 1890s, see Appendix 1.

46. *EMJ*, Apr. 29, 1893; Aug. 11, 1894. In contrast to TCIR, the Knoxville Iron Company had no outstanding bonds from its incorporation in 1868 until 1912. By maintaining a conservative financial policy, the corporation withstood depressions more easily than mining companies that functioned on borrowed capital. Clark, "History of the Knoxville Iron Company," 130.

47. Shook to T. B. Branch, Feb. 21, 1893; Shook to Calhoun, Feb. 21, 1893; Shook to G. B. McCormack, Dec. 17, 1894; Shook to Benton McMillian, Dec. 17, 1894, Shook Papers; TCIR, *Annual Report*, 1894, 6; Fuller, "History of the Tennessee Coal, Iron, and Railroad Company," 384.

48. *Knoxville City Directory*, 1891–92, 698–704; Clark, "History of the Knoxville Iron Company," 8–9, 46, 122–23.

49. *The Coal Trade*, 1877, 65–67; 1896, 42.

50. *Weekly Nashville American*, June 15, 1887, Bowron Scrapbook, 1887–95; *The Coal Trade*, 1896, 42; Fuller, "History of the Tennessee Coal, Iron, and Railroad Company," 199–209; *Grundy County Herald*, Sept. 2, 1976.

51. TCIR Prospectus, 1885, Bowron Scrapbook, 1877–95; "Facts and Figures Concerning . . . the Nashville, Chattanooga & St. Louis Railway," 1895, Killebrew Papers; Gregg, *Origin and Development of the Tennessee Coal, Iron, and Railway Company*, 13–14. Ironically, TCIR's success in pig iron impeded its switch to the manufacture of steel, placing it at a severe disadvantage to its northern competitors. For the wide-ranging nature of TCIR's iron market, see *EMJ*, Oct. 6, 1888; June 8, 1889; Dec. 9, 1893; June 20, 1896; *The Tradesman*, Dec. 26, 1892, Bowron Scrapbook, 1877–95. By 1892, TCIR was the fourth-largest coal and iron company in the world and the only one of the big four that did not produce steel. See, especially, Shook to A. B. Beardman, Dec. 3, 1892, Shook Papers. For the best discussion of horizontal combination and vertical integration in nineteenth-century industry, see Chandler, *The Visible Hand*.

52. This constraint only placed a floor of activity below which east Tennessee operators could not go; they were able to reduce their workforces to some extent. Original Bill, 5, *Jenkins v. TCMC* (1896); TCIR, *Annual Report*, 1897, 11–13.

53. *Memorial and Biographical Record*, 238–511.

54. Bowron Autobiography, June 30, 1886; Bowron to W. D. Spears, Mar. 11, 1896, Bowron Papers; *Tracy City News*, Oct. 14, 1897. For the activity of the Mountain Home Building and Loan Association, see Grundy County Trust Deeds, 1889–98, roll 92. Also see Norrell, *James Bowron*, xvi; Nicholson, *Grundy County*, 68.

55. See, for example, TCIR's sale of a town lot to Dan Moran for $100. Grundy County Deeds, 1889–93, roll 58, 543–47; *National Labor Tribune*, Dec. 12, 1891; Shook to Victor A. Fagaux, May 10, 1894, Shook Papers.

56. *Tracy City News*, Sept. 18, 1886; TPC, 2:18 (*Knoxville Journal*, Nov. 6, 1891); 2:137 (*Knoxville Journal*, Aug. 15, 1892); *Chattanooga Republican*, Sept. 20, 1891; *National Labor Tribune*, Dec. 12, 1891; *New Orleans Daily Picayune*, Aug. 14, 1892; Shook to Victor A. Fagaux, May 10, 1894, Shook Papers; Bowron to W. D. Spears, Mar. 11, 1896, Bowron Papers; *Grundy County Herald*, Sept. 2, 1976.

57. TCIR deed to J. C. Brooks, I. H. Cannon, and John Harris, Grundy County Deeds, 1889–93, roll 58, 1–4; Grundy County Tax Book, 1892, roll 114; *Enumeration of Male Voters*, Grundy-Hickman County, 1891, reel 4; *Tracy City News*, Oct. 12, 1893. For references to TCIR's involvement in the religious life of its employees, see Bowron Diary, Apr. 15, 1885; June 30, 1886; Shook to Sarah Shook, Apr. 12, 1890; Shook to Rev. R. A. Reagan, Jan. 7, 1891; Shook to Rev. G. P. Jackson, Sept. 20, 1892, Shook Papers.

58. Shook to Fattie Sims Goodwin, May 13, 1890; Shook to Middleton and Fitzgerald, July 8, 1890; Shook to Middleton and Fitzgerald, July 14, 1890; Shook to J. C. Brooks, Mar. 21, 1891; Shook to W. C. Smith, Mar. 18, 1891; Shook to E. O. Hopkins, Sept. 18, 1892, Shook Papers; *Chattanooga Republican*, Aug. 4, 1889. The new school became a center of cultural activities in the town. *The Tennessee State Gazetter and Business Directory, 1890–1891*, 769; *Chattanooga Republican*, Mar. 11, 1893; *Tracy City News*, Aug. 29, Sept. 5, 1895; Sept. 10, 1896.

59. Dombrowski interview with Mollie Scoggins (n.d.), SCEF Papers; *Jenkins v. TCMC* (1896). Also see *Clinton Gazette*, 1889–92, for discussions of independent churches, schools, and other community organizations.

60. *Weekly Toiler*, Sept. 25, 1889.

61. Tennessee Commissioner of Labor, *Special Report*, 1891, 16.

62. *Chattanooga Republican*, Aug. 23, 1891.

63. Census Office, *Report on Mineral Industries, 1890*, 410.

64. *Enumeration of Male Voters*, Grundy-Hickman County, 1891, reel 4; TPC, 2:136 (*Knoxville Journal*, Aug. 5, 1892); Dombrowski interviews with I. H. Cannon (Mar. 1937) and Mrs. S. O. Saunders (Apr. 1937), SCEF Papers; *Grundy County Herald*, Sept. 2, 1976. Black employees of TCIR were joined by convict laborers in tending the coke ovens.

65. Census Office, *Compendium, 1890*, pt. 1, 647. Men represented 81.6, 79.4, and 68.5 percent of the black population in Wise, McDowell, and Bell Counties, respectively. Lawrence, "Appalachian Metamorphosis," 100.

66. *Journal of United Labor*, Nov. 5, 1887; Elliott and Moxley, eds., *Tennessee Civil War Veterans Questionnaires*, 458–59.

67. Dombrowski interviews with H. Lee Goodman (July 1938), George Ford (July 1938), I. H. Cannon (Mar. 1937), and Mrs. S. O. Saunders (Apr. 1937), SCEF Papers. Bowron Diary, Apr. 20, 1886; Bowron Autobiography, Apr. 26, 1886. The Tracy City Knights were not alone in sanctioning the inclusion of employers. Knights elsewhere in the country followed this practice, as did some high-ranking UMWA officials. Laurie, *Artisans into Workers*, 165–66.

68. Briceville and Coal Creek had a total of 753 miners—645 whites and 108 blacks. In Oliver Springs, 193 miners were white and 48 black. Tennessee Commissioner of Labor, *Special Report*, 1891, 73–74. In 1890, Anderson County's population was 15,120; whites accounted for 92 percent and blacks 8 percent. Census Office, *Compendium, 1890*, pt. 1, 506,

645, 800. For the increase in the number of blacks living in the Central Appalachian Plateau between 1860 and 1900, see Lawrence, "Appalachian Metamorphosis," 96. The small overall proportion of blacks in Anderson County had its origins in antebellum agricultural patterns. The hilly topography and thin soil of east Tennessee had rendered it unsuitable for plantation agriculture and hence large-scale slaveholding. In 1890, black Tennesseans constituted 24.6 percent of the population. Tennessee Department of Agriculture, "Tennessee," 14.

69. *Clinton Gazette*, June 30, Aug. 4, 1892; *UMWJ*, Apr. 7, 1892. The enumeration of Coal Creek (District 5) in the 1880 and 1900 manuscript census records showed that black and white families were not completely separated from one another. Byron and Barbara Sistler, "1880 Census—Tennessee: Transcription for Anderson County"; 1900 Federal Population Census, reel 1557.

70. *UMWJ*, Sept. 8, 1892. Riley was nominated for national president, vice president, and secretary-treasurer of the UMWA in 1893. *UMWJ*, May 23, 1893. For discussions of the moderate nature of race relations in many parts of Appalachia, see Woodson, "Freedom and Slavery," 132–50; Lewis, *Black Coal Miners in America*, 121–42.

71. TPC, 2:111 (*United Labor*, Mar. 11, 1892); *UMWJ*, Mar. 17, 1892; Mar. 30, 1893. For precedents of racial animosity among white and black coal miners, see *Weekly Negro World*, Nov. 26, 1887; *Chattanooga Republican*, Dec. 15, 1889; Mar. 16, 1890; Dombrowski interview with Mrs. S. O. Saunders (Apr. 1937), SCEF Papers. The 1889–90 legislatures enacted three election laws pertaining to voter registration, the introduction of the secret ballot, and the enactment of a poll tax. Ostensibly color-blind, they served to diminish black political clout. See Hart, *Redeemers, Bourbons, and Populists*, 266–73. For examples of manipulation of race by coal operators, see *Memphis Appeal Avalanche*, July 17, 1891; "Negro Labor in Southern Manufacturers," *The Nation*, Sept. 17, 1891; *UMWJ*, Apr. 14, May 4, May 12, June 30, 1892; Oct. 11, 1894; Tennessee Commissioner of Labor, *Annual Report*, 1893, 142.

72. Elliott and Moxley, eds., *Tennessee Civil War Veterans Questionnaires*, 2245. For discussions of the bitter feelings between supporters of the Union and Confederacy in east Tennessee, see Bailey, *Class and Tennessee's Confederate Generation*, 109–17.

73. Robison, *Bob Taylor and the Agrarian Revolt in Tennessee*, 147; Corlew, *Tennessee*, 374–75.

74. This interpretation rests between the positions adopted in Corbin's *Life, Work, and Rebellion in the Coal Fields* and Eller's *Miners, Millhands, and Mountaineers* on the one hand and Shifflet's *Coal Towns* on the other. Both Corbin and Eller depict Appalachia as a region whose land and culture was severely compromised by southern industrialization. In both their portrayals, the people living in Appalachia were immobilized by "forces" they could not shape or control. Shifflet, by contrast, persuasively emphasizes the significance of economic opportunities and enriched social life in coal towns, but excessively downplays the consequences of the great power wielded by many coal companies. My position is similar to that articulated by Edward Ayers in *The Promise of the New South*.

Chapter 3

1. For the variety of postbellum approaches to convict leasing, see U.S. Commissioner of Labor, *Report on Convict Labor, 1886*, Table 3.

2. U.S. Commissioner of Labor, *Report on Convict Labor, 1886*; Cohen, *At Freedom's Edge*, 221; Cohen, "Negro Involuntary Servitude in the South," 31–60; Ayers, *Vengeance and Justice*, 185–222. For general discussions of convict labor in the South, see Carter, "Politics and Business"; Zimmerman, "Penal Systems and Penal Reforms in the South since the Civil War"; Lichtenstein, "The Political Economy of Convict Labor in the New South"; Crowe,

"Agitation for Penal Reform in Tennessee"; Carleton, *Politics and Punishment*; Crawford, "A History of the Kentucky Penitentiary System."

3. Ayers, *Vengeance and Justice*, 190. In "The Political Economy of Convict Labor in the New South," Lichtenstein discusses how convict labor became both Reconstruction and Redeemer policy. Though convict labor ran counter to the Reconstruction ideology of free labor, it dovetailed with efforts by the U.S. Army and the Freedmen's Bureau to return the freedmen to work and to rebuild the southern economy. For the Redeemers, convict labor meshed with their goals of racial control, fiscal stringency, and limited government.

4. For chronologies of Tennessee's nineteenth-century penal policy, see Tennessee Commissioner of Labor, *Annual Report*, 1891; *House Journal*, 1891 (extra session), 13; Hutson, "The Coal Miners' Insurrection, 1891–92," 16; Green, "Some Aspects of the Convict Lease System in the Southern States," 113; Nicely, "History of the Tennessee Penitentiary," 68–78. The lease payment of 43 cents per inmate per day compared extremely favorably with daily wages for even unskilled labor between 1865 and 1870, which averaged around $1.50. Bureau of the Census, *Historical Statistics*, pt. 1, 165.

5. Control of the penitentiary went to another Nashville firm, Cherry, O'Connor, Morrow & Co., which held two six-year contracts between 1871–77 and 1877–84. Crowe, "The Origin and Development of Tennessee's Prison Problem," 128–31.

6. Carter, "Politics and Business," 54; Nicely, "History of the Tennessee Penitentiary," 18, 80–94; Crowe, "Agitation for Penal Reform," 38.

7. Similar conditions pertained in Georgia and Alabama: coal mining became the mainstay of convict labor in Georgia from the mid-1870s, and in Alabama during the 1880s. Convicts also made a brief and problematic appearance in Kentucky coal mines in the 1880s. In Florida convicts also toiled in mines, but not in the coal industry. After the decline of the turpentine industry in Florida toward the close of the 1880s, convicts were sent to work the new and hazardous phosphate pits. In other southern states, where mining did not provide the same opportunities, convicts continued to work on railroads, levees, and plantations and in prison manufactories. As the 1890s beckoned, prisoners increasingly constructed county roads and planted and harvested crops on state-run penal farms. Despite ample coal reserves, Virginia put most of its state inmates to work in railroad building, shoe manufacture, and county road construction. In Virginia, Texas, and South Carolina, the state leased convicts but remained responsible for feeding, clothing, and guarding them. U.S. Commissioner of Labor, *Report on Convict Labor, 1886*, Table 4; Carleton, *Politics and Punishment*, 22; Zimmerman, "Penal Systems and Penal Reforms in the South since the Civil War," 176–83, 251–58; Carter, "Politics and Business," 68, 77, 83–84; Green, "Some Aspects of the Convict Lease System in the Southern States," 112–23; Lichtenstein, "The Political Economy of Convict Labor in the New South," 135–38; Lewis, *Black Coal Miners in America*, 13. The shift away from the use of convicts in railway construction partly reflected the difficulties that railroad companies encountered in guarding convicts. See Winton, "A History of Brushy Mountain Penitentiary," 5–6; Crowe, "Agitation for Penal Reform," 47–49, 71.

8. For discussions of the introduction of convicts into different Tennessee mining communities, see Tennessee Commissioner of Labor, *Annual Report*, 1892, 142; Fuller, "History of the Tennessee Coal, Iron, and Railroad Company," 288–90; Clark, "History of the Knoxville Iron Company," 56–60.

9. Hill, "Experience in Mining Coal with Convicts," 389. See also *Chattanooga Republican*, Aug. 9, 1891; TPC, 2:22 (*Knoxville Tribune*, Nov. 8, 1891); Crowe, "Agitation for Penal Reform," 50; Carter, "Politics and Business," 61–62; Lewis, *Black Coal Miners in America*, 33.

10. *Knoxville Tribune*, Aug. 28, 1877; *Tracy City News*, Sept. 18, 1886; *New York Tribune*, May 1, 1890, Bowron Scrapbook, 1877–95.

11. *Report of the Joint Committee on the Penitentiary*, 1837; *Report of the Joint Select Committee . . . in Relation to the Penitentiary*, 1840; *Engineering Magazine* (Sept. 1891): 755; TPC, 2:22 (*Knoxville Tribune*, Nov. 8, 1891); Belissary, "The Rise of the Industrial Spirit in Tennessee," 230; Lewis, *Black Coal Miners in America*, 21; Crowe, "Agitation for Penal Reform," 10–12, 39; Zimmerman, "Penal Systems and Penal Reforms in the South since the Civil War," 105–6.

12. For coal prices between 1865 and 1890, see Census Office, *Historical Statistics*, pt. 1, 208–9. Extant company records do not allow comprehensive accounting of production costs in Tennessee mines. Nonetheless, a wide range of evidence indicates the centrality of labor costs in the excavation of the state's coal and the manufacture of its coke and pig iron. In 1888, payments to miners equaled three-fourths of TCIR's marginal cost in producing a ton of coal in mid-Tennessee. *EMJ*, Aug. 18, 1888. Henry J. Evans, an east Tennessee mine operator, reported in 1885 that labor expenses constituted 90 percent of marginal costs related to pig iron production. U.S. Senate, *Testimony as to the Relations between Labor and Capital*, 1885, 4:181–82. According to the Census Office, three-fourths of total annual mining expenditure in Tennessee during 1890 went to wages. *Report on Mineral Industries, 1890*, 351. On the limited technological change in postbellum mining, see Long, *Where the Sun Never Shines*, 24–51, 132–39; Dix, *What's a Coal Miner to Do?*, 1–60. Widespread use of cutting machines in Tennessee mines only began in the late 1890s. Clark, "A History of the Knoxville Iron Company," 47–48.

13. Tennessee Commissioner of Labor, *Annual Report*, 1893, 142, 152; Crowe, "Agitation for Penal Reform," 100–104.

14. *New York Times*, Aug. 22, 1892.

15. On wage reductions, see Crowe, "Agitation for Penal Reform," 296. On conditions of underemployment, see *National Labor Tribune*, Jan. 11, Jan. 18, Aug. 23, 1890; *Journal of the Knights of Labor*, May 21, June 5, June 26, July 10, 1890; *Clinton Gazette*, June 9, Aug. 11, Sept. 8, 1892. On policies surrounding the weighing of coal, see *Smith v. State* (1891); on the imposition of "iron-clad" contracts, see *UMWJ*, May 21, June 11, 1891; Hutson, "The Coal Miners' Insurrection, 1891–92," 106.

16. For the direct costs of using convict labor in Tennessee mines, see U.S. Commissioner of Labor, *Report on Convict Labor, 1886*, Table 10; TPC, 1:149 (*Memphis Appeal Avalanche*, Aug. 18, 1891); *UMWJ*, Nov. 5, 1891; Sept. 15, 1892; Shook to G. B. McCormick, May 4, 1894, Shook Papers; Bowron and Cooper Depositions, Trial Record, 263, 309, *Buchanan v. TCIR* (1897); Clark, "A History of the Knoxville Iron Company," 124–25. On declining wage rates in the Tennessee coalfields, see *Chattanooga Republican*, Sept. 20, 1891; Mar. 12, 1892; Crowe, "Agitation for Penal Reform," 296; Fuller, "History of the Tennessee Coal, Iron, and Railroad Company," 313. Overseers earned slightly more than miners; laborers and boys under sixteen years of age earned considerably less. Census Office, *Report on Mineral Industries, 1890*, 349–50. The decline in piece rates paid to Tennessee miners paralleled the general decline in nineteenth-century prices; thus real wages remained essentially stagnant over the two decades.

17. For a persuasive argument that emancipation signified a fundamental break with the past but that the "absence of slavery did not ensure the presence of a liberal bourgeois economy," see Woodman, "The Reconstruction of the Cotton Plantation in the New South," 106. See also Carter, "Politics and Business," 63; Ayers, *Vengeance and Justice*, 191–92. For general discussions of antebellum industrial slavery, see Starobin, *Industrial Slavery in the Old South*; Delfino, "Antebellum Tennessee Elites and Industrialization," 102–19.

18. Ayers, *Vengeance and Justice*, 196.

19. *House Journal*, 1891, 14. For statistics on lease payments between 1870 and 1890, see Nicely, "History of the Tennessee Penitentiary," 109–10.

20. White, *Messages of the Governors of Tennessee*, 7:418–19; *Sequatchie News*, Sept. 10, 1891.

21. Jones, *Tennessee at the Crossroads*, 5–6; Corlew, *Tennessee*, 368–69.

22. For an outstanding discussion of the origins of Tennessee's debt crisis, see Jones, *Tennessee at the Crossroads*, 3–17. Twenty years later, the state still held the dubious distinction of having the second-largest debt in the nation, ranking fourth in debt per capita. Census Office, *Report on Wealth, Debt, and Taxation, 1890*, pt. 1, 73, and graphs following 130.

23. Jones, *Tennessee at the Crossroads*, 18–148.

24. The warden is quoted in Hutson, "The Coal Miners' Insurrection, 1891–92," 30. See also *Report of the Joint Select Committee . . . on the Resolution to Investigate the State Prison, 1843*; Crowe, "Agitation for Penal Reform," 111–18; Carter, "Politics and Business," 40–42.

25. The convict-lease system soon became rife with abuse, leading Edward Ayers to call the institution "a sort of mutual aid society" for capitalists and politicians of the New South. While capitalists "fixed" the bidding for the lease and greatly influenced other aspects of penal policy, state officials turned to lessees for a variety of favors, including railway passes and tips for stock purchases. Bowron Diary, June 30, 1886; Mar. 2, Apr. 14, 1892; Bowron Autobiography, Jan. 29, 1888; Feb. 4, Feb. 5, 1889; Apr. 14, 1892; Tennessee Commissioner of Labor, *Annual Report*, 1893, 146; Shook to R. Carroll, Mar. 1, 1893, Shook Papers; J. A. Harris to H. Clay Jones, Mar. 14, 1894; J. A. Harris to W. S. Coover, Mar. 21, 1894, Comptroller Letterbook, 1891–94; TPC, 2:128–29 (*Journal of Labor*, July 1, 1892); Ayers, *Vengeance and Justice*, 195.

26. Tennessee Comptroller, *Biennial Report*, 1888, 1890, 1892, 1894.

27. Ibid. In Kentucky, the costs of administering the system of criminal justice also greatly exceeded the revenue brought in by the convict lease. Crawford, "A History of the Kentucky Penitentiary System," 20, 257, 266.

28. Crowe, "Agitation for Penal Reform," 56–57.

29. Ibid., 59. Though these amounts may appear trivial by today's standards, they were not insignificant in the deflationary environment of the period from the mid-1870s to the 1990s.

30. Crowe, "Agitation for Penal Reform," 170; Moulder, "Convicts as Capital," 48.

31. Tennessee Commissioner of Labor, *Special Report*, 1891, 77–104; Crowe, "The Origin and Development of Tennessee's Prison Problem," 123; Tennessee Department of Agriculture, "Tennessee," 13. For a racial breakdown of Tennessee's convicts from 1865 to 1888, see Appendix 2.

32. *House Journal*, 1891, 15. For earlier statements of similar views, see Crowe, "The Origin and Development of Tennessee's Prison Problem," 124.

33. Hill, "Experience in Mining Coal with Convicts," 390; Winton, "A History of Brushy Mountain Penitentiary," 27.

34. Blacks who were new to a place, who lacked a white patron, and who lived in cities or large towns were most at risk of falling foul of the law. Taylor, *The Negro in Tennessee*, 41; Foner, *Reconstruction*, 362–64.

35. The first comment, made in 1872 by Governor James Milton of Georgia, is quoted in Lichtenstein, "The Political Economy of Convict Labor in the New South," 116. Dr. Deering J. Roberts, the surgeon at Tennessee's state penitentiary, made the second assertion. "Response to Sims Report," Jan. 22, 1885, Bowron Scrapbook, 1877–95.

36. On age, see Nicely, "History of the Tennessee Penitentiary," 33. In 1878, the year for

which the commissioner of labor noted the age of inmates, 20 percent were between the ages of ten and nineteen; 53 percent between twenty and twenty-nine; 17 percent between thirty and thirty-nine; and a mere 10 percent between forty and sixty-nine. On gender, see *House Journal*, 1893, 343. Of the 1,560 convicts in 1893, forty-six were women. On education, see Tennessee Commissioner of Labor, *Special Report*, 1891, 93. In 1888, 69 percent of prisoners had no education, 25 percent a "limited education," and a mere 6 percent a "good education." On skill level, see Nicely, "History of the Tennessee Penitentiary," 43. In 1888, 54 percent of prisoners had no trade and 25 percent had farming experience. In 1891, 65 percent of the prison inmates were single. Nicely, "History of the Tennessee Penitentiary," 35–36. The profile of Tennessee's inmates resembled that of Kentucky's. See Crawford, "A History of the Kentucky Penitentiary System," 157–61.

37. *House Journal*, 1891 (extra session), 11; Nicely, "History of the Tennessee Penitentiary," 39–41. The length of a prisoner's sentence included extra time so as to recompense the state for court fees, such as payments to witnesses, lawyers, and judicial officers. Groups that opposed convict leasing, such as the Knights of Labor, advocated the abolition of court fees. *Missouri Republican*, Feb. 25, 1886. In Georgia individuals who had committed nonviolent crimes against property also constituted a significant percentage of state prisoners in the 1870s and 1880s. Lichtenstein, *Twice the Work of Free Labor*, 70–71.

38. On the convicts' geographic origins, see Tennessee Commissioner of Labor, *Special Report*, 1891, 102. For the migration of African Americans to urban areas and conditions in the shantytowns, especially after the turn of the century, see Lamon, *Black Tennesseans*, 26–53; Taylor, *The Negro in Tennessee*, 31–41. For a discussion of crime in the urban South, see Rabinowitz, *Race Relations in the Urban South*, 31–60.

39. Statistics are calculated from figures presented in Nicely, "History of the Tennessee Penitentiary," 39. These findings, along with the high percentage of larceny convictions in Tennessee's major cities, suggest an amendment to the arguments that the historians William Cohen and Pete Daniel have made about the functioning of postbellum southern criminal codes. Cohen and Daniel maintain that the convict lease worked in tandem with laws against vagrancy and enticement of workers already under contract, as well as contract-enforcement statutes. Together with the denial of the vote and a host of extralegal mechanisms, such as debt peonage and violence, these provisions allowed white elites to reassert control over the labor of rural blacks. Cohen, *At Freedom's Edge*, 221–26; Daniel, "The Metamorphosis of Slavery." Also see Wharton, *The Negro in Mississippi*, 237. The passage of vagrancy, anti-enticement, and contract-enforcement laws in Tennessee almost certainly had the aim of enhancing the grip that rural landowners and merchants had on black laborers. But the enforcement of the criminal law in postbellum Tennessee had its greatest impact in the cities rather than the countryside, working to impose a new structure of racial subordination in the state's fast-growing urban areas.

40. McMillen, *Dark Journey*, 139. For the use of the law to redefine property relations and limit rights to commons, see Hahn, *The Roots of Southern Populism*; Perman, *The Road to Redemption*, 242–63; Foner, *Nothing But Freedom*, 39–73. For a discussion of the relationship between changing notions of property and the criminalization of the poor in England, see Linebaugh, *The London Hanged*.

41. Nicely, "History of the Tennessee Penitentiary," 31, 39. For comprehensive statistics of the crimes that sent Tennesseans to state prison between 1866 and 1892, see Appendix 3.

42. Petition for Pardon—Henry Martin, 1892, box 22, Buchanan Papers.

43. Petition for Pardon—Noah Talley, 1892, box 23, Buchanan Papers.

44. Petition for Pardon—George Bridges, 1892, box 20, Buchanan Papers. Also see the

1892 petitions regarding Charles Brown, box 20, James Kelley, box 21, John L. Tanner, box 23, and Andrew Vann, box 23.

45. Petition for Pardon—E. H. Liggett, 1892, box 22, Buchanan Papers.

46. Petition for Pardon—James Denigan, 1892, box 7, Buchanan Papers. Also see William Nance's 1892 Petition, box 22.

47. 1892 Petitions for Pardon: John Brenhem, box 20; George Moore, box 22; James Manual, box 22; Samuel W. Jennings, box 21, Buchanan Papers.

48. If destitution, ill health, drunken behavior, and "moral justification" often served as the grounds for pardon petitions, so too did the claim of innocence or an inadequate trial. Less pervasive but also common arguments included the young age of the convicted felon, a parent's love for a son, and "bad female company." 1892 Petitions for Pardon: William White, box 23; Jackson Judd, box 21; W. F. Leonard, box 22; F. M. Martin, box 22; Sterling McDaniel, box 22; J. A. Brewster, box 20; William Boman, box 20, Buchanan Papers.

49. Ayers, *The Promise of the New South*, 156–57.

50. Petition for Pardon, 1893—Will White, box 23, Buchanan Papers.

51. Murfree, "Drifting Down Lost Creek," 52–59.

52. For examples, see 1892 Petitions for Pardon: George Moore, box 22; James Manual, box 22; S. J. Jennings, box 22; James Archer, box 20, Buchanan Papers.

53. Petition for Pardon—H. Clay King, 1892, box 21, Buchanan Papers.

54. Statistics calculated from figures in Nicely, "History of the Tennessee Penitentiary," 47. Only 1 percent of prisoners served out their full sentences; the remainder either escaped or died in prison. Over 500 prisoners entered and left the prison system every year. *Report of the Joint Committee on the Penitentiary*, 1893, 19. For greater statistical detail, see Appendix 4. A convict who behaved well was eligible for a one-month reduction from his sentence for the first year, two months for his second, three months for each subsequent year to and including his tenth, and four months for each remaining year of his sentence. Nicely, "History of the Tennessee Penitentiary," 41–47.

55. The willingness of black and poor white pardon petitioners to play by the rules of a paternalistic game by no means implies a widespread sense among Tennessee's blacks and poor whites that the state's criminal justice system was legitimate or fair. Nonetheless, that willingness did contribute to the confidence and self-satisfaction of the state's white elite.

56. In an effort to prevent overcrowding in the main penitentiary, the 1889 lease forbade lessees from keeping more than 400 convicts there. Nicely, "History of the Tennessee Penitentiary," 104–5.

57. Tennessee Commissioner of Labor, *Special Report*, 1891, 103; *Report of the Joint Committee on the Penitentiary*, 1893, 3.

58. *Clinton Gazette*, Jan. 9, 1890.

59. Quoted in Crowe, "Agitation for Penal Reform," 29–30.

60. Felix G. Buchanan, "Warden's Report, Dec. 1892–Nov. 1894," Turney Papers.

61. Hill, "Experience in Mining Coal with Convicts," 391–94.

62. *Report of the Joint Committee on the Penitentiary*, 1893, 4; Clark, "History of the Knoxville Iron Company," 59.

63. *Report of the Joint Committee on the Penitentiary*, 1893, 11. Guards routinely whipped prisoners found guilty of sodomy.

64. Ibid., 4–5; *Clinton Gazette*, Apr. 6, 1893.

65. *Report of the Joint Committee on the Penitentiary*, 1893, 6; TPC, 1:6 (*Knoxville Journal*, July 18/19, 1891?).

66. *Report of the Joint Committee on the Penitentiary*, 1893, 10–15. For another review of

Tennessee's branch prisons, see *Harper's Weekly*, Aug. 2, 1890. For detailed discussions of the poor conditions in all of Tennessee's mining camps throughout the lease era, see Crowe, "Agitation for Penal Reform," 72–76, 152–204.

67. Once a convict showed that he could mine more than his allotted task, his overseer invariably increased his workload. *Report of the Joint Committee on the Penitentiary*, 1893, 8–15; *Report of the Joint Committee on Penitentiary Affairs*, 1895, 2–3.

68. *Journal of United Labor*, Aug. 10, 1885; TPC, 1:26 (*Sentinel*, July 1891?); 2:124–25 (*United Labor*, Mar. 1892?); Tennessee Commissioner of Labor, *Annual Report*, 1893, 194; *Report of the Joint Committee on Penitentiary Affairs*, 1895, 2–3; Bowron Deposition, Trial Record, 216–17, *Buchanan v. TCIR* (1897).

69. Reports of how much TCIR convicts collectively earned per year varied between $500 to $4,000. *National Labor Tribune*, May 9, 1885; *Nashville American*, Feb. 24, 1887, Bowron Scrapbook, 1877–95; *Report of the Joint Committee on Penitentiary Affairs*, 1895, 6; Dombrowski interview with I. H. Cannon (Mar. 1937), SCEF Papers.

70. Dombrowski interview with Sarah L. Cleek (July 1938), SCEF Papers.

71. Dombrowski interview with I. H. Cannon (Mar. 1937), SCEF Papers; *Chattanooga Republican*, Feb. 20, 1892; *Report of the Joint Committee on the Penitentiary*, 1893, 8; Crowe, "Agitation for Penal Reform," 186–87, 201. The task system and its attendant whippings were vividly described in "Lone Rock Song," a tune composed by Tracy City inmates during the early 1890s. See Appendix 5.

72. Crowe, "Agitation for Penal Reform," 72–76, 173–74, 181–82.

73. The historiographies of American slavery and Russian serfdom are replete with outstanding analyses of day-to-day resistance. See, for example, Genovese, *Roll, Jordan, Roll*; Kolchin, *Unfree Labor*. For two excellent examples of similar studies in different contexts, see Scott, *Weapons of the Weak*; van Onselen, *Chibaro*.

74. Shook to P. G. Shook, Aug. 1, 1894, Shook Papers; *EMJ*, Aug. 4, 1894.

75. J. W. Renfro to Governor R. L. Taylor, June 20, 1890, Adjutant General's Office, Correspondence of the Governors of Tennessee, 1877–1910; *Clinton Gazette*, Jan. 9, 1890; May 26, 1892; Nov. 9, 1893; TPC, 1:55.

76. John E. Lloyd, "Inspection of the Big Mountain Mine," n.d., Turney Papers; *EMJ*, Sept. 15, 1894.

77. Tennessee Commissioner of Labor, *Annual Report*, 1893, 145. In one unusual case an ex-convict sued TCIR for injuries he sustained while working at Tracy City. Shook to E. O. Nathurst, Sept. 16, 1893; Shook to T. M. Steger, Sept. 16, 1893; Shook to Storey, Goff, & Williams, Sept. 16, 1893, Shook Papers.

78. *Harper's Weekly*, Aug. 2, 1890; *EMJ*, Sept. 15, 1894. See also Bowron Diary, May 31, 1886.

79. TPC, 2:76 (*Nashville Herald*, Jan. 14, 1892); *EMJ*, Sept. 15, 1894. Resistance by convict miners in postbellum Georgia greatly resembled that demonstrated by the inmates working in Tennessee mines; Georgia convict lessees also responded to that resistance in much the same ways as their Tennessee counterparts. Lichtenstein, *Twice the Work of Free Labor*, 126–51.

80. My analysis of the song follows that of Ayers, *Vengeance and Justice*, 202.

81. One branch prison warden advocated the complete separation of white and black convicts because their similar treatment encouraged many African American inmates to contest, through word and deed, the ideology of white supremacy. Felix G. Buchanan, "Warden's Report, Dec. 1892–Nov. 1894," Turney Papers.

82. See van Onselen's *Chibaro* for a similar analysis of resistance in the gold mines of southern Rhodesia.

83. Tennessee Commissioner of Labor, *Annual Report*, 1896, 286.

84. *Journal of the Knights of Labor*, May 29, June 5, June 26, July 10, 1890. Access to the coke and pig iron markets did not release TCIR from concerns about the ups and downs of the cyclical coal market. Shook to E. O. Nathurst, Feb. 11, 1893, Shook Papers.

85. Newspaper clipping, July 20, 1884, Bowron Scrapbook, 1877–95; Bowron Diary, June 2, 1885; Tennessee Commissioner of Labor, *Annual Report*, 1892, 145–46, 229–31; Shook to Felton, Nov. 4, 1892; Shook to Felton, Nov. 9, 1892, Shook Papers.

86. Bowron Autobiography, July 1883. On the east Tennessee operators' desires to restrict the number of convicts in the mines, see *Knoxville Tribune*, Aug. 28, 1877. For evidence about similar problems that postbellum Georgia coal operators encountered with convict labor, see Lichtenstein, *Twice the Work of Free Labor*, 89, 106–8.

87. Bowron Diary, May 25, 1886.

88. Dombrowski interview with Mrs. S. O. Saunders (Apr. 1937), SCEF Papers.

89. *Chattanooga Republican*, Nov. 24, 1889; Apr. 26, 1891; *Weekly Toiler*, May 13, 1891; E. J. Sanford to C. M. McGhee, Nov. 14, 1891, McGhee Papers; Baxter to Buchanan, Aug. 10, 1892, Buchanan Papers; J. A. Harris to M. E. (illegible), Apr. 12, 1894; Harris to John Skillern, Apr. 24, 1894; Harris to L. W. Bates, Aug. 9, 1894; Harris to Dees, Aug. 22, 1894; Harris to M. Deakins, Sept. 12, 1894; Harris to Deakins, Sept. 22, 1894; Harris to James Armitage, Sept. 28, 1894; Harris to W. P. Chester, Nov. 13, 1894, Comptroller Letterbook, 1891–94.

90. *Knoxville Chronicle*, Aug. 24, 1877; Tennessee Commissioner of Labor, *Annual Report*, 1892, 142; Fuller, "History of the Tennessee Coal, Iron, and Railroad Company," 289–90; Crowe, "Agitation for Penal Reform," 102–5.

91. Crowe, "Agitation for Penal Reform in Tennessee," 51, 62–67, 86–99, 107–17, 176–85, 203–21, 235–36.

92. Sanford to McGhee, Nov. 8, 1890; Sanford to H. W. Cannon, Dec. 4, 1890, McGhee Papers.

93. The conflict between Jenkins and his employees began in December 1890. In the middle of winter, when public demand for coal was high, the miners struck, demanding an independent checkweighman. Though Jenkins initially agreed to this condition, he closed his mine four months later, ostensibly for repairs. By the time Jenkins was ready to reopen his mine, the other companies in Briceville had fired their checkweighmen. Jenkins then refused to allow an independent checkweighman at his mine. For Jenkins's side of the story, see *National Labor Tribune*, June 27, 1891; *UMWJ*, July 16, 1891; TPC, 1:15 (*Knoxville Sentinel*, July 21, 1891?); 1:171 (*Knoxville Tribune*, Aug. 6, 1891); 1:149 (*Memphis Appeal Avalanche*, Aug. 18, 1891).

94. *National Labor Tribune*, June 13, 1891; *Knoxville Tribune*, July 17, July 21, 1891; TPC, 1:66 (*Memphis Commercial*, Aug. 16, 1891); 2:26 (*Chattanooga Times*, Nov. 1891?); 2:74 (*Nashville Herald*, Jan. 14, 1892); 1:50; Tennessee Commissioner of Labor, *Annual Report*, 1893, 187–89; "Memoranda of Issues Regarding *Buchanan v. TCIR*," 1896, Turney Papers; Daniel, "The Tennessee Convict War," 279.

95. *Nashville American*, Oct. 18, Oct. 21, Dec. 9, Dec. 10, 1890; *Nashville Republican*, Nov. 12, 1890; Bowron Autobiography, July 20, 1891; *Report of the Tennessee Penitentiary, House Journal Appendix*, 1893, 3.

96. Bowron Diary, June 26, 1891; TPC, 2:34. This agreement underscored the tenuous nature of the state's control over convict laborers. TCIR subleased convicts to William Morrow, who, in turn, arranged for a third party, J. E. Goodwin, to work a share of his convicts at Jenkins's Briceville mine.

97. Sanford to McGhee, Nov. 14, 1891, McGhee Papers. Jenkins agreed to pay Goodwin sixty cents per convict per day. The Knoxville Iron Company, by contrast, paid TCIR eighty cents per convict per day. Clark, "History of the Knoxville Iron Company," 61.

Chapter 4

1. *Knoxville Journal*, July 16, 1891; Tennessee Commissioner of Labor, *Special Report*, 1891, 19.

2. Tennessee Commissioner of Labor, *Special Report*, 1891, 21.

3. For brief sketches of E. B. Wade's political career, see *Weekly Toiler*, Aug. 7, 1889; Hart, *Redeemers, Bourbons, and Populists*, 126–27, 155.

4. *Memphis Appeal Avalanche*, July 16, 1891; *New York Times*, July 16, 1891; *Birmingham Labor Advocate*, July 25, 1891; Rutherford to Buchanan, Nov. 9, 1891, Buchanan Papers; Hutson, "The Overthrow of the Convict Lease System in Tennessee," 104. A great deal of controversy surrounded the governor's actions in calling out the militia; in the views of many observers, an insurrection was not imminent. For references to the legal questions that arose out of his actions, see *Memphis Appeal Avalanche*, July 16–23, 1891; *Knoxville Tribune*, July 18–25, 1891; *New York Times*, July 18–23, 1891; *Clinton Gazette*, Nov. 5, 1891; Buchanan to Rutherford, Aug. 29, 1892, Houk Papers; Morris, "Legal Questions Arising out of Our Recent Labor Troubles," 144–55.

5. Buchanan failed to win reelection in 1892. In his last speech to the legislature, he again raised the issue of the governor's right to call out the militia, arguing that this prohibition curtailed the executive's ability to govern the state. White, *Messages of the Governors of Tennessee*, 7:449.

6. Tennessee Commissioner of Labor, *Special Report*, 1891, 22–23.

7. This biographical sketch is based on Dombrowski interview with Merrell's cousin, Mollie Scoggins (n.d.), SCEF Papers; TPC, 1:15 (*Knoxville Sentinel*, July 21, 1891?); 2:73 (*Nashville Herald*, Jan. 14, 1892); 2:70 (*Journal of Labor*, Jan. 18, 1892); UMWJ, Sept. 10, 1896; Dombrowski, "Fire in the Hole," 72–75. Merrell's small size probably helped secure his reputation as a successful breadwinner in a mining community. Large men were at a distinct disadvantage in the mines. They suffered as they trod the narrow mine stopes, frequently banging their backs against the roof of the low corridors that linked the rooms in which the drilling, blasting, and loading of coal took place. George Orwell's descriptions of his trips into the Wigan Peer mines suggest the pain of a man over six feet whose vertebrae regularly hit the roof of the stopes; one might similarly recall Emile Zola's depiction of Catherine's slight body, hunched over as though on all fours as she manipulated her full tub of coal, to realize the benefit of a small frame and low center of gravity in a coal mine. Orwell, *Road to Wigan Peer*, 18–31; Zola, *Germinal*, 53–55.

8. *House Journal* (extra session), 1891, 19–20; *Knoxville Journal*, July 14, 1891; *Chattanooga Republican*, July 19, 1891; *Sequatchie News*, July 23, 1891.

9. *Knoxville Tribune*, July 21, 1891; *New York Times*, July 21, 1891; UMWJ, July 23, 1891; TPC, 1:32–33 (*Coal Creek Press*, July 25, 1891); U.S. Commissioner of Labor, *Strikes and Lockouts*, 1894, 1:1150.

10. TPC, 1:12 (*Sentinel*, July 21/22, 1891?); *Knoxville Tribune*, July 22, 1891; Tennessee Commissioner of Labor, *Special Report*, 1891, 102.

11. Francis, *Seventy Years in the Coal Mines*, 97–98. On the militant reputation of Kentucky miners, see TPC, 1:145 (*Memphis Appeal Avalanche*, July 1891?); 1:2 (*Sentinel*, July 20–21, 1891?); 1:139 (*Nashville American*, Sept. 19, 1891); *Memphis Appeal Avalanche*, Sept. 19, 1891; EMJ, Sept. 26, 1891.

12. Crawford, "A History of the Kentucky Penitentiary System," 299–320. See also *Louisville Courier Journal* and *Louisville Commercial* throughout March 1886.

13. These companies included the Chickasaw Guards, Bluff City Zouaves, Rosier Zouaves, Memphis Maurelin Cadets, Nashville Light Infantry, Washington Light Artillery, Nashville

Buchanan Rifles, Murfreesborough Stone River Guards, Tullahoma Light Infantry, Shelby-ville Guards, Sewanee Cadets, and Hibernian Rifles. Bowron Diary, July 20, 1891; *New York Times*, July 21, July 22, 1891.

14. Tennessee Commissioner of Labor, *Special Report*, 1891, 27–28; J. C. Roberts to Pow-derly, Dec. 22, 1891, reel 37, Powderly Papers.

15. *Knoxville Tribune*, July 17–22, 1891; *Chattanooga Republican*, July 19, 1891; TPC, 1:10 (*Knoxville Sentinel*, July 21, 1891). The near total absence of blacks from the militia eased fraternization between miners and militia. A few black men served in the militia's ranks but did not occupy positions of equality; their duties primarily involved cooking and cleaning. TPC, 1:36; *Memphis Appeal Avalanche*, July 19, July 23, 1891; *Nashville Banner*, July 24, 1891.

16. *UMWJ*, July 30, 1891. The editor was probably referring to the eight-hour-day strikes in May 1886. For a description of the strike at the Michigan Car Works, see Oestreicher, *Solidarity and Fragmentation*, 150–53. The camaraderie between east Tennessee's miners and militia had several precedents, as did Buchanan's reliance on militiamen who did not come from the same region as the Anderson County mineworkers. During the great railroad strikes of 1877, for example, the adjutant general of Pennsylvania had called in Philadelphia troops to quell the Pittsburgh strike. Foner, *The Great Labor Uprising of 1877*, 58–60.

17. *Weekly Toiler*, May 7, 1890; Allison, ed., *Notable Men of Tennessee*, 285; Hart, *Redeemers, Bourbons, and Populists*, 126.

18. Robison, *Bob Taylor and the Agrarian Revolt in Tennessee*, 1–22; Sharp, "The Entrance of the Farmers' Alliance into Tennessee Politics," 80–81.

19. Though these political factions endured at least until the end of the nineteenth century, they did not always guide the stances of Tennessee Democrats. On one of the state's major issues following the war—settlement of the state debt—a number of Democrats deviated from expected positions. The mining magnate Arthur S. Colyar, for example, advocated scaling back the debt during the 1870s. Colyar has often been described as the leader of the powerful industrial wing of the Democratic Party, but the stand he took on the state debt weakened the position of the business-oriented, state credit faction. The stance of Isham Harris proved just as unexpected as Colyar's. As leader of the states' righters, Harris was generally wary of New South philosophers, yet he aligned himself with the old-line Whigs on the debt issue, backing a state credit position. Jones, *Tennessee at the Crossroads*, 32–68. For an argument that such exceptions vitiate the analytical utility of Robison's tripartite division of postbellum Tennessee Democrats, see Hart, *Redeemers, Bourbons, and Populists*, 224–35.

20. C. M. McGhee to D. S. Williams, Aug. 8, 1890, McGhee Papers; See also *Birmingham Age Herald*, Feb. 26, 1890; *New York Times*, Aug. 13, 1890.

21. *Nashville Banner*, May 20, 1890, cited in Hart, *Redeemers, Bourbons, and Populists*, 142–43. For an analysis of the subtreasury scheme, see Goodwyn, *The Populist Moment*, 90–113.

22. Corlew, *Tennessee*, 349.

23. *Chattanooga Republican*, July 20, 1890. For opposition to Buchanan's nomination from within the Democratic Party, see *Weekly Toiler*, Feb. 19, June 18, July 30, 1890; Oct. 28, 1891; *Nashville American*, Oct. 26, Nov. 6, 1890.

24. For the struggle over the *Nashville American*, see Howell, "The Editorials of Arthur S. Colyar," 263. For the battles over the Knoxville papers, see Queener, "The East Tennessee Republicans in State and Nation," 113.

25. The weekly edition of dailies—copies that circulated in the country districts—had the largest number of subscribers. On small country newspapers, see Clark, "The Tennessee Country Editor," 3–18. For listings of Tennessee newspapers, their editors, size, and circula-tion, see *American Newspaper Annual and Directory*, 1891.

26. *Weekly Toiler*, Jan. 29, 1890; *Nashville American*, Sept. 21, Oct. 18, Oct. 26, Dec. 4, Dec. 9, 1890; *Chattanooga Republican*, Dec. 7, 1890. In pandering to the horror that the Lodge Bill elicited in southern whites, Buchanan did not diverge from the national policy of the Farmers' Alliance. At the 1890 Ocala, Florida, meeting of the Alliance, a Mississippi delegate secured the passage of a resolution condemning the Lodge election bill. This legislative proposal greatly hurt Tennessee Republicans in the 1890 election. See Queener, "The Republican Party of East Tennessee," 222–23. Terence Powderly, general master workman of the Knights of Labor, also opposed Lodge's bill. *Chattanooga Republican*, Aug. 3, 1890; TPC, 1:55 (*Memphis Sentinel*, Aug. 13, 1891). For a discussion of Buchanan's platform, see Sharp, "The Entrance of the Farmers' Alliance into Tennessee Politics," 84–86.

27. *Nashville American*, Sept. 3, 1890, emphasis added. See also *Weekly Toiler*, July 23, 1890; *Nashville American*, Oct. 2, Oct. 26, 1890.

28. Miller, *The Official and Political Manual of the State of Tennessee*, 334. Some east Tennesseans criticized Buchanan soon after the first revolt for his previous support of the convict lease and his decision to call out the militia. TPC, 1:23–24 (*Florida Times Union*, July 21/22, 1891?); 1:33 (*Coal Creek Press*, July 25, 1891).

29. Tennessee Commissioner of Labor, *Special Report*, 1891, 33–36.

30. Ibid., 33–37. For a detailed discussion of these negotiations, see Shapiro, "The Tennessee Coal Miners' Revolts," 104–7.

31. Gibson and Rule were not the best of friends, having engaged in a bitter fight over control of the *Knoxville Journal* in one of Tennessee's periodic "paper wars." TPC, 1:23 (*Florida Times*, July 23, 1891); "Obituary to Thomas J. Smith," *Knoxville Independent*, May 1942, clipping, box 145, SCEF Papers; Sharp, "The Farmers' Alliance in Tennessee Politics," 131; Jones, *Tennessee at the Crossroads*, 47.

32. Tennessee Commissioner of Labor, *Special Report*, 1891, 40; *Knoxville Tribune*, July 25, 1891.

33. *Birmingham Labor Advocate*, Apr. 9, 1892; TPC, 1:38.

34. Tennessee Commissioner of Labor, *Special Report*, 1891, 30–37; TPC, 1:24; Hutson, "The Coal Miners' Insurrection, 1891–92," 75–77.

35. Webb served six consecutive terms on the UMWA's Executive Board during the 1890s. For his role in the Kentucky revolts, see *Louisville Courier Journal*, Mar. 14, 1886. For biographical information about Webb, see Mayer, "Glimpses of Union Activity among Coal Miners in Nineteenth-Century Eastern Kentucky," 217–25; Mayer, "Gone and Nearly Forgotten," 17–19.

36. McGhee to Stanford, July 30, 1891, McGhee Papers.

37. C. W. Heiskel to Buchanan, July 31, 1891; A. J. Harris to Buchanan, July 30, 1891, Buchanan Papers; TPC, 1:40 (*Memphis Commercial*, July 1891?).

38. *New York Times*, July 25, 1891. For references to the divisions among the miners, see *Chattanooga Republican*, July 26, 1891; *Clinton Gazette*, July 30, 1891; *UMWJ*, July 30, 1891; *State v. Monroe*, Murder (1893); Original Bill, Trial Record, 10, *Buchanan v. TCIR* (1897). For references to report back meetings, see TPC, 1:2 (*Knoxville Journal*, July 14, 1891); *Clinton Gazette*, July 23, 1891; *EMJ*, July 25, 1891.

39. TPC, 1:56 (*Memphis Appeal Avalanche*, Aug. 13, 1891).

40. *Clinton Gazette*, Aug. 6, Nov. 5, 1891; *Journal of the Knights of Labor*, Aug. 6, 1891; TPC, 1:119. For an incisive analysis of the role of charismatic leaders in worker politics, see Sewell, "Uneven Development," 604–37.

41. On country stores, see Clark, "The Country Store in Post–Civil War Tennessee."

42. TPC, 1:56 (*Memphis Appeal Avalanche*, Aug. 13, 1891); 2:75–76 (*Nashville Herald*, Jan. 14, 1892); *Chattanooga Republican*, Aug. 27, 1892; Will of Jonas Irish, Mar. 26, 1887, Anderson

County Wills, 1887–1912, roll 27, 29–32; Anderson County Deeds, 1889–92, roll 41, 327–29; Anderson County Deeds, 1892–95, roll 42, 88–89.

43. TPC, 1:176; *Journal of the Knights of Labor*, Aug. 13, 1891.

44. *Memphis Appeal Avalanche*, July 22, 1891; *Chattanooga Republican*, Aug. 2, 1891.

45. *Knoxville Journal*, July 26, 1891; Aug. 19, 1892.

46. TPC, 1:6 (*Knoxville Journal*, July 18/19, 1891?); 1:15 (July 20/21, 1891?); 1:145 (*Knoxville Journal*, Sept. 22, 1891).

47. The term "movement culture" is Lawrence Goodwyn's; see *The Populist Moment*, especially 20–54.

48. TPC, 2:74 (*Nashville Herald*, Jan. 14, 1892). Each mine had three representatives, putting a total of thirty-three men on the miners' committee. *Memphis Appeal Avalanche*, July 30, 1891.

49. *Knoxville Independent*, May 1942, clipping, box 145, SCEF Papers. Alleman's political savvy is well illustrated by the manner in which he shepherded the legislation that created the Bureau of Labor and Mining Statistics through the assembly. Passage of the bill required that two-thirds of the ninety-nine assembly members cast their votes. On the third reading, fifty-two votes were counted for the bill and thirteen against—one short of the quorum of sixty-six. While the speaker held up the roll call, Alleman, along with George Ford, then a Knoxville labor leader, approached John Taylor of Union County, who was antilabor and had refused to vote. Ford "begged him to vote. 'Damn your old labor union, I'll not vote for it.' 'Well if you won't vote for the bill are you man enough to vote against it?' 'Damn you, yes' and he did. And we got our bill through." Dombrowski, notes to "Fire in the Hole."

50. *UMWJ*, Sept. 17, 1891. Miners also marched at the head of the Knoxville parade.

51. TPC, 1:145 (*Memphis Appeal Avalanche*, July 1891?); 1:28 (July 1891); 1:52 (Aug. 12, 1891); 1:57–58; 1:55 (Aug. 13, 1891); 1:85 (Sept. 3–4, 1891?); *New York Times*, July 30, Aug. 29, 1891; *Knoxville Tribune*, July 29, 1891.

52. TPC, 1:46; 1:5 (*Knoxville Journal*, July 18–19, 1891); 1:94; 1:116 (*Nashville Banner*, Sept. 12, 1891); *Chattanooga Republican*, Sept. 20, 1891.

53. *UMWJ*, Sept. 17, 1891; TPC, 1:46; 1:97 (*United Labor*, Sept. 5, 1891); 1:109 (Sept. 10, 1891?); 1:110 (Sept. 10, 1891?); 1:112 (*Nashville Banner*, Sept. 11, 1891); 1:86 (Sept. 1891?); 1:116 (*Nashville Banner*, Sept. 12, 1891); 1:151 (*Coal Creek Press*, Sept. 26, 1891); *Knoxville Tribune*, Sept. 2, 1891; *Clinton Gazette*, Oct. 20, 1892.

54. Rodgers, *Contested Truths*, 3–11. See also Myers, *The Jacksonian Persuasion*, v–ix.

55. TPC, 1:62 (Aug. 1891). At this time both the Knights of Labor and the Farmers' Alliance had adopted policies of non-partisanship.

56. TPC, 1:142 (*Chattanooga Express*, Aug. 19, 1891).

57. "XX," Tracy City to editor, *Chattanooga Republican*, Jan. 23, 1892. For similar analyses by other miners, see *UMWJ*, May 21, 1891; *Chattanooga Republican*, Jan. 9, 1892.

58. TPC, 1:31, 179–81; *UMWJ*, June 1, 1893; *Chattanooga Republican*, Nov. 15, 1891.

59. TPC, 1:183 (Aug. 15, 1891?); 1:59; 2:74 (*Nashville Herald*, Jan. 14, 1892); Schneider, "Republicanism Reinterpreted," 211. Tennessee miners recognized the link between their situation and that of Pennsylvania ironworkers. The southern coal miners readily approved both the Homestead strikers' "defense of home" and their resistance to the Pinkerton guards. At a picnic commemorating the first anniversary of their march on the stockade, the miners passed a resolution urging the Homestead strikers to obey the law but resist the Pinkertons. TPC, 2:130 (*Journal of Labor*, July 20–22, 1892?).

60. TPC, 1:56 (*Memphis Appeal Avalanche*, Aug. 13, 1891). See also *Knoxville Tribune*, July 18, 1891; TPC, 1:173–74 (*Coal Creek Press*, July 18, 1891); 1:87 (Sept. 3–4, 1891?); 1:94; 2:75 (*Nashville Herald*, Jan. 13–14, 1892); Hoskins, *Historical Sketches*, 102.

61. *Chattanooga Republican*, Aug. 23, 1891.

62. House Resolutions, 1–40, 1891, box 1, Secretary of State Papers. See also the petition by the Knoxville Central Labor Union, whose resolution noted that the convicts sent to Coal Creek Valley were putting miners "out of employment, destroying their business and virtually confiscating their homes." *Knoxville Tribune*, July 22, 1891; TPC, 1:2 (*Knoxville Journal*, July 1891?).

63. Stromquist, *A Generation of Boomers*, 174–87; Gutman, "Class, Status, and Community Power," 234–60.

64. TPC, 1:21; *Chattanooga Republican*, July 26, 1891; *UMWJ*, July 30, 1891; Tennessee Commissioner of Labor, *Special Report*, 1891, 30–31.

65. See Foner, *Free Soil, Free Labor, Free Men*.

66. *Journal of Knights of Labor*, June 26, 1890.

67. TPC, 2:75 (*Nashville Herald*, Jan. 14, 1892). See also *Knoxville Journal*, July 21, 1891. This demand for a "just share of the wealth [we] create" led some critics to cast aspersions on the manner in which the miners calculated the value of their labor. In an 1892 speech to legal colleagues, attorney Robert L. Morris snidely remarked that "organized labor regard themselves as owners of a vested right to employment at a given pursuit and place; that their labor has, for the most part, created the business; that they are *quasi*-partners of those furnishing the capital." Morris, "Legal Questions Arising out of Our Recent Labor Troubles," 153.

68. TPC, 1:27 (July 1891); *Knoxville Tribune*, July 17, 1891; *UMWJ*, Aug. 25, Sept. 8, 1892; *New York Times*, Sept. 2, 1891; *Chattanooga Republican*, Dec. 20, 1891. For a general discussion of notions of manhood in the nineteenth century, see Montgomery, *Workers' Control in America*, 13–14.

69. For thorough discussions of the relationship between slavery and liberty in eighteenth-century and antebellum America, see Morgan, *American Slavery, American Freedom*; Foner, *Free Soil, Free Labor, Free Men*.

70. *Knoxville Journal*, July 23, 1891. See also *Knoxville Journal*, July 18, 1891; *UMWJ*, July 30, 1891; May 18, 1893; *National Labor Tribune*, Nov. 7, 1891; TPC, 2:93; 2:99 (*Journal of United Labor*, Feb. 17, 1892); *Chattanooga Republican*, Feb. 20, 1892.

71. For a skillful analysis of the evolution of these distinctions, see Steinfeld, "Property and Suffrage in the Early American Republic," 335–76.

72. *Coal Creek Press*, July 25, 1891. For elite notions of work and honor in the antebellum South, see Wyatt-Brown, *Southern Honor*, 178–79, 327–28. The yeomanry in antebellum Tennessee also placed high social value on manual labor. Bailey, *Class and Tennessee's Confederate Generation*, 67.

73. *UMWJ*, July 30, 1891; TPC, 1:171 (*Coal Creek Press*, July 18, 1891); 1:32 (*Coal Creek Press*, July 25, 1891); 1:56 (*Memphis Appeal Avalanche*, Aug. 13, 1891); 2:82 (*Chattanooga Republican*, Jan. 27, 1892); 2:109 (*Journal of United Labor*, Mar. 4, 1892). The antimonopoly rhetoric occasionally took on an anti-English twist. An editorial in the *UMWJ* attacked "English stockholders of Southern corporations" for their greed. *UMWJ*, July 23, 1891.

74. *Knoxville Journal*, July 23, 1891.

75. *UMWJ*, July 30, 1891, Sept. 8, 1892; TPC, 2:76 (*Nashville Herald*, Jan. 14, 1892). See also TPC, 1:85 (Sept. 1891?); *National Labor Tribune*, Nov. 7, 1891; *Chattanooga Republican*, Nov. 15, 1891; Dombrowski, "Fire in the Hole," 77–78.

76. *Knoxville Tribune*, July 17, 1891. The men signed the affidavit on Sept. 1, 1891. TPC, 1:71.

77. *National Labor Tribune*, Sept. 3, 1892. In the popular mind of the late nineteenth century, Sevier was lionized. One man from Andersonville, Tennessee, noted that Sevier "was very popular with the mass of the people, in consequence of his services in the

Revolution, and his Conduct in many Indian fights." *Clinton Gazette*, June 2, 1892. For a popular treatment of the State of Franklin, see Gerson, *Franklin*. Thomas Abernathy disputes Sevier's democratic impulses, attributing the formation of Franklin to conflicts between different groups of "land jobbers." *From Frontier to Plantation in Tennessee*, 64–90.

78. *Birmingham Labor Advocate*, Apr. 9, 1892. See also *Chattanooga Republican*, May 14, 1892.

79. Dego continued, "They are serious, seldom smiling, but often laughing, feeding on corn and pork, and asking the rest of the world only to stand out of their sunshine and let them alone. The miners are not in any way different from the other mountaineers." TPC, 2:34. See also TPC, 2:18.

80. *National Labor Tribune*, Nov. 7, 1891. For discussions of how notions of Appalachian violence and independence have fed stereotypes in social science and literary scholarship, see McKinney, "Industrialization and Violence in Appalachia"; Shapiro, *Appalachia on Our Mind*. For a broader discussion of cultural images of American frontiersmen, see Smith, *Virgin Land*, 51–58.

81. White, *Messages of the Governors of Tennessee*, 7:415.

82. Tennessee Commissioner of Labor, *Special Report*, 1891, 34; TPC, 2:40 (Nov. 1891?). Tennessee newspapers in 1871 repeatedly poured scorn on the Paris Commune. Belissary, "The Rise of the Industrial Spirit in Tennessee," 201.

Chapter 5

1. Ford Folder, McClung Collection; Dombrowski interview with George Ford (July 1938), SCEF Papers.

2. *UMWJ*, June 25, 1896; Ford Folder, McClung Collection; Dombrowski interview with George Ford (July 1938), SCEF Papers.

3. The company became insolvent a little more than a year after the first revolt. *Jenkins v. TCMC* (1896).

4. "Minutes, Board of Inspectors of the Tennessee Penitentiary, 1877–92," Aug. 3, 1891, Prison Records; Tennessee Commissioner of Labor, *Annual Report*, 1893, 191.

5. *National Labor Tribune*, Feb. 20, 1890; June 2, 1892; William Camack to the editor, *UMWJ*, May 5, 1892. Also see Gutman, "The Negro and the United Mine Workers of America," 161–63.

6. Cartwright, *The Triumph of Jim Crow*, viii, 81, 90; Kousser, *The Shaping of Southern Politics*, 104–7; McKinney, *Southern Mountain Republicans*, 132–39.

7. Tennessee Commissioner of Labor, *Special Report*, 1891, 45–47. Ford's report minimized the complexity of working conditions in Briceville. Though the company flouted the law and showed scant regard for its employees, the miners also bore some responsibility for the unsafe mine. The piece-rate system, which the miners themselves favored, meant that work unrelated to the narrow task of blasting and loading coal frequently received short shrift. Timbering, which was unpaid work but essential to the miners' safety, often went neglected in the miners' haste to fill as many tubs of coal as possible.

8. Ibid., 45, 48.

9. Ibid., 42–48. Commercial papers, labor organs, and trade journals all presented sympathetic accounts of Ford's report. See, for example, *EMJ*, Aug. 2, 1891; *Knoxville Tribune*, Aug. 14, 1891; *New York Times*, Aug. 14, 1891; *Memphis Appeal Avalanche*, Aug. 14, Aug. 18, 1891; *National Labor Tribune*, Aug. 22, 1891.

10. Tennessee Commissioner of Labor, *Special Report*, 1891, 50–51.

11. The attorney general reiterated Ford's finding that conditions in the mine violated

state law. He also reasoned that the convicts were "not outlaws"; as a result, they were "entitled to protection of life and health during their imprisonment." Ibid., 52–55.

12. For discussions of the system of judicial election, see Greene and Avery, *Government in Tennessee*, 152–53; Miller, *The Official and Political Manual of the State of Tennessee*, 301; Caldwell, *Studies in the Constitutional History of Tennessee*, 154.

13. Tennessee Commissioner of Labor, *Special Report*, 1891, 56. See also "Minutes, Board of Inspectors of the Tennessee Penitentiary, 1877–92," Aug. 13, 1891, Prison Records; *Memphis Appeal Avalanche*, Aug. 14, 1891; *National Labor Tribune*, Aug. 22, 1891. The three-man Board of Prison Inspectors consisted of Charles A. Miller, secretary of state; J. W. Allen, comptroller; and Mansfield F. House, treasurer. All three were elected by the legislature, the secretary of state for four years and the comptroller and treasurer for two. The latter two officials were in their second appointments. All three men were Democrats. Miller was from Hardeman County in west Tennessee, Allen and House from Davidson and Williamson Counties, respectively, in mid-Tennessee. Miller, *The Official and Political Manual of Tennessee*, 296–99.

14. Bowron Autobiography, Aug. 14, 1891; TPC, 1:64 (*Knoxville Journal*, Aug. 16, 1891).

15. *Memphis Appeal Avalanche*, Aug. 15, Aug. 16, Aug. 18, 1891; *EMJ*, Aug. 29, 1891. Ford defeated this legal challenge by showing that the act of 1891 had superseded the restrictive clause in the act of 1887. He held his appointment, he successfully argued, under the latter law.

16. *Memphis Appeal Avalanche*, Aug. 15, 1891; *EMJ*, Aug. 29, 1891.

17. *New York Times*, Aug. 19, 1891; *Knoxville Tribune*, Aug. 19, 1891; Tennessee Commissioner of Labor, *Special Report*, 1891, 61–62.

18. According to the complainant's lawyers, the Board of Prison Inspectors had legal authority primarily over the main prison in Nashville; its jurisdiction over the branch prisons was limited to making by-laws and regulations for their administration by the lessees. Tennessee Commissioner of Labor, *Special Report*, 1891, 67–69. For a detailed discussion of the jurisdictional issue, see Tennessee Commissioner of Labor, *Annual Report*, 1893, 203–16. Also see *New York Times*, Aug. 19, 1891; *Knoxville Tribune*, Aug. 19, Aug. 23, 1891; Tennessee Commissioner of Labor, *Annual Report*, 1892, 204.

19. Tennessee Commissioner of Labor, *Special Report*, 1891, 70.

20. Ibid., 72; Bowron Autobiography, Aug. 26, 1891; *Memphis Appeal Avalanche*, Aug. 27, 1891; *Knoxville Tribune*, Aug. 27, 1891.

21. "Minutes, Board of Prison Inspectors of the Tennessee Penitentiary, 1877–92," Sept. 2, Sept. 8, 1891, Prison Records; TPC, 1:78 (*Nashville Herald*, Sept. 2, 1891); 1:104; Tennessee Commissioner of Labor, *Annual Report*, 1893, 206–26.

22. Senate Joint Resolution No. 17, 1891, box 2, Secretary of State Papers.

23. For the wide range of this support, see Hutson, "The Coal Miners' Insurrection, 1891–92," 60–61, 74–78, 82–86; Crowe, "Agitation for Penal Reform in Tennessee," 266–77; Shapiro, "The Tennessee Coal Miners' Revolts of 1891–92," 137–46.

24. Democratic Party fears that a severely divided party would lead to Republican rule were not completely misplaced. In 1880 the Republican gubernatorial candidate won the election, and in 1894 the GOP carried a plurality of the state's voters. Without an outright majority, the bitter election went to the legislature, where Democratic members ensured that one of their candidates entered the governor's mansion. Robison, "Tennessee Politics and the Agrarian Revolt," 378; Kousser, *The Shaping of Southern Politics*, 104. For a history of the Republican Party in Tennessee, see Queener, "The East Tennessee Republicans as a Minority Party," 49–73.

25. Sharp, "The Farmers' Alliance and Tennessee Politics," 97–99; Robison, *Bob Taylor and the Agrarian Revolt in Tennessee*, 148. These calculation are based on Miller, *The Official*

and Political Manual of the State of Tennessee, 246–48. See also Hart, *Redeemers, Bourbons, and Populists*, 159. Formed in 1887, the Farmers' Alliance merged with the older Agricultural Wheel in 1889. For a brief history of the Wheel and the Alliance, see Hart, *Redeemers, Bourbons, and Populists*, 120–21. Of the fifty-four Alliancemen, four were Republicans and fifty Democrats. The legislature also included a number of farmers who were not Alliance members.

26. The Republicans had eight members in the Senate and nineteen in the House.

27. Ralph Davis's proposal gained unanimous support from east Tennessee Republican representatives, but won the votes of only eight Democrats—four Alliancemen and four party regulars. As a result, the measure fell thirty votes short of passage. Hart, *Redeemers, Bourbons, and Populists*, 173–74.

28. Alex Lichtenstein argues that the shift from the convict lease system to road work in the South was the result of Progressive Era alliances between civic reformers and labor leaders. Lichtenstein, *Twice the Work of Free Labor*, 158–85. As the Tennessee Alliance's proposal indicates, in at least some cases the lineage of these reforms extends back to the Populists.

29. TPC, 1:55 (*Memphis Sentinel*, Aug. 13, 1891); Hart, *Redeemers, Bourbons, and Populists*, 173.

30. TPC, 1:148 (*Alliance Tribune*, Aug. 27, 1891); 1:108 (*Weekly Toiler*, Sept. 10, 1891); 1:155–56 (*Weekly Toiler*, Sept. 30, 1891); 2:31 (*Weekly Toiler*, Nov. 18, 1891).

31. Such letters and resolutions appeared regularly in the newspapers from 1888 to 1892. See *Weekly Toiler*, Aug. 15, Sept. 19, Oct. 24, 1888; June 5, Aug. 14, Aug. 28, Nov. 27, 1889; Apr. 20, May 21, July 16, July 23, Aug. 6, 1890; July 3, 1891; Jan. 27, 1892; TPC, 1:107 (*Weekly Toiler*, Sept. 9, 1891); *Clinton Gazette*, Mar. 19, May 7, 1891.

32. TPC, 1:44 (*Memphis Scimitar*, July/Aug. 1891?). See also *Weekly Toiler*, Dec. 12, 1888.

33. In an 1896 report, the warden at the Inman branch prison recalled the long-standing attachment of mid-Tennessee large farmers to the use of convicts in mining. The warden explained that area farmers believed that the increased employment of free miners necessitated by a repeal of the lease would "draw away and demoralize the farm help by offering apparently higher wages." Inman Branch Prison, "Annual Report," 1896, box 24, Prison Records.

34. *Chattanooga Republican*, Aug. 30, 1891.

35. White, *Messages of the Governors of Tennessee*, 7:384–85.

36. *House Journal*, 1891 (extra session), 10–11.

37. Ibid., 14–16.

38. The governor warned against the immediate cancellation of the lease, fearing that such action would drain already overburdened state coffers. He calculated that abrogation of the lease would require appropriations of around $1,000,000 over a two-year period. White, *Messages of the Governors of Tennessee*, 7:418–19; *Sequatchie News*, Sept. 10, 1891.

39. White, *Messages of the Governors of Tennessee*, 7:413–17; *Memphis Appeal Avalanche*, Sept. 1, 1891.

40. *Nashville Banner*, Sept. 5, 1891; *Nashville Herald*, Sept. 8, 1891; *Clinton Gazette*, Sept. 8, 1891; Bowron Diary, Sept. 8, 1891; *Memphis Appeal Avalanche*, Sept. 9, 1891.

41. *Knoxville Tribune*, Sept. 9, 1891; TPC, 1:94 (*Nashville Banner*, Sept. 5, 1891); 1:80–81, 1:106–7; House Resolutions 1–40, 1891, box 1, Secretary of State Papers.

42. *New York Times*, Sept. 3, 1891; *Memphis Appeal Avalanche*, Sept. 15, 1891; House Resolutions 1–40, 1891, box 1; Senate Bills 34 and 62, 1891, box 2, Secretary of State Papers; TPC, 1:77, 79, 80, 105, 117 (*Nashville Herald*, Sept. 12, 1891); 1:129 (*Nashville Herald*, Sept. 19, 1891); 1:141 (*Knoxville Journal*, Sept. 20, 1891).

43. TPC, 1:111 (*Nashville Banner*, Sept. 11, 1891); 1:119 (*Nashville Herald*, Sept. 14, 1891); 1:126 (*Nashville American*, Sept. 16, 1891); 1:129 (*Nashville American*, Sept. 19, 1891); 1:132 (*Nashville Banner*, Sept. 19, 1891); 1:135 (*Nashville American*, Sept. 19, 1891); 1:138 (*Nashville Banner*, Sept. 19, 1891); *Nashville American*, Sept. 20, 1891; *Memphis Appeal Avalanche*, Sept. 16, 1891; Bowron Diary, Sept. 19, 1891; *New York Times*, Sept. 20, 1891; House Resolutions 1–40, 1891, box 1, Secretary of State Papers.

44. Hart, *Redeemers, Bourbons, and Populists*, 173–74; *Memphis Appeal Avalanche*, Sept. 6, 1891; House Resolution 19, 1891, box 1, Secretary of State Papers. For a cynical interpretation of the legislature's initiatives, see *National Labor Tribune*, Sept. 26, 1891.

45. *Acts of the State of Tennessee*, 1891 (extra session), chaps, 7, 8, 13; *New York Times*, Sept. 2, Sept. 6, 1891; *Knoxville Tribune*, Sept. 6, 1891; *Memphis Appeal Avalanche*, Sept. 12, 1891; Hart, *Redeemers, Bourbons, and Populists*, 174.

46. *Memphis Appeal Avalanche*, Sept. 11, Sept. 17, Sept. 18, 1891.

47. *New York Times*, Sept. 5, 1891; *Journal of the Knights of Labor*, Sept. 10, 1891. Senator Alexander was a member of the militia who had gone to Knoxville.

48. *UMWJ*, Sept. 17, 1891.

49. Sanford to McGhee, Nov. 14, 1891, McGhee Papers.

50. *Knoxville Tribune*, Sept. 3, Sept. 12, 1891; *New York Times*, Sept. 4, 1891; *Memphis Appeal Avalanche*, Sept. 12, 1891; House Joint Resolution, 16, 1891, box 1, Secretary of State Papers.

51. *UMWJ*, Sept. 17, 1891; *Memphis Appeal Avalanche*, Sept. 18, 1891. See also TPC, 1:124–25 (*Nashville Banner*, Sept. 15, 1891); 1:159 (*Weekly Toiler*, Oct. 1891?); 1:140 (*Knoxville Journal*, Sept. 20, 1891); *New Orleans Times Democrat*, Sept. 6, 1891; *Memphis Appeal Avalanche*, Sept. 20, 1891.

52. TPC, 1:147 (*Chattanooga Times*, Sept. 24, 1891?).

53. Robison, *Bob Taylor and the Agrarian Revolt in Tennessee*, 158–61; Sharp, "The Farmers' Alliance and the People's Party in Tennessee," 92–93; Hart, *Redeemers, Bourbons, and Populists*, 133–34. Despite the rapid rise of the Farmers' Alliance, it often managed only a shallow organization of members and even leaders. Such was the case in Kansas. McNall, *The Road to Rebellion*, 56, 187.

54. Quoted in Palmer, *"Man over Money,"* 48.

55. Hart, *Redeemers, Bourbons, and Populists*, 165; Robison, *Bob Taylor and the Agrarian Revolt in Tennessee*, 152–53.

56. *Nashville Sun*, June 18, 1896, quoted in Hart, *Redeemers, Bourbons, and Populists*, 163; Robison, *Bob Taylor and the Agrarian Revolt in Tennessee*, 153.

57. Quoted in Robison, *Bob Taylor and the Agrarian Revolt in Tennessee*, 142.

58. Sims, "The Lease System in Tennessee and Other Southern States," 127; Hart, *Redeemers, Bourbons, and Populists*, 26; Sharp, "The Farmers' Alliance in Tennessee Politics," 172; Robison, *Bob Taylor and the Agrarian Revolt in Tennessee*, 156–67.

59. Robison, *Bob Taylor and the Agrarian Revolt in Tennessee*, 141–51; Sharp, "The Entrance of the Farmers' Alliance into Tennessee Politics," 84; Hart, *Redeemers, Bourbons, and Populists*, 143. For the platform of the national Alliance, see Goodwyn, *The Populist Moment*, 108–10, 145, 161.

60. *Chattanooga Republican*, Mar. 16, 1890; *Clinton Gazette*, Oct. 30, 1890. See also Robison, "Tennessee Politics and the Agrarian Revolt"; Hart, *Redeemers, Bourbons, and Populists*, 266.

61. J. A. Harris to Buchanan, June 28, 1891, Buchanan Papers. For Republican challenges to these laws, see *Nashville American*, Oct. 3, 1890; *Chattanooga Republican*, Apr. 12, 1891; May 7, 1892; TPC, 1:131 (*Nashville Banner*, Sept. 19, 1891); *Clinton Gazette*, Dec. 24, 1894.

62. *Memphis Avalanche*, Mar. 27, 1889, quoted in Kousser, *The Shaping of Southern Politics*, 111.

63. Kousser, *The Shaping of Southern Politics*, 110–16.

64. Sharp, "The Farmers' Alliance and Tennessee Politics," 137.

65. Kousser, *The Shaping of Southern Politics*, 116–21. For concern about the effect of these laws on white voters, see George Baxter to Col. C. M. McGhee, Sept. 13, 1890, McGhee Papers; John Chandler to Houk, Oct. 13, 1891; Thomas G. Stanberg to Houk, Oct. 27, 1891; Republican State Executive Committee to Houk, Sept. 28, 1892, Houk Papers.

66. TPC, 1:135 (*Knoxville Journal*, Sept. 18, 1891); *Clinton Gazette*, Nov. 5, 1891; Robison, *Bob Taylor and the Agrarian Revolt in Tennessee*, 154.

67. Disfranchisement laws impeded Populist success in most states where the Democrats implemented voting registration prior to statewide populist campaigns—including Tennessee, Florida, Mississippi, and Arkansas. Palmer, *"Man over Money,"* 196.

68. Sharp, "The Farmers' Alliance in Tennessee Politics," 114–18.

69. Many poorer Alliance members also opposed ending the convict lease, if doing so meant higher property taxes for economically strapped farmers. Sims, "The Lease System in Tennessee and Other Southern States," 125–26.

70. Woodward, *Origins of the New South*, 204; See also Palmer, *"Man over Money,"* 142, 195.

71. Quoted in Conway, ed., *The Welsh in America*, 203.

72. The local *Coal Creek Press* criticized his dismissal, commenting that, "he has made many friends who will regret to have him go." TPC, 1:166 (*Coal Creek Press*, Oct. 24, 1891).

73. To bolster this claim, Colyar cited at length the duties of prison inspectors and superintendents. These arguments ran counter to those presented a few months earlier by J. E. Goodwin, the convict sublessee who had argued that the Board of Prison Inspectors had no say over branch or secondary prisons. The ease with which the convict lessees put forward wildly divergent positions confirmed the amorphous nature of the convict-lease law and its failure to confer unambiguous responsibility on any particular branch or office of government. TPC, 1:153 (*Knoxville Journal*, Oct. 2, 1891).

74. In an effort to diminish Williams's popularity among traditionally Republican constituents, the paper reported that he had supported the universal application of voter registration laws. If the previous legislature had not narrowed the laws to apply principally to town districts, the *Journal* observed, many of the miners would have been disenfranchised. Williams denied this accusation, saying that he had favored registration laws only in urban areas, where "bribery and corruption" were likely to occur. TPC, 1:146 (*Knoxville Journal*, Sept. 23, 1891); 1:146 (*Nashville Sentinel*, Sept. 24, 1891); 1:160 (*Nashville Banner*, Oct. 12, 1891); 1:162 (*Nashville Sentinel*, Oct. 24, 1891); C. Bonhum to Houk, Oct. 15, 1891, Houk Papers.

75. Williams also drew on judicial precedent, reaching back into Tennessee's antebellum history. The attorney likened a convict's period of incarceration to slavery, drawing on a case in which a slaveholder had successfully sued a man to whom he had rented his slave for a specific purpose, but who, in turn, had rented the slave. TPC, 1:153 (*Knoxville Journal*, Oct. 2, 1891).

76. TPC, 1:162; 1:154–55 (*Knoxville Journal*, Oct. 3, 1891); *Knoxville Tribune*, Oct. 3, 1891; *EMJ*, Oct. 3, 1891; *UMWJ*, Oct. 8, 1891; Dombrowski, "Fire in the Hole," 104–5.

77. Bowron Diary, Oct. 2, 1891.

78. *State v. Jenkins*, 582, 584 (1891); See also TPC, 1:160 (*Knoxville Journal*, Oct. 14, 1891).

79. *Payne v. Western & Atlanta Rail Road*, 81 Tenn. 507 (1884), quoted in Hogler, "Labor History and Critical Labor Law," 180–81. See also Forbath, "The Ambiguities of Free Labor," 786, 798–807. The judicial drift toward the upholding of owners' property rights under the

employment-at-will doctrine was not without contrary rulings, even in the area of mining. Not every Tennessee legal decision undercut miners' interests and weakened their legal rights. The first case the Anderson County miners pursued, also about the weighing of coal, ended successfully, with the Supreme Court's Judge Lea declaring final judgment during the same month that the miners' other two cases reached conclusion. In this case, miners gained a criminal indictment against John Smith, a weighman of the Coal Creek Mining Company, for "knowingly, willfully, and unlawfully [taking] more pounds for a ton of coal than is now provided by law." Again the 1887 checkweighman law was at issue. The miners argued that if the beam of the scale "kicked up," indicating the car weighed over 2,500 pounds, Smith ran the car off the scales and credited the miner with only 2,500; with payment fixed at fifty cents per ton, this practice substantially reduced the miners' income. The defense offered a common law argument, suggesting that since this manner of weighing had been in vogue for a number of years, the miners had tacitly agreed to it. Judge Lea rejected this position and sentenced Smith to imprisonment for three months. Even Chief Justice Turney concurred because the miner concerned had not agreed to "the system of weighing and paying in force by this company." Perhaps a signed contract would have resulted in a dissenting vote from Turney or a different ruling altogether. Nonetheless, the ruling against Smith serves as a reminder that the state's higher courts were not wholeheartedly and consistently arraigned against the workingmen of east Tennessee. *State v. Smith* (1890). The *Clinton Gazette*, *Knoxville Journal*, and *Nashville Sentinel* covered this case. See their reports for October 13–15, 1891.

80. *State v. Jack* (1891); TPC, 1:163, 165; *New York Times*, Nov. 1, 1891.

Chapter 6

1. The phrase is from Dombrowski, "Fire in a Hole," 106.

2. TPC, 1:169 (*Knoxville Sentinel*, Oct. 31, 1891); *Coal Creek Press*, Nov. 5, 1891; *National Labor Tribune*, Nov. 7, 1891; UMWJ, Nov. 19, 1891; Byron and Barbara Sistler, "1880 Census—Tennessee: Transcription for Anderson County," household 287.

3. *Knoxville Tribune*, Oct. 31, Nov. 1, 1891; *UMWJ*, Nov. 1, Nov. 19, 1891; *New York Times*, Nov. 1, 1891; *Coal Creek Press*, Nov. 5, 1891.

4. TPC, 1:167 (*Knoxville Journal*, Oct. 29, 1891). The union men were J. M. Turner, S. R. Pickering, W. R. Harrington, C. M. Woodward, John Sharp, and W. Pickett.

5. Maier, *From Resistance to Revolution*, 37 n.

6. *National Labor Tribune*, Nov. 21, 1891; TPC, 2:3 (*Knoxville Journal*, Oct. 31, 1891); 2:74 (*Nashville Herald*, Jan. 14, 1892).

7. *Alabama Sentinel*, Nov. 7, 1891.

8. *National Labor Tribune*, Nov. 21, 1891. See also *Memphis Appeal Avalanche*, Sept. 19, 1891; TPC, 1:139 (*Nashville American*, Sept. 19, 1891); 1:167 (*Knoxville Journal*, Oct. 27, 1891); *EMJ*, Sept. 26, 1891; *UMWJ*, Nov. 5, 1891; May 31, 1892; *Birmingham Labor Advocate*, Nov. 7, 1891; Daniel, "The Tennessee Convict War," 285. Clothing stores quickly incorporated the latest town events into their advertising. One company ran an advertisement entitled "The Convicts" in which it suggested that "if tonight a convict should decide to wear your suit away leaving his instead, remember large stripes in black and white are not stylish; do not wear them but come at once to us and get a wool brown suit." TPC, 2:16 (Nov. 1891?).

9. *National Labor Tribune*, Nov. 7, Nov. 21, 1891; *Chattanooga Republican*, Nov. 8, 1891.

10. Quoted in Dombrowski, "Fire in a Hole," 109; *Knoxville Tribune*, Nov. 1, 1891; TPC, 2:11.

11. Quoted in Dombrowski, notes to "Fire in the Hole"; TPC, 1:170; *UMWJ*, Nov. 5, 1891; *Clinton Courier*, Feb. 6, 1975.

12. *Oliver Springs News*, Sept. 14, Nov. 16, 1887; *Clinton Gazette*, July 24, Nov. 13, Dec. 11, 1890; *Chattanooga Republican*, Apr. 16, May 14, 1892.

13. Miscellaneous files, CCM&MC Papers; CCM&MC Company, Letterbook 1885–88, June 30, 1888, McClung Collection; *Chattanooga Republican*, May 11, 1890; *Clinton Gazette*, Jan. 12, 1891; Jan. 19, Feb. 9, Apr. 13, May 11, Nov. 16, 1893; Mar. 18, Oct. 23, 1895; Hoskins, *Historical Sketches*, 100.

14. *Tennessee State Gazetter and Business Directory*, 1890–91, 677; Hoskins, *Historical Sketches*, 166. Travelers Cecile and Albert Chavannes characterized the town in 1900 as "a little village insignificant in itself, but of some importance as a railroad station in a mining district, and also for being a summer resort on account of its mineral waters." *East Tennessee Sketches*, 26.

15. TPC, 2:34 (*Dispatch*, Nov. 1891?).

16. Dombrowski, notes to "Fire in the Hole"; *National Labor Tribune*, Nov. 7, Nov. 21, 1891.

17. TPC, 2:34 (*Dispatch*, Nov. 1891?); Dombrowski, notes to "Fire in the Hole."

18. TPC, 1:169 (*Knoxville Sentinel*, Oct. 31, 1891); 1:174; *New York Times*, Nov. 2, 1891; *Knoxville Tribune*, Nov. 3, Nov. 6, Nov. 13, 1891; *Birmingham Age Herald*, Nov. 12, 1891.

19. *New York Times*, Nov. 3, 1891; *Clinton Gazette*, Nov. 5, Nov. 12, 1891; *Knoxville Tribune*, Nov. 10, 1891; TPC, 2:213 (*Nashville Tribune*, Mar. 22, 1892); 2:12; Original Bill, Trial Record, 12, *Buchanan v. TCIR* (1897).

20. Bowron Diary, Nov. 4, 1891; Hutson, "The Coal Miners' Insurrection, 1891–92," 115. State officials later contended that the branch prisons had been understaffed at the time of the fall 1891 attacks because TCIR had refused to pay for additional guards. Amended Bill, Trial Record, 53–54, *Buchanan v. TCIR* (1897).

21. Hutson, "The Coal Miners' Insurrection, 1891–92," 114. See also Answer to Original Bill, Trial Record, 42, *Buchanan v. TCIR* (1897).

22. Sanford to McGhee, Nov. 14, 1891, McGhee Papers. McGhee was also in the habit of blaming prison employees for siding with the miners. See McGhee to S. M. Felton, Aug. 3, 1891, McGhee Papers. Although the appointment of prison officials provided an important avenue of patronage, it also gave the convicts a minimal form of protection. Allowing the coal companies to appoint officials at the stockades may have subjected the convicts to even greater abuse.

23. Bowron Diary, Nov. 2, 1891; Bowron Autobiography, Nov. 2, 1891.

24. McGhee to Sanford, Nov. 12, 1891; Sanford to McGhee, Nov. 14, 1891, McGhee Papers.

25. *Chattanooga Republican*, Nov. 8, 1891. See also *Clinton Gazette*, Nov. 19, 1891.

26. *UMWJ*, Nov. 5, 1891; *Alabama Sentinel*, Nov. 7, 1891; *Birmingham Labor Advocate*, Nov. 7, 1891.

27. *Journal of the Knights of Labor*, Nov. 12, 1891. See also ibid., Nov. 5, Nov. 26, 1891; TPC, 2:41 (*Nashville Journal of Labor*, Nov. 24, 1891); 2:105 (*Knoxville Sentinel*, Mar. 5, 1892); 2:110 (*Knoxville Journal*, Mar. 11, 1892).

28. George Ford to Powderly, Dec. 22, 1891; J. C. Roberts to Powderly, Dec. 22, 1891, Powderly Papers.

29. Powderly wrote to John A. Wilson, Local 3552, Coal Creek, W. F. Miller, Local 2957, Briceville, J. G. Guess, Local 3527, Coal Creek, J. A. Goens, Local 3549, Coal Creek, and Robert Young, Local 2855, Coal Creek, all on Jan. 2, 1892. All of this correspondence is in the Powderly Papers. At least two local miners replied, asking Powderly to arbitrate on their

behalf. See Sam R. Pickering to Powderly, Jan. 12, 1892; John R. Rhodes to Powderly, Jan. 16, 1892, Powderly Papers.

30. *Memphis Appeal Avalanche*, July 22, 1891; *Chattanooga Republican*, July 26, 1891; TPC, 1:21 (*Knoxville Sentinel?*); Tennessee Commissioner of Labor, *Special Report*, 1891, 30–31.

31. *Knoxville Tribune*, Nov. 3, Nov. 4, 1891; *Nashville American*, Dec. 18, 1891; *Knoxville Journal*, Jan. 2, 1892.

32. TPC, 2:12 (*Knoxville Journal*, Nov. 1891?).

33. *Knoxville Tribune*, Nov. 6, 1891; *National Labor Tribune*, Nov. 7, 1891; *Clinton Gazette*, Nov. 12, Nov. 26, 1891; *Birmingham Labor Advocate*, Nov. 14, 1891; *Chattanooga Republican*, Nov. 22, 1891; *Coal Trade Journal*, Dec. 2, Dec. 9, 1891; TPC, 2:19; 2:28 (*Knoxville Journal*, Nov. 16, 1891); 2:32 (*Coal Creek Press*, Nov. 21, 1891); 2:26 (*Chattanooga Times*, Nov. 1891?); *UMWJ*, Dec. 3, 1891; Tennessee Commissioner of Labor, *Annual Report*, 1893, 33, 164, 174.

34. *Chattanooga Republican*, Dec. 6, 1891.

35. Bowron Diary, Nov. 4, 1891; *Alabama Sentinel*, Nov. 21, 1891; J. A. Pitts to Buchanan, Nov. 24, 1891, Buchanan Papers; *Chattanooga Republican*, Dec. 27, 1891.

36. Original Bill, Trial Record, 13–14, *Buchanan v. TCIR* (1897); J. A. Pitts to G. W. Pickle, July 2, 1892, Turney Papers.

37. G. W. Pickle to Buchanan, Nov. 30, 1891, Buchanan Papers.

38. *Savannah Tribune*, Dec. 5, 1891; *National Labor Tribune*, Dec. 12, 1891.

39. G. W. Pickle to Buchanan, Nov. 20, Nov. 30, 1891, Buchanan Papers; *Clinton Gazette*, Dec. 15, 1891, cited in Hutson, "The Coal Miners' Insurrection, 1891–92," 115.

40. Bowron Diary, Nov. 4, 1891; George Ford to Buchanan, Jan. 15, 1892, Buchanan Papers; TPC, 2:63 (Jan. 1892?).

41. Tennessee Commissioner of Labor, *Annual Report*, 1892, 141–47; Baxter Deposition, Trial Record, 83, *Buchanan v. TCIR* (1897).

42. TCIR made such a request in late November. Nathaniel Baxter to Board of Prison Inspectors, Nov. 27, 1891, Prison Records; *Savannah Tribune*, Dec. 5, 1891.

43. Bowron Diary, Dec. 17, Dec. 19, 1891. Prior to meeting the mine leaders themselves, TCIR officials had sent delegates from local labor unions to Coal Creek "to urge the cessation of lawlessness." These efforts failed. Bowron Diary, Nov. 23, Nov. 27, 1891; *Knoxville Journal*, Jan. 9, 1892; TPC, 2:62 (Jan. 1892); *Nashville Herald*, Jan. 14, 1892.

44. TPC, 2:47 (*Nashville American*, Dec. 1891?); 2:52 (*Chattanooga Times*, Dec. 24, 1891); *Clinton Gazette*, Dec. 3, 1891; Jan. 7, 1892; *Alabama Sentinel*, Dec. 5, 1891; *Sequatchie News*, Dec. 11, 1891; Tennessee Adjutant General, *Biennial Report*, 1891–92, 15; Captain Anderson to H. H. Norman, Nov. 15, 1892, Adjutant General Papers; *UMWJ*, June 8, 1893; Hutson, "The Coal Miners' Insurrection, 1891–92," 116–20.

45. "Memorandum of Agreement between TCIR and the State," Trial Record, 26–27, *Buchanan v. TCIR* (1897). The hastily drawn and loosely worded provisions about the payment of salaries for the militia laid the foundation for a serious dispute between government and company officials when relations between those groups soured in 1892.

46. *Clinton Gazette*, Dec. 3, 1891; *Birmingham Labor Advocate*, Dec. 5, 1891; *Knoxville Journal*, Jan. 1, 1892; *UMWJ*, Jan. 7, 1892; TPC, 2:79 (*Coal Creek Press*, Jan. 8, 1892).

47. TPC, 2:74 (*Nashville Herald*, Jan. 14, 1892); 2:153–59, Merrell to Buchanan, n.d.; Buchanan to Merrell, Jan. 16, 1892.

48. TPC, 2:69 (*Knoxville Sentinel*, Jan. 15, 1892); George Ford to Buchanan, Jan. 15, 1892, Buchanan Papers.

49. *Clinton Gazette*, Feb. 25, 1892. TCIR later concurred that the militia had no role other than resisting insurrection. Answer to Original Bill, Trial Record, 46–47, *Buchanan v. TCIR* (1897).

50. *Alabama Sentinel*, Jan. 9, Jan. 23, 1892; *Knoxville Journal*, Feb. 7, Aug. 9, 1892; *Clinton Gazette*, Feb. 11, Aug. 4, 1892; *New York Times*, Feb. 26, 1892; Hutson, "The Coal Miners' Insurrection," 126; TPC, 2:76 (*Nashville Herald*, Jan. 14, 1892); 2:97 (*Journal of United Labor*, Feb. 16, 1892?); 2:130 (*Nashville Sentinel*, July 20–22, 1892); 1:179–81; Dombrowski, notes to "Fire in the Hole"; Daniel, "The Tennessee Convict War," 287.

51. J. A. Draughn to H. H. Norman, July 23, 1892, Buchanan Papers. For Captain Anderson's disparaging view of the local population, see TPC, 2:103 (*Nashville Herald*, Mar. 1, 1892?).

52. *Clinton Gazette*, Feb. 25, 1892; *Chattanooga Republican*, June 25, 1892.

53. *Chattanooga Republican*, Feb. 20, 1892; *Clinton Gazette*, Feb. 25, Mar. 3, 1892; *UMWJ*, Mar. 24, June 16, 1892; TPC, 2:81 (*Journal of United Labor*, Jan. 1892?); 2:68 (Jan. 15, 1892?); 2:109 (Mar. 5, 1892?); 2:99 (*Journal of United Labor*, Feb. 1892?). Slackness in the coal market most likely helped to convince J. W. Renfro to accept a transfer of the coal mining lease for Oliver Springs's Big Mountain Mine from his company to TCIR in late January 1892.

54. *Clinton Gazette*, July 31, 1890; Mar. 7, Mar. 14, 1894; Apr. 29, 1896. Although white miners and black citizens of Anderson County both continued to find hope in the Republican Party, their shared political loyalty did not necessarily provide a bond between them. For an example of racial tension in the political realm, see *Clinton Gazette*, Oct. 31, 1894.

55. *UMWJ*, Mar. 30, 1893. For a comparison of relations between black and white miners in the Lower South and Appalachia, see Lewis, "Job Control and Race Relations in Coal Fields," 35–64.

56. *UMWJ*, May 5, 1892. See also *UMWJ*, July 28, Aug. 4, 1892; Mar. 30, 1893.

57. *UMWJ*, Feb. 7, July 28, Aug. 4, 1892.

58. *UMWJ*, Mar. 3, Mar. 17, Jan. 2, 1892; TPC, 2:124 (Apr. 1892?). Riley attributed the problems to adverse economic conditions, some white miners' fear of competition from blacks, some black miners' refusal to stand up for their rights, and the cowardly behavior of both groups—what he called "nigger-like" or "dog-like" behavior. Postbellum agreements in workplaces to apportion employment opportunities between white and black union members were not always honored in the breach. See Arnesen, *Waterfront Workers of New Orleans*, 249–51.

59. *Clinton Gazette*, Dec. 3, 1891; *Coal Trade Journal*, Dec. 9, 1891; TPC, 2:39–43; *Chattanooga Republican*, June 18, 1892; Tennessee Commissioner of Labor, *Annual Report*, 1893, 143.

60. *UMWJ*, Mar. 24, May 5, 1892. See also *UMWJ*, Mar. 17, May 19, 1892. For union activity in the social and political lives of the towns, see *UMWJ*, Sept. 24, 1891; May 19, 1892; *Knoxville Journal*, Feb. 20, 1892; TPC, 2:111 (*Journal of United Labor*, Mar. 11, 1892?); *Journal of the Knights of Labor*, May 26, 1892; S. W. Taylor et al. to Houk, July 18, 1892; J. P. McLearn to Houk, July 18, 1892; Houk to J. P. McLearn, July 20, 1892; E. G. Miller et al. to Houk, July 22, 1892, Houk Papers.

61. *UMWJ*, Dec. 3, Dec. 17, 1891; May 5, 1892.

62. *Chattanooga Republican*, Feb. 27, 1892; TPC, 2:108 (*Journal of United Labor*, Mar. 4, 1892); 2:111 (Mar. 11, 1892); *UMWJ*, Mar. 17, 1892; Tennessee Commissioner of Labor, *Annual Report*, 1893, 183. For a discussion of employer abuses of the piece-rate system, see Dix, *What's a Coal Miner to Do?*, 15–16.

63. *UMWJ*, May 12, May 19, May 26, June 2, June 9, June 16, 1892. Union participants who would figure prominently during the cataclysmic 1892 revolt, such as D. B. Monroe, began to consolidate their leadership positions in this struggle. Other union leaders included G. W. Black, L. Goins, and Samuel Pickering. TPC, 2:124 (*Journal of United Labor*, May 9, 1892).

64. *Knoxville Journal*, Feb. 13, 1892; *EMJ*, Feb. 20, 1892; Tennessee Commissioner of Labor, *Annual Report*, 1893, 232.

65. TPC, 2:100 (*Knoxville Journal*, Feb. 28, 1892); 2:106, 109.

66. TPC, 2:89 (*Knoxville Sentinel*, Sept. 22, 1891); 2:106; Tennessee Commissioner of Labor, *Annual Report*, 1893, 230.

67. *Knoxville Journal*, Feb. 28, 1892.

68. *Savannah Times*, Feb. 20, 1892; Ford to Powderly, Mar. 18, 1892, Powderly Papers; TPC, 2:96, 107; 2:117 (*Memphis Unionist*, Apr. 9, 1892).

69. TPC, 2:95 (Feb. 1892?).

70. *UMWJ*, Sept. 29, 1892. By 1894, the promise of the Jellico mine had fizzled and the miners who had invested in the mine had lost their securities. "Prospectus for Jellico and Bird-Eye Coal Company, Kentucky, Mar. 2, 1892," Powderly Papers; *UMWJ*, Aug. 11, 1892; Mar. 22, 1894; *Journal of United Labor*, Aug. 10, 1895. For an overview of the Knights' cooperative philosophy, see Dulles and Dubofsky, *Labor in America*, 129–31.

71. *UMWJ*, Feb. 25, 1892; TPC, 2:100 (*Knoxville Journal*, Feb. 29, 1892); 2:109 (*Knoxville Sentinel*, Mar. 8, 1892); B. A. Jenkins to Powderly, Mar. 21, 1892, Powderly Papers. For the endorsement of the Central Labor Unions, see TPC, 2:105 (*Knoxville Journal*, Mar. 4, 1892); 2:116 (*Knoxville Sentinel*, Apr. 8, 1892); 2:120 (*Memphis Unionist*, Apr. 22, 1892).

72. *UMWJ*, Mar. 31, 1892.

73. Powderly to Ford, Apr. 1, 1892, Powderly Papers. Powderly immediately wrote to Jenkins seeking assurance that the company would divide its profits among the workmen, only employ Knights of Labor men, and sell stock to these unionists. Powderly to Jenkins, Apr. 1, 1892, Powderly Papers.

74. William T. Love to Powderly, Mar. 2, 1892, Powderly Papers. The Knoxville Central Labor Union also expressed concern about the scheme, but endorsed it on the basis that half a loaf was better than none. TPC, 2:116 (*United Labor*, Apr. 1, 1892).

75. TPC, 2:105.

76. *Chattanooga Republican*, May 14, 1892. See also ibid., Nov. 29, 1891; TPC, 2:79 (*Journal of United Labor*, Jan. 15, 1892).

77. *Clinton Gazette*, Aug. 18, 1892; TPC, 1:162; 2:114 (*Weekly Toiler*, Mar. 24, 1892).

78. *Chattanooga Republican*, Nov. 29, 1891; TPC, 2:41 (Nov. 1891?). For the pamphlet in which the Nashville Central Labor Union called for the formation of a State Labor Congress, see TPC, 1:174.

79. TPC, 2:115 (Feb. 27, 1892?). See also *UMWJ*, Dec. 3, 1891; TPC, 2:64 (*Journal of Labor*, Jan. 7, 1892?); 2:100 (Feb. 28, 1892?).

80. TPC, 2:104 (*Nashville Herald*, Mar. 2, 1892); 2:108 (*Nashville American*, Mar. 2, 1892); 2:102–5 (*Nashville American*, Mar. 3, 1892); Shahan, "The Limits of Agrarian Reform," 92. For a refutation of these charges, see TPC, 2:114 (*Weekly Toiler*, Mar. 24, 1892).

81. TPC, 2:104; Sharp, "The Farmers' Alliance and the People's Party," 97–98. The Republicans tried to make political capital out of the splits within the Democratic Party. Houk to John H. McDowell, Sept. 23, 1892, Houk Papers.

82. *Chattanooga Republican*, Mar. 12, Apr. 16, May 21, May 28, June 18, 1892; TPC, 2:122 (*Knoxville Journal*, Mar. 14, 1892); *Weekly Toiler*, Mar. 30, Oct. 26, 1892; A. K. Shelton, Oliver Springs, to E. B. Wade, June 14, 1892, Buchanan Papers; Allison, ed., *Notable Men of Tennessee*, 115–17.

83. The Coal Creek and Briceville delegation consisted of Merrell, Pickering, Miller, Bennett, and Wilson, and the Tracy City delegation of Brown and Jenkins. TPC, 2:100.

84. The remaining prescriptions had a wider application, including demands for a law compelling arbitration between employers and employees; the prohibition of hiring children under fifteen to work in mines, workshops, and factories; compulsory education for children between the ages of eight and twelve; the expansion of the office of the commis-

sioner of labor to include three assistants (one for mines, a second for factories and work-shops, and a third for boilers); the establishment of reform schools for criminals under the age of eighteen; and the extension of the length of a voting day from 6 A.M. to 6 P.M.—presumably to allow workingmen to reach the polls more easily. *Weekly Toiler*, Mar. 30, 1892.

85. Ibid.

Chapter 7

1. Miller, *The Official and Political Manual of the State of Tennessee*, 246–47; Elliott and Moxley, eds., *Tennessee Civil War Veterans Questionnaires*, 458–59.

2. *Grundy County Herald*, Sept. 2, 1976.

3. *Journal of United Labor*, Sept. 25, 1884; July 10, 1885; June 30, 1888; Feb. 7, Apr. 11, Apr. 25, 1889.

4. *Chattanooga Republican*, Feb. 6, 1892.

5. The price of Southern Grey Forge iron dropped from $17.25 a ton to $11.00 a ton between 1889 and 1892. Fuller, "History of the Tennessee Coal, Iron, and Railroad Company," 101, 385–88. For the financial health of TCIR's Tennessee operations during 1891, see *EMJ*, Aug. 8, Nov. 21, 1891; Shook to C. O. Baldwin, Sept. 11, 1891, Shook Papers. For Bowron's views on the failure of Baring Brothers, see Norrell, *James Bowron*, 94–95.

6. *Chattanooga Republican*, Sept. 20, 1891.

7. See Chapter 2 for an extended discussion of life and work in TCIR-dominated towns.

8. *Knoxville Journal*, Aug. 14, 1892; Nathaniel Baxter to Buchanan, Aug. 16, 1892, Buchanan Papers.

9. *UMWJ*, Aug. 18, 1892.

10. Grundy County Trust Deeds, 1889–98, roll 92, 265–70; Woodward, *Tracy City from 1893 to 1919*.

11. Grundy County Tax Book, 1892, District 11, 15; Dombrowski, "Fire in the Hole," 115–17.

12. Dombrowski interviews with Jake Hargis (n.d.); I. H. Cannon (Mar. 1937), SCEF Papers; Bowron to Buchanan, Aug. 13, 1892, Buchanan Papers.

13. Dombrowski interviews with I. H. Cannon (Mar. 1937); H. Lee Goodman (July 1938), SCEF Papers; *UMWJ*, Aug. 18, 1892; *National Labor Tribune*, Aug. 20, 1892; *Report of the Warden, Superintendent, and Other Officers of the Tennessee Penitentiary*, 1893, 9; *Memorial and Biographical Record*, 238–40.

14. Baxter to Buchanan, Aug. 10, 1892; Baxter to Buchanan, Aug. 15, 1892, Buchanan Papers; Bowron Diary, Aug. 10, 1892; *New Orleans Daily Picayune*, Aug. 14, 1892.

15. Buchanan to Baxter, Aug. 10, 1892, Buchanan Papers.

16. Wade to Buchanan, Aug. 11, 1892; Wade to Buchanan, Aug. 12, 1892, Buchanan Papers; *Report of the Warden, Superintendent, and Other Officers of the Tennessee Penitentiary*, 1893, 9.

17. In a letter to Buchanan, Nathaniel Baxter accused Morrison of being one of the miners' leaders. The governor later reprimanded the sheriff for shirking his duty. Buchanan to Morrison, Aug. 13, 1892; Baxter to Buchanan, Aug. 15, 1892; Buchanan to Morrison, Aug. 24, 1892; Morrison to Buchanan, Aug. 24, 1892; Morrison to Buchanan, Aug. 29, 1892; Buchanan Papers.

18. Baxter to Buchanan, Aug. 15, 1892; Buchanan to Baxter, Aug. 15, 1892, Buchanan Papers; Bowron Diary, Aug. 15, 1892; TPC, 2:137 (*Knoxville Journal*, Aug. 15, 1892); *New York Times*, Aug. 16, 1892; *Knoxville Journal*, Aug. 16, 1892; *EMJ*, Aug. 20, 1892. In Whitwell, 22 percent of the 355 miners were black. Tennessee Commissioner of Labor, *Special Report*, 1891, 73.

19. *Knoxville Journal*, Aug. 16, 1892. The miners were not averse to using strong-arm

tactics. According to newspaper reports, the Whitwell miners caught and severely whipped a company messenger who tried to leave Whitwell to inform the Inman officials of the miners' impending march toward their town. The miners also demonstrated a willingness to take on larger groups of men. Baxter complained to Buchanan that the "mob" had prevented the men working at TCIR's Victoria coke ovens from keeping the ovens running. Baxter to Buchanan, Aug. 15, 1892, Buchanan Papers; TPC, 2:137 (*Knoxville Journal*, Aug. 15, 1892). For a discussion of the destructive actions of New England mobs, particularly in response to the Stamp Act, see Maier, *From Resistance to Revolution*, 57.

20. *New York Times*, Aug. 17, 1892; *Knoxville Journal*, Aug. 17, 1892.

21. Baxter to Buchanan, Aug. 15, 1892, Buchanan Papers; Tennessee Division Report, Jan. 31, 1893; A. M. Shook Report, n.d., Business Reports, 1883–1903, Shook Papers.

22. Though TCIR's management strongly denied these allegations, both Assistant General Manager Gaines and the company's Tracy City superintendent, E. O. Nathurst, made statements indicating tacit complicity in the assault. *Knoxville Journal*, Aug. 15, 1892; Baxter to Buchanan, Aug. 16, 1892, Buchanan Papers; Bowron Autobiography, Aug. 16, 1892; *UMWJ*, Aug. 18, 1892; Nathurst to Shook, Aug. 24, 1892, Shook Papers.

23. Byron and Barbara Sistler, "1880 Census—Tennessee: Transcription for Anderson County," 10, 19; Anderson County Tax Book, 1891–92, District 13, 54, 75; Powderly to John A. Wilson, Jan. 2, 1892, Powderly Papers; *New York Times*, Aug. 6, 1892; "Petition from Citizens of Coal Creek to Governor Buchanan," Aug. 15, 1892, Buchanan Papers; *Clinton Gazette*, Aug. 18, 1892; *Knoxville Journal*, Aug. 23, 1892. Republican congressman John C. Houk endorsed the Coal Creek petition. Houk to Buchanan, Aug. 15, 1892, Houk Papers.

24. TPC, 2:134 (*Knoxville Sentinel*, Aug. 15, 1892).

25. *Knoxville Journal*, Aug. 16, 1892; TPC, 2:134 (*Knoxville Sentinel*, Aug. 15, 1892); 2:136.

26. J. A. Pitts to Buchanan, Aug. 17, 1892, Turney Papers; "Minutes of Inspectors of the Tennessee Penitentiary," Aug. 17–23, 1892, Prison Records; *Knoxville Journal*, Aug. 18, Aug. 23, Aug. 24, 1892; Bowron Autobiography, Aug. 18, 1892; Bowron Diary, Aug. 20, Aug. 23, 1892; Shook to Platt, Aug. 25, 1892; Shook to T. J. Hillman, Aug. 25, 1892; Shook to G. B. McCormack, Aug. 25, 1892, Shook Papers; *National Labor Tribune*, Aug. 27, 1892; *EMJ*, Aug. 27, 1892.

27. *Knoxville Journal*, Aug. 18, 1892.

28. TPC, 2:138 (Aug. 16, 1892?); Baxter to Buchanan, Aug. 16, 1892, Buchanan Papers; Bowron Diary, Aug. 16, 1892; *New York Times*, Aug. 17, 1892.

29. *Knoxville Journal*, Aug. 16, Aug. 17, 1892.

30. Baxter to Buchanan, Aug. 16, 1892, Buchanan Papers; Bowron Diary, Aug. 16, 1892; *Knoxville Journal*, Aug. 16, Aug. 17, 1892.

31. *Knoxville Journal*, Aug. 17, Aug. 18, 1892; *Clinton Gazette*, Aug. 18, 1892.

32. *Knoxville Journal*, Aug. 17, Aug. 18, 1892; Bowron Diary, Aug. 17, 1892; *New Orleans Daily Picayune*, Aug. 18, 1892; *Clinton Gazette*, Aug. 18, 1892; *Chattanooga Republican*, Aug. 20, 1892.

33. TPC, 2:145–46; *New York Times*, Aug. 19, 1892; *Knoxville Journal*, Aug. 23, 1892.

34. *New Orleans Daily Picayune*, Aug. 18, 1892; *Knoxville Journal*, Aug. 18, Sept. 2, 1892; A. Milan to H. H. Norman, Aug. 19, 1892; E. S. Mallony to H. H. Norman, Aug. 24, 1892, Buchanan Papers; TPC, 2:144–45.

35. *Knoxville Journal*, Aug. 19, 1892. See also F. K. Huger to H. H. Norman, Aug. 18, 1892, Telegrams, 1892–93, Buchanan Papers.

36. *New Orleans Daily Picayune*, Aug. 19, 1892; TPC, 2:144. For an account of the 1877 strikes, see Foner, *The Great Labor Uprising of 1877*.

37. *Knoxville Journal*, Aug. 19, 1892. For Commissioner of Labor George Ford's recollec-

tion of the event, see *Knoxville Independent*, May 1942, box 145; Dombrowski interview with Jessie Sparks (Oct. 1938), SCEF Papers.

38. Just a week before, Gammon had complained that TCIR had not paid the guards, who increasingly suspected that they would not be paid "this side of the superior court and then, possibly, three or four years hence." He informed prison superintendent Wade that there would not be an extra guard on duty after September 1 if they did not receive some assurance that their pay would be forthcoming. Gammon to Wade, Aug. 12, 1892, Buchanan Papers; *Knoxville Journal*, Aug. 19, Aug. 25, 1892.

39. F. K. Huger to H. H. Norman, Aug. 18, 1892; Alleman to Buchanan, Aug. 18, 1892, Telegrams 1892–93, Buchanan Papers; *Chattanooga Republican*, Aug. 27, 1892; *Harper's Weekly*, Aug. 27, 1892.

40. *Knoxville Journal*, Aug. 19, Aug. 20, 1892; *New Orleans Daily Picayune*, Aug. 21, 1892; *Harper's Weekly*, Aug. 27, 1892; Dombrowski, "Fire in the Hole," 124–28; *Clinton Courier*, Feb. 13, 1975.

41. D. D. Anderson, an officer in the Knox County company, gave a rather scathing description of his men at Colonel Woolford's court martial: "I was in command of a lot of fellows . . . picked from everywhere, and every man thought he was Captain or Lieutenant or Brigadier General, and knew more about it than the officer in command." "Proceedings of a Court of Inquiry," Sept. 15, 1892, 48, 122, 144–45, 174, Adjutant General Papers.

42. Carnes to H. H. Norman, n.d., box 9, Buchanan Papers. Decades after these events, participant M. W. Scoggins continued to maintain that the militia had killed their own men, despite efforts by the press to attribute these deaths to the miners. Grace Roberts interview with M. W. Scoggins (n.d.), box 146, SCEF Papers.

43. *Knoxville Journal*, Aug. 20, 1892; *Clinton Gazette*, Oct. 6, 1892; Mintz, "The Miners Who Tore Down the Walls," 199.

44. *Knoxville Journal*, Aug. 24, 1892. Though Monroe would acknowledge a role in the rebellion, he would vigorously deny serving as the militant leader described in press reports and court proceedings. Rather, he would stress his position as head of the committee elected to restrain the more belligerent impulses of the miners.

45. Byron and Barbara Sistler, "1880 Census—Tennessee: Transcription for Anderson County," 18; Anderson County Tax Book, 1891, District 5, 63; *Knoxville Journal*, Aug. 25, 1892; Dombrowski, "Fire in the Hole," 133.

46. *Knoxville Journal*, Aug. 17, Aug. 23, 1892; *New York Times*, Aug. 18, 1892, cited in Mintz, "The Miners Who Tore Down the Walls," 179–80.

47. UMWA officials strongly denied the presence of an oath-bound organization. District 19's second president, S. P. Herron, maintained that the UMWA and the Knights had not sanctioned the miners' actions and that those members who had participated in the recent attacks did so in disregard of union guidelines. *Knoxville Journal*, Aug. 19, 1892; *UMWJ*, Sept. 22, 1892.

48. *UMWJ*, Sept. 22, 1892.

49. *New York Times*, Aug. 17, 1892; *Knoxville Journal*, Aug. 17, Aug. 18, Aug. 19, 1892; F. K. Huger to H. H. Norman, Aug. 18, 1892, Telegrams, 1891–93, Buchanan Papers; *Clinton Gazette*, Aug. 18, 1892. The miners' interference with the railroads led the East Tennessee, Virginia & Georgia Railroad to offer a $200 reward for the capture of the men who had taken over the trains.

50. *Knoxville Journal*, Aug. 21, 1892. Anderson County citizens strongly opposed the *Journal*'s coverage of the miners' revolts, particularly the designation of the miners as anarchists. Their objections were sufficiently intense to spark rumors in September 1892 that Anderson County residents would boycott the paper. *Clinton Gazette*, Sept. 8, Sept. 22,

Sept. 29, 1892; Mar. 9, 1893. For a sampling of critical responses to the miners' lawlessness in papers from around the state, including the Memphis, Nashville, Knoxville, and Chattanooga press, see Crowe, "Agitation for Penal Reform," 290. The *Chattanooga Republican* and *National Labor Tribune* also emphasized the theme of law and order in their coverage, but continued to analyze events in the context of the oppressiveness of the convict lease. *Chattanooga Republican*, Aug. 20, 1892; *National Labor Tribune*, Aug. 27, 1892.

51. *Knoxville Journal*, Aug. 19, Aug. 20, 1892; W. M. Scott to Buchanan, Aug. 19, 1892; W. G. Smith to H. H. Norman, Aug. 19, 1892; H. K. Bryson to H. H. Norman, Aug. 19, 1892; J. A. Armstrong to Buchanan, Aug. 19, 1892; R. L. Watkins and W. P. McClatchy to H. H. Norman, Aug. 25, 1892, Telegrams, 1892–93, Buchanan Papers; *New Orleans Daily Picayune*, Aug. 20, 1892; *Journal of the Knights of Labor*, Aug. 25, 1892. For the tone of Buchanan's request for volunteers, see Governor Buchanan's appeal "To the Law Abiding People of Tennessee, August 1892," box 3, Turney Papers.

52. F. K. Huger to H. H. Norman, Aug. 20, 1892, Telegrams 1892–93, Buchanan Papers; *Knoxville Journal*, Aug. 20, Aug. 21, 1892.

53. *New York Times*, Aug. 21, 1892; *Knoxville Journal*, Aug. 22, 1892; *UMWJ*, Aug. 25, 1892; *National Labor Tribune*, Aug. 27, 1892; *Chattanooga Republican*, Sept. 3, 1892.

54. TPC, 2:146 (*Knoxville Journal*, Aug. 18, 1892). For a similar account of the Tracy City miners' military organization, see *Report of the Warden, Superintendent, and Other Officers of the Tennessee Penitentiary*, 1893, 9.

55. "Union Veterans," Tennessee, 1890 Federal Census, roll 95. See also *New Orleans Daily Picayune*, Aug. 18, 1892.

56. *Savannah Tribune*, Aug. 27, 1892.

57. Conservative voices in the miners' internal deliberations had raised the specter of federal military intervention as early as July 1891. Hutson, "The Coal Miners' Insurrection, 1891–92," 77. For contemporary analogies between the situation in the Tennessee coalfields and the strikes in Homestead and Buffalo, see *Knoxville Journal*, Aug. 17, Aug. 18, 1892; *UMWJ*, Aug. 25, 1892.

58. Carnes to H. H. Norman, Aug. 22, 1892, Telegrams 1892–93, Buchanan Papers.

59. J. A. Pitts to Carnes, Aug. 22, 1892, Buchanan Papers. See also H. H. Norman to F. K. Huger, Aug. 18, 1892, Buchanan Papers; "J. A. Pitts on Martial Law," n.d., box 3, Turney Papers; *New York Times*, Aug. 21, 1892.

60. Quoted in Mintz, "The Miners Who Tore Down the Walls," 202; *Knoxville Journal*, Aug. 20, 1892.

61. *UMWJ*, Aug. 25, Sept. 8, 1892; Kentucky Assembly 3010 to Powderly, Sept. 11, 1892; John A. Wilson to Powderly, Sept. 24, 1892, reel 39, Powderly Papers. For a firsthand account of the fear and destruction created by the militia in the coal towns, see Dombrowski interview with S. O. Saunders (Apr. 1937), SCEF Papers.

62. *UMWJ*, Sept. 1, 1892; *Clinton Gazette*, Sept. 29, 1892. Carnes also attempted to influence public opinion by publishing a camp newspaper during his stay in Anderson County. The general, who possessed a well-developed sense of self-importance, both renamed Fort Anderson Camp Carnes and entitled his publication the *Camp Carnes Anti-Bushwhacker*. Only two editions of the paper survive, carrying dates of Aug. 24 and 26, 1892.

63. *UMWJ*, Dec. 8, 1892.

Chapter 8

1. TPC, 2:122 (*Knoxville Journal*, Apr. 14, 1892); *Chattanooga Republican*, May 7, May 28, Aug. 27, 1892.

2. *New Orleans Daily Picayune*, Aug. 14, 1892; Hart, *Redeemers, Bourbons, and Populists*, 179–98.

3. *Knoxville Journal*, Oct. 6, 1892.

4. Hart, *Redeemers, Bourbons, and Populists*, 195, 198. Turney won the election with over 127,000 votes, 26,000 more than Winstead. Buchanan trailed badly with a mere 31,500.

5. Kentucky Assembly 3010 to Powderly, Sept. 11, 1892, reel 39, Powderly Papers.

6. Anderson County Execution Dockets, 1891–93; Anderson County Circuit Court Criminal Minutes, 1891–93; Winton, "A History of Brushy Mountain Penitentiary," 14.

7. For brief biographical sketches of Hicks, see *Clinton Gazette*, Feb. 21, Feb. 24, 1894.

8. *Clinton Gazette*, Sept. 29, 1892. See also *Knoxville Journal*, Sept. 27, 1892.

9. In Briceville, for example, 125 residents were listed as "gone" in the 1893 tax records. Only 11 of the 125 owned property. The rest paid poll taxes but were not property owners. Anderson County Tax Books, 1892–93, Districts 5, 7, and 13.

10. *Clinton Gazette*, Sept. 30, 1896; Crowe, "Agitation for Penal Reform in Tennessee," 289.

11. The miners made public appeals for money to help them defray their legal costs. *UMWJ*, Mar. 9, 1893.

12. Anderson County Execution Dockets, 1891–93, 164, 172, 342, 405, 436, 519, 549; Anderson County Circuit Court Criminal Minutes, 1894–97, C:10, 66, 87.

13. Anderson County Execution Dockets, 1891–93, 496, 546; Anderson County Circuit Court Criminal Minutes, 1894–97, C:39. See also Mintz, "The Miners Who Tore Down the Walls," 262–66.

14. Hicks suggested that Moore's mere presence with the rifle would constitute felonious behavior. *State v. Moore* (1893).

15. Anderson County Wills, 1887–1912, roll 127-B, 292; Anderson County Tax Books, 1891, Districts 5 and 13; *State v. Moore*, 271, 305, 481, 486, 492 (1893).

16. *Knoxville Journal*, Aug. 27, Sept. 28, 1892.

17. *State v. Monroe*, Felony (1893); *State v. Monroe*, Murder (1893).

18. *Knoxville Journal*, Aug. 29, 1892; Trial Record, 30–55, 92–156, *State v. Monroe*, Felony (1893).

19. Trial Record, 102–18, *State v. Monroe*, Felony (1893). Taking charge of the committee to maintain town order was not Monroe's first official duty on behalf of the miners. In May 1892 he served on Knights of Labor committees that sought the reinstatement of members dismissed by coal companies and solicited funds for out-of-work members. TPC, 2:124 (*United Labor*, May 9, 1892); *UMWJ*, May 19, 1892; *Knoxville Journal*, Aug. 26, Aug. 27, 1892.

20. Anderson County Circuit Court Criminal Minutes, 1891–93, 350–52, *State v. Monroe*, Felony (1893); *State v. Moore* (1893). The common-law argument may have represented an effort on the part of Monroe's and Moore's attorneys to lay the grounds for an appeal.

21. *Clinton Gazette*, Oct. 13, 1892; Jan. 2, Feb. 9, 1893; *State v. Monroe*, Murder (1893).

22. Trial Record, 157–58, *State v. Monroe*, Felony (1893).

23. Trial Record, 159–61, ibid. Union leader S. P. Herron compared Monroe's fate to that of the abolitionist John Brown. *UMWJ*, Feb. 9, 1893. The convicted insurrectionary seems to have served his full sentence.

24. S. P. Herron intimated in October 1892 that there was an explicit arrangement along these lines, reporting that General Carnes had paid Hatmaker's bail. *UMWJ*, Oct. 27, 1892. One of the state prosecutors, J. A. Fowler, may similarly have paid George Irish's legal fees and court costs. In March 1893 Irish assigned real estate in Briceville to a trustee in order to secure the payment of almost $600 to Fowler. Anderson County Trust Deeds, 1892–94, roll 40, 55–57.

25. In mid-Tennessee's Marion County, the sheriff also refused to serve the warrants of arrest. *New Orleans Daily Picayune*, Aug. 18, 1892.

26. TPC, 1:3 (*Knoxville Tribune*, July 19, 1891); 1:35; Bony Craig Application for Reward, Jan. 15, 1894, box 29; Petition for Pardon—Bony Craig, Feb. 3, 1894, box 20, Turney Papers.

27. *Knoxville Journal*, Aug. 20–21, 1892; Petition for Pardon—Bony Craig, Feb. 3, 1894; Kellar Anderson to Peter Turney, Feb. 6, 1894, box 20, Turney Papers; Grace Roberts interview with W. M. Scoggins (n.d.), box 146, SCEF Papers.

28. Anderson County Execution Dockets, 1891–93, 242, 458, 462, 482, 499, 547, 554, 581.

29. Petition for Pardon—Bony Craig, box 20, Turney Papers.

30. *Clinton Gazette*, Mar. 9, 1893; Feb. 21, Mar. 4, 1894.

31. While some miners left for the Kentucky border, others chose to go south to seek work in the Birmingham district. *Birmingham Labor Advocate*, Sept. 3, 1892; *Alabama Sentinel*, Sept. 10, 1892.

32. *Chattanooga Republican*, Jan. 28, Feb. 11, Feb. 18, 1893.

33. *Knoxville Journal*, Aug. 16, 1892. See also J. A. Pitts to Turney, Pickle, and Morgan, Jan. 12, 1894, Turney Papers.

34. Baxter to Allen, House, and Miller, Penitentiary Inspectors, Aug. 15, 1892, Buchanan Papers.

35. Minutes of Tennessee Penitentiary Board of Inspectors, 1877–92, Aug. 29, 1892, Prison Records; Bowron Diary, Sept. 1, Sept. 3, 1892; Shook to Hillman, Sept. 3, 1892, Shook Papers.

36. This legal controversy probably encouraged miners in both mid- and east Tennessee to adopt militant tactics against convict labor in the following month.

37. Original Bill, Trial Record, 5–7, *Buchanan v. TCIR* (1897).

38. Bowron Autobiography, July 6, 1892; Bowron Diary, July 1892; *Knoxville Journal*, July 7, 1892; Norrell, *James Bowron*, xv. The Supreme Court ruling in the Warren matter was not nearly as clear-cut as Bowron would have had it. Justice Turney only ruled that the status of branch prisons was a matter for the Board of Prisons to decide and that the prisoner in question lacked standing to sue.

39. Original Bill, Trial Record, 8–9, *Buchanan v. TCIR* (1897).

40. Answer to Original Bill, Trial Record, 33–36, *Buchanan v. TCIR* (1897).

41. Ibid., 36–37. TCIR's directors were notorious for playing musical chairs. See Armes, *The Story of Coal and Iron in Alabama*; Fuller, "History of the Tennessee Coal, Iron, and Railroad Company."

42. Answer to Original Bill, Trial Record, 43–51, *Buchanan v. TCIR* (1897).

43. Bowron Diary, July 25, 1892; June 29, July 5, July 6, Oct. 19, Oct. 20, Dec. 11, 1893; Baxter to Turney, Craig, and Harris, July 1, 1893, Turney Papers.

44. Shook to G. B. McCormack, Dec. 21, 1892, Shook Papers; Bowron Autobiography, Jan. 2, 1893.

45. Fuller, "History of the Tennessee Coal, Iron, and Railroad Company," 386.

46. "Report of the Penitentiary Purchasing and Building Committee ," 1893, box 3, Turney Papers.

47. *Acts of Tennessee*, 1893, Chapter 127.

48. Bowron Diary, May 25, 1893; Baxter, Shook, and Bowron Depositions, Trial Record, 65–66, 97–98, 166, 215, *Buchanan v. TCIR* (1897).

49. Baxter and Bowron Depositions, Trial Record, 84, 193–97, *Buchanan v. TCIR* (1897).

50. Bowron Diary, Jan. 17–27, 1894; *EMJ*, Aug. 11, 1894.

51. Biographical sketches of Jere Baxter portray him as a man of remarkable business acumen. See, for example, Allison, ed., *Notable Men of Tennessee*, 43–45; Speer, *Sketches of*

Prominent Tennesseans, 570–72; Fuller, "History of the Tennessee Coal, Iron, and Railroad Company," 129.

52. Bowron Autobiography, Jan. 26, 1894. See also Shook to S. M. Felton, Apr. 29, 1893; Shook to Felton, Nov. 1, 1893, Shook Papers; Bowron Diary, Sept. 20, 1893; Jan. 2, Mar. 15, July 24, 1894; *Tracy City News*, Oct. 12, 1893. Jere Baxter's difficulties in providing for the convicts eventually caused state officials to demand that TCIR remove the prisoners from his care. Shook to Nathaniel Baxter, Sept. 4, Oct. 14, Oct. 15, 1895; Shook to J. H. Trice, Oct. 31, 1895; Shook to S. Kirkpatrick, Oct. 31, 1895, Shook Papers; Bowron Diary, Sept. 26, 1895.

53. Tennessee Commissioner of Labor, *Annual Report*, 1893, 40; *The Coal Trade*, 1895, 50.

54. Shook to G. B. McCormack, Nov. 25, 1892; Aug. 8, Oct. 12, 1893, Shook Papers; Bowron Autobiography, Aug. 15, Aug. 31, 1893; May 10, June 5, 1894; TCIR, *Annual Report*, 1893, 4; 1895, 3; John C. Haskell, "To the Executive Committee," Dec. 1, 1895, Bowron Scrapbook, 1877–95.

55. *CCM&MC v. TCIR* (1900); Shook to Steger, Wash, and Jackson, Sept. 4, 1895, Shook Papers. See also *Clinton Gazette*, Apr. 13, Aug. 10, Sept. 14, Oct. 5, 1893; May 6, 1896; *Journal of the Knights of Labor*, Jan. 11, 1894; *National Labor Tribune*, Feb. 6, July 23, 1896; T. H. Heald to CCM&MC, Feb. 21, 1896, CCM&MC Papers.

56. Bowron Autobiography, Nov. 20, 1893; Bowron Diary, Nov. 28, Dec. 7, 1893; Feb. 23, 1895; "Grundy County Wins . . . Suit against TCIR," n.d., Bowron Scrapbook, 1877–95.

57. R. M. Edwards to H. H. Norman, Sept. 15, 1892; C. Dabney Jr., "Additional Items of Damage Done by State Troops," n.d., box 3, Buchanan Papers; Edgar Stevens to J. Taylor Stratton, Apr. 24, 1893, Turney Papers; Sims, "The Lease System in Tennessee and Other Southern States," 128.

58. The state's account was as follows: $167,000, rent; $12,000, capture of convicts; $15,000, back taxes; $47,000, military expenses. J. A. Pitts to Turney, Craig, and Harris, n.d., Turney Papers; Baxter Deposition, Trial Record, 114, *Buchanan v. TCIR* (1897).

59. Bowron Deposition, Trial Record, 202, *Buchanan v. TCIR* (1897).

60. The courts eventually indicted sixteen soldiers for Drummond's murder. The outcome of the charges against them and the investigation into Laugherty's murder remain unclear. *Knoxville Journal*, Aug. 9, Aug. 16, Aug. 18, 1893; *Clinton Gazette*, Aug. 17, Aug. 24, Sept. 14, Sept. 21, Sept. 28, Oct. 5, 1893; Feb. 14, Mar. 14, 1894; Governor Turney, "To the People of Tennessee," Aug. 19, 1893, box 3, Turney Papers; *Tracy City News*, Oct. 12, 1893; Dombrowski interview with George Ford (July 1938), SCEF Papers.

61. Baxter and Bowron Depositions, Trial Record, 78, 201–2, *Buchanan v. TCIR* (1897).

62. Settlement between TCIR and the State, Dec. 14, 1893; Consent Decree, Dec. 14, 1893, both cited in *Buchanan v. TCIR*, 1–6 (1897).

63. Bowron Autobiography, Dec. 14, 1893; TCIR, *Annual Report*, 1894, 6–7; *Buchanan v. TCIR*, 2–6 (1897).

64. For a detailed discussion of these policy shifts, see Shapiro, "The Tennessee Coal Miners' Revolts," 339–41.

65. William Morgan to E. R. Tuck, Apr. 9, 1894; Morgan to J. T. Edwards, July 25, 1894, Turney Papers.

66. J. A. Harris to Nathaniel Baxter, Apr. 20, 1894, Comptroller Letterbook, 1891–94; Bowron Diary, Sept. 29, 1894. TCIR charged Nashville between 75 cents and $1.40 per day for an unskilled laborer, and the Knoxville Iron Company 35 cents. Shook to J. L. Gaines, Nov. 1, 1895, Shook Papers; Nixon Deposition, Trial Record, 255–74, *Buchanan v. TCIR* (1897).

67. Chancery Decree, Feb. 26, 1896, Trial Record, 72–74, *Buchanan v. TCIR* (1897).

68. Bowron Diary, Sept. 26, 1894; Baxter, Shook, and Bowron Depositions, Trial Record, 75–227; TCIR Supreme Court Brief, 3–25, *Buchanan v. TCIR* (1897).

69. TCIR Supreme Court Brief, 25–29, *Buchanan v. TCIR* (1897).

70. Young, Craig, Carroll, and Morgan Depositions, Trial Record, 242–51, 421–89; State of Tennessee Supreme Court Reply Brief, 6–12, *Buchanan v. TCIR* (1897).

71. *Buchanan v. TCIR*, 14 (1897).

72. Ibid., 7–19.

73. "Grundy County Wins . . . Suit against TCIR," n.d., Bowron Scrapbook, 1877–95.

74. Bowron to J. Swann, Jan. 22, 1897, Bowron Papers; Armes, *The Story of Coal and Iron in Alabama*, 423–90; Fuller, "History of the Tennessee Coal, Iron, and Railroad Company," 176–77.

75. *UMWJ*, Sept. 29, 1892; July 6, July 20, 1893. See also Coal Creek Local 3552 to Powderly, Feb. 12, 1893, Powderly Papers.

76. At least two men died as a result of wounds sustained during the attack. Illegible to Governor Peter Turney, Apr. 19–21, 1893, Turney Papers; Bowron Diary, Apr. 20–25, 1893; Bowron Autobiography, Apr. 20, 1893; *EMJ*, Apr. 22, 1893; Shook to G. B. McCormack, Apr. 25, 1893, Shook Papers; *Clinton Gazette*, Apr. 27, 1893; Tennessee Commissioner of Labor, *Annual Report*, 1894, 7; Dombrowski, "Fire in the Hole," 134–39; "Tracy City, Second Battle," box 145, SCEF Papers.

77. The companies may not have had an alternative. With the 1890s nationwide depression at its worst, cash and credit were in short supply. *UMWJ*, Aug. 10, Nov. 2, 1893; Feb. 1, 1894; *Clinton Gazette*, Aug. 17, 1893; *EMJ*, Aug. 19, 1893; *Tracy City News*, Oct. 12, 1893; U.S. Commissioner of Labor, *Strikes and Lockouts*, 1894, 1:1166–69.

78. *UMWJ*, Mar. 30, May 23, 1893. W. L. Wilson to Powderly, Jan. 28, 1893, reel 40; Powderly to Wilson, Feb. 4, 1893, reel 58; Gibson to Powderly, June 1, 1893, reel 42, Powderly Papers.

79. Bowron Diary, Apr. 3, 1894. The Whitwell miners suffered as a result of their decision to support the nationwide strike. TCIR summarily closed the mine, throwing 500 men out of work and crippling the town's economy. When 200 miners returned to work in August, they did so at reduced pay. Bowron Diary, May 3, May 8, Aug. 15, Aug. 22, Aug. 28, Aug. 30, 1894; Bowron Autobiography, May 19, 1894; TCIR, *Annual Report*, 1895, 4–5.

80. Newspaper clipping, May 8, 1894, Bowron Scrapbook, 1877–95; *EMJ*, June 2, 1894; Fuller, "History of the Tennessee Coal, Iron, and Railroad Company," 386.

81. *Clinton Gazette*, Apr. 18, Apr. 25, May 9, June 13, June 20, 1894; *North Alabamian*, May 4, 1894. Between sixty and seventy Coal Creek "semi-leaders" were blacklisted for their involvement in the 1894 strike. Tennessee Commissioner of Labor, *Annual Report*, 1895, 42–58.

82. *UMWJ*, Oct. 29, 1896. As late as 1898, commentators still noted the difference in the commitment to unionization by the Coal Creek miners before and after the 1891 and 1892 revolts. *UMWJ*, May 5, June 9, 1898, clipping in box 146, SCEF Papers. For the similar decline of unionism in Tracy City, see *Birmingham Labor Advocate*, July 23, Nov. 5, Nov. 12, 1898.

83. *Birmingham Labor Advocate*, June 22, 1895.

84. Laurie, *Artisans into Workers*, 139–40, 188–89.

85. The National Trade Assemblies consisted of classic trade unions and fell directly under the general assembly of the Knights of Labor rather than under state or district assemblies. Richmond Convention Notes, Oct. 1886, reel 67, 265, Powderly Papers.

86. For references to early squabbles in the Kentucky-Tennessee district, see *National Labor Tribune*, Feb. 15, Feb. 22, 1890; *UMWJ*, June 2, 1892.

87. *Knoxville Journal*, Nov. 19, 1892; Herron to Powderly, Apr. 15, 1893, reel 41; Powderly to Herron, Apr. 20, 1893, reel 58; McBride to Powderly, July 26, 1893, reel 42; all in Powderly Papers.

88. Herron to Powderly, June 13, 1893, reel 42, Powderly Papers; *UMWJ*, June 15, Oct. 26, 1893; Nov. 21, 1895.

89. Herron to Powderly, June 13, 1893, reel 42, Powderly Papers; *Journal of the Knights of Labor*, Mar. 14, 1895.

90. *UMWJ*, July 6, Aug. 3, 1893; Mar. 28, July 31, 1895; *Journal of the Knights of Labor*, Mar. 24, 1895.

91. *UMWJ*, July 20, Oct. 26, 1893; *Journal of the Knights of Labor*, Apr. 11, 1895.

92. *Journal of the Knights of Labor*, Aug. 15, 1895.

93. *UMWJ*, July 7, Aug. 24, 1892. "Willing Hands," a black organizer from Indiana, congratulated Riley on his success in organizing District 19's black and white miners. Riley later responded by mentioning that parts of Tennessee had confounded his organizing skills largely because of his black skin. *UMWJ*, May 19, July 14, July 28, Aug. 4, 1892.

94. *UMWJ*, Mar. 30, 1893.

95. Ibid., Aug. 4, 1892. Herron was not the first person to lean toward a class analysis; his comments reflected a shift in emphasis, not a complete break with the past. For two early examples of reasoning similar to Herron's, see *Journal of United Labor*, Dec. 31, 1887; *Weekly Toiler*, Apr. 24, 1889.

96. *UMWJ*, Dec. 8, 1892.

97. Ibid., Sept. 8, 1892.

98. "Coal Creek Troubles," a local song written in the wake of the convict wars, vividly encapsulated this ideological shift. The song suggests that disillusionment with democracy in an industrial age was prompted by the state government's repeated refusals "to lend a helping hand, to help the struggling miner or remove the convict band." See Appendix 6.

Chapter 9

1. For descriptions of the 1892 New Orleans general strike, see Arnesen, *Waterfront Workers of New Orleans*, 115–17; Woodward, *Origins of the New South*, 231–32. For analyses of the 1894 strike of coal miners in the Birmingham district, see Ward and Rogers, *Labor Revolt in Alabama*; Letwin, "Race, Class, and Industrialization in the New South," 259–80.

2. Saloutos, "The American Society of Equity in Kentucky," 348–53; Grantham, "Black Patch War," 216–19; Campbell, *The Politics of Despair*, 30–37.

3. Campbell, *The Politics of Despair*, 76–97, 171–80; Grantham, "Black Patch War," 219–25; Saloutos, "The American Society of Equity in Kentucky," 354–63.

4. Youngman, "The Tobacco Pools of Kentucky and Tennessee," 39; McCulloch-Williams, "The Tobacco War in Kentucky," 179; Campbell, *The Politics of Despair*, 40–45.

5. In 1910 African Americans constituted roughly 10 percent of all farmers in the Black Patch. Campbell, *The Politics of Despair*, 124. For a discussion of the African American communities in Anderson and Grundy Counties, Tennessee, see Chapter 2.

6. Saloutos, Grantham, and Campbell all stress that the Black Patch was home to tens of thousands of sharecroppers, renters, and indebted farm owners who struggled to meet mortgage payments. Campbell also emphasizes that the toll of debt increased significantly between 1880 and 1910, as Black Patch farmers confronted tobacco prices that barely exceeded the cost of production. Yet farm owners in the Black Patch continued to outnumber tenants and sharecroppers by a considerable margin in 1910, and growers who owned their land free of encumbrances constituted a considerable proportion of farm owners. In Montgomery County, Tennessee—the one county for which Campbell provides comprehensive statistics—over two in five farmers owned their land outright. Propertied growers, moreover, were particularly active in the PPA, dominating its leadership and determining its

policies. Campbell's narrative makes clear that the cooperative struggled to attract croppers and tenants, both because the organization did not make issues relating to indebtedness a priority and because sharecroppers and renters had great difficulty in withholding their tobacco from the market for any length of time. Campbell, *The Politics of Despair*, 13, 58–71; Saloutos, "The American Society of Equity in Kentucky," 351–54; Gregory, "Robertson County and the Black Patch War," 352; Grantham, "Black Patch War," 215–16.

7. Saloutos, "The American Society of Equity in Kentucky," 351; Grantham, "Black Patch War," 221–24; Campbell, *The Politics of Despair*, 46–58.

8. Saloutos, "The American Society of Equity in Kentucky," 352–54; Gregory, "Robertson County and the Black Patch War," 349–50; Campbell, *The Politics of Despair*, 41–44. The PPA's first large-scale rally in 1904 similarly received impressive political backing, as the two congressmen who represented the Black Patch both attended and endorsed the organization.

9. Lichtenstein, *Twice the Work of Free Labor*, 73, 214 n.

10. On the size of the labor force in and around the Birmingham coalfields and for the relative proportion of black and white miners, see Letwin, "Race, Class, and Industrialization in the New South," 48. Alabama miners by no means welcomed the convicts in their midst. Instead, they regularly complained about the destructive impact that the convict lease had on the moral and material conditions under which the free miners labored, the deleterious effect that convicts had on the financial situation in the district, and the corrupting influence of the penitentiary ring on Alabama politics. Opposition invariably took constitutional forms and always came to naught. The convict lease in Alabama survived longer than in any other state, ending only in 1928. Letwin, "Race, Class, and Industrialization in the New South," 90–91.

11. Carleton, *Politics and Punishment*, 14, 35.

12. Laurie, *Artisans into Workers*, 173–74; Gould, "The Strike of 1887," 45–55.

13. Crawford, "A History of the Kentucky Penitentiary System," 311; for a description of the Kentucky rebellion and its aftermath, see 309–20. Between March and May 1886, the *Louisville Courier Journal* and the *Louisville Commercial* carried regular articles about the attack on the stockade and the political machinations that followed.

14. *Louisville Courier Journal*, Mar. 14, 1886. The strong correspondence in Tennessee between militance and miners with a permanent stake in their communities suggests a different pattern from that described by Stephen Brier in some West Virginian coal towns. Brier argues that transient African American miners in West Virginia were more inclined to embark on strikes and other militant action precisely because they had less to lose. Brier, " 'The Most Persistent Unionists,' " 98.

15. Grantham, "Black Patch War," 221; Campbell, *The Politics of Despair*, 90–93.

16. For a similar analysis of the role that the United Mine Workers played in curbing racial tensions in Alabama, see Letwin, "Interracial Unionism, Gender, and 'Social Equality' in the Alabama Coalfields."

17. The lease was resurrected briefly in 1896. When prison officials found that they could not accommodate all the convicts, they leased 125 men to TCIR in June of that year. The company put the men to work at their Inman mine and housed them in the old prison stockade. Winton, "A History of Brushy Mountain Penitentiary," 34 n.

18. *Acts of Tennessee*, 1893, 96–195, cited in Winton, "A History of Brushy Mountain Penitentiary," 16. In setting up a new penal system, Tennessee alone of the southern states bought a coal mine as a means of providing work for its prisoners.

19. *House Journal*, 1897, 31.

20. Shook to E. O. Nathurst, Sept. 16, 1893, Shook Papers.

21. TPC, 2:74 (*Nashville Herald*, Jan. 14, 1892). See also *Chattanooga Republican*, Nov. 29,

1891, Jan. 23, 1892; TPC, 1:87; 2:94 (*Chattanooga Republican*, Feb. 4, 1892). The miners might also have expected that the state would not sell convict-mined coal on the open market. When Governor Buchanan had floated the proposal for a state mine, he suggested that public institutions would serve as its sole consumers.

22. *Appleton's 1890*, 669; *Appleton's 1898*, 718–19; Zimmerman, "Penal Systems and Penal Reforms in the South Since the Civil War," 343–44, 437.

23. See Winton, "A History of Brushy Mountain Penitentiary," for the production of coke (67–97); the establishment of gardens (47); the payment of bonuses to prisoners (46); the linkage between performance and parole or privileges (49–52); and the careful selection of prisoners sent to Brushy Mountain (43–44). For the management of convict labor at the state mine, see Hill, "Experience in Mining Coal with Convicts," 392–93. When Hill instituted bonuses for convicts who mined more than their allotted tasks, he was following the example set by TCIR, which had also offered such payments.

24. Winton, "A History of Brushy Mountain Penitentiary," 71–72.

25. *Atlanta Constitution*, Mar. 11, 1895; *UMWJ*, July 7, 1898.

26. *Appleton's 1896*, 726; *National Labor Tribune*, Mar. 28, Apr. 4, 1895; J. T. Hill to W. M. Nixon, Dec. 13, 1895, box 10, Prison Records; *House Journal*, 1897, 31.

27. Winton, "A History of Brushy Mountain Penitentiary," 90–91.

28. TPC, 2:74 (*Nashville Herald*, Jan. 14, 1892).

BIBLIOGRAPHY

Manuscript Collections

Birmingham, Alabama
Birmingham Public Library
    James Bowron Scrapbooks, 1877–1928
    Erskine Ramsey Papers
    Alfred M. Shook Papers and Scrapbooks

Boston, Massachusetts
Harvard Business School
    R. G. Dun Records for Anderson, Grundy, and Knox Counties, Tennessee

Knoxville, Tennessee
Coal Creek Mining & Manufacturing Headquarters
    Coal Creek Mining & Manufacturing Company Papers
Lawson McGhee Library
    Coal Creek Coal Company Letterbook, Aug. 1876–Oct. 1877
    Coal Creek Mining & Manufacturing Company Letterbook, 1885–88
    "Coal" Folder
    "Arthur St. Clair Colyar" Folder
    "George W. Ford" Folder
    "Grundy County" Folder
    Katherine B. Hoskins, "History of Anderson County"
    John C. Houk Papers
    C. C. Justus, "Grundy County History"
    Calvin M. McClung Historical Collection
    Charles McClung McGhee Papers
    Thomas A. R. Nelson Papers
    William Rule Papers
    "Strikes" Folder
    Wiley-McAdoo Papers
University of Tennessee
    Special Collections
        Oliver Perry Temple Papers
        Campbell Wallace Papers
        Jack Wayland Scrapbook, 1881–1919

Nashville, Tennessee
Nashville Public Library
    W. C. Tatom, "Press Clippings on Coal Creek," 2 vols.
Tennessee State Library and Archives
    John Price Buchanan, Governor's Papers

Edward W. Carmack Papers
Ziphia Horton Papers
Morton B. Howell Collection
Joseph B. Killebrew Papers and Autobiography
Secretary of State Papers, 1891–92
Tennessee Coal, Iron, and Railroad Company, "Prospectus," n.d.
Peter Turney, Governor's Papers
War Records Department
Adjutant General Papers

New Haven, Connecticut
Yale University Library
Thomas C. Platt Papers
Terence Vincent Powderly and John Hayes Papers

Tracy City, Tennessee
William Ray Turner, Private Historical Collection

Tuscaloosa, Alabama
University of Alabama
James Bowron Papers, Diary, and Autobiography

Tuskegee, Alabama
Tuskegee University
Southern Conference Education Fund Papers

Washington, D.C.
Library of Congress
Calvin Stewart Brice Papers
Benjamin F. Tracy Papers

Government and Institutional Documents

Proceedings of the Annual Congress of the National Prison Association of the United States,
1886–1900.
Tennessee. *Acts of the State of Tennessee,* 1881–93.
Tennessee. Adjutant General. *Biennial Reports,* Nashville, 1888–94.
———. *Regulations for the National Guard.* Nashville, 1890.
Tennessee. Anderson County. Deeds, 1889–96.
———. Execution Dockets, 1891–93.
———. Tax Books, 1888–96.
———. Trust Deeds, 1882–94.
———. Wills, 1887–1912.
Tennessee. Anderson County Chancery Court. Criminal Minutes, 1885–1902.
Tennessee. Anderson County Circuit Court. Minutes, 1884–97.
———. Clerks Record, 1893.
Tennessee. Army National Guard, National Guard Center, Nashville. "Proceedings of a
Court of Inquiry to Investigate the Accusation of Cowardice and Incompetency against
Colonel Cator Woolford." Sept. 1892.

Tennessee. Board of Prison Commissioners. *Annual Reports*, 1889–99.

Tennessee. Bureau of Agriculture, Statistics, and Mines. *Biennial Reports*, 1891–92.

——. "Coal," by Henry E. Colton. Nashville, 1883.

——. "Iron and Coal in Tennessee," by J. B. Killebrew. Nashville, 1881.

——. "Minerals and Agricultural Resources of the Portion of Tennessee along the Cincinnati Southern and Knoxville and Ohio Railroad," by J. B. Killebrew. Nashville, 1876.

Tennessee. *The Codes of Tennessee*, compiled by W. A. Williken and John J. Vertrees. Nashville: Marshall & Bruce, 1884.

Tennessee. *Code Supplement Embracing the Public and Permanent Statutes of the State of Tennessee, from 1885 to 1893*. Nashville, 1893.

Tennessee. Commissioner of Labor and Inspector of Mines. *Annual Reports*, 1891–97.

Tennessee. Comptroller. *Biennial Reports*, Nashville, 1888–94.

——. *Digest of the Taxes on Privileges in the State of Tennessee for 1891 and 1892*, by J. W. Allen. Nashville, 1891.

——. *Letterbook*, 1891–94.

Tennessee. Department of Agriculture. "Tennessee: Its Resources, Capabilities and Development, 1892," by D. G. Godwin. Nashville, 1892.

Tennessee. Department of Education. Division of Geology. "The Southern Tennessee Coal Field," by Wilbur A. Nelson. Nashville, 1925.

Tennessee. *1891 Enumeration of Male Voters*.

Tennessee. Grundy County. Tax Books, 1888–93.

——. Trust Deeds, 1889–98.

——. Wills, 1875–1941.

Tennessee. *Journal of the House of Representatives of the General Assembly of the State of Tennessee*, 1891–97.

Tennessee. *Journal of the Senate of the General Assembly of the State of Tennessee*, 1891–93.

Tennessee. National Guard. Souvenir of Company "C," First Regiment, 1893. Nashville: St. Lewis, Woodward & Tiernon Print Co., 1893.

Tennessee. *Penitentiary Code*, by H. C. King. Nashville, 1899.

Tennessee. Prison Records, 1831–1922.

Tennessee. *Public and Permanent Statutes of a General Nature Being an Annotated Code of Tennessee, 1896*, compiled by R. T. Shannon. Nashville: Marshall & Bruce, 1896.

Tennessee. *Report of the Joint Committee on Penitentiary Affairs under Senate Joint Resolution #46*. Nashville, 1893.

Tennessee. *Report of the Joint Committee on Penitentiary Affairs under Senate Joint Resolution #31*. Nashville, 1895.

Tennessee. *Report of the Joint Committee on the Penitentiary*. Nashville: S. Nye & Co., 1837.

Tennessee. *Report of the Joint Penitentiary Investigating Committee*. Nashville, 1897.

Tennessee. *Report of the Joint Select Committee of the Senate and House of Representatives, on the Resolutions to Investigate the State Prison*. Nashville, 1843.

Tennessee. *Report of the Joint Select Committee to Whom Was Referred Sundry Resolutions and a Memorial in Relation to the Penitentiary*. Nashville, 1840.

Tennessee. *Report of the Penitentiary Purchasing and Building Committee*. Nashville, 1894–95.

Tennessee. *Report of the Warden, Superintendent, and Other Officers of the Tennessee Penitentiary*. Nashville, 1892.

Tennessee. *Reports of the Inspectors, Warden, Superintendent, Physician and Chaplain of the Tennessee Penitentiary*. Nashville, 1884.

Tennessee. Treasurer. *Biennial Reports*, Nashville, 1890–94.

U.S. Bureau of Labor. Commissioner of Labor. *Report on Convict Labor, 1886*. Washington, D.C.: GPO, 1887.

——. *Strikes and Lockouts, 1887*. Washington, D.C.: GPO, 1888.

——. *Strikes and Lockouts, 1894*. Vol. 1. Washington, D.C.: GPO, 1896.

U.S. Department of Commerce and Labor. Census Office. *Special Reports, Mines and Quarries 1902*. Washington, D.C.: GPO, 1905.

——. *Historical Statistics of the United States: Colonial Times to 1970*. 2 pts. Washington, D.C.: GPO, 1975.

——. "The Union Movement among Coal-Mine Workers," by Frank Julian Warne. Bulletin of the Bureau of Labor, no. 51, March 1904.

U.S. Department of the Interior, Census Office. *Abstract of the Eleventh Census, 1890*. Washington, D.C.: GPO, 1896.

——. *Compendium of the Eleventh Census, 1890*. Pt. 1.

——. *Manuscript Census, 1870 and 1900*. Anderson County, Tennessee, District 5.

——. *Report on Agriculture at the Twelfth Census of the United States, 1900*. Pt. 1.

——. *Report on Farms and Homes: Proprietorship and Indebtedness in the United States at the Eleventh Census, 1890*.

——. *Report on Mineral Industries in the United States at the Eleventh Census, 1890*.

——. *Report on Mineral Industries in the United States at the Tenth Census, 1880*.

——. *Report on Population at the Twelfth Census of the United States, 1900*. Pt. 1.

——. *Report on Population of the United States at the Eleventh Census, 1890*. Pt. 2.

——. *Report on the Productions of Agriculture as Returned at the Tenth Census, 1880*.

——. *Report on the Statistics of Agriculture in the United States at the Eleventh Census, 1890*.

——. *Report on Transportation Business in the United States at the Eleventh Census, 1890*. Pt. 1.

——. *Report on Wealth, Debt, and Taxation at the Eleventh Census, 1890*. Pts. 1 and 2.

——. *Special Schedules of the Eleventh Census Enumerating Union Veterans and Widows of Union Veterans of the Civil War, 1890*. Anderson County, Districts 5, 7 and 13; Morgan County, District 10; Grundy County, District 11.

——. *Statistics of the Population of the United States, Tenth Census, 1880*. Vol. 1.

U.S. Industrial Commission. *Report on the Relations and Conditions of Capital and Labor Employed in the Mining Industry*. Washington, 1901.

U.S. Senate. *Report of the Committee of the Senate on Relations between Labor and Capital*. Washington, 1885.

U.S. Senate. *Testimony as to the Relations between Labor and Capital*, 4 vols. Washington, 1885.

Newspapers, Periodicals, and Annuals

Alabama Sentinel, 1891–92

Appelton's Annual Cyclopaedia, 1890–1900

Atlantic Monthly, July–Oct. 1885

Birmingham Labor Advocate, 1891–95

Camp Carnes Anti-Bushwhacker, Aug. 1892

Chattanooga Republican, 1888–93

Chattanooga Sunday Times, Jan. 31, 1937

Clinton Courier, Feb. 6, 1975

Clinton Gazette, 1887–96

The Coal Trade, 1874–97
Coal Trade Journal, 1891–92
The Colored Tennessean, Aug–Oct. 1865; March 1866
Engineering and Mining Journal, 1886–96
The Engineering Magazine, 1891
Grundy County Herald, Sept. 2, 1976
Harper's New Monthly Magazine, 1890–95
Harper's Weekly, 1890–92
Journal of the Knights of Labor, 1890–95
Journal of United Labor, 1884–92
Knoxville Chronicle, 1877
Knoxville Independent, 1894–1900
Knoxville Journal, 1890–93
Knoxville Republican, 1891–94
Knoxville Tribune, 1877, 1891–92
Louisville Commercial, 1886
Louisville Courier Journal, 1886, 1891–92
Manufacturers' Record, 1886–96
Memphis Appeal Avalanche, 1891–92
Missouri Republican, Feb. 15, 1886
Nashville American, 1890–91
Nashville Banner, 1891–92
Nashville Herald, 1891–92
Nashville Republican, Sept.–Dec. 1890
Nashville Sentinel, 1891–92
The Nation, 1891–92
National Labor Tribune, 1885–96
New Orleans Daily Picayune, 1891–92
New York Times, 1890–92
North Alabamian, 1894
Oliver Springs News, 1887–88
Republican Chronicle, 1884
Savannah Times, 1892
Savannah Tribune, 1892
Scranton Truth, Feb.–March 1885
Seattle Post Intelligencer, 1891
Sequatchie News, 1891
Tennessee Star, Nov. 25, 1887
Town Crier, 1892
Tracy City News, 1886–1903
United Mine Workers Journal, 1891–98
Weekly Negro World, Oct.–Nov. 1887
Weekly Toiler, 1888–92

Court Cases

B. A. Jenkins v. Tennessee Coal Mining Company. Tennessee Court of Chancery Appeals,
    April 2, 1896. Tennessee State Library and Archives, Nashville.
Coal Creek Mining & Manufacturing Company v. Tennessee Coal, Iron, and Railroad

Company. Tennessee Supreme Court, 1900. Respondent's Brief. University of Tennessee Archives, Knoxville.

Cullen et al. v. Coal Creek Mining & Manufacturing Company et al. 42 Southwestern Reporter 693 (Tennessee Court of Chancery Appeals, July 7, 1897).

D. A. Wood v. Black Diamond Coal Company. Anderson County Chancery Court, 1896. Tennessee State Library and Archives, Nashville.

John P. Buchanan et al. v. Tennessee Coal, Iron, and Railroad Company et al. Davidson County Chancery Court, June 1896. Tennessee State Library and Archives, Nashville.

John P. Buchanan et al. v. Tennessee Coal, Iron, and Railroad Company, et al. Tennessee Court of Chancery Appeals, February 1897. Tennessee State Library and Archives, Nashville.

Smith v. State of Tennessee. 6 Pickle 575 (Tennessee Supreme Court, October 13, 1891).

State of Tennessee v. B. A. Jenkins. 6 Pickle 580 (Tennessee Supreme Court, October 13, 1891).

State of Tennessee v. Bony Craig. Anderson County Circuit Court, February 2, 1894. Anderson County Criminal Minutes, 1894–97.

State of Tennessee v. D. B. Monroe, Felony. Anderson County Circuit Court, February 1893. Anderson County Criminal Minutes, 1891–93; Trial Record. Tennessee State Library and Archives, Nashville.

State of Tennessee v. D. B. Monroe, Murder. Supreme Court, East Tennessee Division, June 1893. Anderson County Criminal Minutes, 1891–93.

State of Tennessee v. Sam D. Moore. Anderson County Circuit Court, June 19, 1893. Anderson County Criminal Minutes, 1891–93.

State of Tennessee, ex rel. Warren v. Jack. 18 Southwestern Reporter 257 (Tennessee Supreme Court, October 24, 1891).

Directories and Pamphlets

American Newspaper Annual and Directory. Philadelphia: N. W. Ayer & Son, 1891.

Armstead, George H. *The Commercial Club Manual, Business Guide and Directory of Nashville*. Nashville: Parker Brother Printers, 1893.

Branson, H. M. *Annual Handbook of Knoxville, Tennessee for the Year 1892*. Knoxville: N.p., 1892.

Briceville: The Town That Coal Built. Compiled by Marshall McGhee and Gene White. Jacksboro, Tenn.: Action Printing, 1991.

Coal Creek/Lake City: Visions of the Past. A History of Lake City, Tennessee, and the People and Communities of the Coal Creek Valley, 1986. Lake City, Tenn.: N.p., 1986.

Dictionary of American Biography. Edited by Allen Johnson and Dumas Malone. 21 vols. New York: Charles Scribner's Sons, 1928–37.

East Tennessee, Virginia & Georgia Railroad Company. "Reports of the Officers to the Stockholders," 1870–86.

From the Mountains to the Gulf. A Tour of the Regions Traversed by East Tennessee, Virginia & Georgia Railroad and Its Connections. New York: Giles Co., n.d.

Guide to Summer Resorts and Watering Places of East Tennessee. Memphis: S. C. Toof and Co., 1880.

Jones, James B. *Railroad Development in Tennessee, 1865–1920*. Nashville: Tennessee Historical Commission, 1987.

Knoxville City Directory, 1890–1900.

McBride, Robert M., ed. *Bibliographical Directory of the Tennessee General Assembly, 1861–*

1901. Vol. 2. Nashville: Tennessee State Library and Archives and Tennessee Historical Commission, 1979.

Memorial and Biographical Record: An Illustrated Compendium of Biography. Containing a Compendium of Local Biography Including Biographical Sketches of Prominent Old Settlers and Representative Citizens of Part of the Cumberland Region of Tennessee. Chicago: George A. Ogle, 1898.

Nashville City Directory, 1890.

Nashville Commercial Club. *Committee on the Removal of the Penitentiary*. Nashville: N.p., [1890].

Page, Bonnie. *Anderson County: Its Cities, Towns and Points of Interest*. Lake City, Tenn.: Bonnie Page, 1986.

Poor's Manual of Railroads, 1891–92.

Prospector's Guide: Showing Resources and Advantages of East Tennessee and of Her Central and Largest City, Knoxville. Knoxville: W. B. Ragsdale, 1888.

Reflections in the Water: Coal Creek to Lake City. A History of Lake City, Tennessee. Compiled by David Rogers. Lake City: N.p., 1976.

Resources of East Tennessee Adjacent to the Line of the East Tennessee, Virginia & Georgia Railroad Company. Knoxville: Ogden Press, 1890.

Tennessee Coal, Iron, and Railroad Company. *Annual Reports*, 1890–97.

Tennessee Coal, Iron, and Railroad Company. *Charter and By-Laws*. Nashville: Brandon Printing, 1893.

Tennessee State Gazetter and Business Directory, 1876–1877. Nashville: R. L. Polk & Co., 1876.

Tennessee State Gazetter and Business Directory, 1890–1891. Memphis: R. L. Polk & Co., 1891.

Who's Who of Tennessee: A Biographical Reference Book of Notable Tennesseans of Today. Memphis: Paul & Douglass Co., 1911.

Wiebel, Arthur V. *Biography of a Business: Tennessee Coal & Iron Division*. Fairfield, Ala.: U.S. Steel Corporation, 1960.

Woodward, I. B. *Tracy City from 1893 to 1910: Important Events, Deaths, Marriages, Etc., That Have Occurred Here in the Past Eighteen Years*. [Tracy City]: N.p., 1910.

Books and Articles

Abernathy, Thomas P. *From Frontier to Plantation in Tennessee: A Study in Frontier Democracy*. Chapel Hill: University of North Carolina Press, 1932.

Adamson, Christopher R. "Punishment after Slavery: Southern State Penal Systems, 1865–1900." *Social Problems* 30 (1983): 555–69.

Allison, John, ed. *Notable Men of Tennessee: Personal and Genealogical with Portraits*. Vols. 1 and 2. Atlanta: Southern Historical Association, 1905.

Ansley, Fran, and Brenda Bell. "Miners' Insurrection/Convict Labor." *Southern Exposure* 1 (1974): 144–59.

Armes, Ethel. *The Story of Coal and Iron in Alabama*. Birmingham: Chamber of Commerce, 1910.

Arnesen, Eric. *Waterfront Workers of New Orleans: Race, Class, and Politics, 1863–1923*. New York: Oxford University Press, 1991.

Ash, Stephen V. *Middle Tennessee Society Transformed, 1860–1870: War and Peace in the Upper South*. Baton Rouge: Louisiana State University Press, 1988.

Aurand, Harold W. *From the Molly Maguires to the UMW: The Social Ecology of an Industrial Union, 1869–1897*. Philadelphia: Temple University Press, 1971.

Avrich, Paul. *The Haymarket Tragedy*. Princeton, N.J.: Princeton University Press, 1984.

Ayers, Edward L. "Narrating the New South." *Journal of Southern History* 61 (1995): 555–66.

———. *The Promise of the New South: Life after Reconstruction*. New York: Oxford University Press, 1992.

———. *Vengeance and Justice: Crime and Punishment in the 19th-Century South*. New York: Oxford University Press, 1984.

Bailey, Fred Arthur. *Class and Tennessee's Confederate Generation*. Chapel Hill: University of North Carolina Press, 1987.

Ball, L. "The Public Career of Col. A. S. Colyar, 1870–1877." *Tennessee Historical Quarterly* 12 (1953): 106–28.

Bartley, Numan V. "In Search of the New South: Southern Politics after Reconstruction." *Reviews in American History* 10 (1982): 150–63.

Belissary, Constantine G. "Industry and the Industrial Philosophy in Tennessee, 1850–1860." *East Tennessee Historical Society Publications* 23 (1951): 46–57.

———. "The Rise of Industry and the Industrial Spirit in Tennessee, 1865–85." *Journal of Southern History* 14 (1953): 193–215.

———. "Tennessee and Immigration, 1865–1880." *Tennessee Historical Quarterly* 7 (1948): 229–48.

Bergeron, Paul H. *Paths of the Past: Tennessee, 1770–1970*. Knoxville: University of Tennessee Press, 1979.

Brier, Stephen. "The Career of Richard L. Davis Reconsidered: Unpublished Correspondence from the National Labor Tribune." *Labor History* 21 (1980): 420–29.

———. "Interracial Organizing in the West Virginia Coal Industry: The Participation of Black Mine Workers in the Knights of Labor and the United Mine Workers, 1880–1894." In *Essays in Southern Labor History: Selected Papers, Southern Labor History Conference, 1976*, edited by Gary M. Fink and Merle E. Reed, 18–35. Westport, Conn.: Greenwood Press, 1977.

Brophy, John. *A Miner's Life*. Madison: University of Wisconsin Press, 1964.

Burgoyne, Arthur G. *The Homestead Strike of 1892*. Pittsburgh: University of Pittsburgh Press, 1979.

Cable, George W. "The Convict Lease System in the Southern States." *Century Illustrated Monthly Magazine* 27 (1883–84): 582–99.

———. "Paper on the Convict Lease System in the Southern States." In *Proceedings of the Tenth Annual National Conference of Charities and Corrections, 1883*, 265–301. Madison, Wisc.: Midland Publishing, 1884.

———. *The Silent South: Together with the Freedman's Case in Equity and the Convict Lease System*. New York: Scribner's Sons, 1885.

Caldwell, Joshua W. *Studies in the Constitutional History of Tennessee*. Cincinnati: Robert Clarke, 1907.

Campbell, Tracy. *The Politics of Despair: Power and Resistance in the Tobacco Wars*. Lexington: University of Kentucky Press, 1993.

Carleton, Mark T. *Politics and Punishment: The History of the Louisiana State Penal System*. Baton Rouge: Louisiana State University Press, 1971.

Cartwright, Joseph H. *The Triumph of Jim Crow: Tennessee Race Relations in the 1880s*. Knoxville: University of Tennessee Press, 1976.

Chandler, Alfred D., Jr. *The Visible Hand: The Managerial Revolution in American Business*. Cambridge: Harvard University Press, 1977.

Chavannes, Cecile, and Albert Chavannes. *East Tennessee Sketches*. Knoxville: Albert Chavannes, 1900.

Clark, Thomas D. "The Country Newspaper: A Factor in Southern Opinion, 1865–1930."
    Journal of Southern History 14 (1948): 3–33.
——. "The Country Store in Post–Civil War Tennessee." *East Tennessee Historical Society
    Publications* 17 (1945): 3–21.
——. "The Tennessee Country Editor." *East Tennessee Historical Society Publications* 21
    (1949): 3–18.
Cobb, James C. "Beyond Planter and Industrialists: A New Perspective on the New South."
    Journal of Southern History 54 (1988): 45–68.
——. *Industrialization and Southern Society, 1877–1984*. Chicago: Dorsey Press, 1988.
Cohen, William. *At Freedom's Edge: Black Mobility and the Southern White Quest for Racial
    Control, 1861–1915*. Baton Rouge: Louisiana State University Press, 1991.
——. "Negro Involuntary Servitude in the South, 1865–1940: A Preliminary Analysis."
    Journal of Southern History 42 (1976): 31–60.
Commons, John R. *History of Labor in the United States*. Vol. 2. New York: Macmillan,
    1961.
Conway, Alan, ed. *The Welsh in America: Letters from Immigrants*. Minneapolis: University
    of Minnesota Press, 1961.
Corbin, David A. *Life, Work, and Rebellion in the Coal Fields: The Southern West Virginia
    Miners, 1880–1922*. Urbana: University of Illinois Press, 1981.
Corlew, Robert E. *Tennessee: A Short History*. Knoxville: University of Tennessee Press,
    1981.
Crow, Jeffrey J., Paul D. Escott, and Charles L. Flynn, Jr., eds. *Race, Class, and Politics in
    Southern History: Essays in Honor of Robert F. Durden*. Baton Rouge: Louisiana State
    University Press, 1989.
Crowe, Jesse C. "The Origin and Development of Tennessee's Prison Problem, 1831–1871."
    Tennessee Historical Quarterly 15 (1956): 111–35.
Daniel, Pete. "The Metamorphosis of Slavery, 1865–1900." *Journal of American History* 66
    (1979): 88–99.
——. "The Tennessee Convict War." *Tennessee Historical Quarterly* 34 (1975): 273–92.
Delfino, Susanna. "Antebellum Tennessee Elites and Industrialization: The Examples of the
    Iron Industry and Internal Improvements." *East Tennessee Historical Society Publications*
    56–57 (1984–85): 102–19.
Dix, Keith. *What's a Coal Miner to Do? The Mechanization of Coal Mining*. Pittsburgh:
    University of Pittsburgh Press, 1988.
Doyle, Don H. *Nashville in the New South, 1880–1930*. Knoxville: University of Tennessee
    Press, 1985.
——. *New Men, New Cities, New South: Atlanta, Nashville, Charleston, Mobile, 1860–1910*.
    Chapel Hill: University of North Carolina Press, 1990.
Dulles, Forster Rhea, and Melvyn Dubofsky. *Labor in America: A History*. Arlingon
    Heights, Ill.: Harlan Davidson, 1984.
Eller, Ronald D. "The Coal Barons of the Appalachian South, 1880–1930." *Appalachian
    Journal* 4 (1977): 195–207.
——. "Land and Family: An Historical View of Preindustrial Appalachia." *Appalachian
    Journal* 6 (1979): 83–109.
——. *Miners, Millhands, and Mountaineers: Industrialization of the Appalachian South,
    1880–1930*. Knoxville: University of Tennessee Press, 1982.
——. "Toward a New History of the Appalachian South." *Appalachian Journal* 5 (1977): 74–
    81.
Elliott, Colleen Morse, and Louise Armstrong Moxley, eds. *Tennessee Civil War Veterans*

Questionnaires, compiled by Gustavus W. Dyer and John Trotwood Moore. Easley, S.C.: Southern Historical Press, 1985.

Evans, Chris. *A History of the United Mine Workers of America, 1860–1900*. 2 vols. Indianapolis: N.p., 1918.

Fields, Barbara Jeane. "The Advent of Capitalist Agriculture: The New South in the Bourgeois World." In *Essays on the Postbellum Southern Economy*, edited by Thavolia Glymph and John J. Kushma, 73–94. College Station: Texas A&M University Press, 1985.

———. "Slavery, Race, and Ideology in the United States of America." *New Left Review* 181 (1990): 95–118.

Fink, Leon. *Workingmen's Democracy: The Knights of Labor and American Politics*. Urbana: University of Illinois Press, 1982.

Flynn, Charles L., Jr. *White Land, Black Labor: Caste and Class in Late Nineteenth-Century Georgia*. Baton Rouge: Louisiana State University Press, 1983.

Folmsbee, Stanley J. "The Beginnings of the Railroad Movement in East Tennessee." *East Tennessee Historical Society Publications* 5 (1933): 81–104.

———. "The Origins of the Nashville and Chattanooga Railroad." *East Tennessee Historical Society Publications* 6 (1934): 81–95.

Foner, Eric. *Free Soil, Free Labor, Free Men: The Ideology of the Republican Party before the Civil War*. New York: Oxford University Press, 1970.

———. *Nothing But Freedom: Emancipation and Its Legacy*. Baton Rouge: Louisiana State University Press, 1983.

———. *Reconstruction: America's Unfinished Revolution, 1863–1877*. New York: Harper & Row. 1988.

Foner, Phillip S. *The Great Labor Uprising of 1877*. New York: Monad, 1977.

Forbath, William E. "The Ambiguities of Free Labor: Labor and the Law in the Gilded Age." *Wisconsin Law Review* 4 (1985): 767–817.

Ford, Lacy K. *Origins of Southern Radicalism: The South Carolina Upcountry, 1800–1860*. New York: Oxford University Press, 1988.

———. "Rednecks and Merchants: Economic Development and Social Tensions in the South Carolina Upcountry, 1865–1900." *Journal of American History* 71 (1984): 294–318.

Francis, Phillip. *Seventy Years in the Coal Mines*. Edited by George D. Dominick. N.p.: N.p., 1943.

Gaither, Gerald H. *Blacks and the Populist Revolt: Ballots and Bigotry in the New South*. Birmingham: University of Alabama Press, 1977.

———. "The Negro Alliance Movement in Tennessee, 1888–1891." *West Tennessee Historical Society Publications* 27 (1973): 50–62.

Gardiner, John Rolfe. *Great Dream from Heaven: A Novel*. New York: E. P. Dutton, 1974.

Garlock, Jonathan. *Guide to the Local Assemblies of the Knights of Labor*. Westport, Conn.: Greenwood Press, 1982.

Garrett, William R., and Albert V. Goodpasture. *History of Tennessee: Its People and Its Institutions*. Nashville: Brandon Printing, 1900.

Gaston, Paul Morton. *The New South Creed: A Study in Mythmaking*. New York: Knopf, 1970.

Gaventa, John. *Power and Powerlessness: Quiescence and Rebellion in an Appalachian Valley*. Urbana: University of Illinois Press, 1980.

Genovese, Eugene D. *Roll, Jordan, Roll: The World the Slaves Made*. New York: Vintage, 1976.

Gerson, Noel B. *Franklin: America's "Lost State."* New York: Crowell-Collier Press, 1968.

Gildemeister, Glen. *Prison Labor and Convict Competition with Free Workers in Industrializing America, 1840–1890*. New York: Garland Publishing, 1987.

Goodrich, Carter. *The Miner's Freedom: A Study of the Working Life in a Changing Industry*. Boston: Marshall Jones, 1925.

Goodspeed's History of Tennessee. Nashville: Goodspeed Publishing, 1887; reprint, Easley, S.C.: Southern Historical Press, 1979.

Goodwyn, Lawrence. *The Populist Moment: A Short History of the Agrarian Revolt in America*. New York: Oxford University Press, 1978.

Gould, Jeffrey. "The Strike of 1887: Louisiana Sugar War." *Southern Exposure* 12 (1984): 45–55.

Graebner, William. "Great Expectations: The Search for Order in Bituminous Coal, 1890–1917." *Business History Review* 48 (1974): 49–72.

Grantham, Dewey W., Jr. "Black Patch War: The Story of the Kentucky and Tennessee Night Rider, 1905–1909." *South Atlantic Quarterly* 59 (1960): 215–25.

——. *The Life and Death of the Solid South: A Political History*. Lexington: University of Kentucky Press, 1988.

——. *Southern Progressivism: The Reconciliation of Progress and Tradition*. Knoxville: University of Tennessee Press, 1983.

Green, Archie. *Only a Miner: Studies in Recorded Coal Mining Songs*. Urbana: University of Illinois Press, 1972.

Green, Fletcher M. "Some Aspects of the Convict Lease System in the Southern States." *James Sprunt Studies in History and Political Science* 31 (1949): 112–23.

Greene, James. "The Brotherhood of Timber Workers, 1910–1913: A Radical Response to Industrial Capitalism in the Southern USA." *Past and Present* 60 (1973): 161–200.

Greene, Lee Seifert, and Robert Sterling Avery. *Government in Tennessee*. Knoxville: University of Tennessee Press, 1966.

Gregg, Robert. *Origin and Development of the Tennessee Coal, Iron, and Railroad Company*. New York: Newcomen Society of England, 1945.

Gregory, Rick. "Robertson County and the Black Patch War, 1904–1909." *Tennessee Historical Quarterly* 39 (1980): 341–58.

Gutman, Herbert. "Class, Status, and Community Power in Nineteenth-Century American Industrial Cities: Paterson, New Jersey: A Case Study." In *Work, Culture, and Society in Industrializing America: Essays in American Working-Class and Social History*, 234–60. New York: Vintage Books, 1977.

——. "The Negro and the United Mine Workers of America: The Career and Letters of Richard L. Davis and Something of their Meaning, 1890–1900." In *Work, Culture, and Society in Industrializing America: Essays in American Working-Class and Social History*, 121–208. New York: Vintage Books, 1977.

——. "Protestantism and the American Labor Movement: The Christian Spirit in the Gilded Age." In *Work, Culture, and Society in Industrializing America: Essays in American Working-Class and Social History*, 79–117. New York: Vintage Books, 1977.

Gutman, Herbert, and Ira Berlin. "Class Composition and the Development of the American Working Class, 1840–1890." In *Power and Culture: Essays on the American Working Class*, edited by Ira Berlin, 380–94. New York: Pantheon Books, 1987.

Hahn, Steven. "Class and State in Postemancipation Societies: Southern Planters in Comparative Perspective." *American Historical Review* 95 (1990): 75–98.

——. "Hunting, Fishing, and Foraging: Common Rights and Class Relations in the Postbellum South." *Radical History Review* 26 (1982): 37–64.

——. *The Roots of Southern Populism: Yeoman Farmers and the Transformation of the Georgia Upcountry, 1850–1890*. New York: Oxford University Press, 1983.

——. "The 'Unmaking' of Southern Yeomanry: The Transformation of the Georgia Upcountry, 1860–1890." In *The Countryside in the Age of Capitalist Transformation*, edited by Steven Hahn and Jonathan Prude, 179–203. Chapel Hill: University of North Carolina Press, 1985.

Hall, Jacquelyn Dowd. "Disorderly Women: Gender and Labor Militancy in the Appalachian South." *Journal of American History* 73 (1986): 354–82.

Hall, Jacquelyn Dowd, James Leloudis, Robert Korstad, Mary Murphy, Lu Ann Jones, and Christopher B. Daly. *Like a Family: The Making of a Southern Cotton Mill World*. New York: W. W. Norton, 1987.

Hamer, Philip M., ed. *Tennessee: A History, 1673–1932*. 4 vols. New York: American Historical Society, 1933.

Hart, Roger L. *Redeemers, Bourbons, and Populists: Tennessee 1870–1896*. Baton Rouge: Louisiana State University Press, 1975.

Hicks, J. D. *The Populist Revolt: A History of the Farmers' Alliance and the People's Party*. Minneapolis: University of Minnesota Press, 1931; reprint, Lincoln: University of Nebraska Press, 1961.

Hill, Herbert. "Myth-Making as Labor History: Herbert Gutman and the United Mine Workers of America." *International Journal of Politics, Culture, and Society* 2 (1988): 132–200.

Hill, Jesse T. "Experience in Mining Coal with Convicts." In *Proceedings of the Annual Congress of the National Prison Association of the United States, 1897*, 388–98. Pittsburgh: Shaw Brothers, 1898.

Hogler, Raymond L. "Labor History and Critical Labor Law: An Interdisciplinary Approach to Workers' Control." *Labor History* 30 (1989): 165–92.

Holt, Wyath. "The New American Labor Law History." *Labor History* 30 (1989): 275–93.

Hoskins, Katherine B. *Anderson County*. Memphis: Memphis State University Press, 1979.

——. *Anderson County: Historical Sketches*. Clinton, Tenn.: Courier News, 1987.

Howell, Sarah McCanless. "The Editorials of Arthur S. Colyar, Nashville Prophet of the New South." *Tennessee Historical Quarterly* 27 (1968): 262–76.

Hutson, Andrew C., Jr. "The Coal Miners' Insurrection of 1891 in Anderson County, Tennessee." *East Tennessee Historical Society Publications* 7 (1935): 103–21.

——. "The Overthrow of the Convict Lease System in Tennessee." *East Tennessee Historical Society Publications* 8 (1936): 82–103.

Hyman, Michael R. *The Anti-Redeemers: Hill-Country Political Dissenters in the Lower South from Redemption to Populism*. Baton Rouge: Louisiana State University Press, 1990.

Ignatieff, Michael. *A Just Measure of Pain*. New York: Pantheon, 1978.

Jaynes, Gerald. *Branches without Roots: The Genesis of the Black Working Class in the American South, 1862–1882*. New York: Oxford University Press, 1986.

Jones, Robert B. *Tennessee at the Crossroads: The State Debt Controversy, 1870–1883*. Knoxville: University of Tennessee Press, 1977.

Kann, Kenneth. "The Knights of Labor and the Southern Black Worker." *Labor History* 18 (1977): 49–70.

Kelley, Robin D. G. " 'We Are Not What We Seem': Rethinking Black Working-Class Opposition in the Jim Crow South." *Journal of American History* 80 (1993): 75–112.

Kessler, Sidney H. "The Organization of Negroes in the Knights of Labor." *Journal of Negro History* 37 (1952): 248–76.

Keve, Paul W. *The History of Corrections in Virginia*. Charlottesville: University Press of Virginia, 1986.

Keyssar, Alexander. *Out of Work: The First Century of Unemployment in Massachusetts.* New York: Cambridge University Press, 1986.

Kiger, Joseph C. "Social Thought as Voiced in Rural Middle Tennessee Newspapers, 1878–1898." *Tennessee Historical Quarterly* 9 (1950): 131–54.

Killebrew, Joseph B. *Introduction to the Resources of Tennessee.* Nashville: Tavel, Eastman & Howell, 1874.

——. *Iron and Coal of Tennessee.* Nashville: Tavel & Howell, 1881.

Kloosteboer, W. *Involuntary Labour since the Abolition of Slavery: A Survey of Compulsory Labour throughout the World.* Leiden: E. J. Brill, 1960.

Klotter, James C. "The Black South and White Appalachia." *Journal of American History* 66 (1980): 832–49.

Kolchin, Peter. *Unfree Labor: American Slavery and Russian Serfdom.* Cambridge: Harvard University Press, 1987.

Kousser, J. Morgan. *The Shaping of Southern Politics: Suffrage Restriction and the Establishment of the One-Party South, 1880–1910.* New Haven: Yale University Press, 1974.

Krausse, Paul. *The Battle for Homestead, 1880–1892: Politics, Culture, and Steel.* Pittsburgh: University of Pittsburgh Press, 1992.

Kurns, T. C. *The Government of the People of the State of Tennessee.* Philadelphia: Elredge & Brother, 1897.

Lamon, L. C. *Black Tennesseans, 1900–1930.* Knoxville: University of Tennessee Press, 1977.

Laurie, Bruce. *Artisans into Workers: Labor in Nineteenth-Century America.* New York: Noonday Press, 1989.

Letwin, Daniel. "Interracial Unionism, Gender, and 'Social Equality' in the Alabama Coalfields, 1878–1908." *Journal of Southern History* 61 (1995): 519–54.

Lewis, Ronald L. *Black Coal Miners in America: Race, Class, and Community Conflict, 1780–1980.* Lexington: University Press of Kentucky, 1987.

——. "From Peasant to Proletarian: The Migration of Southern Blacks to the Central Appalachian Coalfields." *Journal of Southern History* 55 (1989): 77–102.

——. "Job Control and Race Relations in Coal Fields, 1870–1920." *Journal of Ethnic Studies* 12 (1985): 35–64.

——. "Race and the United Mine Workers' Union in Tennessee: Selected Letters of William R. Riley, 1892–1898." *Tennessee Historical Quarterly* 36 (1977): 524–36.

Lichtenstein, Alex. "Good Roads and Chain Gangs in the Progressive South: 'The Negro Convict as Slave.'" *Journal of Southern History* 59 (1993): 85–110.

——. "Racial Conflict and Racial Solidarity in the Alabama Coal Strike of 1894: New Evidence for the Gutman-Hill Debate." *Labor History* 36 (1995): 63–76.

——. *Twice the Work of Free Labor: The Political Economy of Convict Labor in the New South.* London: Verso Press, 1996.

Lindsey, Almont. *The Pullman Strike.* Chicago: University of Chicago Press, 1942.

Linebaugh, Peter. *The London Hanged: Crime and Civil Society in the Eighteenth Century.* New York: Cambridge University Press, 1992.

Litwack, Leon. "Trouble in Mind: The Bicentennial and the Afro-American Experience." *Journal of American History* 72 (1987): 315–37.

Long, Priscilla. *Where the Sun Never Shines: A History of America's Bloody Coal Industry.* New York: Paragon House, 1989.

MacArthur, William J., Jr. "The Early Career of Charles McClung McGhee." *East Tennessee Historical Society Publications* 45 (1972): 3–13.

MacArthur, William Joseph, Jr., and Justin Fuller. *Charles McClung McGhee, Southern Financier.* Ann Arbor, Mich.: University Microfilms, 1975.

McCulloch-Williams, Martha. "The Tobacco War in Kentucky." *Review of Reviews* 37 (1908): 168–70.

McKelvey, Blake. *American Prisons: A Study in American Social History Prior to 1915.* Chicago: University of Chicago Press, 1936.

——. "Penal Slavery and Southern Reconstruction." *Journal of Negro History* 20 (1935): 153–79.

McKenzie, Robert Tracy. "Freedmen and the Soil in the Upper South: The Reorganization of Tennessee Agriculture, 1865–1880." *Journal of Southern History* 59 (1993): 63–84.

——. *One South or Many? Plantation Belt and Upcountry in Civil War-Era Tennessee.* New York: Cambridge University Press, 1994.

McKinney, Gordon Bartlett. "Industrialization and Violence in Appalachia in the 1890's." In *An Appalachian Symposium: Essays Written in Honor of Cratis D. Williams*, edited by J. W. Williamson, 131–44. Boone, N.C.: Appalachian State University Press, 1977.

——. "The Mountain Republicans and the Negro." *Journal of Southern History* 41 (1975): 493–516.

——. "The Political Uses of Appalachian Identity after the Civil War." *Appalachian Journal* 7 (1980): 200–9.

——. "The Rise of the Houk Machine in East Tennessee." *East Tennessee Historical Society Publications* 45 (1973): 61–77.

——. *Southern Mountain Republicans, 1865–1900: Politics and the Appalachian Community.* Chapel Hill: University of North Carolina Press, 1978.

McLaurin, Melton. *The Knights of Labor in the South.* Westport, Conn.: Greenwood Press, 1978.

McMath Robert C., Jr. *American Populism: A Social History, 1877–1898.* New York: Hill & Wang, 1993.

——. *Populist Vanguard: A History of the Southern Farmers' Alliance.* Chapel Hill: University of North Carolina Press, 1975.

——. "Sandy Land and Hogs in the Timber: (Agri)cultural Origins of the Farmers' Alliance in Texas." In *The Countryside in the Age of Capitalist Transformation*, edited by Steven Hahn and Jonathan Prude, 205–29. Chapel Hill: University of North Carolina Press, 1985.

McMillen, Neil R. *Dark Journey: Black Mississippians in the Age of Jim Crow.* Urbana: University of Illinois Press, 1990.

McNall, Scott G. *The Road to Rebellion: Class Formation and Kansas Populism, 1865–1900.* Chicago: University of Chicago Press, 1988.

McWhirter, A. J. *Revised Hand-Book of Tennessee.* Nashville: Albert B. Tavel,1885.

Maier, Pauline. *From Resistance to Revolution: Colonial Radicals and the Development of American Opposition to Britain, 1765–1776.* New York: Knopf, 1972.

Mancini, Matthew J. "Race, Economics, and the Abandonment of Convict Leasing." *Journal of Negro History* 63 (1978): 339–92.

Mayer, Henry C. "Glimpses of Union Activity among Coal Miners in Nineteenth-Century Eastern Kentucky." *Register of the Kentucky Historical Society* 86 (1988): 216–29.

——. "Gone and Nearly Forgotten: William Webb." *Coal People Magazine* 15 (1990): 17–19.

Miller, Charles A. *The Official and Political Manual of the State of Tennessee.* Nashville: Marshall & Bruce, 1890.

Montgomery, David. *Beyond Equality: Labor and the Radical Republicans, 1862–1872.* Urbana: University of Illinois Press, 1967.

——. *Citizen Worker: The Experience of Workers in the United States with Democracy and the Free Market during the Nineteenth Century*. New York: Cambridge University Press, 1993.

——. "Labor and the Republic in Industrial America: 1860–1920." *Le Mouvement Social* 3 (1980): 201–15.

——. *Workers' Control in America*. New York: Cambridge University Press, 1979.

Moore, James Tice. "Agrarianism and Populism in Tennessee, 1886–1896: An Interpretative Overview." *Tennessee Historical Quarterly* 42 (1983): 76–94.

——. "Redeemers Reconsidered: Change and Continuity in the Democratic South, 1870–1900." *Journal of Southern History* 44 (1978): 357–78.

Moore, John Trotwood. *Tennessee: The Volunteer State, 1769–1923*. Vol. 1. Nashville: S. J. Clarke, 1923.

Morgan, Edmund S. *American Slavery, American Freedom: The Ordeal of Colonial Virginia*. New York: W. W. Norton, 1975.

Morris, Robert L. "Legal Questions Arising out of Our Recent Labor Troubles." In *Proceedings of the Eleventh Annual Meeting of the Bar Association of Tennessee 1892*, 144–55. Nashville: Marshall & Bruce, 1892.

Moulder, Rebecca Hunt. "Convicts as Capital: Thomas O'Connor and the Leases of the Tennessee Penitentiary System, 1871–1883." *East Tennessee Historical Society Publications* 48 (1976): 40–70.

——. *May the Sod Rest Lightly: Thomas O'Conner*. Tucson, Ariz.: Skyline Publishing, 1977.

Murfree, Mary Noailles [Charles Egbert Craddock]. "Drifting Down Lost Creek." In *In the Tennessee Mountains*, 1–79. Boston: Houghton Mifflin, 1892; reprint, Knoxville: University of Tennessee Press, 1970.

Myers, Marvin. *The Jacksonian Persuasion: Politics and Beliefs*. New York: Vintage, 1960.

Newby, I. A. *Plain Folk in the New South: Social Change and Cultural Persistence, 1880–1915*. Baton Rouge: Louisiana State University Press, 1989.

Nicholson, James L. *Grundy County*. Memphis: Memphis State University Press, 1982.

Nobles, Gregory. "Capitalism in the Countryside: The Transformation of Rural Society in the United States." *Radical History Review* 41 (1988): 163–76.

Norrell, Robert J. *James Bowron: The Autobiography of a New South Industrialist*. Chapel Hill: University of North Carolina Press, 1991.

Northrup, Herbert. *Organized Labor and the Negro*. New York: Harper & Brothers, 1944.

Oestreicher, Richard Jules. *Solidarity and Fragmentation: Working People and Class Consciousness in Detroit, 1875–1900*. Urbana: University of Illinois Press, 1986.

Orwell, George. *Road to Wigan Peer*. London: Victor Gollancz, 1937; reprint, London: Penguin, 1986.

Owsley, Frank L. *Plain Folk of the Old South*. Baton Rouge: Louisiana State University Press, 1949.

Owsley, Frank L., and Harriet C. "The Economic Structure of Rural Tennessee, 1840–1860." *Journal of Southern History* 8 (1942): 162–82.

Palladino, Grace. *Another Civil War: Labor, Capital, and the State in the Anthracite Regions of Pennsylvania*. Urbana: University of Illinois Press, 1990.

Palmer, Bruce. *"Man over Money": The Southern Populist Critique of American Capitalism*. Chapel Hill: University of North Carolina Press, 1980.

Perman, Michael. *The Road to Redemption: Southern Politics, 1869–1879*. Chapel Hill: University of North Carolina Press, 1984.

Queener, Verton M. "A Decade of East Tennessee Republicanism, 1867–1876." *East Tennessee Historical Society Publications* 14 (1942): 59–85.

——. "The East Tennessee Republicans as a Minority Party, 1870–1896." *East Tennessee Historical Society Publications* 15 (1943): 49–73.

——. "The East Tennessee Republicans in State and Nation, 1870–1900." *Tennessee Historical Quarterly* 2 (1943): 99–128.

——. "The Origin of the Republican Party in East Tennessee." *East Tennessee Historical Society Publications* 13 (1941): 66–90.

Rabinowitz, Howard N. *Race Relations in the Urban South, 1865–1890*. New York: Oxford University Press, 1978.

Rachleff, Peter J. *Black Labor in the South: Richmond, Virginia, 1865–1890*. Philadelphia: Temple University Press, 1984.

Roberts, Derrell. "Joseph E. Brown and His Georgia Mines." *Georgia Historical Quarterly* 52 (1968): 285–92.

Robison, Daniel M. *Bob Taylor and the Agrarian Revolt in Tennessee*. Chapel Hill: University of North Carolina Press, 1935.

——. "Tennessee Politics and the Agrarian Revolt, 1886–1896." *Mississippi Valley Historical Review* 20 (1934): 365–80.

Rodgers, Daniel T. *Contested Truths: Keywords in American Politics since Independence*. New York: Basic, 1987.

——. "Republicanism: The Career of a Concept." *Journal of American History* 79 (1992): 11–38.

Rothrock, Mary V. *The French Broad-Holston County: A History of Knox County, Tennessee*. Knoxville: East Tennessee Historical Society, 1946.

Roy, Andrew. *A History of the Coal Miners of the United States: From the Development of the Mines to the Close of the Anthracite Strike of 1902*. Westport, Conn.: Greenwood Press, 1970.

Saloutos, Theodore. "The American Society of Equity in Kentucky: A Recent Attempt in Agrarian Reform." *Journal of Southern History* 5 (1939): 347–63.

Saunders, Robert. "Southern Populists and the Negro, 1893–1895." *Journal of Negro History* 54 (1969): 240–61.

Schneider, Linda. "The Citizen Striker: Workers' Ideology in the Homestead Strike of 1892." *Labor History* 23 (1982): 47–66.

——. "Republicanism Reinterpreted: American Ironworkers, 1860–1892." In *In the Shadow of the Statue of Liberty*, edited by Marianne Debouzy, 199–214. Saint-Denis, France: Presses Universitaires de Vincennes, 1988.

Scott, James C. *Weapons of the Weak: Everyday Forms of Peasant Resistance*. New Haven: Yale University Press, 1985.

Seeger, Pete. "Coal Creek Rebellion." *Sing Out* (1955): 19–21.

Seeger, Pete, and Bob Reisner. *Carry it On! A History in Song and Picture of the Working Men and Women of America*. New York: Simon & Schuster, 1985.

Sewell, William H. "Uneven Development, the Autonomy of Politics, and the Dockworkers of Nineteenth-Century Marseille." *American Historical Review* 93 (1988): 604–37.

Shalhope, Robert E. "Republicanism and Early American Historiography." *William and Mary Quarterly* 39 (1982): 334–56.

——. "Towards a Republican Synthesis: The Emergence of an Understanding of Republicanism in American Historiography." *William and Mary Quarterly* 29 (1972): 49–80.

Shapiro, Henry D. "Appalachia and the Idea of America: The Problem of the Persisting Frontier." In *An Appalachian Symposium: Essays Written in Honor of Cratis D. Williams*, edited by J. W. Williamson, 43–55. Boone, N.C.: Appalachian State University Press, 1977.

——. *Appalachia on Our Mind: The Southern Mountains and Mountaineers in the American Consciousness, 1870–1920.* Chapel Hill: University of North Carolina Press, 1978.

Sharp, Joseph A. "The Entrance of the Farmers' Alliance into Tennessee Politics." *East Tennessee Historical Society Publications* 9 (1937): 77–92.

——. "The Farmers' Alliance and the People's Party in Tennessee." *East Tennessee Historical Society Publications* 10 (1938): 91–113.

Shelden, Randall G. "From Slave to Caste Society: Penal Changes in Tennessee, 1830–1915." *Tennessee Historical Quarterly* 38 (1979): 463–78.

Shifflet, Crandall A. *Coal Towns: Life, Work, and Culture in Company Towns of Southern Appalachia, 1880–1960.* Knoxville: University of Tennessee, 1991.

Sims, P. D. "The Lease System in Tennessee and Other Southern States." In *Proceedings of the Annual Congress of the National Prison Association of the United States, 1893,* 123–34. Chicago: Knight, Leonard & Co., 1893.

Smith, Henry Nash. *Virgin Land: The American West as Symbol and Myth.* Cambridge: Harvard University Press, 1978.

Smith, Samuel Boyd. "Joseph Buckner Killebrew and the New South Movement in Tennessee." *East Tennessee Historical Society Publications* 37 (1965): 5–22.

Sorge, Friedrich A. *Labor Movement in the United States: A History of the American Working Class from 1890 to 1896,* translated by Kai Schoenhals. Westport, Conn.: Greenwood Press, 1987.

Speer, William S. *Sketches of Prominent Tennesseans.* Nashville: A. B. Tavel, 1888.

Spero, Sterling D., and Abram L. Harris. *The Black Worker: The Negro and the Labor Movement.* New York: Columbia University Press, 1931.

Sprague, Stuart Seely. "The Great Appalachian Iron and Coal Town Boom of 1889–1893." *Appalachian Journal* 4 (1977): 216–23.

Starobin, Robert S. *Industrial Slavery in the Old South.* New York: Oxford University Press, 1970.

Steinfeld, Robert J. "Property and Suffrage in the Early American Republic." *Stanford Law Review* 41 (1989): 335–76.

Stover, John Ford. *The Railroads of the South, 1865–1900: A Study in Finance and Control.* Chapel Hill: University of North Carolina Press, 1955.

Stromquist, Shelton. *Generation of Boomers: The Pattern of Railroad Labor Conflict in Nineteenth-Century America.* Urbana: University of Illinois Press, 1987.

Taylor, Alrutheus Ambush. *The Negro in Tennessee, 1865–1880.* Washington, D.C.: Associated Publishers, 1941.

Taylor, A. Elizabeth. "The Abolition of the Convict Lease System in Georgia." *Georgia Historical Quarterly* 26 (1942): 273–87.

——. "The Origin and Development of the Convict Lease System in Georgia." *Georgia Historical Quarterly* 26 (1942): 113–28.

Trotter, Joe William, Jr. *Coal, Class, and Color: Blacks in Southern West Virginia, 1915–32.* Urbana: University of Illinois Press, 1990.

Turner, William H., and Edward J. Cabbell, eds. *Blacks in Appalachia.* Lexington: University Press of Kentucky, 1985.

Van Onselen, Charles. *Chibaro: African Mine Labour in Southern Rhodesia, 1900–1933.* Johannesburg: Ravan Press, 1980.

Walker, Anne Kendrick. *Life and Achievements of Alfred Montgomery Shook.* Birmingham: Birmingham Publishing, 1952.

Waller, Altina L. *Feud: Hatfields, McCoys, and Social Change in Appalachia, 1860–1900.* Chapel Hill: University of North Carolina Press, 1988.

Ward, Robert D., and William W. Rogers. *Convicts, Coal, and the Banner Mine Tragedy*. Birmingham: University of Alabama Press, 1987.

———. *Labor Revolt in Alabama: The Great Strike of 1894*. Birmingham: University of Alabama Press, 1965.

Weiss, Robert P. "Humanitarianism, Labour Exploitation, or Social Control? A Critical Survey of Theory and Research on the Origin and Development of Prisons." *Social History* 12 (1987): 331–50.

Wharton, Vernon Lane. *The Negro in Mississippi, 1865–1890*. Chapel Hill: University of North Carolina Press, 1947.

White, Charles P. "Early Experiments with Prison Labor in Tennessee." *East Tennessee Historical Society Publication* 12 (1950): 45–69.

White, Gene. *Briceville through the Years*. Jacksboro, Tenn.: Action Printing, 1994.

White, Robert H. *Messages of the Governors of Tennessee*. Vol. 7. Nashville: Tennessee Historical Commission, 1967.

———. *Tennessee: Its Growth and Progress*. Nashville: N.p., 1936.

Wiebe, Robert H. *The Search for Order, 1877–1920*. New York: Hill & Wang, 1967.

Wiener, Jonathan M. "Class Structure and Economic Development in the American South, 1869–1955." *American Historical Review* 84 (1979): 970–92.

Williams, Cratis D. "The Southern Mountaineer in Fact and Fiction." *Appalachian Journal* 3 (1975): 8–41.

———. "Who Are the Southern Mountaineers?" *Appalachian Journal* 1 (1972): 48–55.

Wilson, Walter. *Forced Labor in the United States*. New York: International Publishers, 1933.

Winters, Donald L. " 'Plain Folk' of the Old South Reexamined: Economic Democracy in Tennessee." *Journal of Southern History* 53 (1987): 565–86.

Woodman, Harold. "Economic Reconstruction and the Rise of the New South, 1865–1900." In *Interpreting Southern History: Historiographical Essays in Honor of Sanford W. Higgenbotham*, edited by John B. Boles and Evelyn Thomas Nolen, 254–307. Baton Rouge: Louisiana State University Press, 1987.

———. "The Reconstruction of the Cotton Plantation in the New South." In *Essays on the Postbellum Southern Economy*, edited by Thavolia Glymph and John J. Kushma, 95–119. College Station: Texas A&M University Press, 1985.

———. "Sequel to Slavery: The New History Views the Postbellum South." *Journal of Southern History* 43 (1977): 523–54.

Woodson, Carter G. "Freedom and Slavery in Appalachia America." *Journal of Negro History* 1 (1916): 132–50.

Woodward, C. Vann. *Origins of the New South, 1877–1913*. Baton Rouge: Louisiana State University Press, 1951.

———. *The Strange Career of Jim Crow*. New York: Oxford University Press, 1966.

———. *Tom Watson: Agrarian Rebel*. New York: Oxford University Press, 1963.

Worthman, Paul. "Black Workers and Labor Unions in Birmingham, Alabama, 1897–1904." *Labor History* 10 (1969): 375–407.

———. "Black Workers in the New South, 1865–1915." In *Key Issues in the Afro-American Experience*, edited by Nathan I. Huggins, Martin Kilson, and Daniel M. Fox, 47–69. New York: Harcourt Brace Jovanovich, 1972.

Wright, Gavin. *Old South, New South: Revolutions in the Southern Economy since the Civil War*. New York: Basic Books, 1986.

Wyatt-Brown, Bertram. *Southern Honor: Ethics and Behavior in the Old South*. New York: Oxford University Press, 1982.

Youngman, Anna. "The Tobacco Pools of Kentucky and Tennessee." *Journal of Political Economy* 18 (1910): 34–49.

Zimmerman, Hilda. "The Penal Reform Movement in the South during the Progressive Era, 1890–1917." *Journal of Southern History* 17 (1951): 462–92.

Zola, Emile. *Germinal*. London: Penguin, 1954.

Theses and Unpublished Papers

Archer, Claude A. "The Life of John Chiles Houk." M.A. thesis, University of Tennessee, 1941.

Ball, Clyde. "The Public Career of Col. A. S. Colyar, 1870–77." M.A. thesis, Vanderbilt University, 1937.

Belissary, Constantine G. "The Rise of the Industrial Spirit in Tennessee, 1865–1885." Ph.D. diss., Vanderbilt University, 1949.

Berry, David Charles. "Free Labor He Found Unsatisfactory: James W. English and Convict Lease Labor at the Chattahoochee Brick Company." M.A. thesis, Georgia State University, 1991.

Brier, Stephen Burnett. " 'The Most Persistent Unionists': Class Formation and Class Conflict in the Coal Fields and the Emergence of Interracial and Interethnic Unionism, 1880–1904." Ph.D. diss., University of California, Los Angeles, 1992.

Brown, Virginia Holmes. "The Development of Labor Legislation in Tennessee." M.A. thesis, University of Tennessee, 1945.

Carter, Dan T. "Politics and Business: The Convict Lease System in the Post–Civil War South." M.A. thesis, University of Wisconsin, 1964.

Clark, Joseph H. "History of the Knoxville Iron Company." M.Sc. thesis, University of Tennessee, 1949.

Corlew, Robert E. "The Negro in Tennessee: 1870–1900." Ph.D. diss., University of Alabama, 1954.

Crawford, R. G. "A History of the Kentucky Penitentiary System, 1865–1937." Ph.D. diss., University of Kentucky, 1955.

Crowe, Jesse C. "Agitation for Penal Reform in Tennessee, 1870–1900." Ph.D. diss., Vanderbilt University, 1954.

Dombrowski, James. "Fire in the Hole." Notes and Manuscript, Highlander Center, Tennessee, ca. 1938.

Donovan, William F. "The Growth of the Industrial Spirit in Tennessee, 1890–1910." Ph.D. diss., George Peabody College, 1955.

Fox, Elbert Leonard. "A History of Populism in Tennessee." M.A. thesis, George Peabody College for Teachers, 1950.

Fuller, Justin. "History of the Tennessee Coal, Iron, and Railroad Company, 1852–1907." Ph.D. diss., University of North Carolina, 1966.

Hersh, Alan. "The Development of the Iron Industry in East Tennessee." M.Sc. thesis, University of Tennessee, 1958.

"Historical Sketch," Inventory of the County Archives of Tennessee, no. 1, Anderson County. Nashville: Tennessee Historical Records Survey, July 1941.

Howell, Sarah Hardcastle McCanless. "The Editorial Career of Arthur S. Colyar: 1882–1888." M.A. thesis, Vanderbilt University, 1967.

———. "Scholars of the Urban Industrial Frontier: 1880–1889." Ph.D. diss., Vanderbilt University, 1970.

Hutson, Andrew C., Jr. "The Coal Miners' Insurrection, 1891–92." M.A. thesis, University of Tennessee, 1933.

Lawrence, Randall Gene. "Appalachian Metamorphosis: Industrializing Society on the Central Appalachian Plateau, 1860–1913." Ph.D. diss., Duke University, 1983.

Letwin, Daniel L. "Race, Class, and Industrialization in the New South: The Coal Miners of Alabama, 1878–1897." Ph.D. diss., Yale University, 1991.

Lichtenstein, Alexander C. "Convict Labor and Racial Ideology in the New South." Paper presented to the Southern Historical Association, Nov. 1992.

———. "The Political Economy of Convict Labor in the New South." Ph.D. diss., University of Pennsylvania, 1990.

MacArthur William Joseph., Jr. "Charles McClung McGhee, Southern Financier." Ph.D. diss., University of Tennessee, 1975.

Mancini, Matthew. "One Dies, Get Another": How to Think about Convict Leasing." Paper presented to the Southern Historical Association, Nov. 1989.

Mintz, Robert. "The Miners Who Tore Down the Walls." Ph.D. diss., University of California, Berkeley, 1974.

Nicely, Verdel. "History of the Tennessee Penitentiary, 1865–1890." M.A. thesis, University of Tennessee, 1933.

Oshinsky, David M. "Prison Plantation: Parchman Prison and Forced Labor." Paper presented to the Southern Historical Association, Nov. 1989.

Queener, Verton Madison. "The Republican Party of East Tennessee, 1865–1900." Ph.D. diss., Indiana University, 1940.

Seeber, Clifford R. "A History of Anderson County, Tennessee." M.A. thesis, University of Tennessee, 1928.

Shahan, Joseph M. "The Limits of Agrarian Reform: The Tennessee Alliance Movement, 1888–92." M.A. thesis, Vanderbilt University, 1973.

———. "Reform and Politics in Tennessee, 1906–1914." Ph.D. diss., Vanderbilt University, 1981.

Shapiro, Karin A. "The Tennessee Coal Miners' Revolts of 1891–92: Industrialization, Politics, and Convict Labor in the Late Nineteenth-Century South." Ph.D. diss., Yale University, 1991.

Sharp, Joseph A. "The Farmers' Alliance in Tennessee Politics, 1890–1892." M.A. thesis, University of Tennessee, 1931.

Sistler, Byron, and Barbara Sistler. "1880 Census—Tennessee: Transcription for Anderson County." Calvin M. McClung Historical Collection, Knoxville Public Library.

Smith, Samuel Boyd. "Joseph Buckner Killebrew and the New South Movement in Tennessee." Ph.D. diss., Vanderbilt University, 1962.

Walker, Joseph E. "The Negro in Tennessee Politics, 1865–1880." M.A. thesis, Fisk University, 1941.

Westphal, Corinne. "The Farmers' Alliance in Tennessee." M.A. thesis, Vanderbilt University, 1929.

Wilson, Mary Ellen. "The Rise and Fall of Convict Labor in the Central Georgia Lumber Industry." Paper presented to the Southern Historical Association, Nov. 1992.

Winton, Ruth. "A History of Brushy Mountain Penitentiary." M.A. thesis, University of Tennessee, 1937.

Zimmerman, Hilda J. "Penal Systems and Penal Reforms in the South since the Civil War." Ph.D. diss., University of North Carolina, Chapel Hill, 1947.

INDEX

Adkins, J. R., 106
African Americans. *See* Blacks
Agricultural Wheel, 89, 281 (n. 25)
Agriculture: vs. industrialization and min-
ing in late nineteenth century, 21, 22,
28–29, 33, 260 (n. 9); post–Civil War
decline in value of products of, 53–54.
See also Farmers; Farms
Alabama, 27–28, 168, 189, 236; TCIR hold-
ings and operations in, 35, 177, 214,
221–22, 224; convict lease in, 48, 53,
239–40, 267 (n. 7), 298 (n. 10)
Alabama Sentinel, 148
Alexander, T. J., 103, 128, 282 (n. 47)
Alleman, Charles, 101, 115, 128, 135, 277
(n. 49)
Allen, J. W., 280 (n. 13)
Alliance/Alliancemen. *See* Farmers'
Alliance
Alston, Richard, 225
Altamont, Ky., 160
American Federation of Labor, 11
American Revolution: miners draw on
legacy of, 83, 84, 109, 111, 138, 141, 170, 231
American Tobacco Company (ATC),
236–39, 241
Anderson, D. D., 291 (n. 41)
Anderson, Kellar, 153, 185, 187, 191, 205, 206,
209, 210
Anderson County, 21, 28, 72, 98, 101, 137,
185, 201, 244, 284 (n. 79), 292 (n. 62); July
1891 insurrection in, 1, 79–81, 86, 87, 94,
154; agricultural background of migrants
to, 3; as setting for convict wars, 4, 83,
84, 110, 140, 141, 144, 150, 153, 155, 174, 183,
191, 192, 202, 203, 207–8, 217, 218, 235–36,
246–47, 259 (n. 3), 291 (n. 50); differences between Tracy City and mining
communities in, 16, 35–44; as a leading
coal-producing county, 17, 26; geography and geology of, 17, 30, 36, 142–43;

railroads in, 20, 25; postbellum population growth in, 27; CCM&MC owns and
leases coal lands in, 29, 34, 39; Knights of
Labor in, 31; as site of numerous small
coal companies and mines, 36; homeownership among residents of, 41, 105;
union activity in, 42, 43, 223–24, 243;
blacks in, 42–43, 159, 265–66 (n. 68);
race relations in, 43–44, 159–60, 210, 287
(n. 54); Unionist/Republican leanings of,
44, 287 (n. 54); convict labor in, 49, 75,
77, 79; October-November 1891 insurrection in, 144, 145, 147, 148; August 1892
insurrection in, 184. *See also* Briceville;
Coal Creek; Coal Creek Valley; Oliver
Springs
Arkansas, 283 (n. 67); convict lease in, 48
Asheville, N.C., 163
Atlanta, Ga., 163, 245

Barinds, Sim L., 61
Baxter, Jere, 216, 294 (n. 51), 295 (n. 52)
Baxter, Nathaniel, 22, 127, 147, 180, 184, 211,
216, 220, 289 (n. 16), 290 (n. 20)
Bell County, Ky., 42
Bennett, Rufus, 182–83, 288 (n. 83)
Big Mountain Mine, 49, 152, 287 (n. 53)
Birmingham, Ala., 12, 56, 215, 222, 236, 240,
294 (n. 31), 298 (n. 10)
Black, G. W., 287 (n. 63)
Black, George, 207
Black Diamond Coal Company, 162
Black Diamond Mine, 162
Black Patch war, 236–39, 241–43, 297–98
(n. 6)
Blacks: as convicts, 2, 7, 47, 56–57, 61, 62,
64–65, 155, 252, 269 (n. 34), 271 (n. 55),
272 (n. 81); in mid-Tennessee, 12, 13,
41–42; and unions, 12, 31–32, 42, 43, 44,
115, 159–61, 178, 228–29, 232, 242, 287
(n. 58), 297 (n. 93); and race relations in

321

mining communities, 12–13, 41, 42, 43–44, 45, 115, 159–61, 209–10, 228–29, 238, 266 (n. 69); 287 (nn. 54, 58), 297 (n. 93); in east Tennessee, 12–13, 41, 42–43, 262 (n. 25), 265–66 (n. 68), 266 (n. 69); and Republican Party, 12–13, 116, 159, 287 (n. 54); as mineworkers, 27–28, 41–44, 160, 240, 265 (n. 64); in Tennessee's urban centers, 57–58; and gender relations, 60–61; and disfranchisement, 131–32, 266 (n. 71), 270 (n. 39); and boundaries of dissent, 239, 240; and Black Patch war, 242–43; in militia, 275 (n. 15). *See also* Slavery; White supremacy

Board of Prison Inspectors: inspects TCMC mine, 117; and jurisdiction over mines using convict labor, 117–20, 121–22, 126, 137, 219, 280 (n. 18), 283 (n. 73), 294 (n. 38); and removal of convicts from TCMC mine, 118–20, 121, 133, 138; and subleasing of convicts, 135, 136, 138, 212, 213; composition of, 280 (n. 13)

Bowron, James, Sr., 261 (n. 17)

Bowron, James, Jr., 224, 263–64 (n. 39); and financial management of TCIR, 23–24, 38, 147, 216; personality and career of, 23–25, 37, 38; paternalism of, 23–25, 38; as Republican, 25, 44; opposition to labor activism, 38; and Knights of Labor, 42; and disadvantages of convict lease, 73, 87, 147; and TCIR conflict with state over convict lease, 120, 212, 217, 220; and controversy over subleasing, 135, 212, 218, 294 (n. 38)

Bradley, Hendricks, 135, 136

Brice, Calvin S., 23, 261 (n. 19)

Briceville, 17, 23, 102, 103, 104, 134, 191, 209, 293 (n. 9); residents of participate in convict wars, 1, 11, 81, 87, 142, 202, 203, 205, 243; relationship with Coal Creek, 1–2, 30, 81; July 1891 insurrection in, 1–2, 79–81, 83, 87, 105, 110–11, 128, 149, 243; agricultural background of migrants to, 4, 44; race relations in, 12–13, 228–29; as emblem of New South, 15, 35; TCMC facilities and operations in, 20, 34, 79, 114–15, 116–17, 162–66, 273 (n. 93), 279 (n. 7); blacks in, 27, 265 (n. 68); lacked

traits of company town, 29, 82; boosterism and community in, 30, 32, 82, 144, 259 (n. 3); convict labor in, 34, 64, 76–77, 79, 82, 94, 95, 110, 114, 121, 122, 135, 169; conditions for convicts at, 66, 116–17, 118; homeownership among residents of, 82, 262 (n. 28); militia sent to, 84, 86, 89; Merrell as community leader in, 85, 97, 99, 101; relations of militia with miners and residents of, 89; Irish as community leader in, 99, 101; union activity in, 106, 161, 171, 223–24, 263 (n. 32); October 1891 insurrection in, 139, 140, 142, 143, 149; discontinuation of convict labor in, 152, 153, 163, 166; State Labor Congress delegation from, 169, 171

Brown, W. H., 153

Brownlow, William G., 54, 83

Brushy Mountain Mine, 244–46

Buchanan, John P., 143, 244, 289 (n. 17), 290 (n. 19), 299 (n. 21); and convict lease, 53, 84, 93–94, 125, 126–27, 151, 152, 183–84, 185, 276 (n. 28); and increase in criminality, 56–57; and petitions for pardons, 59–61, 62; miners' appeals to and expectations of, 81–82, 89, 91, 94, 97, 111, 125, 169; reaction to miners' July 1891 insurrection, 83–84, 86, 89, 94, 109, 238, 272 (n. 4), 276 (n. 28); and governor's power to call out the militia, 83–84, 145, 155, 174, 180, 186, 274 (n. 5); places priority on maintenance of law and order, 84, 86, 97; background of, 89–90; and Farmers' Alliance, 89–90, 91–92, 111, 126, 127, 129, 131; and Democrats, 90–92, 93; Populist views of, 92, 93, 94, 111, 131–32; and reform of criminal justice system, 94, 125–26, 127, 137–38; and special session of legislature, 95, 96, 111, 113, 123, 125–26, 127, 131, 137–38; relations with operators, 97, 145–47; creates Bureau of Labor, 101, 111; and new penitentiary, 125; and disfranchisement, 132–33; reaction to miners' October-November 1891 insurrection, 144, 145–47, 151–52, 222; and TCIR, 152, 180, 183, 185, 196, 211; and conduct of militia in Anderson County, 154–55, 158, 182–83, 196, 206, 275 (n. 16); and 1892 reelection campaign, 168, 200,

Dandridge, 118
Davidson County, 57, 185
Davis, Ralph, 281 (n. 27)
Davis, T. J., 115
Dayton, 105
DeBardeleben Coal and Iron Company, 176
Declaration of Independence, 141
Dego, C. L., 110, 144, 145, 279 (n. 79)
Democrats, 3, 31, 95, 115, 134, 193, 210; and Farmers' Alliance, 9, 91–92, 123, 127, 129, 133, 138, 168, 175–76, 281 (n. 25); political control of mid-Tennessee by, 13, 44; and white supremacy, 13, 91, 93; and industrialization, 22, 25, 91, 92; and coal barons, 25, 27; old-line Whigs, 25, 91, 92, 123, 129, 130, 275 (n. 19); and issue of state debt, 54, 91, 275 (n. 19); and convict lease, 75, 91, 127, 201, 281 (n. 27); Buchanan and, 83, 84, 90–92, 93, 201; factions among, 90–91, 92, 123, 129, 130, 275 (n. 19), 280 (n. 24); Harris (states' rights), 91, 92, 93, 123, 129, 275 (n. 19); Jacksonian, 91, 123; press organs of, 92–93, 129, 201; and Prison Board, 120; and reform of criminal justice system, 127; and governor's power to call out militia, 128; and Populists, 129–30; and disfranchisement, 131–33; unsympathetic to miners, 135, 150, 201; and State Labor Congress, 168. See also Redeemers/Redemption
Department of Justice (U.S.), 239
Diggs, Wood, 117
Disfranchisement, 131–33, 159, 270 (n. 39), 283 (nn. 67, 74)
District 19. See United Mine Workers of America
Dombrowski, James, 74, 114
Dortch Law, 132
Drummond, Richard, 218, 295 (n. 60)

East Tennessee National Bank, 75–76
East Tennessee, Virginia & Georgia Railroad, 20, 25, 75, 291 (n. 49)
Empire Mine, 162
Evans, Henry J., 268 (n. 12)
Ewing, Felix, 242

Family: miners' militance rooted in a defense of, 41, 81
Farmers: side with miners during convict wars, 1, 81, 82, 145, 148; political alliance of miners with, 2, 170, 171; and migration, 3–4, 29, 262 (n. 27); and Populism, 8; and convict lease, 8, 124–25, 281 (n. 33); Jacksonian Democrats and, 91; Buchanan and, 93; and Black Patch war, 236–39, 241–43, 297–98 (n. 6). See also Agriculture; Farmers' Alliance; Farms
Farmers' Alliance, 99, 276 (n. 26), 277 (n. 55); opposition to capitalists/monopolists, 8, 40, 111, 131; electoral successes of, 8, 82, 123; and convict lease, 8, 123, 124–25, 126, 127–28, 130, 131, 169, 176, 281 (n. 27), 283 (n. 67); internal conflicts in, 8, 125; political inexperience and failures of, 8–9, 129, 282 (n. 53); and Democrats, 9, 91–92, 123, 127, 129, 133, 138, 168, 175–76, 281 (n. 25); and miners, 82, 91, 97, 124, 140, 149, 169, 243; Buchanan and, 83, 89, 90, 91–92, 97, 111; and Republicans, 123, 130, 138, 281 (n. 25); supports governor's power to call out militia, 128; and industrial development, 130–31, 133; conservatism of in Tennessee, 131; and disfranchisement, 131–32, 283 (n. 67); and State Labor Congress, 167–68; Colored Farmers' Alliance, 202; in Black Patch, 237
Farms: migration of mine and industrial workers from, 3–4, 27, 28–29. See also Agriculture; Farmers
Fayette County, 92
Federal Election Bill (Lodge Bill), 93, 132, 276 (n. 26)
Ferris (Oliver Springs warden), 184, 185, 189, 204–5
Florida, 283 (n. 67); convict lease in, 47–48, 267 (n. 7)
Ford, George, 185, 277 (n. 49), 280 (n. 15); and Knights of Labor, 84, 114, 120; as commissioner of labor and inspector of mines, 84, 114, 120, 121; and negotiations following July 1891 insurrection, 94; background and career of, 114, 137; and Knoxville Independent, 114, 190; inspects and condemns conditions at TCMC

mine, 114–17, 120–21, 133, 137; operators'
disparagement of, 120, 128; forced to
permit reopening of TCMC mine, 122;
urges miners' to act within the law, 149;
and TCMC mine cooperative, 162–63
Fort Anderson (Militia Hill, Coal Creek),
153, 154, 161, 162, 187, 206, 208, 209, 292
(n. 62)
Four Mile Law, 32
Fowler, J. A., 208, 293 (n. 24)
Franklin, State of: miners draw on legacy
of, 83, 110, 112
Franklin County, 103, 128, 135, 168
Frazier, Jim, 179
Frontier heritage: miners draw on, 109–10,
111, 193–94, 231
Fyffe, Perry, 187, 189, 209

Gaines, James, 147, 290 (n. 22)
Gammon (Coal Creek warden), 187, 291
(n. 38)
General Assembly of Tennessee, 167, 239;
special session of called to consider convict lease, 2, 94, 96, 102, 113; reluctance
of to reform criminal justice system,
7, 55–56; legislative reform by as only
appropriate means to end convict lease,
84, 95, 96, 148–49; fails to reform penal
system or convict lease, 122–28, 129, 133,
137–38; influence of operators on, 128,
142; and governor's power to call out
militia, 128, 155, 174, 274 (n. 5); passes
law making obstruction of convict labor
illegal, 128, 203; and disfranchisement,
132; and end of convict lease, 215, 223,
233, 244
George, Henry, 232
Georgia: convict lease in, 48, 239–40, 267
(n. 7), 272 (n. 79)
Gibson, Henry R., 95, 97, 107, 108, 231
Gibson County, 124
Givens, Butch, 188
Goins, L., 287 (n. 63)
Goodman, H. Lee, 42
Goodwin, J. E., 76, 120, 121, 273 (nn. 96, 97),
283 (n. 73)
Grand Army of the Republic, 99
Grand Rapids Workman, 89
Grangers, 237

Greenbackers, 237
Grundy County, 28, 72, 99, 185, 259 (n. 3);
agricultural background of migrants
to, 4; as setting for convict wars, 4, 177,
192, 235–36, 246–47; as a leading coal-
producing county, 17, 22; geography of,
17–18; postbellum population growth
in, 27; Knights of Labor in, 31, 42; TCIR
influence on community life in, 37–39,
40; blacks in, 41–42; race relations in, 42,
44; union activity in, 42, 175, 223, 224,
243; Secessionist/Democratic leanings
of, 44; convict labor in, 49, 175; conditions for convicts in, 66; TCIR facilities
and operations in, 122, 181–82, 221, 244;
residents of participate in convict wars,
180, 181. *See also* Inman; Tracy City

Hamilton County, 185
Harriman Railroad, 245–46
Harris, Isham, 91, 275 (n. 19)
Hatmaker, John, 102, 128, 141–42, 184, 187,
189–90, 204–5, 293 (n. 24)
Hayes, Rutherford B., 186
Haymarket massacre, 10, 11–12
Hayward County, 92
Herron, S. P., 109, 165, 195, 232, 291 (n. 47),
293 (nn. 23, 24); espouses class conflict
ideology, 229–31, 247, 297 (n. 95)
Hicks, W. R., 203, 204, 205, 212
Hightower, John "Tip," 141, 206
Hill, J. T., 49–50, 56–57, 65, 245
Holloway (Morgan County sheriff), 185
Homeownership: among Tennessee
mineworkers, 4, 29, 30, 44–45, 82, 230,
238–39, 262 (n. 28); miners' militance
rooted in a defense of, 11, 83, 104–5, 107,
108–9, 111–12, 183, 195; TCIR encouragement and control of, 25, 29, 37–38, 40,
41, 178; and sense of community, 30;
Anderson County mining companies
have little control over, 39; contrast in
symbolic meanings attached to in mid-
and east Tennessee, 40–41
Homestead, Pa., 10, 104, 192, 195, 260 (n. 7),
277 (n. 59)
Houk, John, 116, 134, 185, 191, 206, 290
(n. 23)
Houk, Leonidas, 116

House, Mansfield F., 280 (n. 13)
Huber, Richard, 143
Hurt, Babe, 117

Industrialists. *See* Operators
Industrialization: vs. agriculture in late nineteenth century, 3–4, 22, 33, 260 (n. 9); constraints on in Tennessee, 4–5, 33–35, 263–64 (n. 39); and growth of mining communities, 15–16; Republican support for, 22, 25, 54; Democratic support for, 22, 25, 91; and convict lease, 50, 137; Farmers' Alliance leaders' support for, 130, 133; general state support for, 233; miners' acceptance of, 246; consequences of in Appalachia, 266 (n. 74)
Ingraham, Marcena: as leader during convict wars, 95, 98, 99, 102, 109, 141–42, 150, 189; and Knights of Labor, 99; operators' attempts to discredit, 128; and TCMC mine cooperative, 162–63; and State Labor Congress, 167; leaves Anderson County, 226
Inman: TCIR facilities and operations at, 37, 64, 215, 259 (n. 3); convict labor in, 64, 144, 175, 211, 298 (n. 17); August 1892 insurrection in, 173, 180–82, 184, 211, 290 (n. 19); union activity in, 178, 263 (n. 72)
Inman, John, 22, 261 (n. 19)
Irish, George; as leader during convict wars, 98, 99, 101, 102, 141–42, 189, 204; and Knights of Labor, 99; arguments advanced by in defense of miners' cause, 103–5; operators' attempts to discredit, 128; prosecuted in connection with August 1892 insurrection, 204, 205, 207, 293 (n. 24)

Jack, Samuel W., 134
Jackson, Andrew, 8, 22, 93, 175
James K. Shook School (Tracy City), 39
Jasper, 180
Jefferson County, 118
Jellico, Ky., 87, 102, 139, 185, 191, 224–25, 263 (n. 33); cooperative mine at, 165, 166, 288 (n. 70)
Jenkins, B. A., 40, 178; personality and career of, 25–27; use of convict labor by, 76–77, 79, 82, 94, 110, 212, 273 (nn. 96,

97); and origins of convict wars, 77, 102, 213; complains about miners and their leaders, 103, 128; sees state actions against TCMC as politically motivated, 120; and conflict over independent checkweighman, 135–36, 273 (n. 93); discontinues use of convict labor, 152, 163; relations with TCIR, 152, 212; and TCMC mine cooperative, 162–66, 288 (n. 73); and State Labor Congress, 288 (n. 83)
Jim Crow, 3, 12, 130, 229
Johnson, Andrew, 91, 93
Joint Committee on the Penitentiary, 65
Jones, J. J., 228
Journal of the Knights of Labor, 148, 227

Kentucky, 27–28, 145, 245, 294 (n. 31); miners from participate in Tennessee convict wars, 3, 87, 100, 139, 142–43, 184–85, 224, 195; convict lease in, 48, 267 (n. 7), 269 (n. 27); miners' 1886 action against convict labor in, 87, 96, 241. *See also* Black Patch war
King, Henry Clay, 62
Knights of Labor, 84, 85, 96, 114, 224, 229, 232, 241, 246, 265 (n. 67), 277 (n. 55), 296 (n. 85); moderate, cooperative principles of, 31, 42, 149, 165, 171, 182; interracialism in, 31, 242; and TCIR, 42; racism in, 42, 242; role of in convict wars, 97, 98, 99, 147, 148, 149, 170, 171, 175, 183, 193, 270 (n. 37), 293 (n. 19); and TCMC, 120, 162; urge miners to refrain from violence, 148, 149, 170, 291 (n. 47); and cooperative industries and mines, 162, 165, 288 (n. 73); hostility of courts to, 202; and UMWA, 225; factionalism within, 226–29
Knox County, 99, 101, 128, 185, 218
Knoxville, 25, 36, 57, 84, 85, 89, 93, 99, 115, 134, 142, 165, 186, 193, 215, 277 (n. 50); released convicts sent to, 2, 81, 87, 150; meetings held in to gain support for miners, 102, 107, 108
Knoxville Independent, 114, 190
Knoxville Iron Company, 36, 151, 193, 208; use of convict labor by, 34, 49, 87, 219, 273 (n. 97), 295 (n. 66); subcontracts care of convicts to third party by, 65, 74; and TCIR, 72, 178, 216, 219, 264 (n. 46),

273 (n. 97), 295 (n. 66); miners release
convicts working for, 87, 139, 187
Knoxville Journal, 95, 134, 150, 187, 190, 191,
202, 283 (n. 74), 291 (n. 50)
Knoxville Sentinel, 92
Knoxville Tribune, 66, 92, 140, 150
Knoxville Woolen Mills, 85

Labor: supply of as constraint on southern
industrialization, 4–5, 49–51; convicts
as answer to operators' desire to reduce
militance of, 6, 51–52; convicts as answer
to operators' need to reduce cost of,
51–52, 72–73. *See also* Central Labor
Union(s); Convict lease/labor; Knights
of Labor; Unions; United Mine Workers
of America
Labor Day: observance of, 97, 101, 111
Lake City, 17. *See also* Coal Creek
Laugherty, William, 218, 295 (n. 60)
Lea (Tennessee Supreme Court justice),
136, 284 (n. 79)
Leahy, Dennis, 95
Legislature. *See* General Assembly of
Tennessee
Lewis, John, 182–83
Lewis, Obie, 117
"Life in Southern Prisons" (*Harper's
Weekly*), 69
Liggett, E. H., 60
Lodge, Henry Cabot, 93
"Lone Rock Song," 255–56, 272 (n. 71)
Louisiana, 54; convict lease in, 48, 240
Louisville & Nashville Railroad, 20, 27–28
Louisville, New Orleans and Texas Rail-
road, 61
Love, William T., 166

McDowell, John H., 90, 168
McDowell County, W.Va., 42
McGhee, Charles McClung, 22, 25, 77,
91–92, 97, 147, 261 (n. 19), 285 (n. 22)
Management. *See* Capital; Operators
Marion County, 49, 64, 66, 135, 175, 178,
180–82, 185, 192, 294 (n. 25)
Martin, Henry, 59
Maryland: convict lease in, 48
Memphis, 57, 61, 62, 99, 102, 124, 215
Memphis Appeal Avalanche, 61, 92, 129

Memphis Avalanche, 132
Memphis Commercial, 92
Memphis Scimitar, 124
Merrell, Eugene, 111, 137, 177; as leader
during convict wars, 40, 85–86, 87, 97,
98–99, 101, 102, 141–42, 153, 189; background and career of, 84–85, 274 (n. 7);
and Knights of Labor, 97, 99; arguments
advanced by in defense of miners' cause,
103–5, 108–9; operators' attempts to discredit, 128; complains about conduct of
militia in Anderson County, 154–55; and
TCMC mine cooperative, 162–65; and
State Labor Congress, 167, 288 (n. 83);
leaves Anderson County, 226; espouses
ideology grounded in idea of commonwealth, 229–30
Merrell, John, 85
Militia: fighting between miners and, 2,
186–89, 203; level of performance of, 9,
188–89, 196, 291 (nn. 41, 42); sent to
Anderson County, 84, 86, 89, 95, 153–54,
169, 186, 236, 238; relations with miners
and mining community residents, 89,
154–58, 174, 182–83, 193–94, 195, 209, 218,
275 (nn. 15, 16); governor's power to call
out, 128, 155, 174, 180, 186, 274 (n. 5);
financial responsibility for, 153, 155, 200,
212, 214, 217, 286 (n. 45); withdrawal of
from Anderson County, 158, 184, 204,
218; capitulation of miners to, 191–92,
200
Miller, Charles A., 280 (n. 13)
Miller, William F., 162, 288 (n. 83)
Mining communities: migration to, 3–4,
16, 27, 28–29, 44–45; general character
of, 4, 15, 27–32, 44–45, 82, 111–12, 144–45,
195; boosterism and growth in, 15–16, 27,
44–45; differences among, 35–44, 145.
See also Briceville; Coal Creek; Inman;
Oliver Springs; Tracy City
Mississippi, 283 (n. 67); convict lease in, 48
Missouri: convict lease in, 48
"Molly Maguires," 11–12
Monopolies/Monopolists: Farmers'
Alliance opposition to, 8, 40, 130, 133;
TCIR as, 40, 108; Jacksonian Democrats'
suspicion of, 91, 108; Buchanan's criti-
cism of, 93, 111; miners' opposition to,

104, 108, 111, 231; state seen as corrupted by, 108, 129, 170, 190–91, 230, 231, 238; ATC as, 236, 238; Knights' support for nationalization of, 246

Monroe, D. B., 187, 189, 205–8, 209, 287 (n. 63), 291 (n. 44), 293 (n. 19)

Montgomery County, 297 (n. 6)

Moon (circuit court judge), 180

Moore, S. D., 205, 207

Morgan County, 34, 49, 87, 185, 192, 244, 246

Morris, Robert L., 278 (n. 67)

Morrison, J. W., 180–81, 289 (n. 17)

Morrow, William, 22, 64, 76–77, 94, 213, 214, 273 (n. 96)

Nashville, 22, 57, 99, 101, 102, 186, 193, 215; as home of Tennessee penitentiary, 54, 125

Nashville American, 22, 92, 93, 125, 129, 202

Nashville, Chattanooga & St. Louis Railroad, 20, 179

Nashville Banner, 92

Nashville Herald, 101, 168

Nashville Union, 22

Nathurst, E. O., 38, 42, 179, 290 (n. 22)

National Federation of Miners and Mine Laborers, 226

National Labor Tribune, 110, 142, 292 (n. 50)

Newcomb, 102, 115, 160

New Orleans, La., 12, 84–85, 236

New Orleans Daily Picayune, 186

New York Times, 97

Norfolk and Western Railroad, 20

O'Connor, Thomas, 22

Oliver Springs, 87, 102, 191, 217; race relations in, 12–13, 43, 160–61; as emblem of New South, 15, 35; lacked traits of company town, 29; boosterism and community in, 30, 32, 144, 259 (n. 3); Cumberland Coal Mining Company facilities and operations in, 34, 49; convict labor in, 34, 49, 51, 64, 75, 94, 122, 135, 152, 153, 211; relative independence of miners in, 40; blacks in, 43, 265 (n. 68); agricultural background of migrants to, 44; November 1891 insurrection in, 142–43, 147, 151;

residents of participate in convict wars, 143, 203, 243; compared with Briceville and Coal Creek, 143–44; TCIR operations at, 152, 216, 287 (n. 53); militia sent to, 153–54, 155; relations of militia with miners and residents of, 158; militia withdrawn from, 158, 184; State Labor Congress delegation from, 169; August 1892 insurrection in, 184–85, 202, 206, 210, 211; homeownership among residents of, 262 (n. 28); union activity in, 263 (n. 32)

Operators: industrial ambitions of, 5, 21–22, 27, 50; and origins of convict lease, 5, 22; and problem of labor supply, 5, 49–50, 51, 150; and advantages of convict lease, 5–6, 22, 49–52, 74–75, 76–77, 146–47, 259 (n. 5); and costs and disadvantages of convict lease, 5–6, 72–73, 146, 163, 174, 181–82, 195–96, 211–20, 259 (n. 5); and labor relations, 6, 51–52, 74–75, 148, 150, 161–62, 178; miners' criticism of corrupting, monopolistic influence of, 11, 40, 108, 111, 141–42, 169–70, 230, 231, 246; social and geographic origins of, 22–27; and miners' homeownership, 29–30, 37–38, 39, 40–41; influence of over miners' lives, 32, 37–41, 173, 178; competitive disadvantages of, 33–35, 51; necessity of low labor/production costs for, 35, 50, 51–52, 268 (n. 12); and unions, 41, 42, 51, 52, 150, 160–61, 178, 225; use race to discourage labor solidarity, 41, 44–45, 178; and convicts' acts of resistance, 69; and conflict over independent checkweighman, 76, 106, 136, 150, 161, 169, 273 (n. 93); disagreements with state over administration of convict lease, 117–22, 135–36, 146–47, 153–54, 174, 183–84, 196, 200, 211–20, 232; state favors interests of at expense of miners, 138, 141–42, 195, 218, 222, 231, 232, 233, 246; oppose state-owned mine, 244, 245–46. *See also individual companies and managers*

Palmer, Bruce, 129

Panic of 1873, 20, 51

Panic of 1893, 51, 225

Paterson, N.J., 105
Penitentiary (Brushy Mountain), 244–46
Penitentiary (Nashville), 65, 73, 76, 122, 135, 145; employment of convicts housed in, 48, 63–64, 214; physical condition of, 54, 211; convict lease as means of relieving pressure on, 54–55; kinds of criminals sent to, 56, 124, 126; plans to build a replacement for, 75, 125, 127, 169, 215, 218–19, 244; miners send released convicts to, 179, 181, 185, 211, 238
Pickering, Samuel, 287 (n. 63), 288 (n. 83)
Pickle, George W.: and negotiations following July 1891 insurrection, 94; and Prison Board jurisdiction, 117–18, 120, 121–22; background of, 118, 137; and ruling on subleasing, 126–27, 133, 134, 135, 137, 147, 212; reaction to October-November 1891 insurrection, 151
Pinkerton guards, 10, 277 (n. 59)
Pioneer Co-Operative Mercantile and Manufacturing Association, 165
Pitts, John A., 192–93, 212–13, 217
Planters' Protective Association (PPA), 236–39, 241, 242, 297–98 (n. 6), 298 (n. 8)
Plunkitt, George Washington, 129–30
Polk, James K., 93
Poplar Creek Coal & Iron Company, 264 (n. 43)
Populism/Populists, 3, 8, 129–30, 131, 133, 243, 283 (n. 67). See also Farmers' Alliance
Porter, Robert P., 165
Powderly, Terence, 149, 165, 166, 229, 276 (n. 26), 285–86 (n. 29), 288 (n. 73)
Prison Board. See Board of Prison Inspectors
Property: legal penalties for crimes against, 5, 57–58, 65; convicts' destruction of, 6, 72; operators' desire to protect, 10, 147, 195, 232; miners' acceptance of economy based on, 11; miners act in defense of, 81, 103, 104–7, 108, 109, 111–12, 238, 246; miners' respect for during convict wars, 87, 100, 105, 140, 149–50, 185, 190, 195; labor as, 107, 108; miners' destruction of during convict wars, 139–40, 150, 235, 236; public opinion turns against miners for destruction of, 148, 150, 170; cost to

operators of miners' destruction of, 152, 182, 195–96, 214, 218, 220, 221; role of state in protection of, 232, 233; destruction of in Black Patch war, 237, 241
Pulaski County, Ky., 241
Pullman Railroad Car Company, 10

Race relations, 3, 210; in Tennessee coalfields, 43–44, 159–61, 210. See also Blacks; Jim Crow; Slavery; Whites; White supremacy
Rae, John, 229
Railroads, 178, 190, 215, 236, 245, 246, 262 (n. 27), 291 (n. 49); and industrialization, 3, 19–20, 23, 33–34, 54; and development of coal mining, 5, 20, 21, 33–34, 35; and labor conflict, 10, 186, 275 (n. 16); use of convict labor for building of, 47, 49, 216, 267 (n. 7); post–Civil War condition of, 53; state assistance in development of, 54, 91, 93; and state taxation/regulation of, 91, 93, 130
Redeemers/Redemption, 9, 48, 54, 55, 56, 92, 240, 267 (n. 3). See also Democrats
Renfro, J. W., 152, 160, 287 (n. 53)
Republicans, 3, 31, 83–84, 134, 193, 210; political control of east Tennessee by, 8, 12, 44, 92, 104; and coal barons, 25, 27; and industrialization, 54; and issue of state debt, 54; opposition to convict lease, 75, 123–24, 130, 167, 201, 281 (n. 27); and race relations, 91, 287 (n. 54); overall strength of, 92, 123, 280 (n. 24); press organs of, 93, 190, 201–2; and miners' support committee, 95, 107; and miners' leaders with, 104, 106; and black voters, 116, 159, 167, 287 (n. 54); and Farmers' Alliance, 123, 130, 138, 281 (n. 25); and governor's power to call out the militia, 128; and disfranchisement, 132; turn against miners when they take law into their own hands, 150, 201–2
Rhea County, 105
Ridley, G. S., 60
Riley, William, 31–32, 43, 159–60, 161, 223, 226–29, 266 (n. 70), 297 (n. 93)
Roane County, 34, 185, 262 (n. 26)
Roberts, J. C., 149
Rockwood, 102

insurrection, 173, 179–80, 196, 218, 290
(n. 22); transfer of most operations of to
Alabama, 221–22; and April 1893 insurrection, 223

Tennessee Coal and Railroad Company
(TCR), 20, 22, 23, 36, 49. *See also*
Tennessee Coal, Iron, and Railroad
Company

Tennessee Coal Mining Company (TCMC),
34, 40; miners release convicts from
stockade of, 1–2, 79–81, 86–87; Jenkins's
founding and running of, 26–27; use of
convict labor by, 34, 76, 86, 94, 114, 122,
212–13; Ford inspects and criticizes conditions at mine of, 114–17, 120–21, 137,
279 (n. 7); Prison Board inspects and
removes convicts from mine and stockade of, 118–20, 121, 122; miners burn
stockade of, 139; and TCIR, 152, 163, 178,
212–13; and formation of mine cooperative, 162–66; abandons use of convict
labor, 163

Tennessee Supreme Court, 62, 118, 127,
136, 138, 203, 212, 220–21, 284 (n. 79), 294
(n. 38)

Texas: convict lease in, 48, 267 (n. 7)

Thibodaux, La., 240

Thomas, Samuel, 261 (n. 19)

Toronto Labor Advocate, 89

Tracy, Samuel Franklin, 23

Tracy City, 23, 44, 60, 67, 74, 102, 104, 261
(n. 23), 272 (n. 77); residents of participate in convict wars, 11, 176–77, 179, 243;
race relations in, 12, 13, 41, 42; as emblem
of New South, 15, 16, 35; differs from
east Tennessee mining communities, 16,
35–44; TCIR facilities and operations in,
20, 36–37, 73, 127, 135, 173, 177, 182, 214,
224, 259 (n. 3); convict labor in, 22, 68,
73, 144, 174–75, 176, 211; homeownership
among residents of, 25, 29, 38, 40–41;
blacks in, 27, 41–42; lacked traits of company town, 29; boosterism and community in, 30, 32, 259 (n. 3); Knights of
Labor in, 31, 42, 175; TCIR influence on
community life of, 37–39, 40; agricultural background of migrants to, 44;
August 1892 insurrection in, 173, 174,
179–80, 182, 185, 206, 211; political lean-

ings of residents of, 175–76; State Labor
Congress delegation from, 176–77; union
activity in, 178, 223, 224, 263 (n. 32);
April 1892 insurrection in, 223

Transportation: lack and expense of as
constraint on southern industrialization, 4–5, 19–20, 33–34, 35, 51. *See also*
Railroads

Turney, Peter: as Supreme Court justice,
135–37, 284 (n. 79), 294 (n. 38); as gubernatorial candidate, 168–69, 200; as
governor, 202, 210, 218, 293 (n. 4); and
building of new penitentiary, 215, 243–
44; and end of convict lease, 243–44

Unions: operators' relations with, 3, 10, 40,
41, 52, 161, 162, 178, 225; and politics, 11;
as community institutions, 30; blacks
and, 42, 43–44, 178, 228–29, 232; use of
convicts to dampen activity of in mines,
51, 144; growth and maturation of in
Tennessee coalfields, 82, 97; role of in
convict wars, 97, 99–100, 102, 123, 148,
150, 200, 243; opposition to convict
lease, 123, 175; hostility of courts to, 202;
negative impact of convict wars on,
210–11, 223–29, 243, 296 (n. 82); and
race relations, 241, 242, 287 (n. 58). *See
also* Central Labor Union(s); Knights
of Labor; United Mine Workers of
America

United Mine Workers Journal, 31, 89, 109,
128, 140, 148, 159, 165, 180, 182, 190, 225,
227

United Mine Workers of America
(UMWA), 96, 231; loyalty of black
mineworkers to, 12, 228–29; interracialism in, 31, 115, 159, 161, 228–29, 242;
growth of during convict wars, 31, 161;
TCIR resistance to, 42; racial tensions
within, 159–61, 226, 228–29, 242; and
cooperative industries and mines, 162,
165; role in convict wars, 193, 291 (n. 47);
weakness of following convict wars, 223,
225, 228, 229; and Knights of Labor, 226;
factionalism within, 226–29. *See also*
Unions

University of Tennessee (Knoxville), 89